I, PARROT

BY DEB OLIN UNFERTH & ELIZABETH HAIDLE

ALSO BY DEB OLIN UNFERTH

Wait Till You See Me Dance

Revolution

Vacation

Minor Robberies

I, PARROT

BY DEB OLIN UNFERTH & ELIZABETH HAIDLE

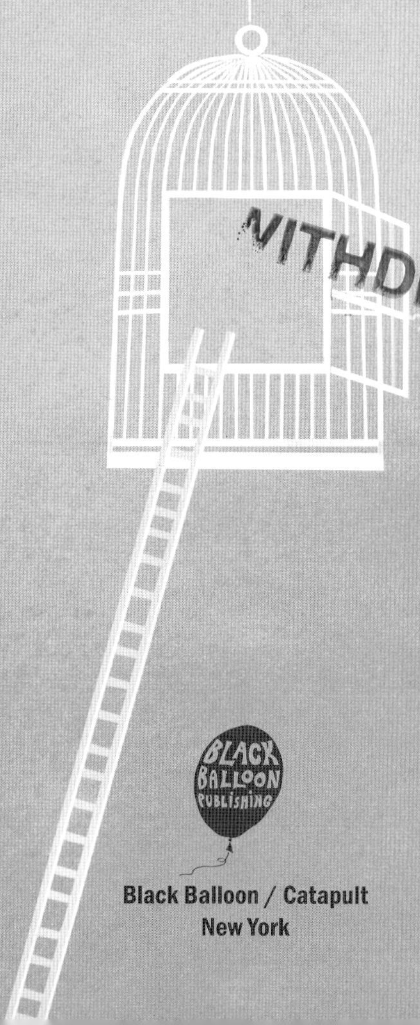

BLACK BALLOON PUBLISHING

Black Balloon / Catapult
New York

PUBLISHED BY BLACK BALLOON, AN IMPRINT OF CATAPULT
catapult.co
TEXT COPYRIGHT © 2017 BY DEB OLIN UNFERTH
ILLUSTRATIONS COPYRIGHT © 2017 BY ELIZABETH HAIDLE

ISBN: 978-1-936787-65-4

Catapult titles are distributed to the trade by
Publishers Group West.

LIBRARY OF CONGRESS CONTROL NUMBER: 2016959630

PRINTED IN CHINA

10 9 8 7 6 5 4 3 2 1

for
KATHERINE COLCORD
AND ELI SONNY-BOY JOHNSON

in memory of
NOAH KENNETH COLCORD

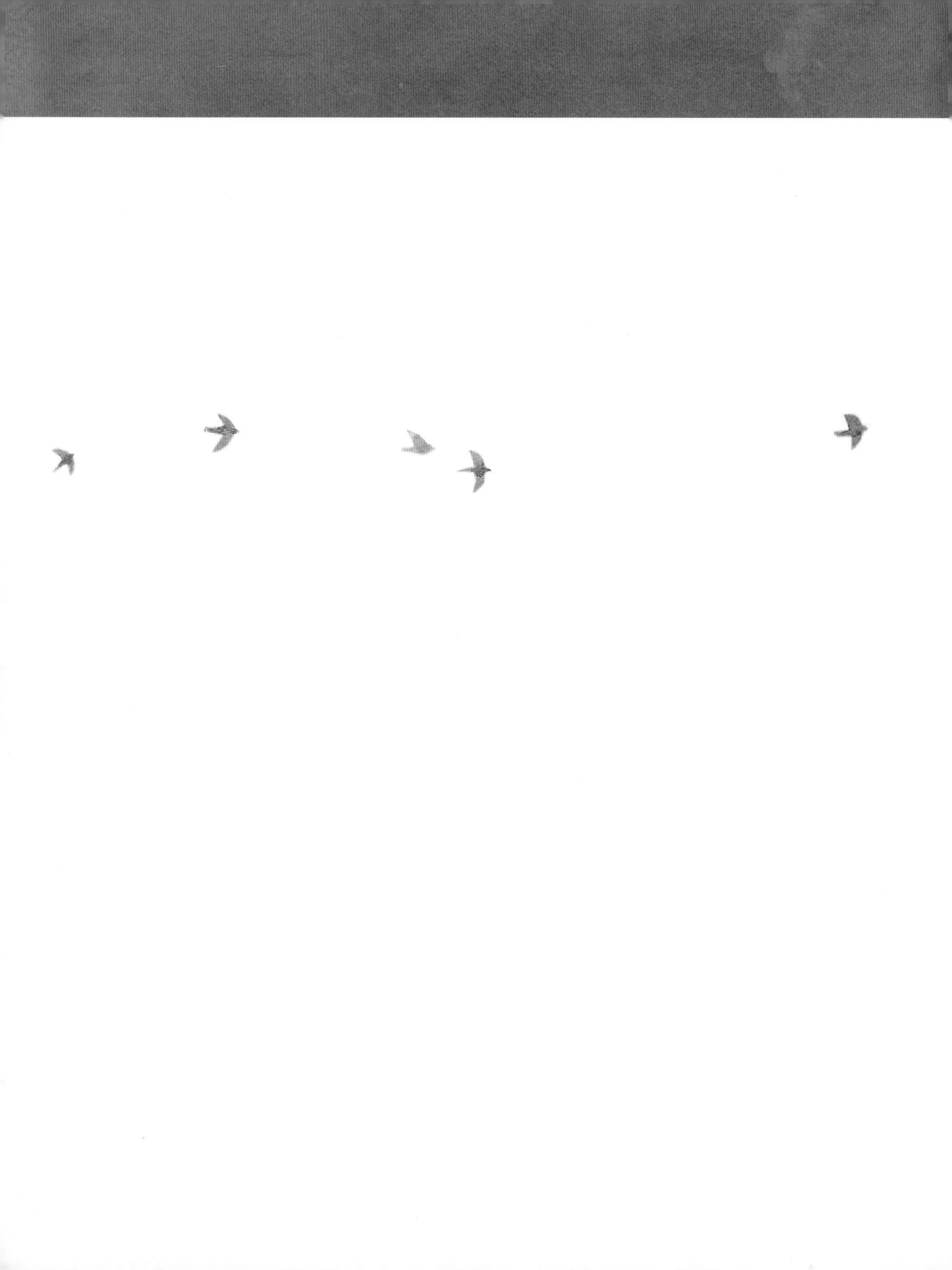

CHAPTER 1: YOU ARE A BEAUTIFUL PERSON

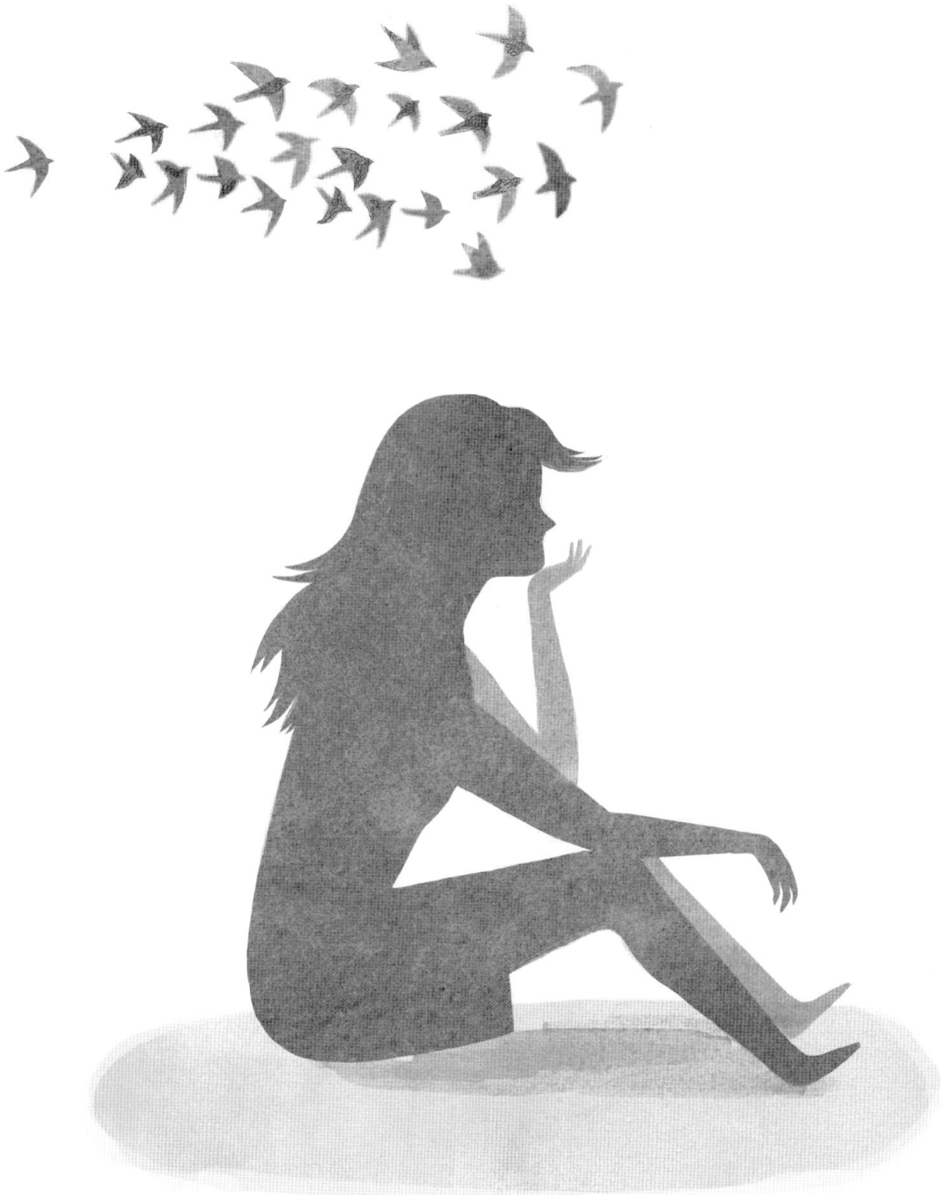

I FINALLY FOUND A JOB.

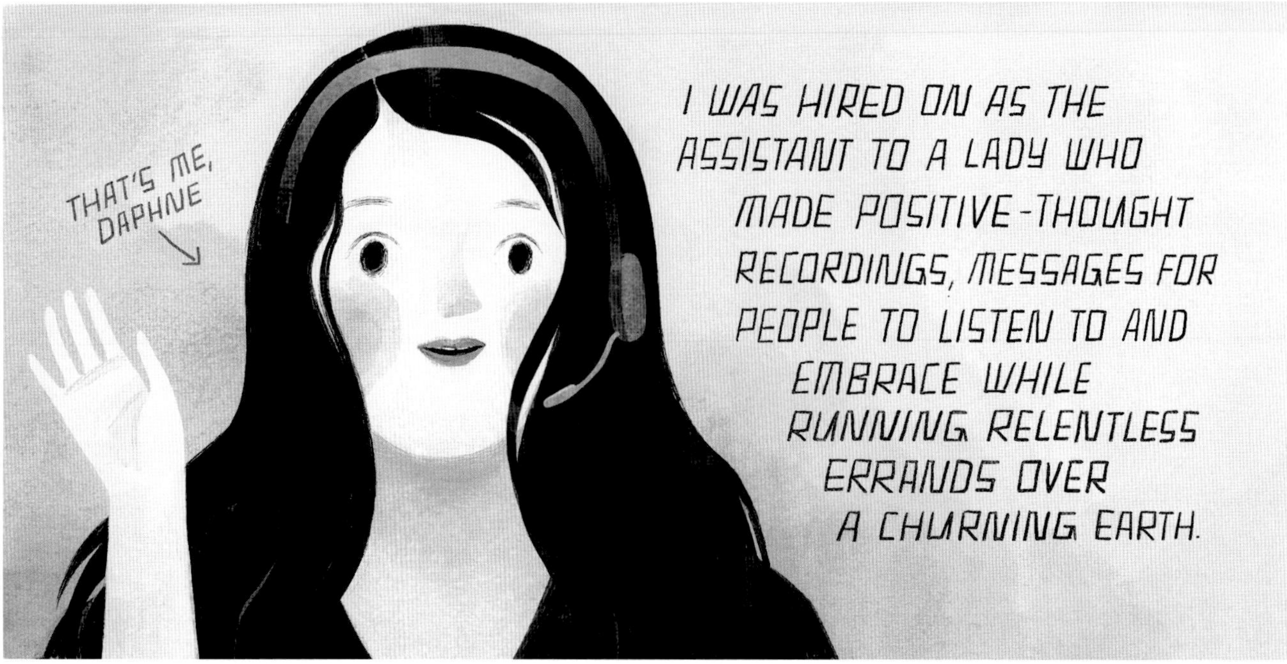
THAT'S ME, DAPHNE
I WAS HIRED ON AS THE ASSISTANT TO A LADY WHO MADE POSITIVE-THOUGHT RECORDINGS, MESSAGES FOR PEOPLE TO LISTEN TO AND EMBRACE WHILE RUNNING RELENTLESS ERRANDS OVER A CHURNING EARTH.

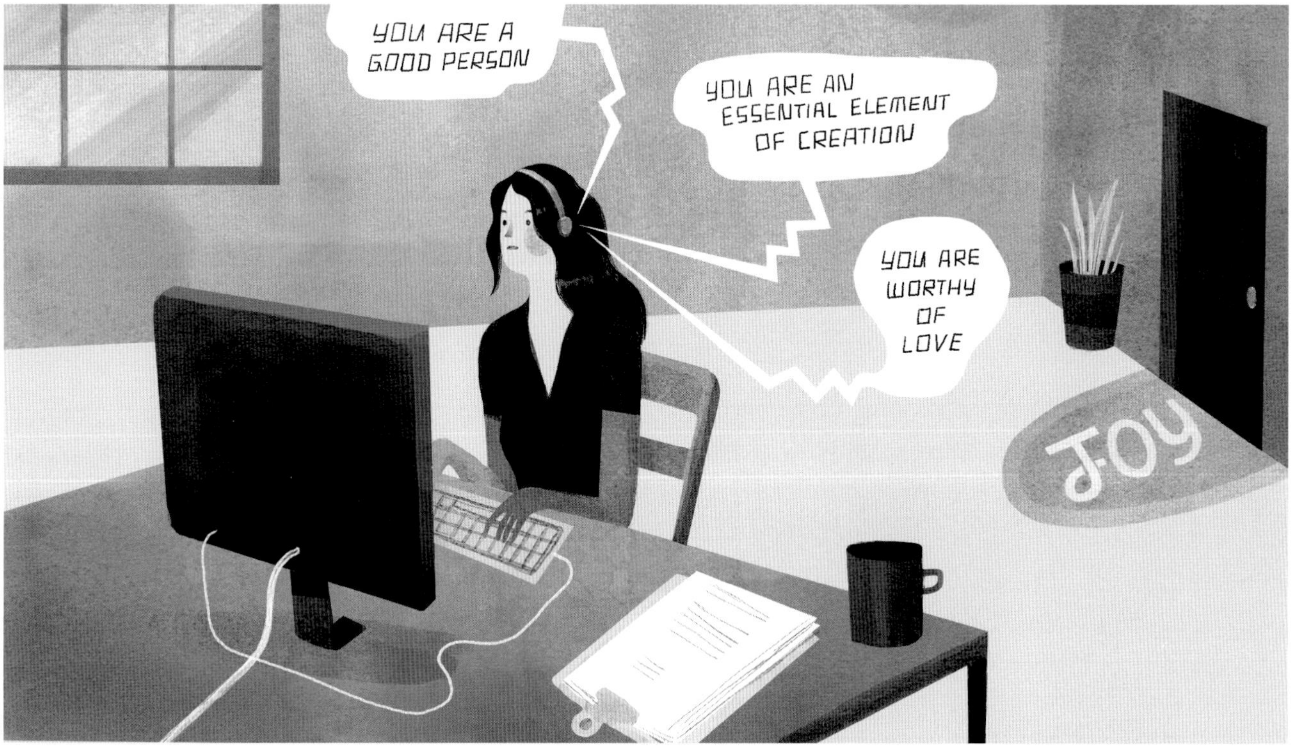
YOU ARE A GOOD PERSON
YOU ARE AN ESSENTIAL ELEMENT OF CREATION
YOU ARE WORTHY OF LOVE
JOY

THE MESSAGES WEREN'T ALL THAT SPECIFIC, REALLY, OR CONVINCING, BUT THEY DID SHUT DOWN, SHUT OUT, OR OTHERWISE IMPEDE THE ROAR OF THE UNHAPPY MIND (WHICH FRANKLY MAY HAVE HAD A MORE PERSUASIVE ARGUMENT).

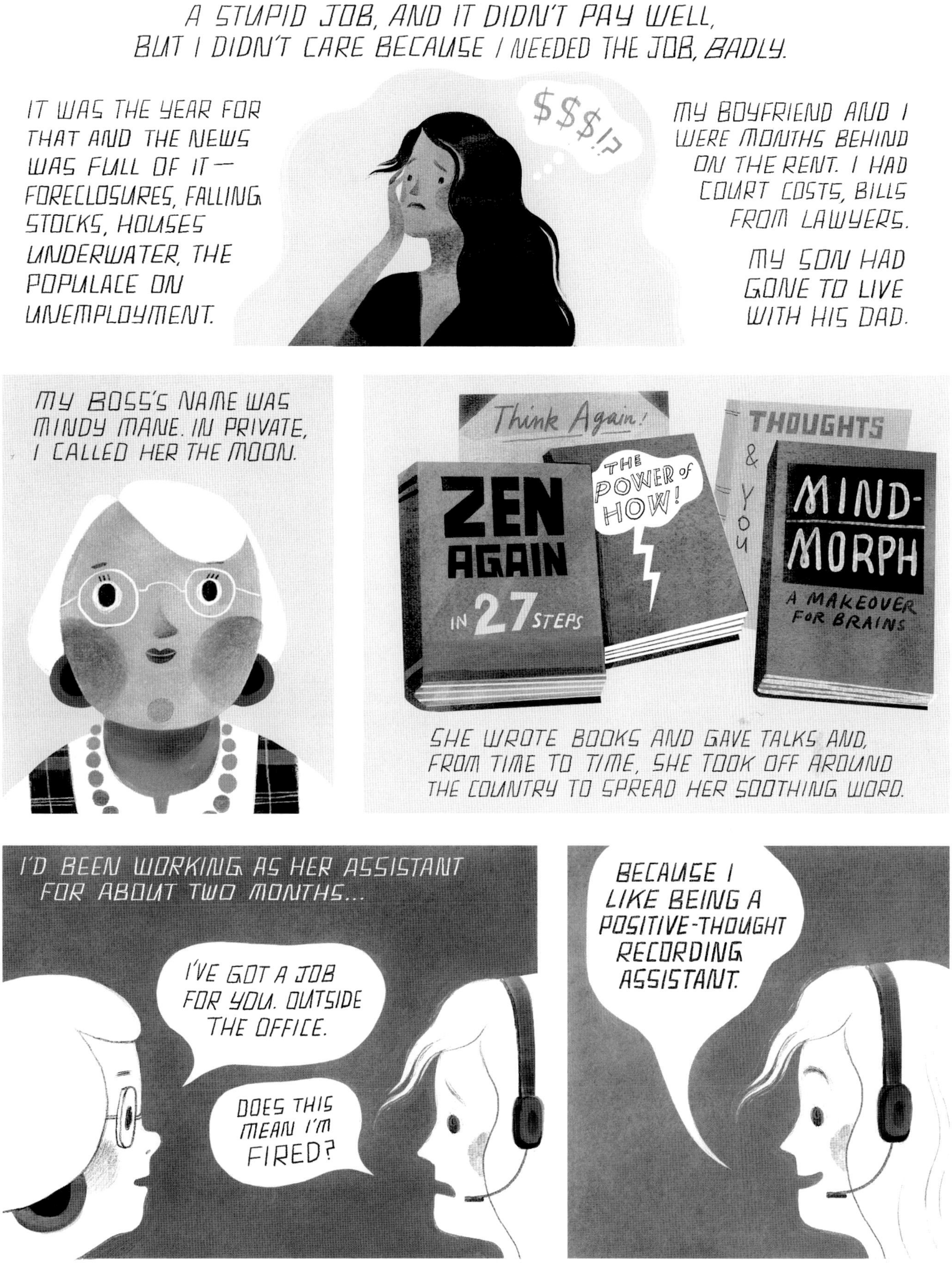
A STUPID JOB, AND IT DIDN'T PAY WELL, BUT I DIDN'T CARE BECAUSE I NEEDED THE JOB, BADLY.
IT WAS THE YEAR FOR THAT AND THE NEWS WAS FULL OF IT— FORECLOSURES, FALLING STOCKS, HOUSES UNDERWATER, THE POPULACE ON UNEMPLOYMENT.
$$$!?
MY BOYFRIEND AND I WERE MONTHS BEHIND ON THE RENT. I HAD COURT COSTS, BILLS FROM LAWYERS.
MY SON HAD GONE TO LIVE WITH HIS DAD.
MY BOSS'S NAME WAS MINDY MANE. IN PRIVATE, I CALLED HER THE MOON.
Think Again!
THOUGHTS & YOU
ZEN AGAIN IN 27 STEPS
THE POWER of HOW!
MIND-MORPH
A MAKEOVER FOR BRAINS
SHE WROTE BOOKS AND GAVE TALKS AND, FROM TIME TO TIME, SHE TOOK OFF AROUND THE COUNTRY TO SPREAD HER SOOTHING WORD.
I'D BEEN WORKING AS HER ASSISTANT FOR ABOUT TWO MONTHS...
I'VE GOT A JOB FOR YOU. OUTSIDE THE OFFICE.
DOES THIS MEAN I'M FIRED?
BECAUSE I LIKE BEING A POSITIVE-THOUGHT RECORDING ASSISTANT.

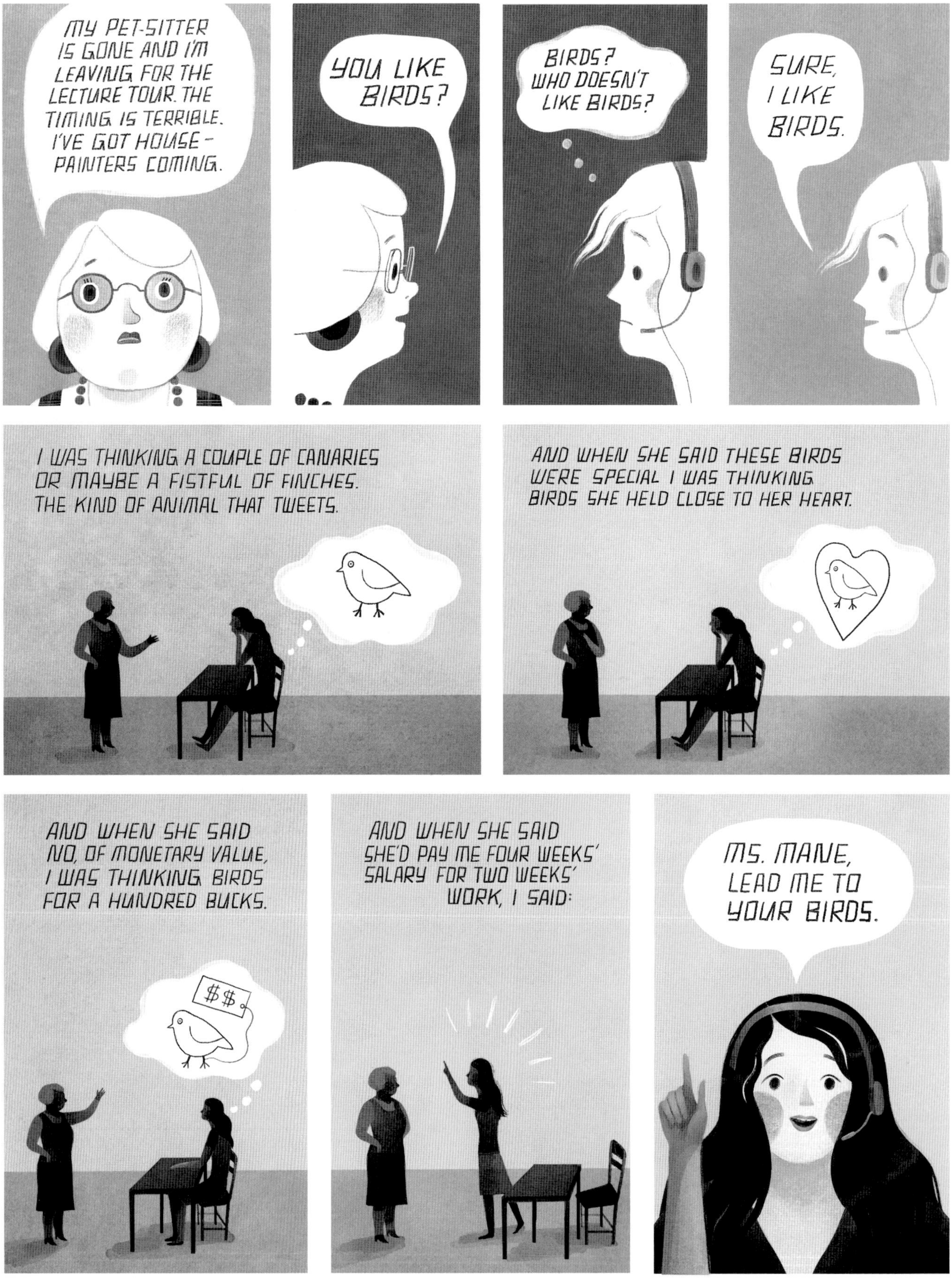
MY PET-SITTER IS GONE AND I'M LEAVING FOR THE LECTURE TOUR. THE TIMING IS TERRIBLE. I'VE GOT HOUSE-PAINTERS COMING.
YOU LIKE BIRDS?
BIRDS? WHO DOESN'T LIKE BIRDS?
SURE, I LIKE BIRDS.
I WAS THINKING A COUPLE OF CANARIES OR MAYBE A FISTFUL OF FINCHES. THE KIND OF ANIMAL THAT TWEETS.
AND WHEN SHE SAID THESE BIRDS WERE SPECIAL I WAS THINKING BIRDS SHE HELD CLOSE TO HER HEART.
AND WHEN SHE SAID NO, OF MONETARY VALUE, I WAS THINKING BIRDS FOR A HUNDRED BUCKS.
$$
AND WHEN SHE SAID SHE'D PAY ME FOUR WEEKS' SALARY FOR TWO WEEKS' WORK, I SAID:
MS. MANE, LEAD ME TO YOUR BIRDS.

BIRDS WERE ALL OVER THE NEWS THAT MONTH. IT WAS ANOTHER THING THAT WAS HAPPENING. SOME KIND OF BIRD THOUGHT LONG EXTINCT, THE PASSENGER PIGEON, HAD BEEN SIGHTED, OR MAYBE SIGHTED, THEN CONFIRMED, OR POSSIBLY CONFIRMED, ENOUGH TIMES THAT IT SEEMED IT COULD BE TRUE.

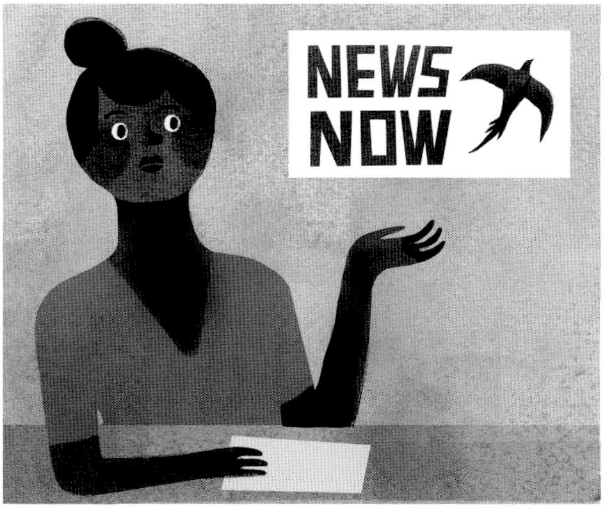
NEWS NOW

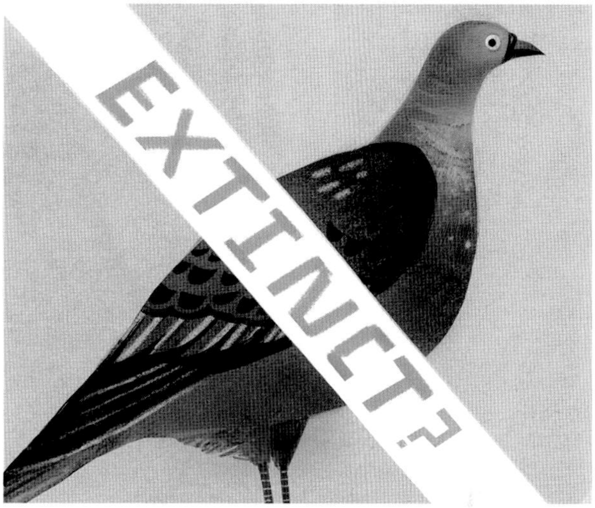
EXTINCT?

PEOPLE WERE OFF THEIR HEADS ABOUT IT, MAKING EXPEDITIONS, FLYING AROUND THEIR DRONES, HOPING TO BE THE NEXT TO CATCH A GLIMPSE.

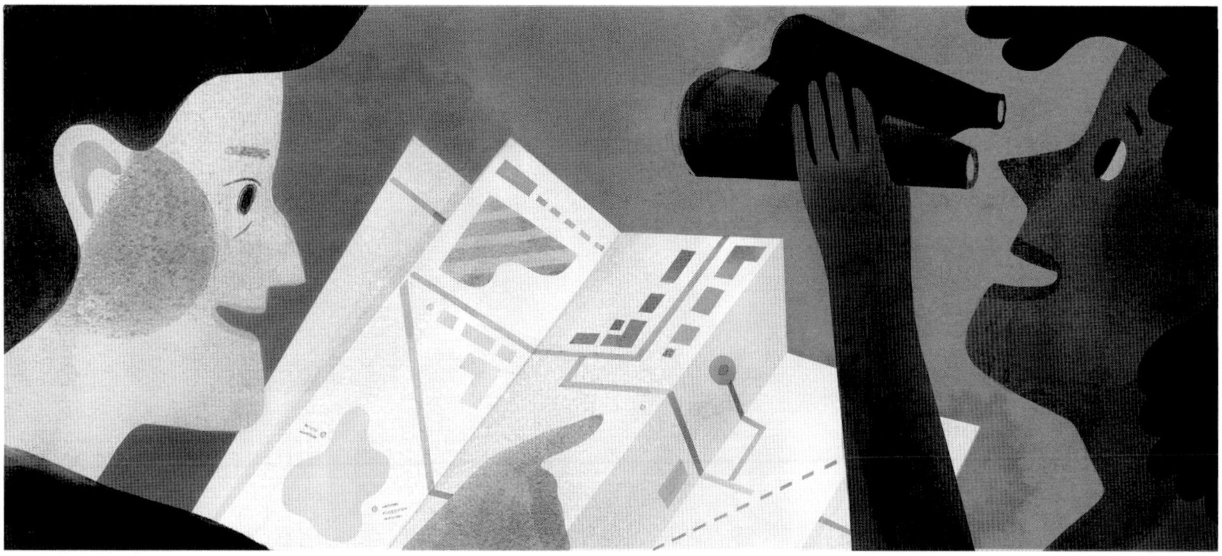

TO SOME IT SIGNALED THE END OF THE WORLD, TO OTHERS THE START OF A NEW ONE.

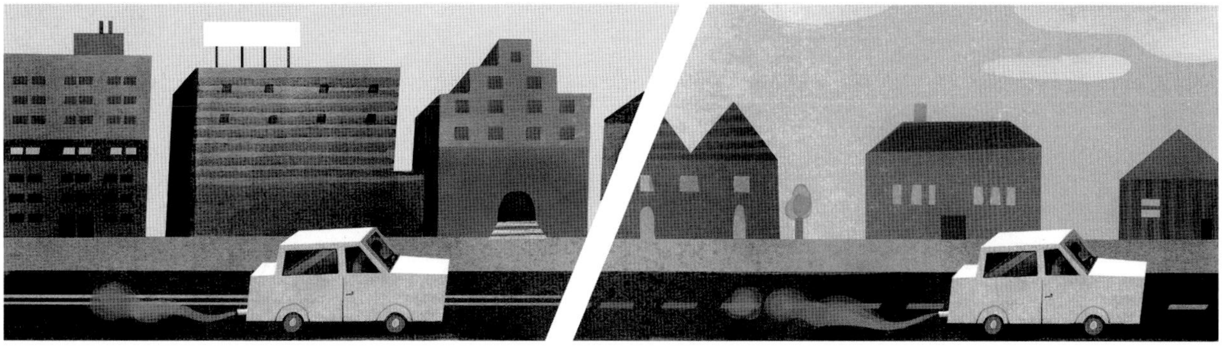

I HAD OTHER WORRIES.

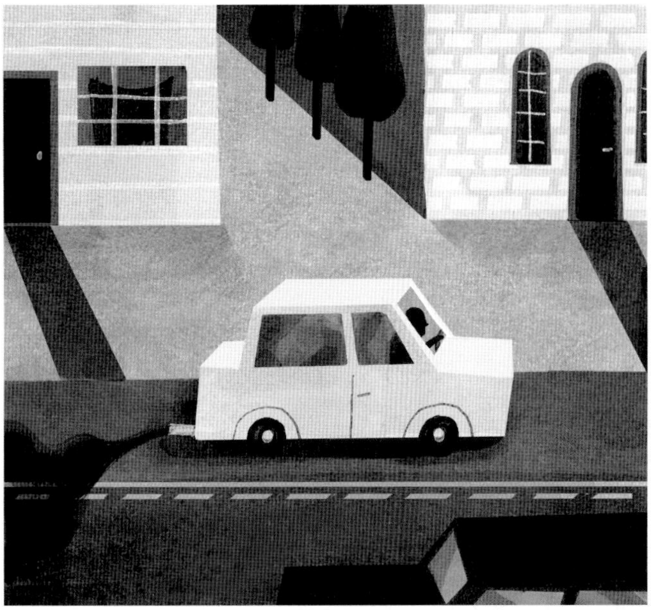

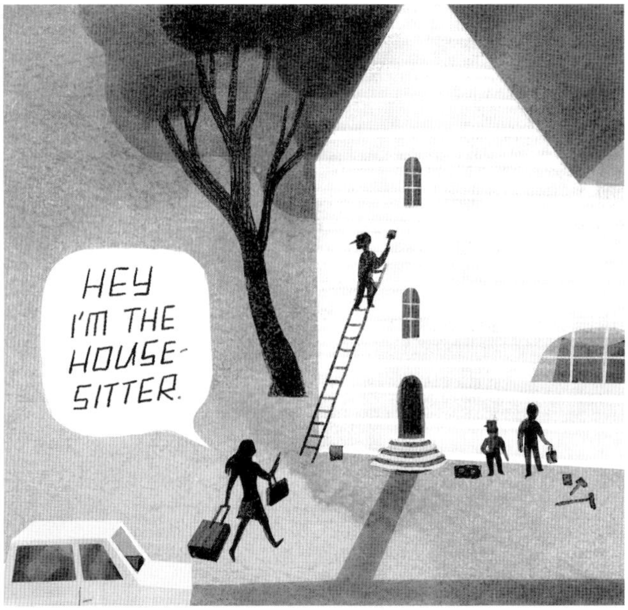
HEY I'M THE HOUSE-SITTER.

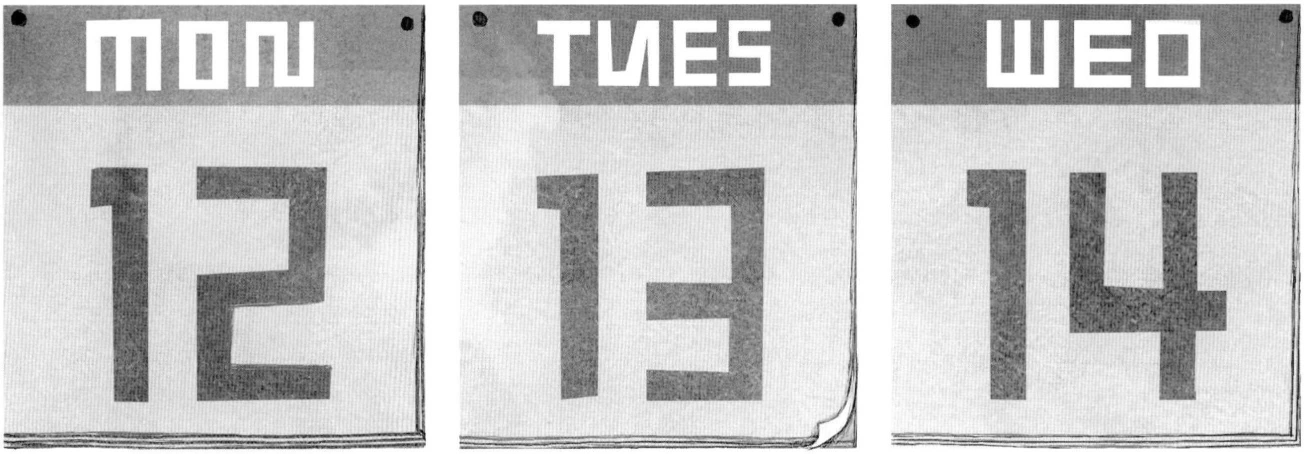
MON
12
TUES
13
WED
14

A COUPLE DAYS IN...

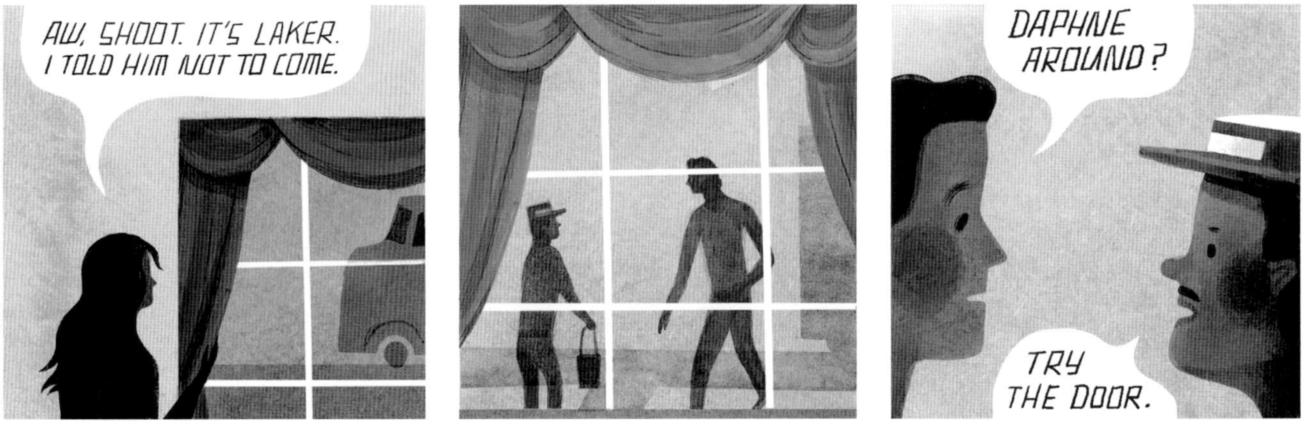
AW, SHOOT. IT'S LAKER. I TOLD HIM NOT TO COME.
DAPHNE AROUND?
TRY THE DOOR.

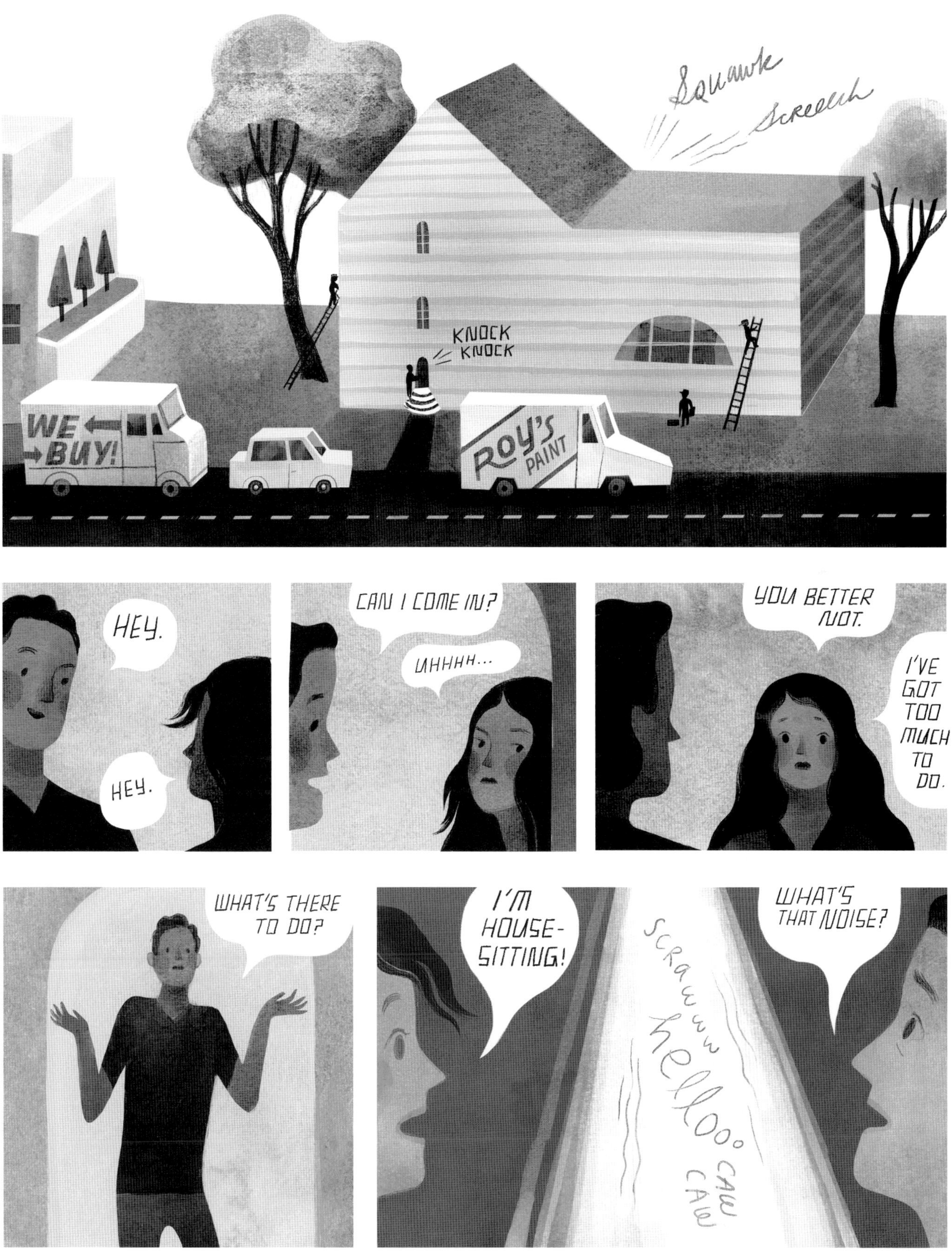
Squawk
Screech
KNOCK KNOCK
WE BUY!
ROY'S PAINT
HEY.
HEY.
CAN I COME IN?
UHHHH...
YOU BETTER NOT.
I'VE GOT TOO MUCH TO DO.
WHAT'S THERE TO DO?
I'M HOUSE-SITTING!
WHAT'S THAT NOISE?
SCRAWWW
hellooo
CAW CAW

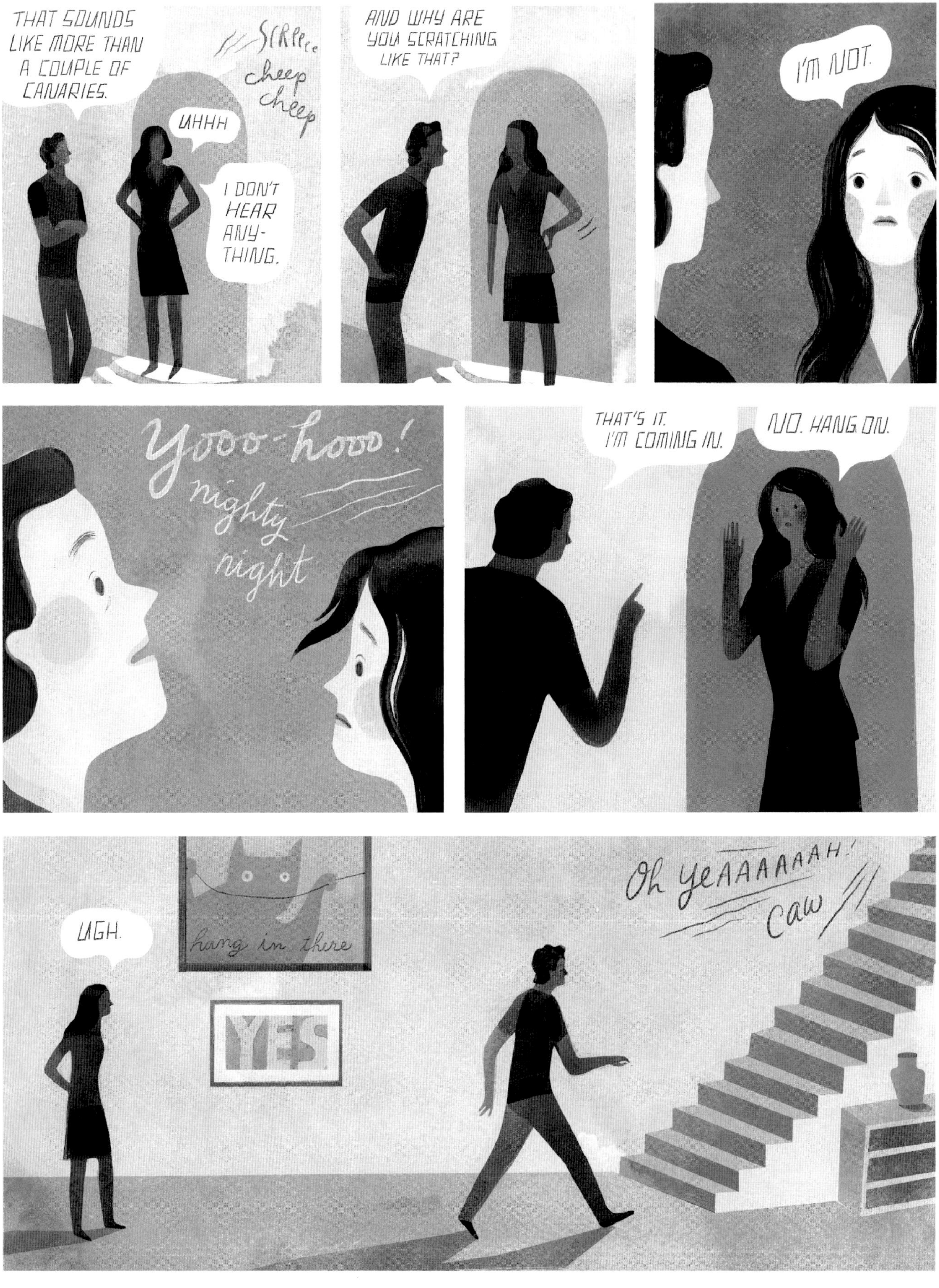
THAT SOUNDS LIKE MORE THAN A COUPLE OF CANARIES.
SCREEee
cheep cheep
UHHH
I DON'T HEAR ANY-THING.
AND WHY ARE YOU SCRATCHING LIKE THAT?
I'M NOT.
Yooo-hooo!
nighty night
THAT'S IT. I'M COMING IN.
NO. HANG ON.
hang in there
UGH.
YES
Oh yeAAAAAAH!
caw

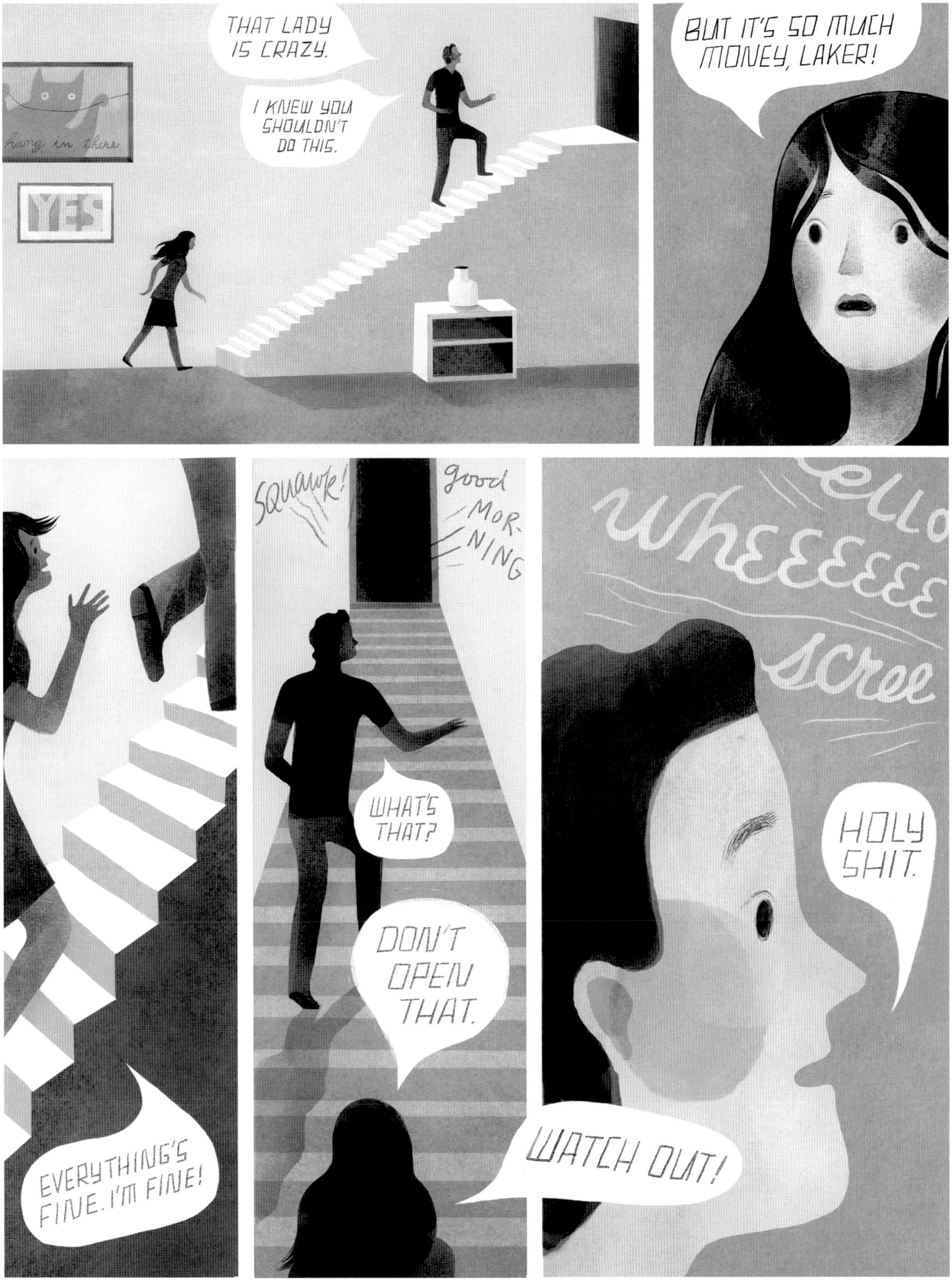

THAT LADY IS CRAZY.
I KNEW YOU SHOULDN'T DO THIS.
hang in there
YES
BUT IT'S SO MUCH MONEY, LAKER!
EVERYTHING'S FINE. I'M FINE!
SQUAWK!
good MOR-NING
WHAT'S THAT?
DON'T OPEN THAT.
WATCH OUT!
WHEEEEEE
scree
HOLY SHIT.

HOW COULD I HAVE KNOWN THAT BY "BIRDS" THE MOON MEANT 100,000 DOLLARS' WORTH OF PARROTS?

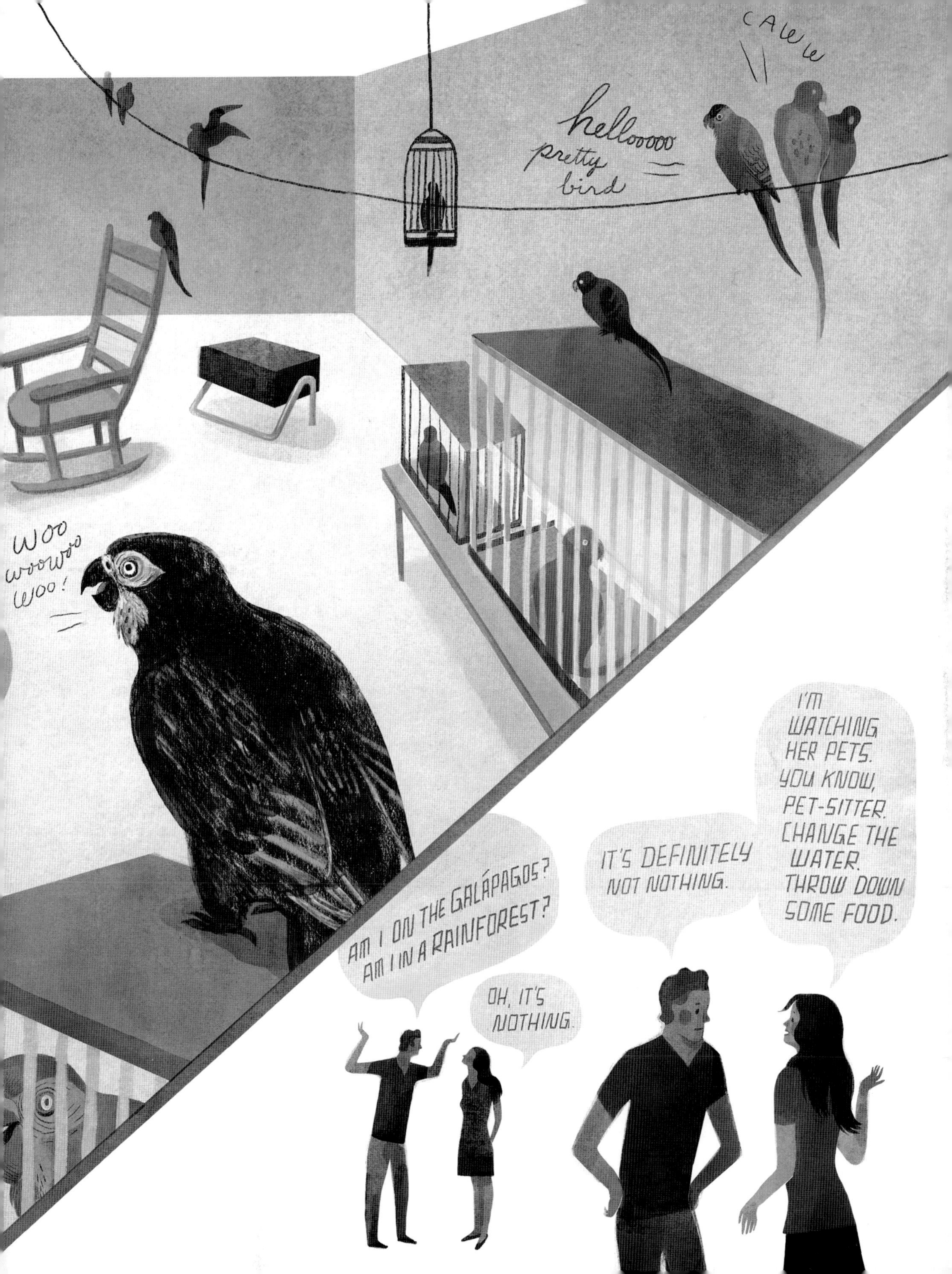
CAWW
hellooooo pretty bird
WOO woowoo woo!
AM I ON THE GALÁPAGOS? AM I IN A RAINFOREST?
OH, IT'S NOTHING.
IT'S DEFINITELY NOT NOTHING.
I'M WATCHING HER PETS. YOU KNOW, PET-SITTER. CHANGE THE WATER. THROW DOWN SOME FOOD.

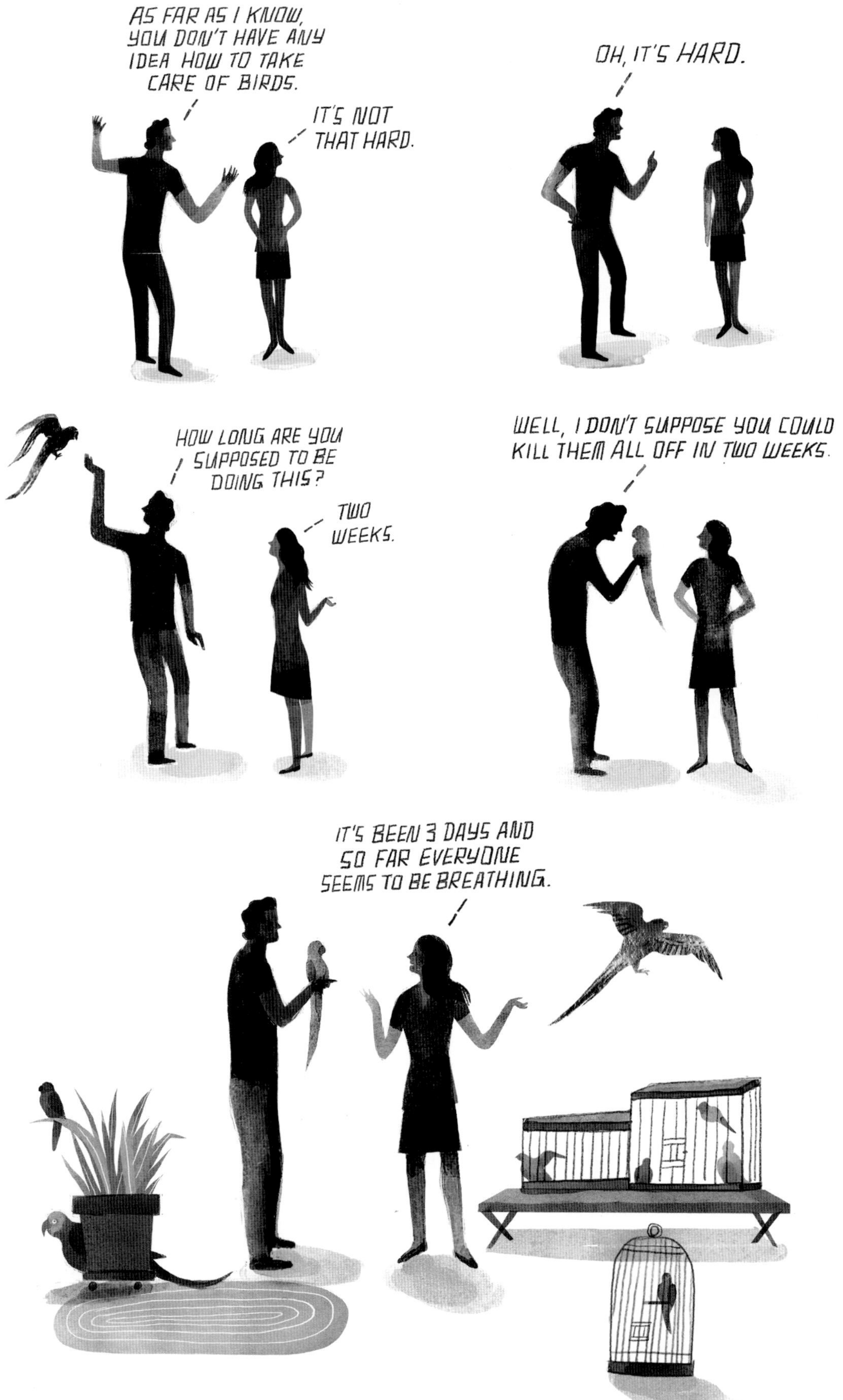
AS FAR AS I KNOW, YOU DON'T HAVE ANY IDEA HOW TO TAKE CARE OF BIRDS.
IT'S NOT THAT HARD.
OH, IT'S HARD.
HOW LONG ARE YOU SUPPOSED TO BE DOING THIS?
TWO WEEKS.
WELL, I DON'T SUPPOSE YOU COULD KILL THEM ALL OFF IN TWO WEEKS.
IT'S BEEN 3 DAYS AND SO FAR EVERYONE SEEMS TO BE BREATHING.

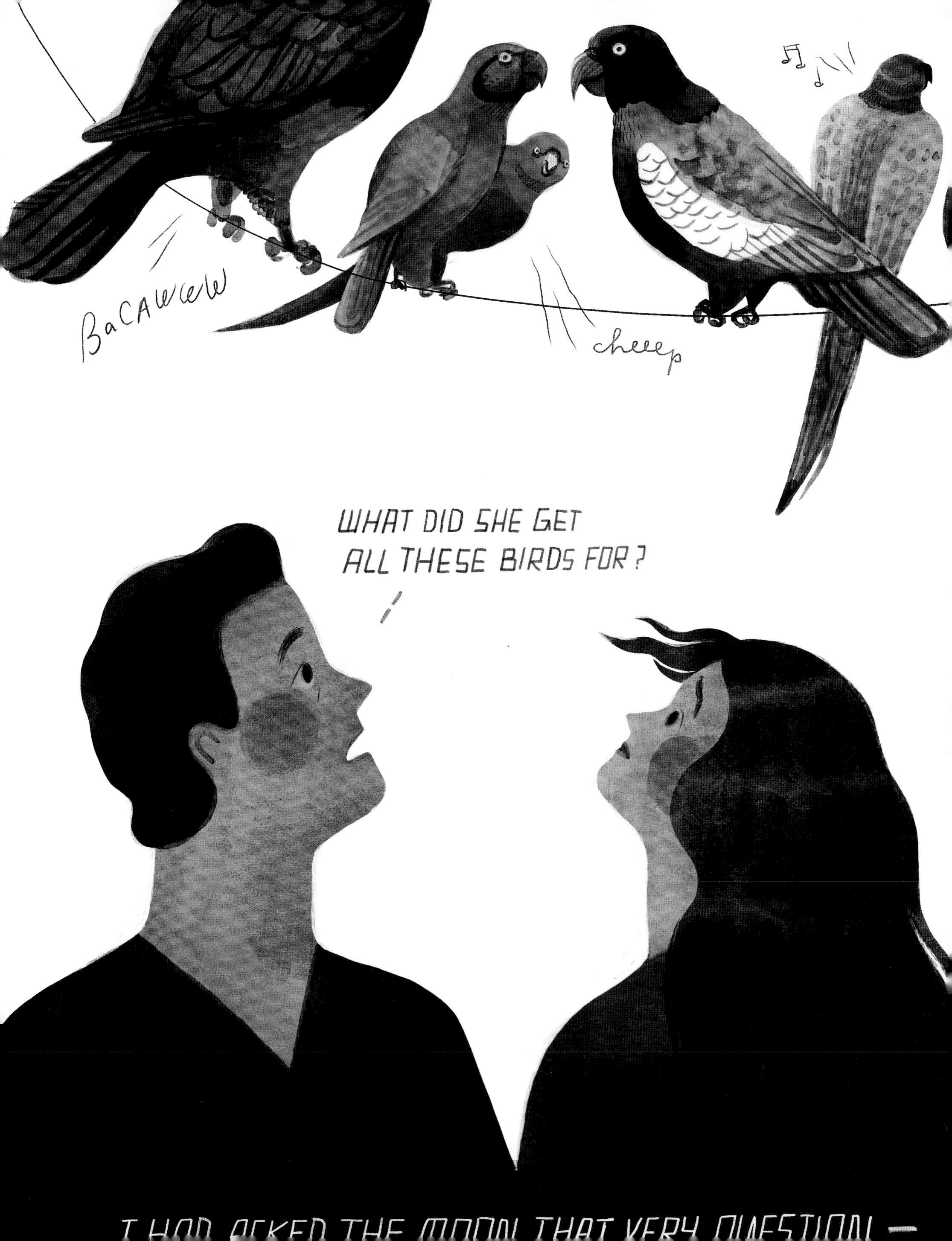
BaCAWWW
cheeep
WHAT DID SHE GET ALL THESE BIRDS FOR?
I HAD ASKED THE MOON THAT VERY QUESTION —

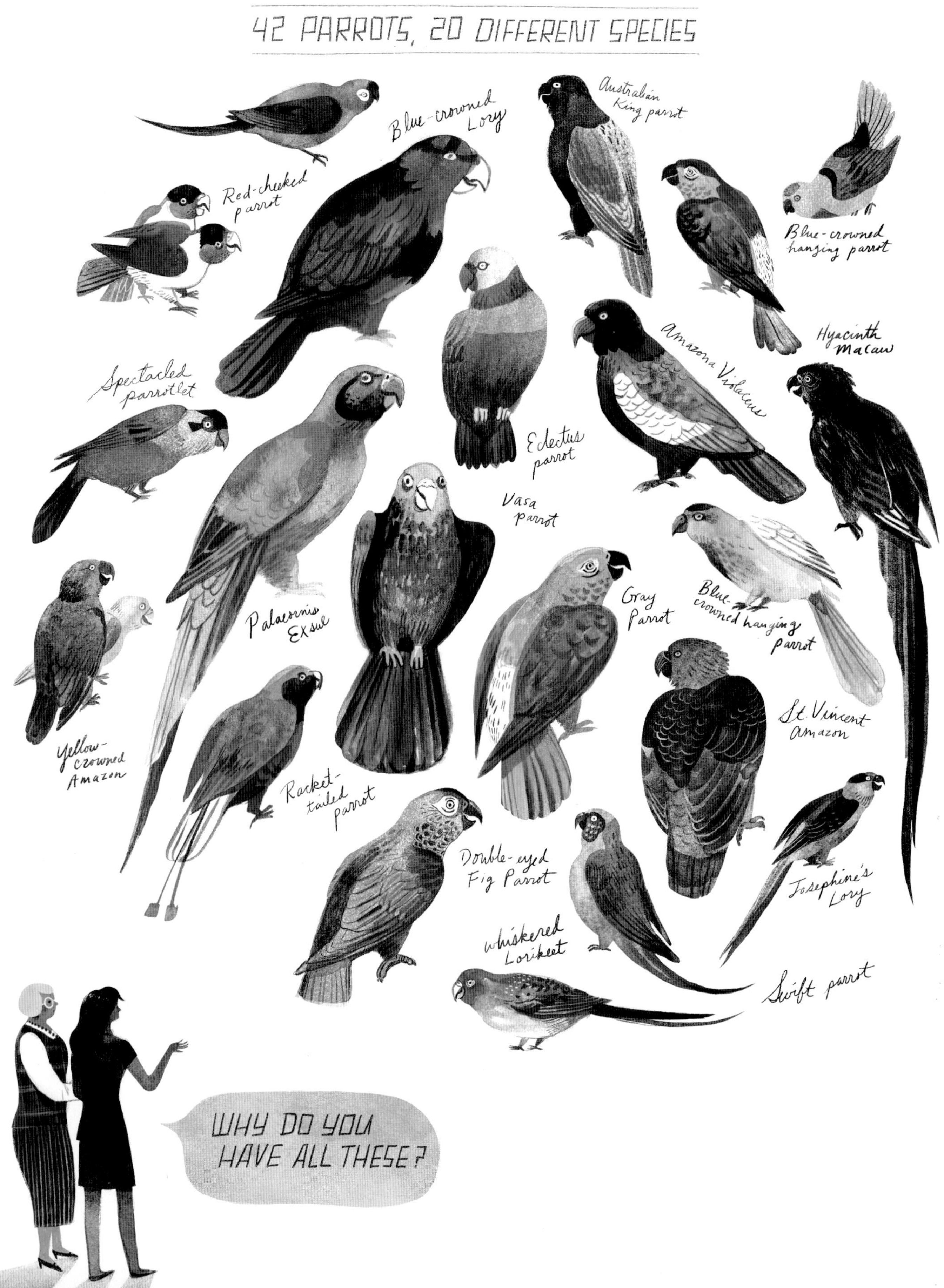
42 PARROTS, 20 DIFFERENT SPECIES
Blue-crowned Lory
Australian King parrot
Red-cheeked parrot
Blue-crowned hanging parrot
Hyacinth Macaw
Amazona Violaceus
Spectacled parrotlet
Eclectus parrot
Vasa parrot
Palaeornis Exsul
Gray Parrot
Blue-crowned hanging parrot
Yellow-crowned Amazon
St. Vincent Amazon
Racket-tailed parrot
Double-eyed Fig Parrot
Josephine's Lory
whiskered Lorikeet
Swift parrot
WHY DO YOU HAVE ALL THESE?

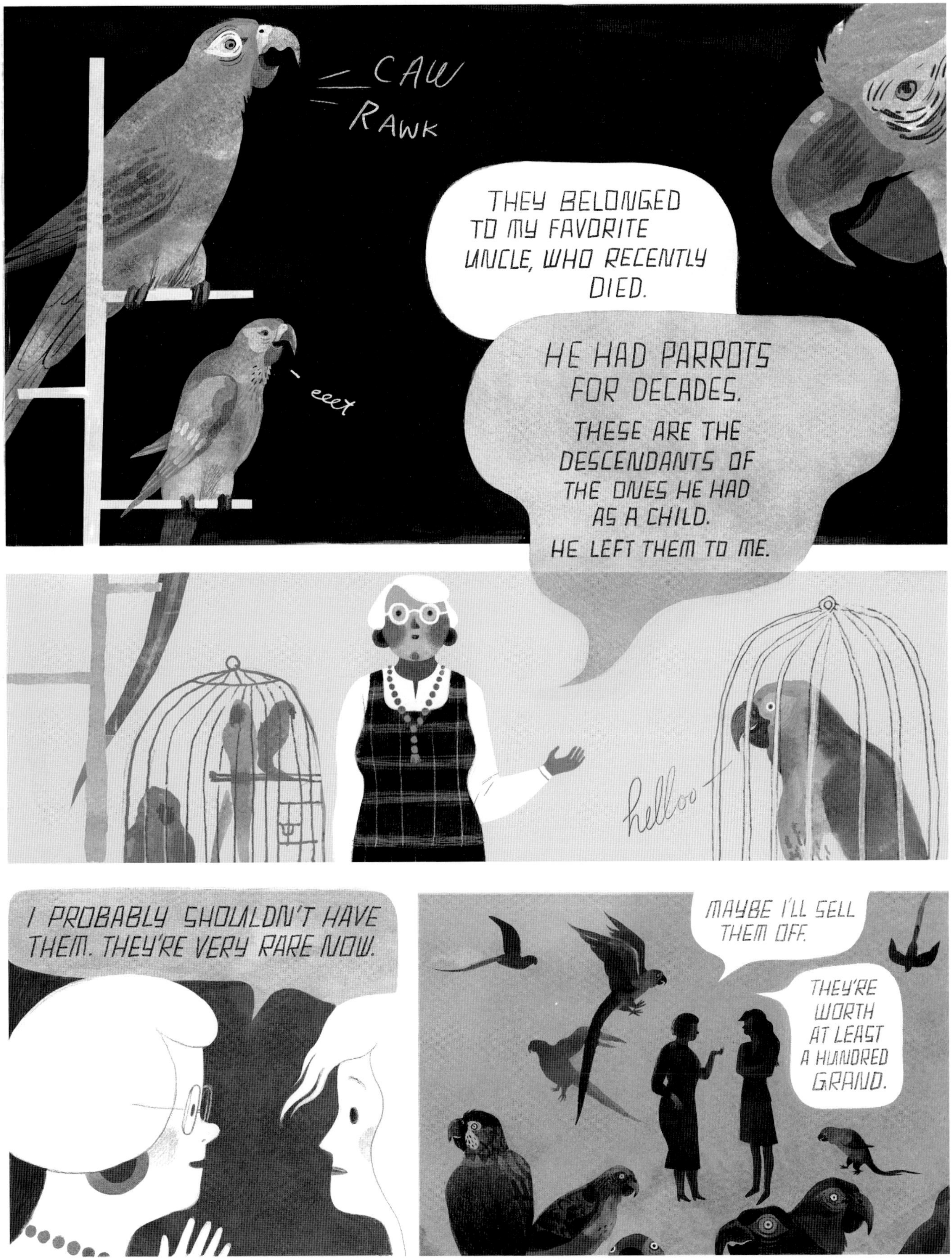
CAW
RAWK
THEY BELONGED TO MY FAVORITE UNCLE, WHO RECENTLY DIED.
eeet
HE HAD PARROTS FOR DECADES.
THESE ARE THE DESCENDANTS OF THE ONES HE HAD AS A CHILD.
HE LEFT THEM TO ME.
helloo
I PROBABLY SHOULDN'T HAVE THEM. THEY'RE VERY RARE NOW.
MAYBE I'LL SELL THEM OFF.
THEY'RE WORTH AT LEAST A HUNDRED GRAND.

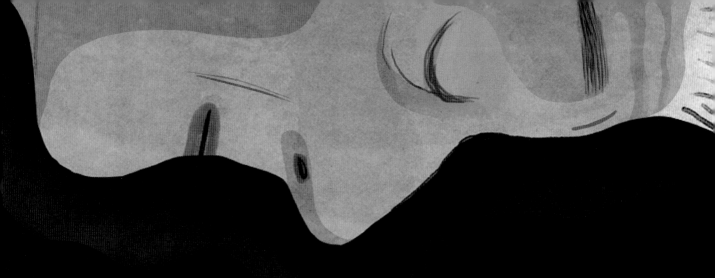

BUT THEY REMIND ME OF HIM.

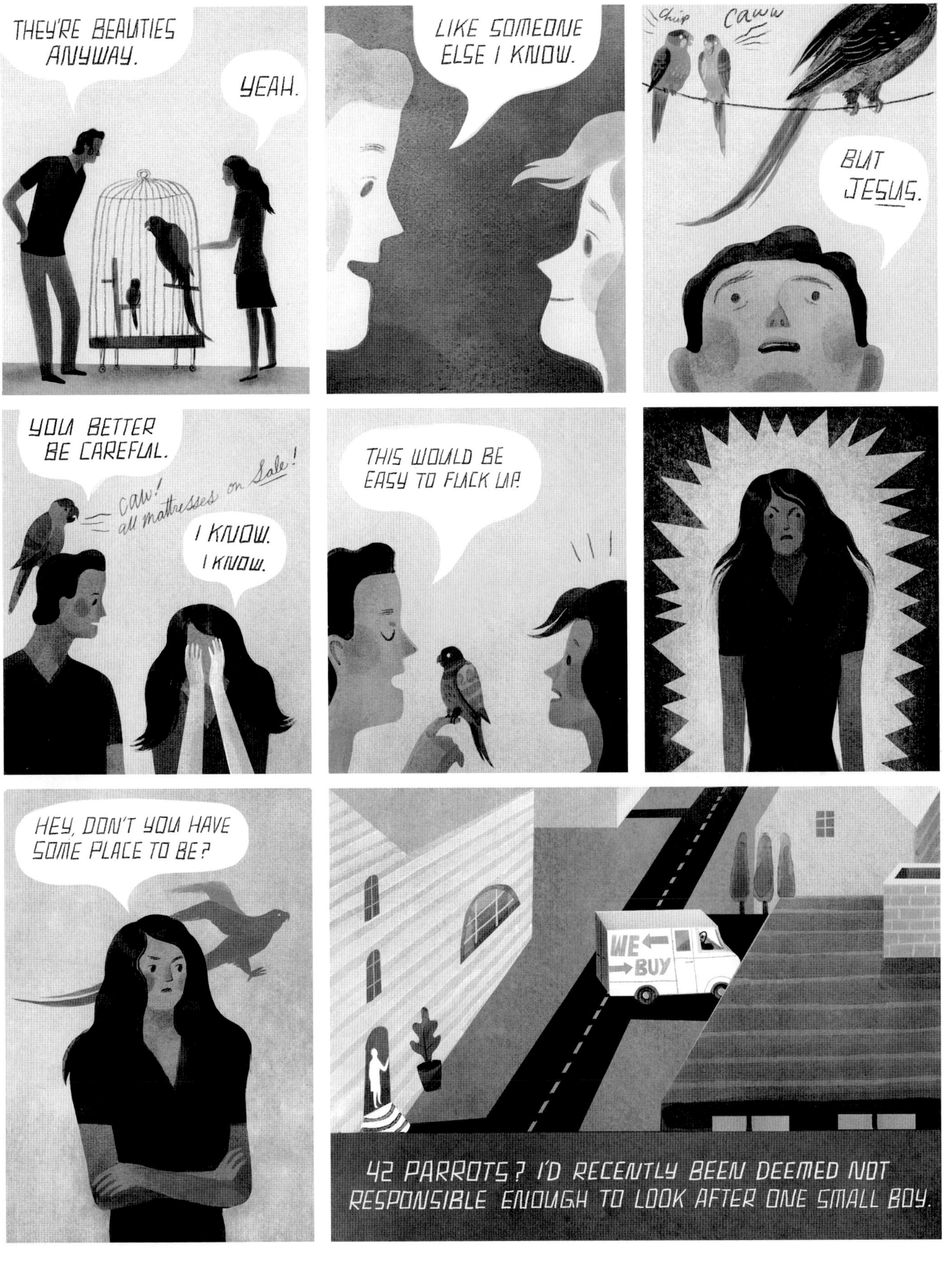
THEY'RE BEAUTIES ANYWAY.
YEAH.
LIKE SOMEONE ELSE I KNOW.
Chirp
Caww
BUT JESUS.
YOU BETTER BE CAREFUL.
Caw! all mattresses on Sale!
I KNOW. I KNOW.
THIS WOULD BE EASY TO FUCK UP.
HEY, DON'T YOU HAVE SOME PLACE TO BE?
WE BUY
42 PARROTS? I'D RECENTLY BEEN DEEMED NOT RESPONSIBLE ENOUGH TO LOOK AFTER ONE SMALL BOY.

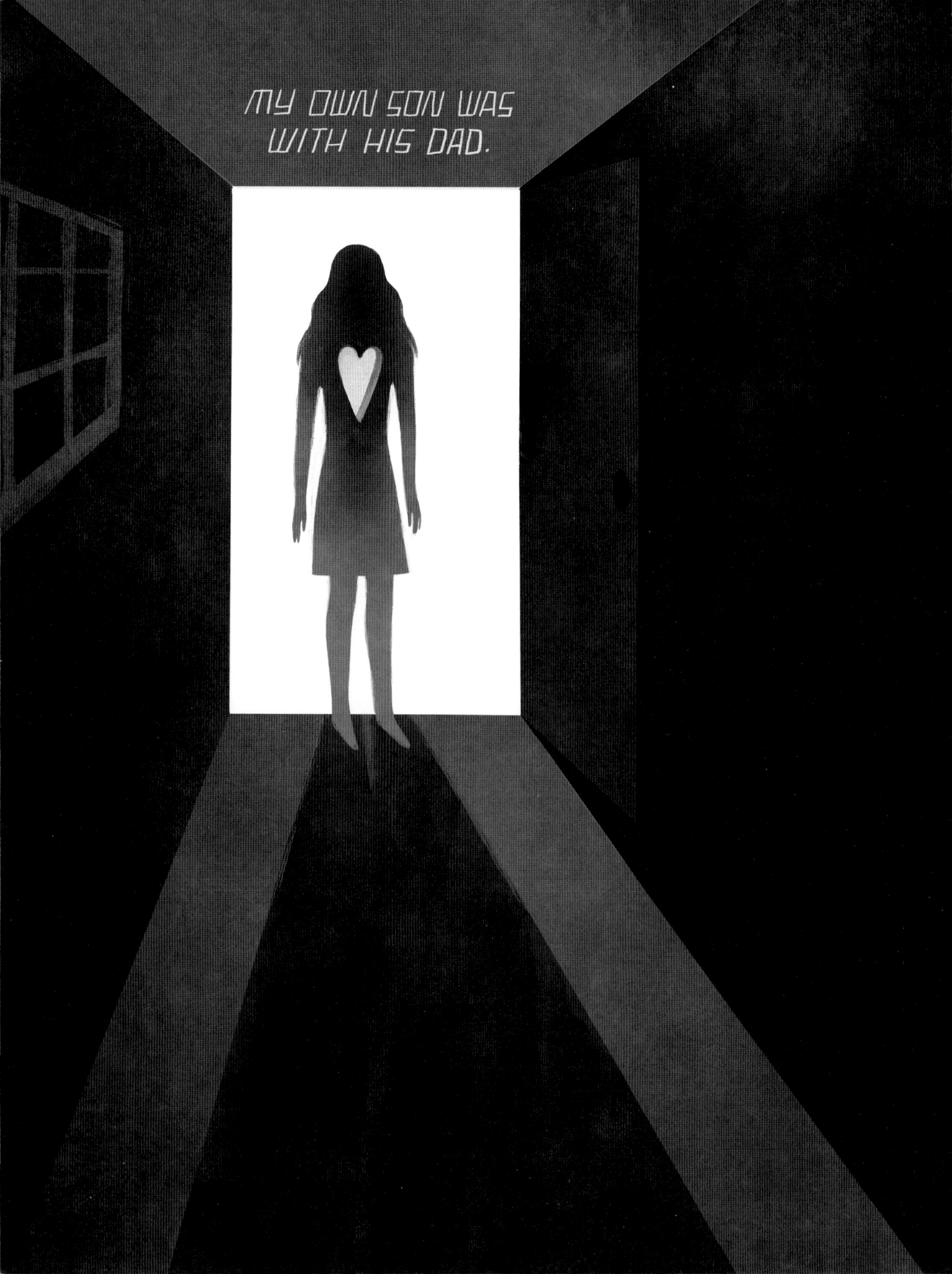
MY OWN SON WAS
WITH HIS DAD.

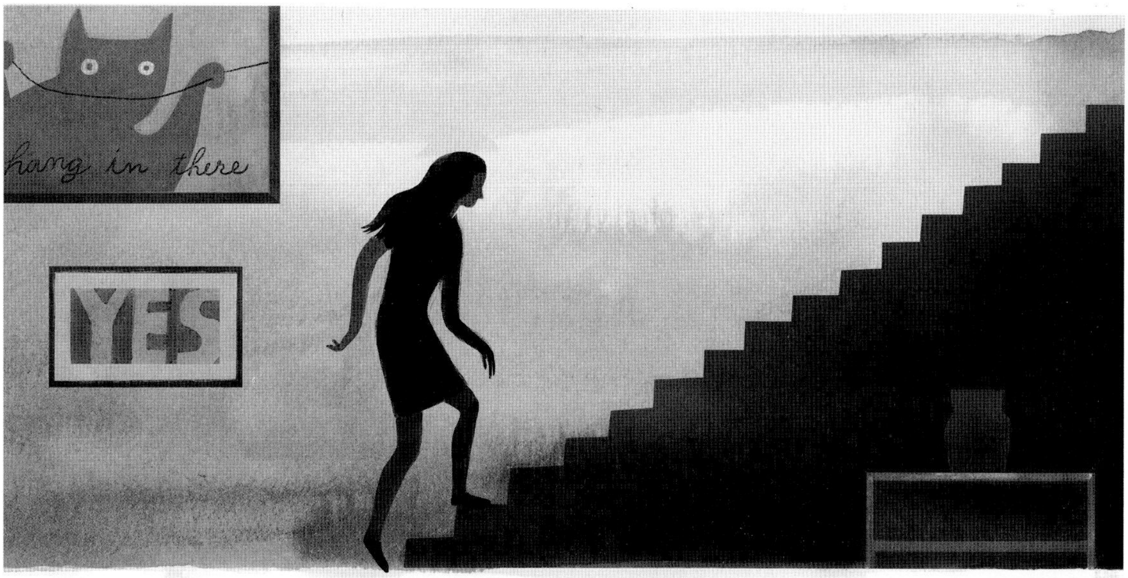
hang in there
YES

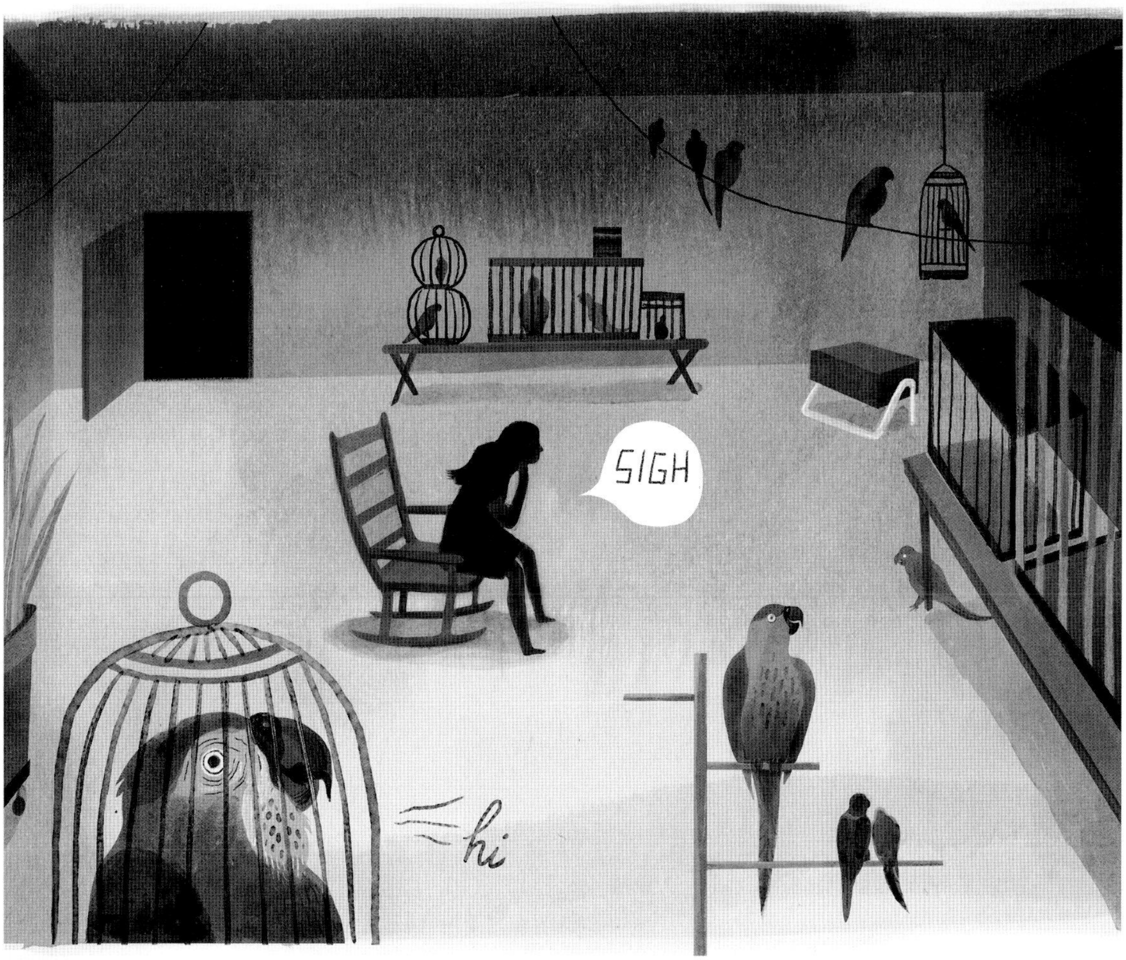
SIGH
hi

CHAPTER 2: CUSTODIAL CATASTROPHE

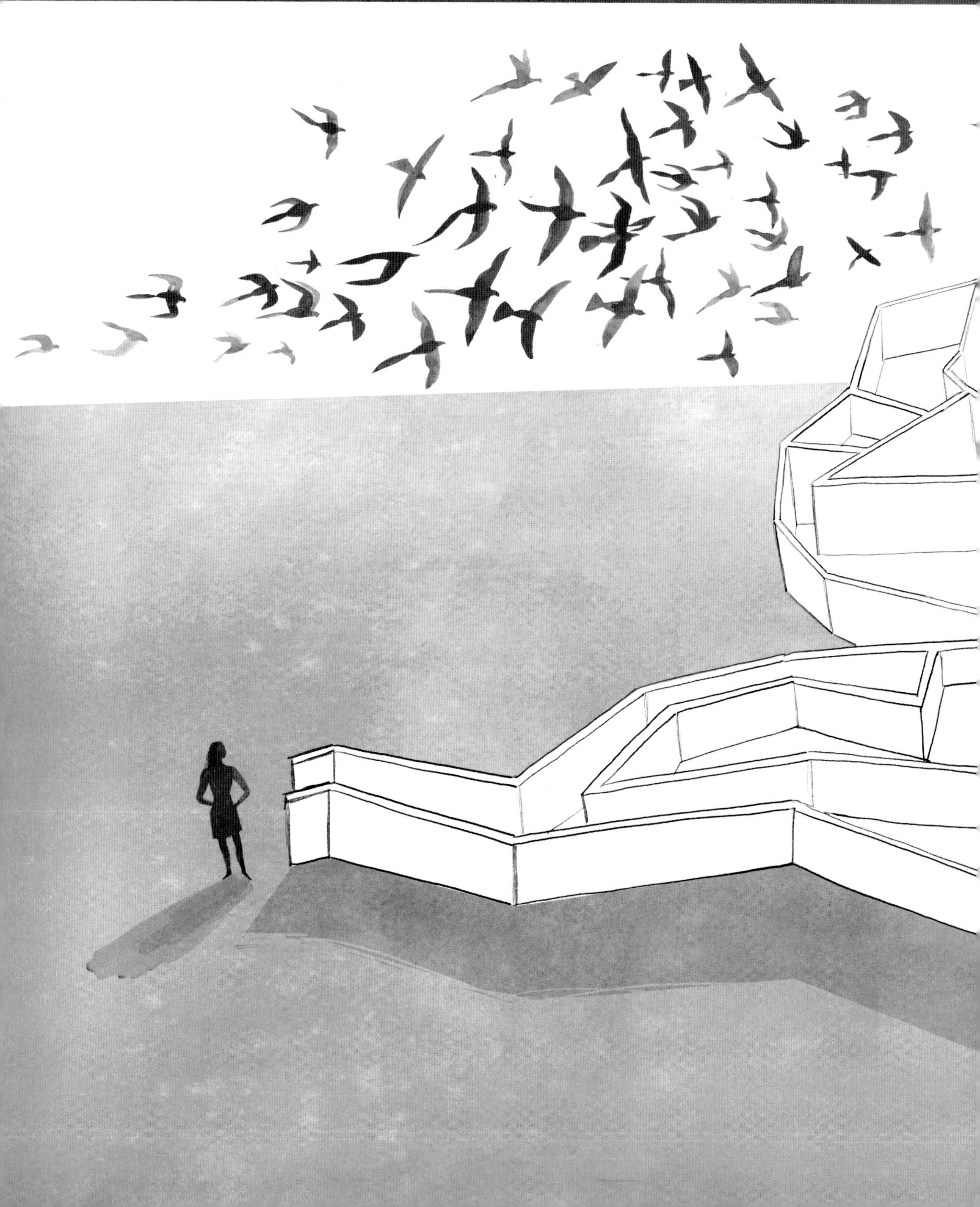

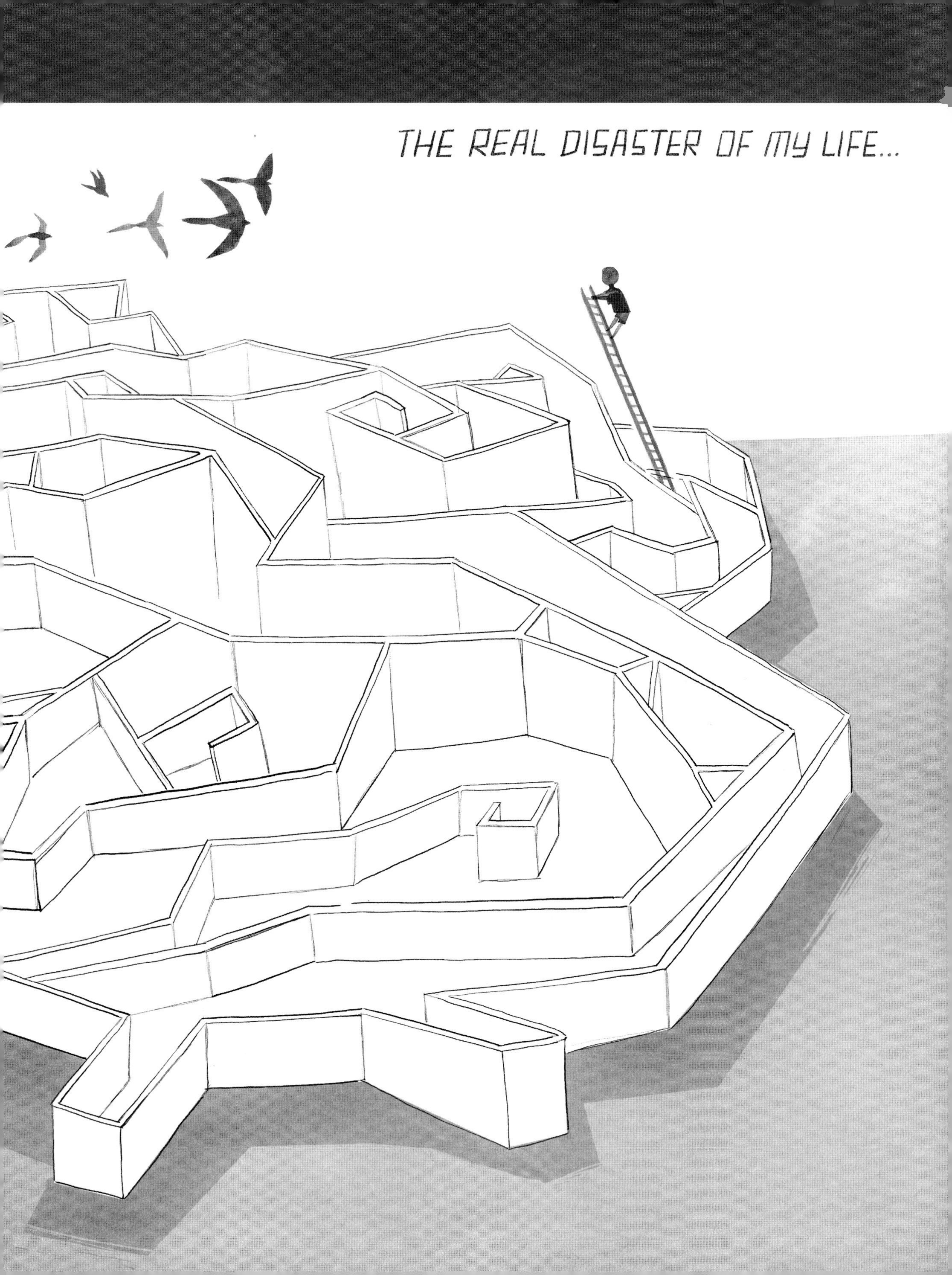
THE REAL DISASTER OF MY LIFE...

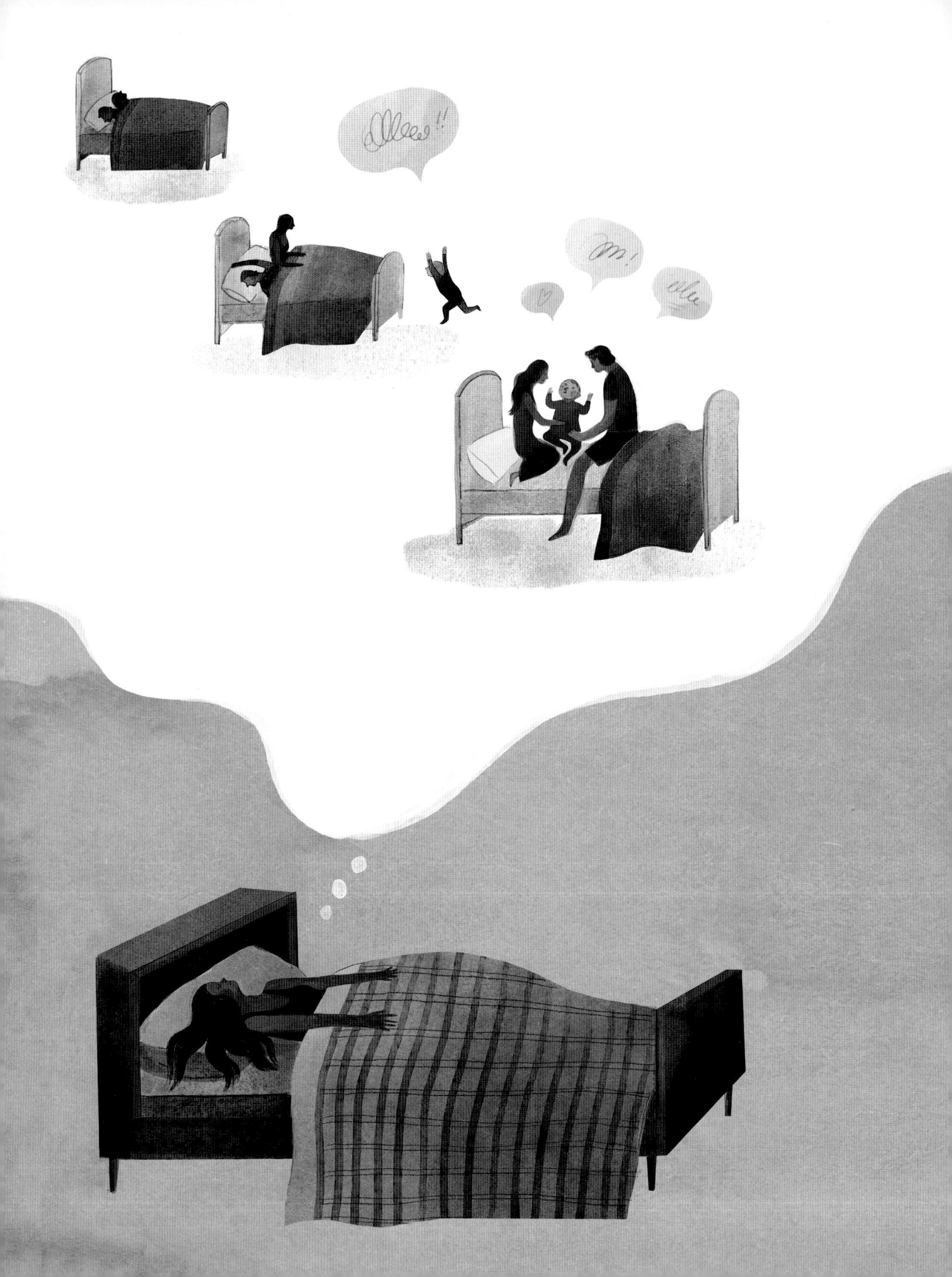

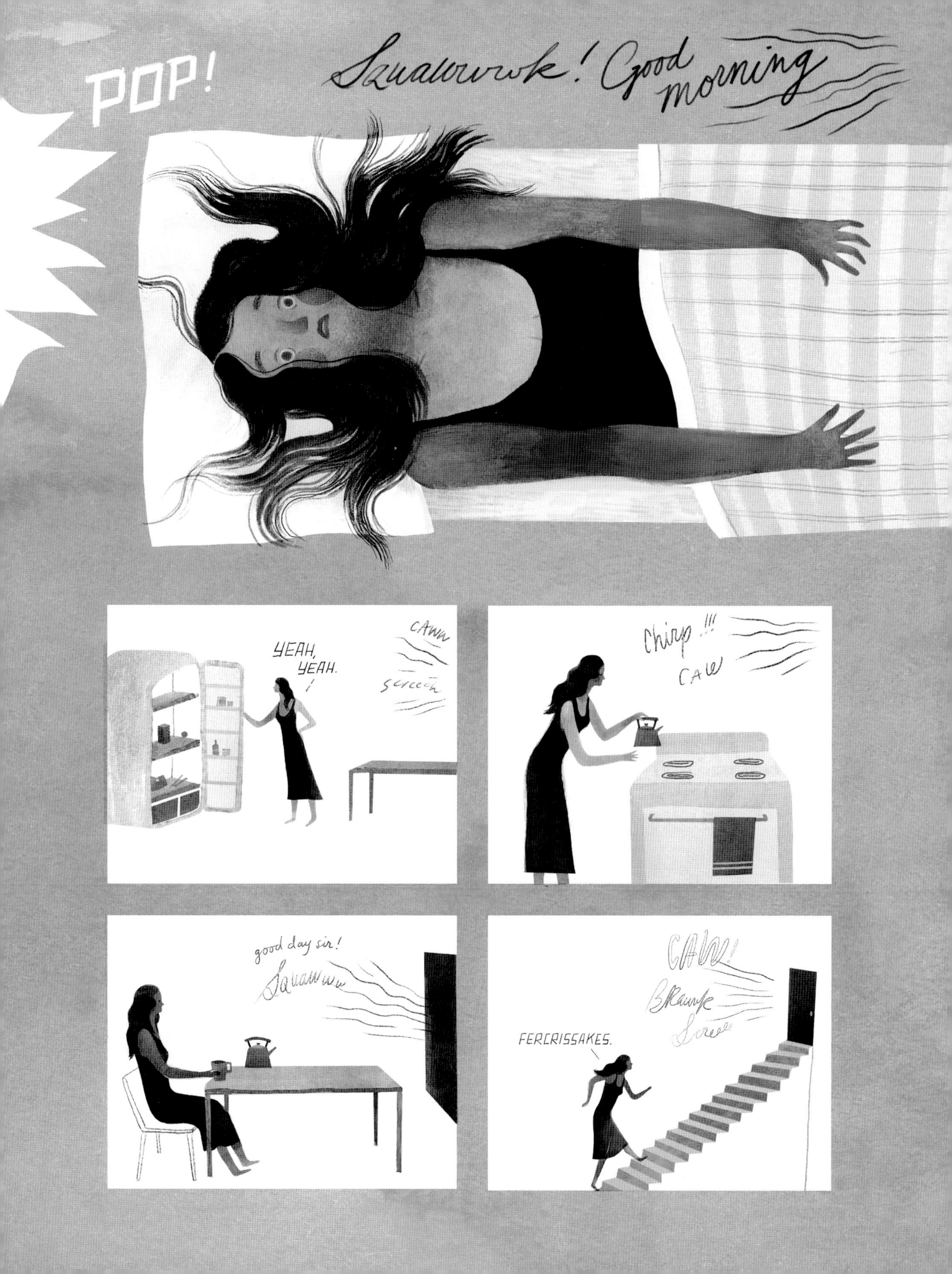

POP!
Squawwwk! Good morning
YEAH, YEAH.
CAWW
screech
Chirp !!!
CAW
good day sir!
Squawwww
FERCRISSAKES.
CAW!
Brawk
Screee

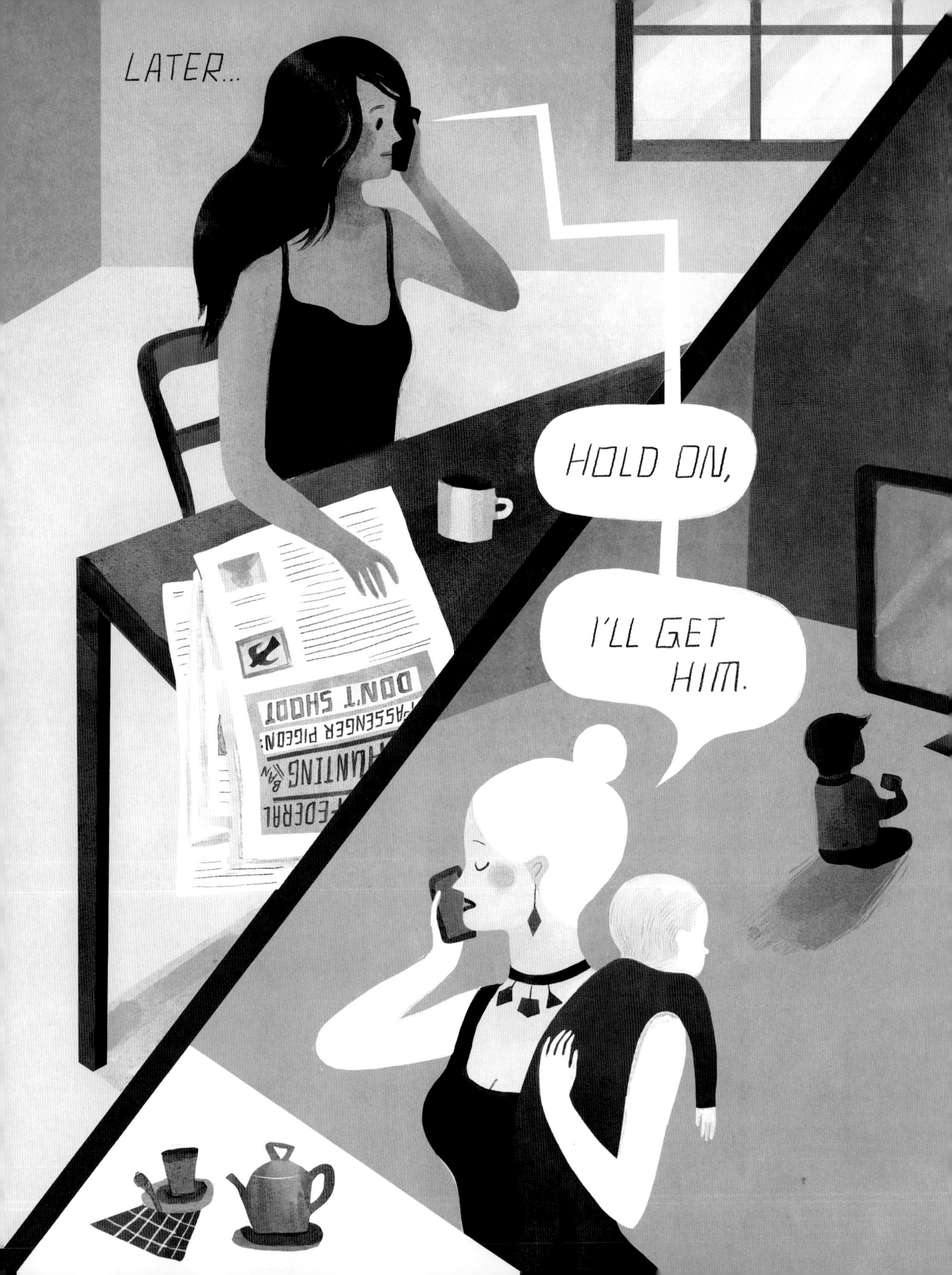
LATER...
HOLD ON,
I'LL GET HIM.
DON'T SHOOT

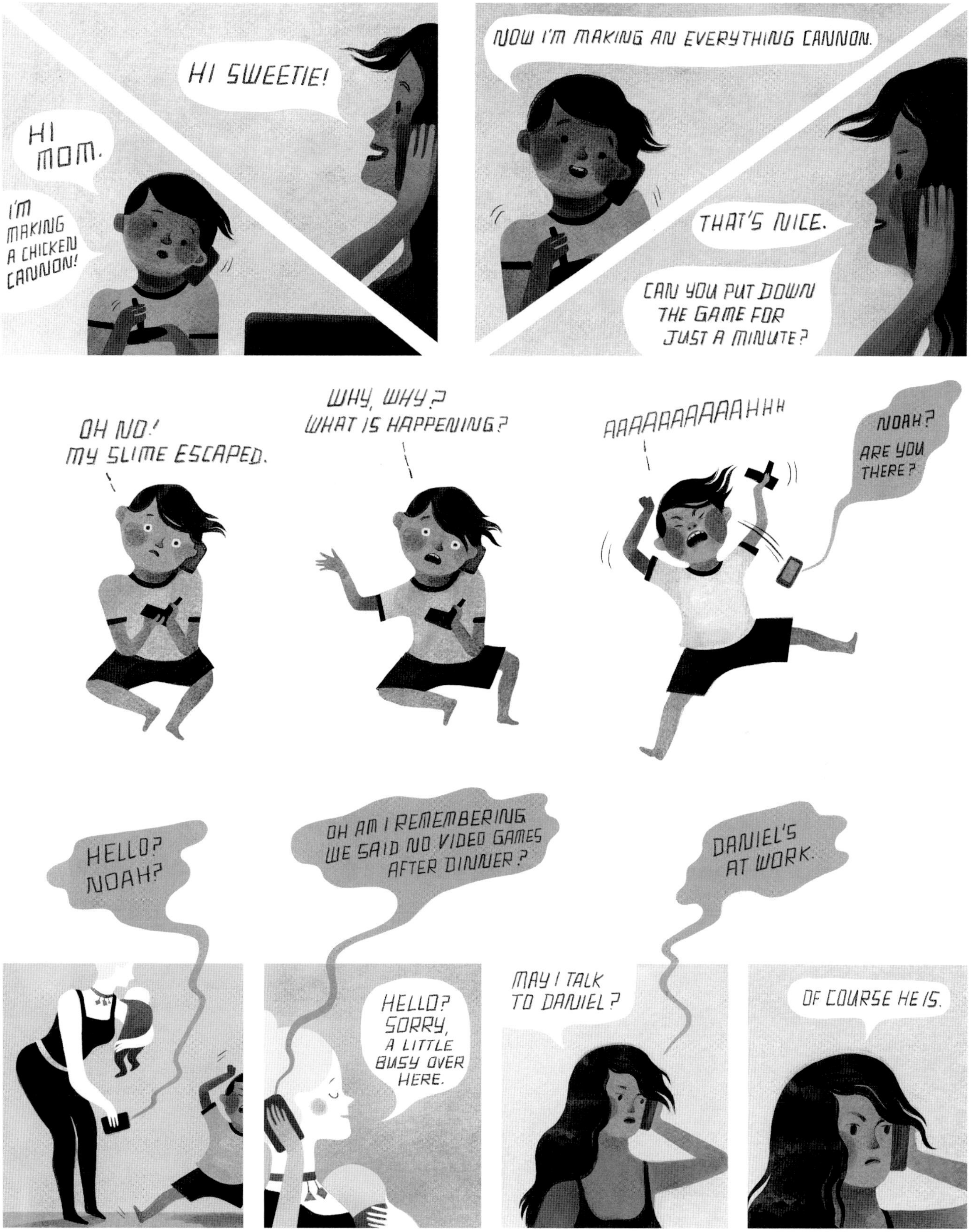
HI SWEETIE!
HI MOM.
I'M MAKING A CHICKEN CANNON!
NOW I'M MAKING AN EVERYTHING CANNON.
THAT'S NICE.
CAN YOU PUT DOWN THE GAME FOR JUST A MINUTE?
OH NO! MY SLIME ESCAPED.
WHY, WHY? WHAT IS HAPPENING?
AAAAAAAAAAAHHH
NOAH? ARE YOU THERE?
HELLO? NOAH?
OH AM I REMEMBERING WE SAID NO VIDEO GAMES AFTER DINNER?
HELLO? SORRY, A LITTLE BUSY OVER HERE.
MAY I TALK TO DANIEL?
DANIEL'S AT WORK.
OF COURSE HE IS.

THE REAL DISASTER OF MY LIFE (OR THE MOST RECENT ONE, OTHER THAN THIS HERD OF BIRDS) WAS MY EX-HUSBAND'S MARRIAGE TO A NEW WOMAN.

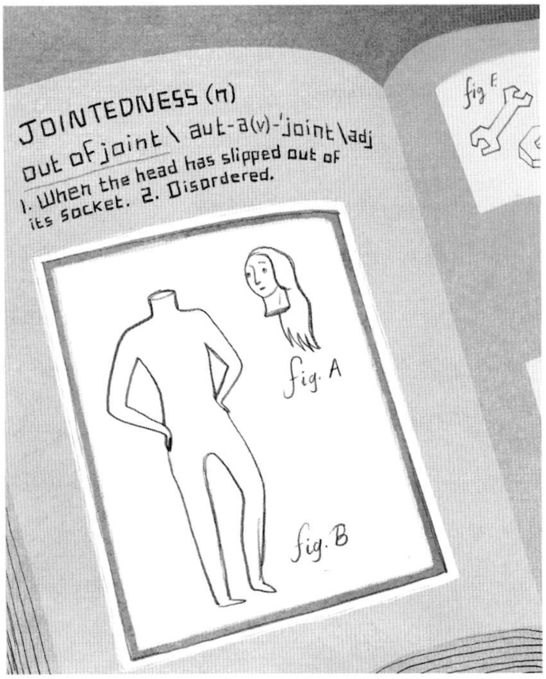
JOINTEDNESS (n)
out of joint
adj
1. When the head has slipped out of its socket. 2. Disordered.
fig. F
fig. A
fig. B

SOMEHOW IN THE FALLOUT FROM HIS PIÑATA OF HAPPINESS, THE PHRASE "JOINT CUSTODY" SUDDENLY SHIFTED FROM MEANING "EQUAL CUSTODY," OR EVEN "TIE GOES TO THE MOTHER CUSTODY," TO A JOINT CUSTODY THAT SEEMED VERY MUCH OUT OF JOINT, WITH ME GETTING CUSTODY EVERY OTHER WEEKEND, HALF THE HOLIDAYS, AND THREE THIN SUMMER WEEKS, WHILE THE NEW HAPPY COUPLE GOT CUSTODY OF EVERYTHING ELSE.

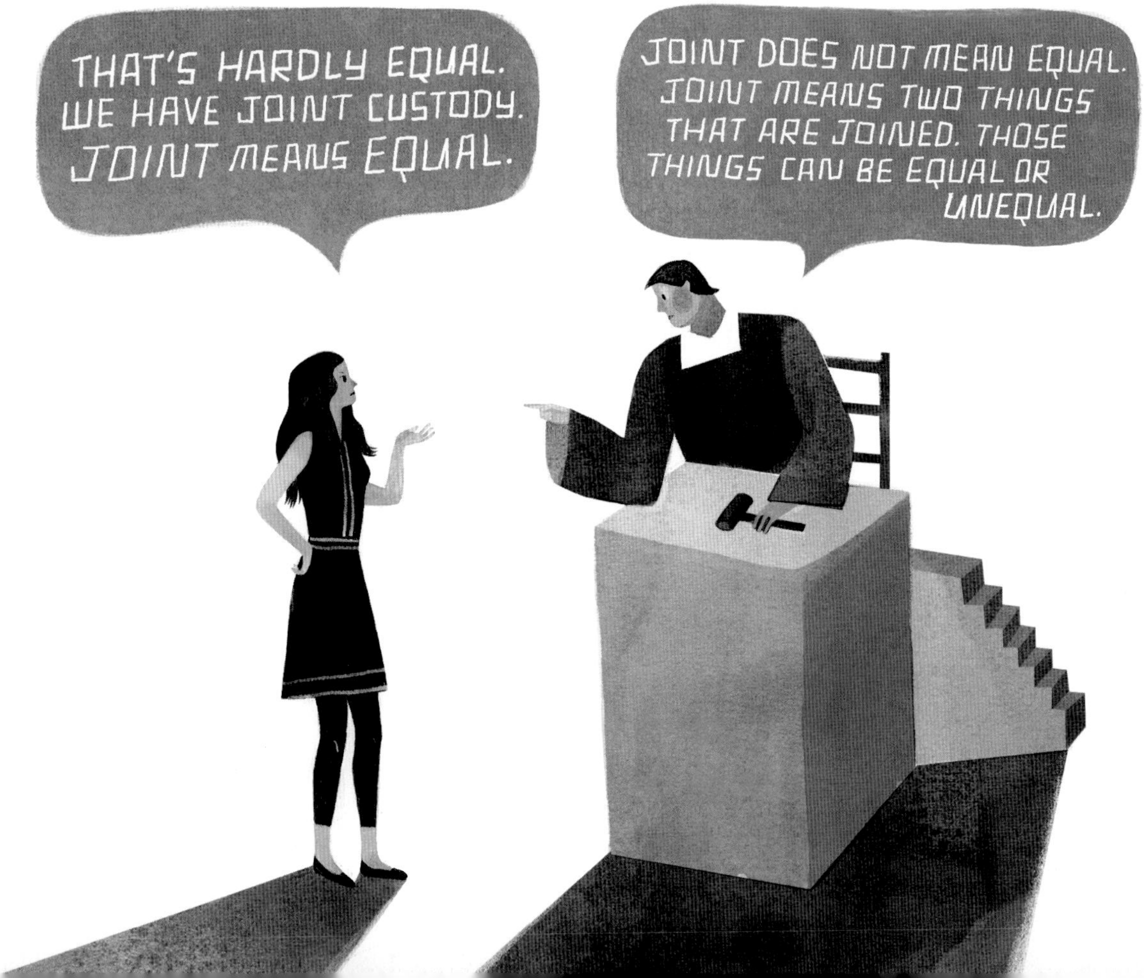
THAT'S HARDLY EQUAL. WE HAVE JOINT CUSTODY. JOINT MEANS EQUAL.
JOINT DOES NOT MEAN EQUAL. JOINT MEANS TWO THINGS THAT ARE JOINED. THOSE THINGS CAN BE EQUAL OR UNEQUAL.

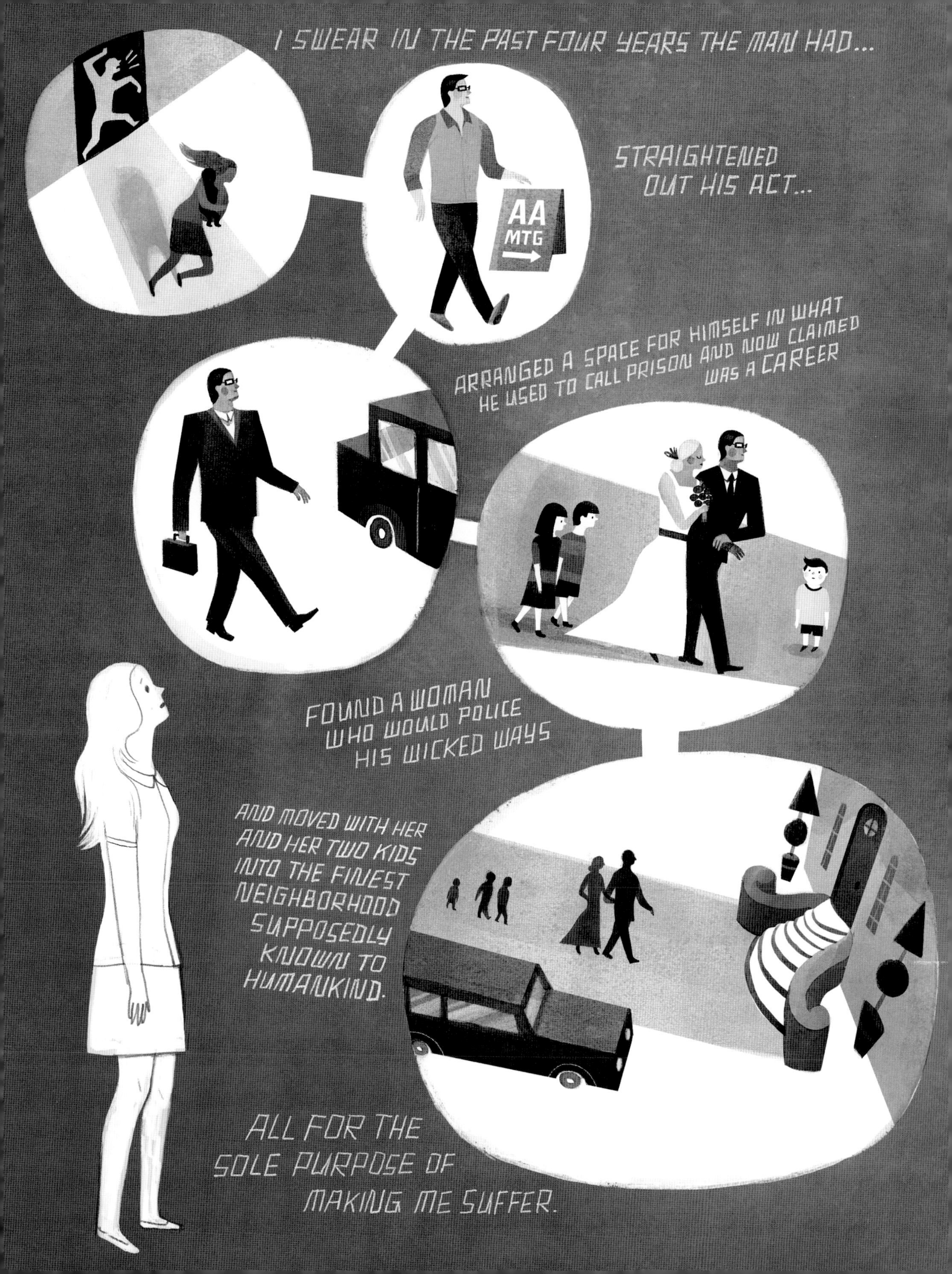
I SWEAR IN THE PAST FOUR YEARS THE MAN HAD...
STRAIGHTENED OUT HIS ACT...
AA MTG
ARRANGED A SPACE FOR HIMSELF IN WHAT HE USED TO CALL PRISON AND NOW CLAIMED WAS A CAREER
FOUND A WOMAN WHO WOULD POLICE HIS WICKED WAYS
AND MOVED WITH HER AND HER TWO KIDS INTO THE FINEST NEIGHBORHOOD SUPPOSEDLY KNOWN TO HUMANKIND.
ALL FOR THE SOLE PURPOSE OF MAKING ME SUFFER.

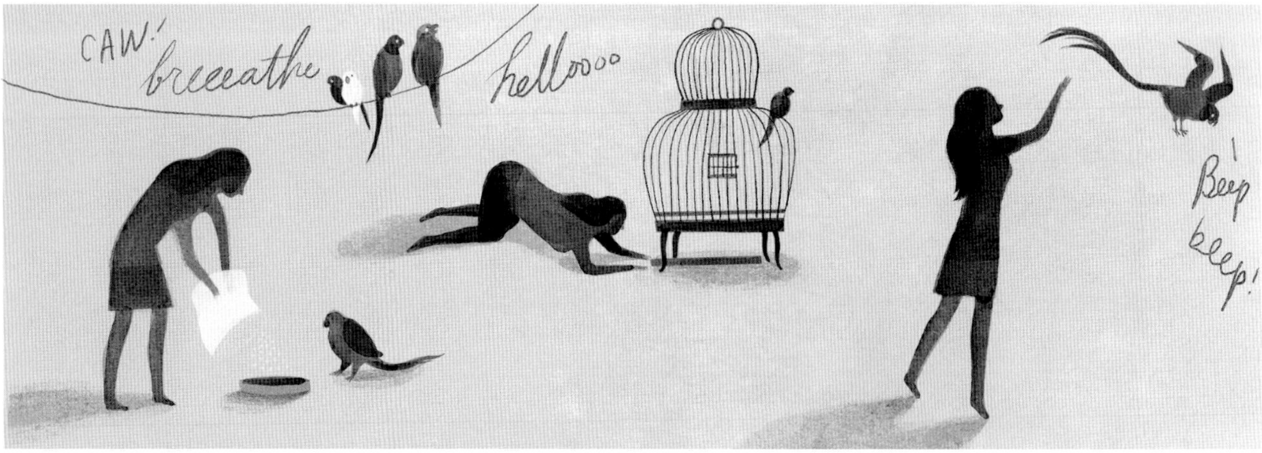
CAW!
breeeathe
hellooo
Beep beep!

IF I COULD KEEP THE JOB FOR SIX MONTHS, ACCORDING TO MY LAWYER,
WELL, NO PROMISES, BUT NO ONE WANTS TO KEEP A KID FROM HIS MOM.

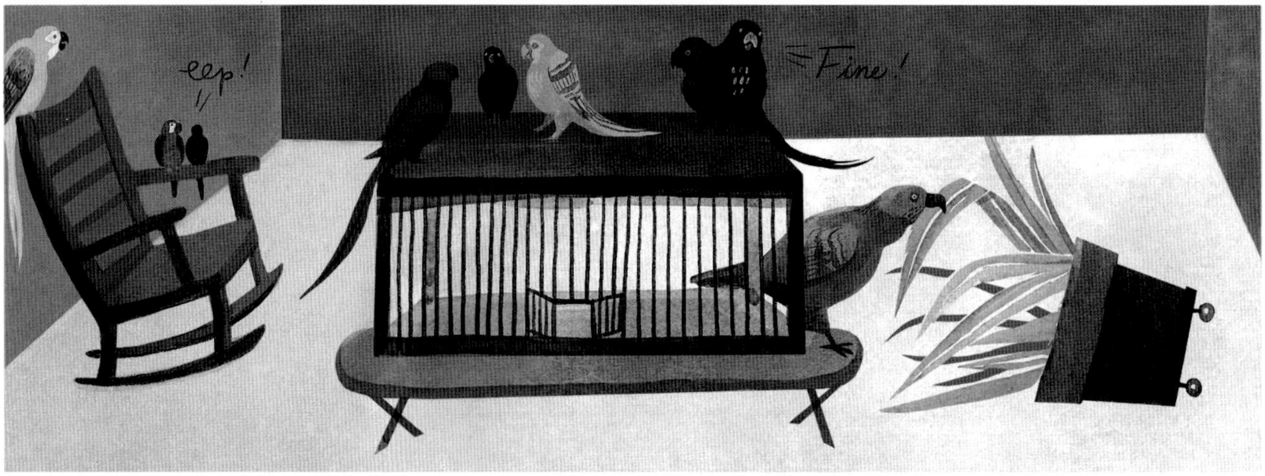
eep!
Fine!

SO IF THE MOON WANTED ME TO WATCH 100,000 DOLLARS' WORTH OF BIRDS...

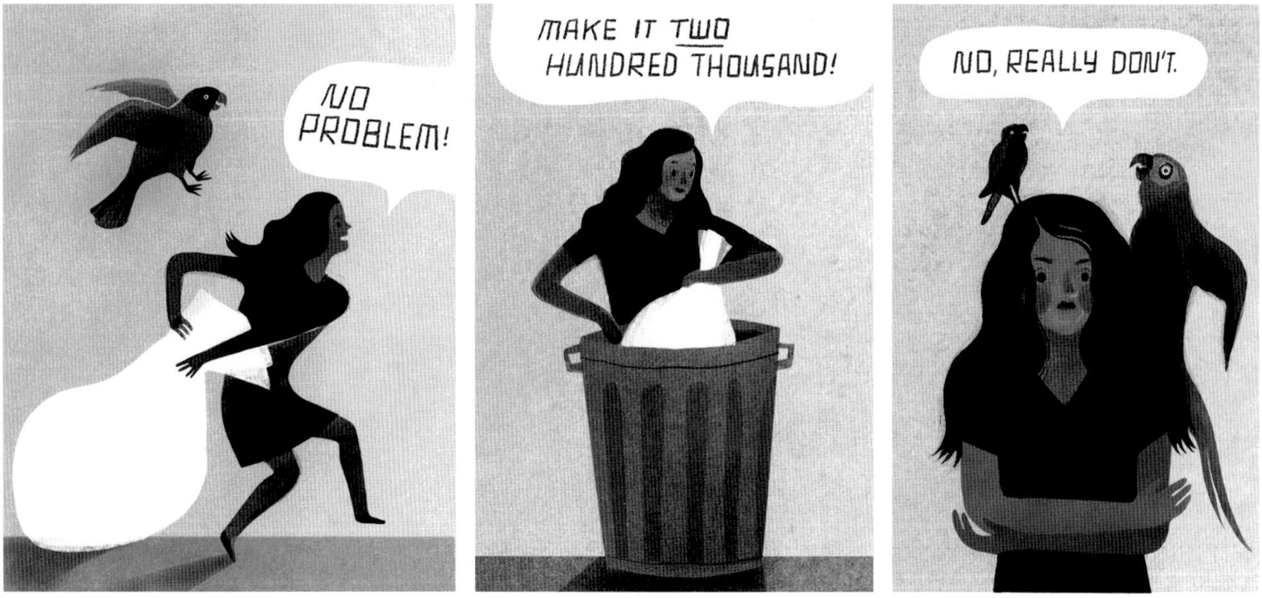
NO PROBLEM!
MAKE IT TWO HUNDRED THOUSAND!
NO, REALLY DON'T.

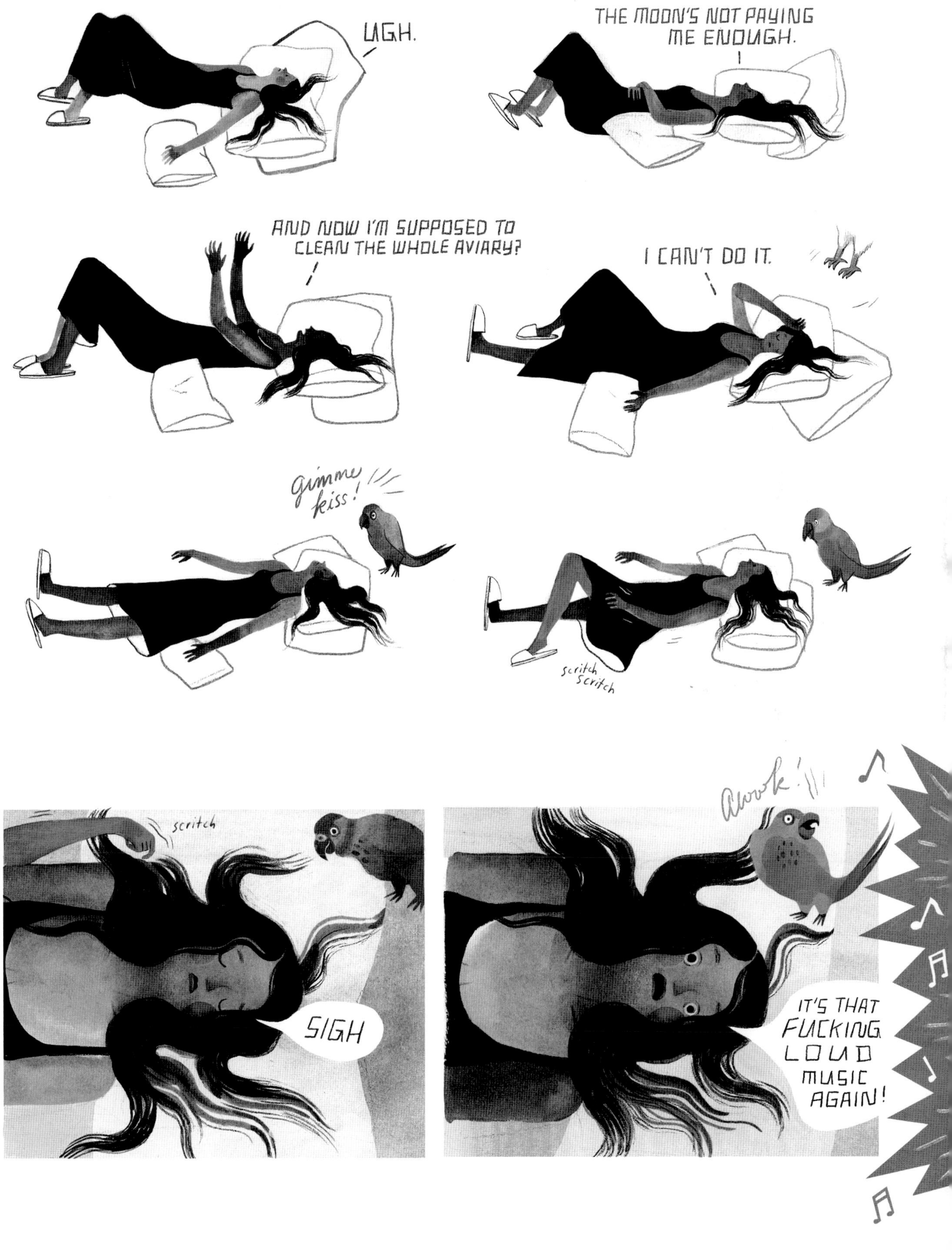
UGH.
THE MOON'S NOT PAYING ME ENOUGH.
AND NOW I'M SUPPOSED TO CLEAN THE WHOLE AVIARY?
I CAN'T DO IT.
gimme kiss!
scritch scritch
scritch
SIGH
Awok!
IT'S THAT FUCKING LOUD MUSIC AGAIN!

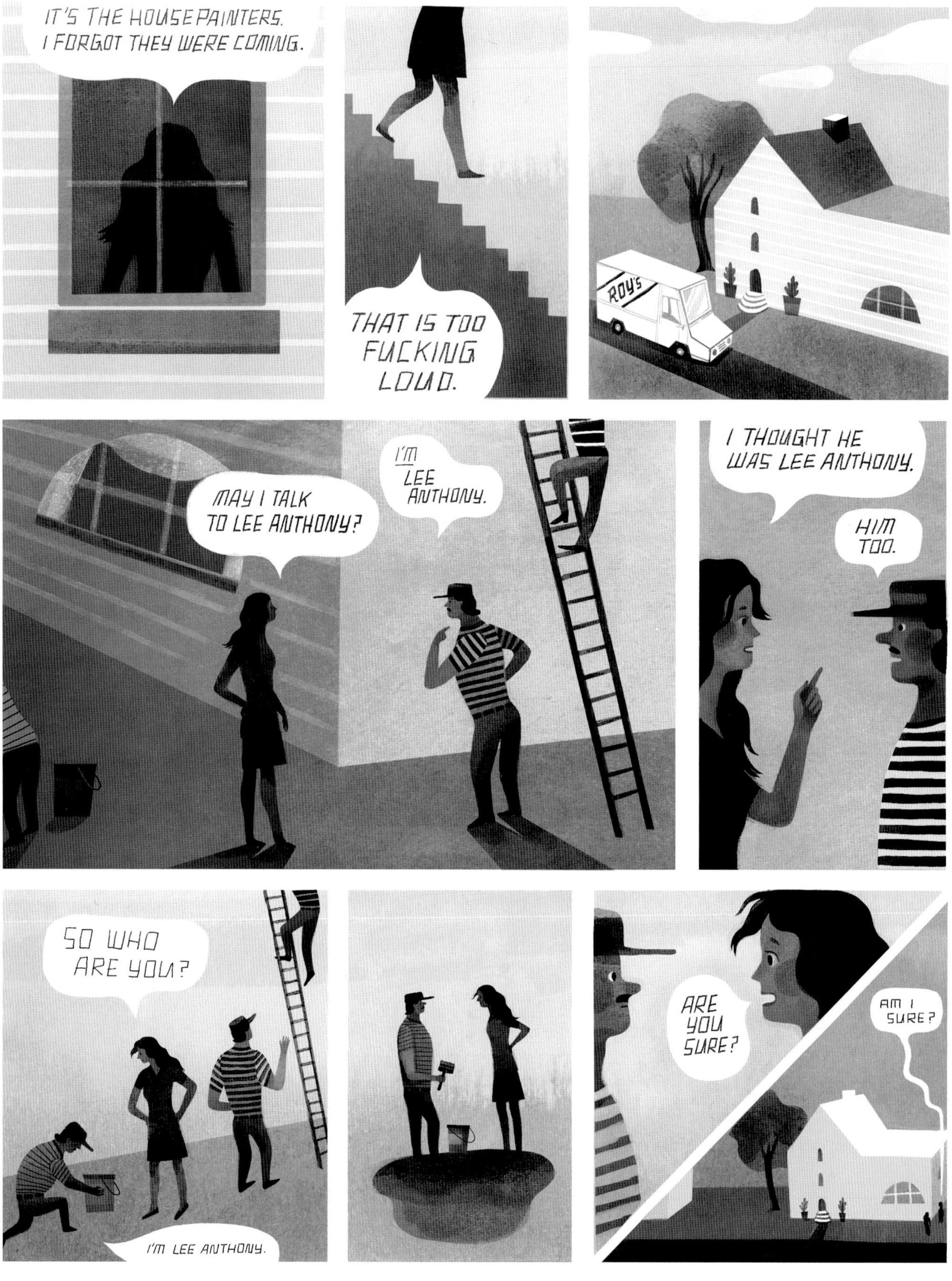
IT'S THE HOUSEPAINTERS. I FORGOT THEY WERE COMING.
THAT IS TOO FUCKING LOUD.
ROY'S
MAY I TALK TO LEE ANTHONY?
I'M LEE ANTHONY.
I THOUGHT HE WAS LEE ANTHONY.
HIM TOO.
SO WHO ARE YOU?
I'M LEE ANTHONY.
ARE YOU SURE?
AM I SURE?

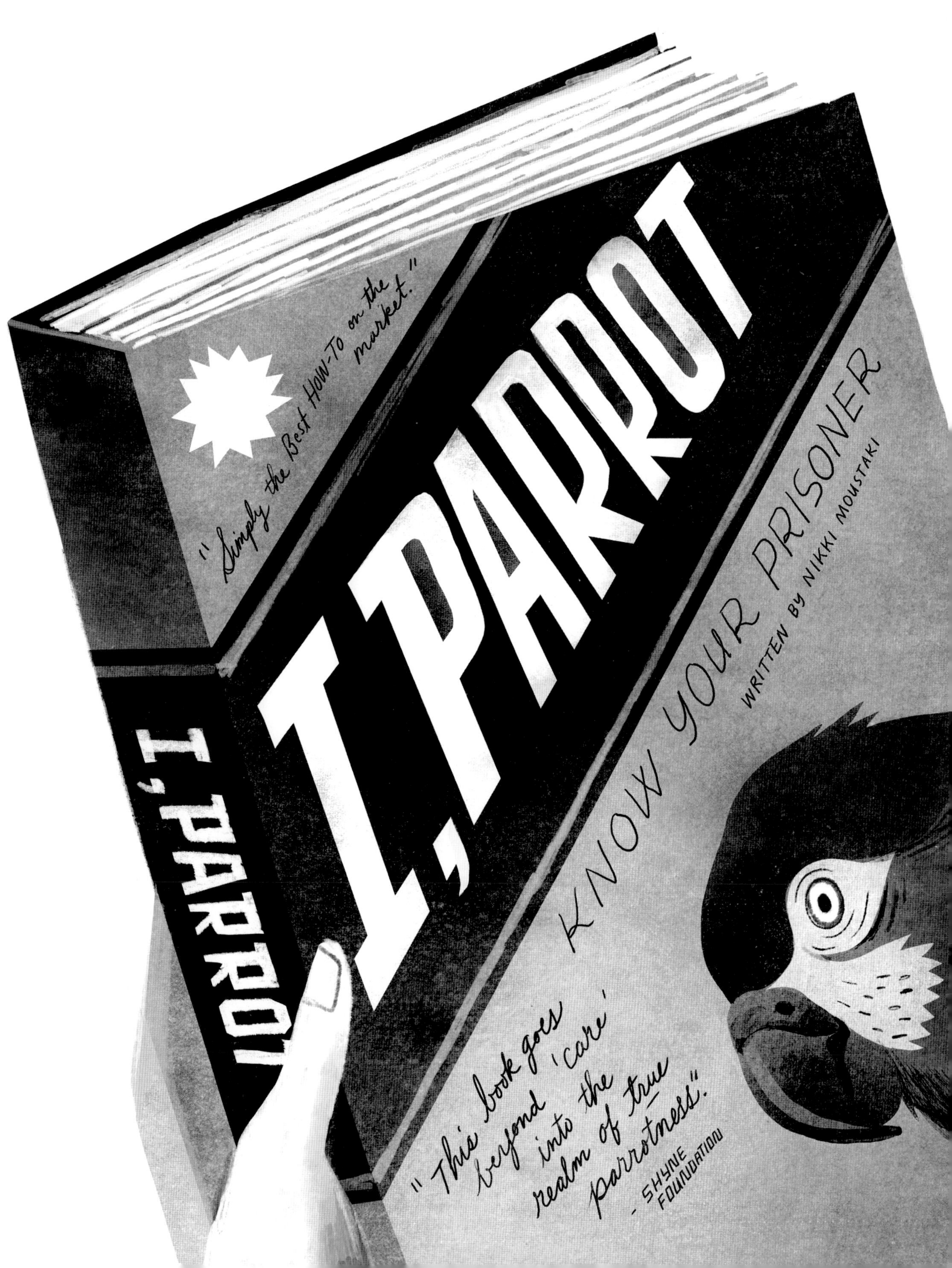

"Simply the Best HOW-TO on the market."
I, PARROT
KNOW YOUR PRISONER
WRITTEN BY NIKKI MOUSTAKI
"This book goes beyond 'care' into the realm of true parrotness".
- SHYNE FOUNDATION
I, PARROT

INTRODUCTION

IF YOU HAVE A PARROT, YOU CAN BE PRETTY CERTAIN THIS BOOK IS FOR YOU BECAUSE ANYONE WITH A PARROT DOESN'T UNDERSTAND HIM. ANYONE WHO HAS A PARROT IS NOT UP TO THE TASK.

Fig. 2.1 Be sure to bring your avian friend in a safe, sturdy carrier when visiting the vet.

HOW DO YOU THINK HE LIKES BEING LOCKED IN A SMALL DARK BOX FOR HIS ENTIRE LIFE? DO YOU THINK YOU CAN DO ANYTHING OTHER THAN TRY UNSUCCESSFULLY TO KEEP THE BIRD FROM SLIDING INTO CRIPPLING, SUICIDAL DEPRESSION WHILE YOU SLOWLY SQUASH EVERY INSTINCT HE HAS? FAILURE IS ALL YOU CAN HOPE FOR.

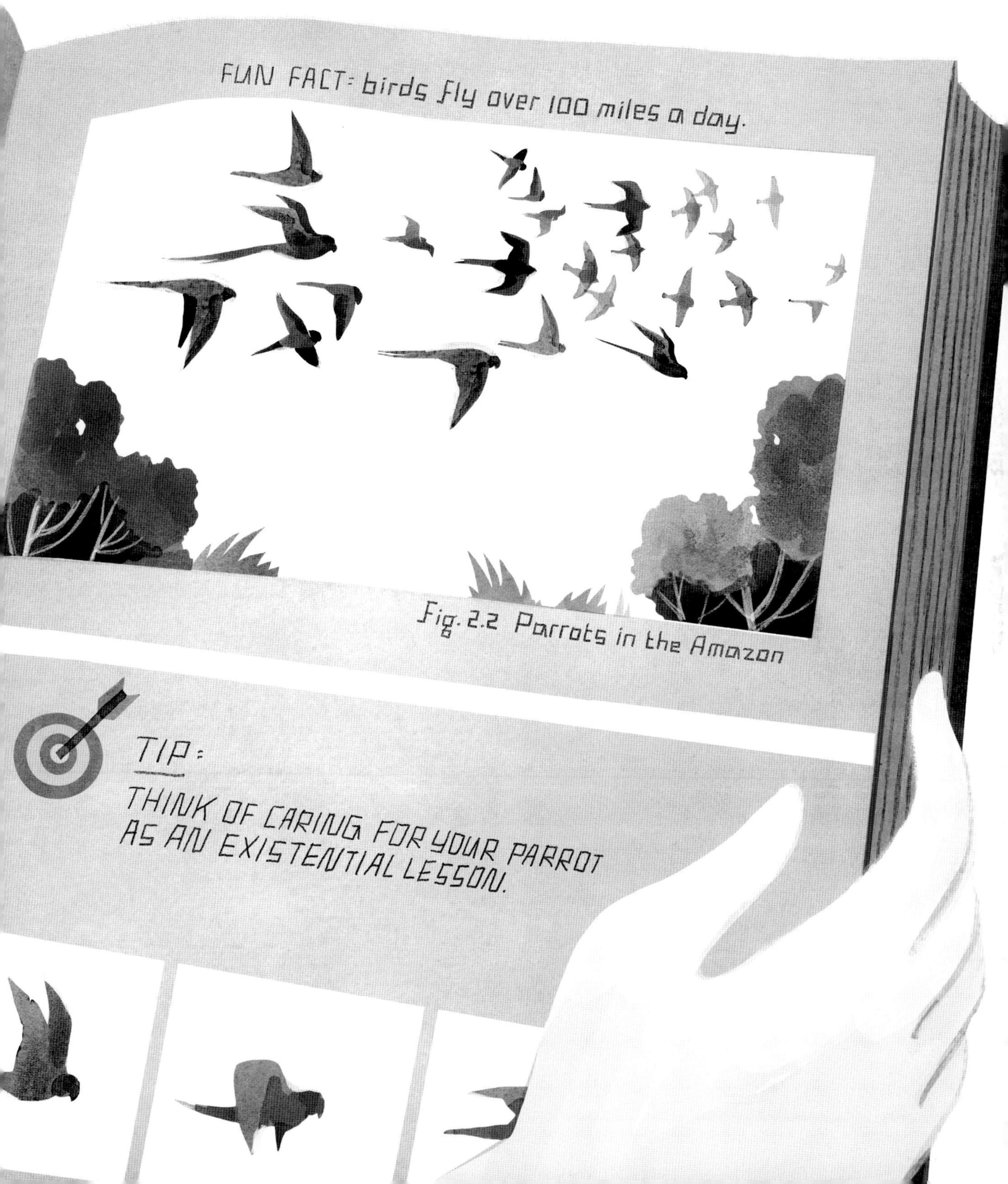
FUN FACT: birds fly over 100 miles a day.
Fig. 2.2 Parrots in the Amazon
TIP:
THINK OF CARING FOR YOUR PARROT AS AN EXISTENTIAL LESSON.

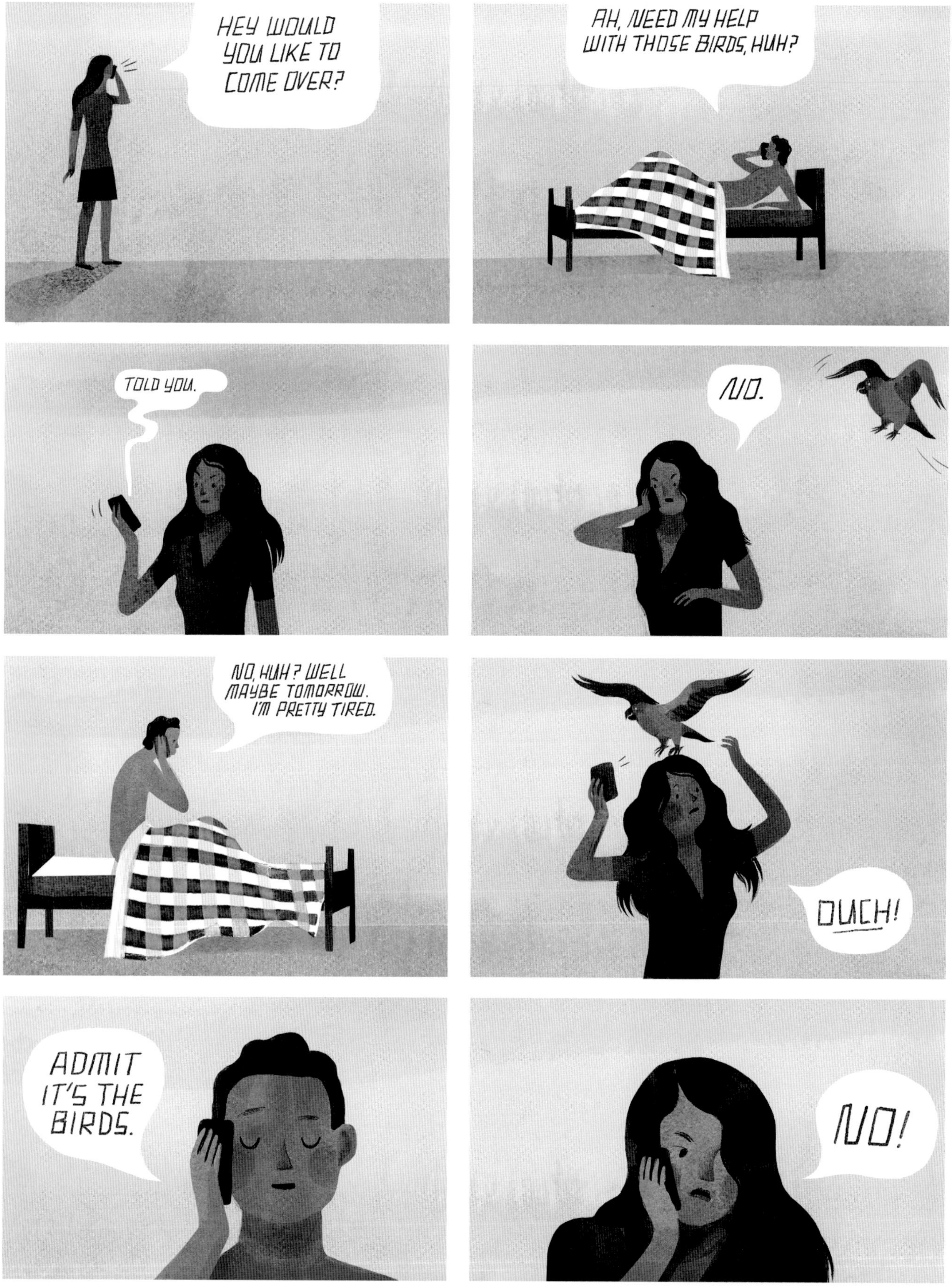
HEY WOULD YOU LIKE TO COME OVER?
AH, NEED MY HELP WITH THOSE BIRDS, HUH?
TOLD YOU.
NO.
NO, HUH? WELL MAYBE TOMORROW. I'M PRETTY TIRED.
OUCH!
ADMIT IT'S THE BIRDS.
NO!

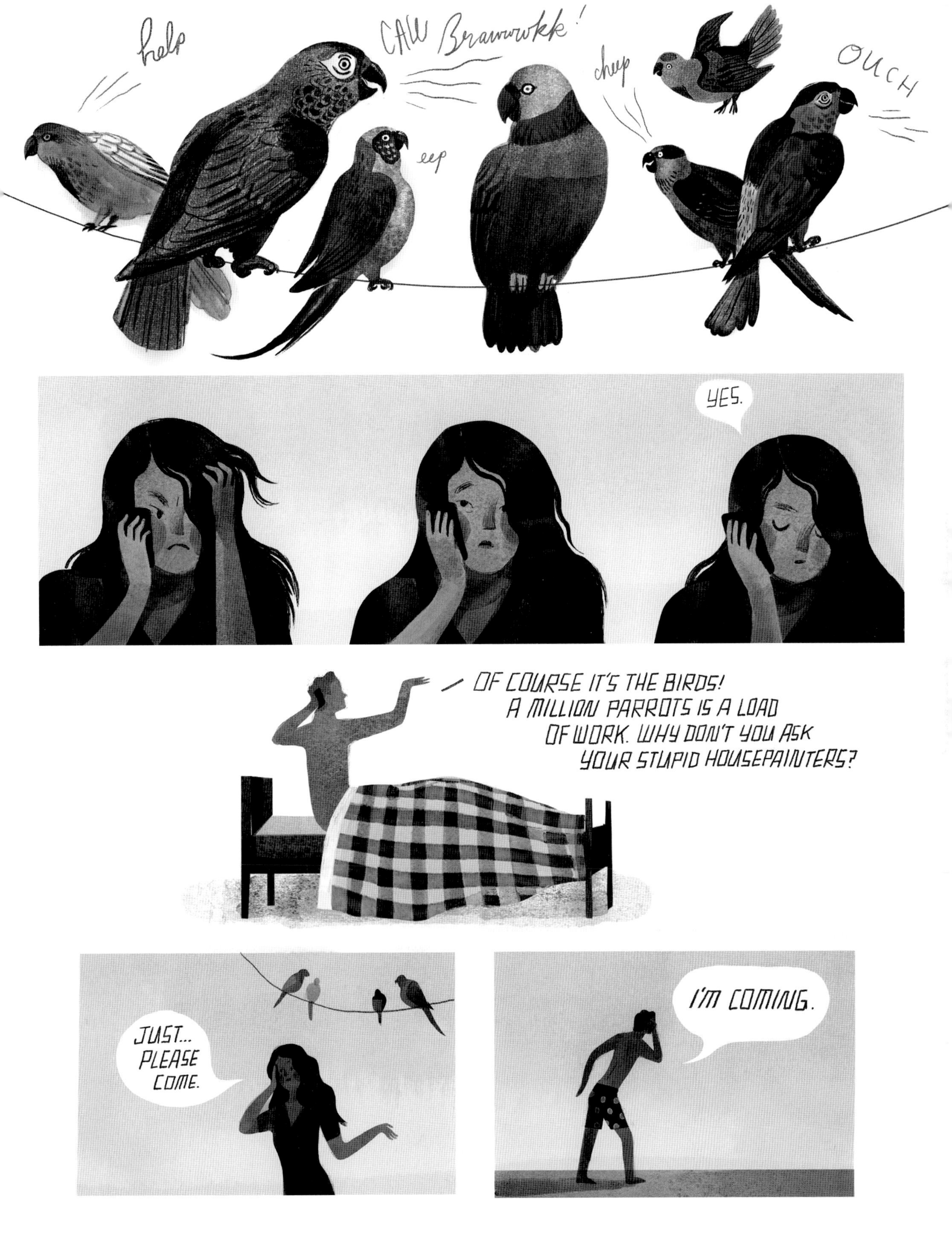
help
CAW Brawwwkk!
eep
cheep
OUCH
YES.
OF COURSE IT'S THE BIRDS! A MILLION PARROTS IS A LOAD OF WORK. WHY DON'T YOU ASK YOUR STUPID HOUSEPAINTERS?
JUST... PLEASE COME.
I'M COMING.

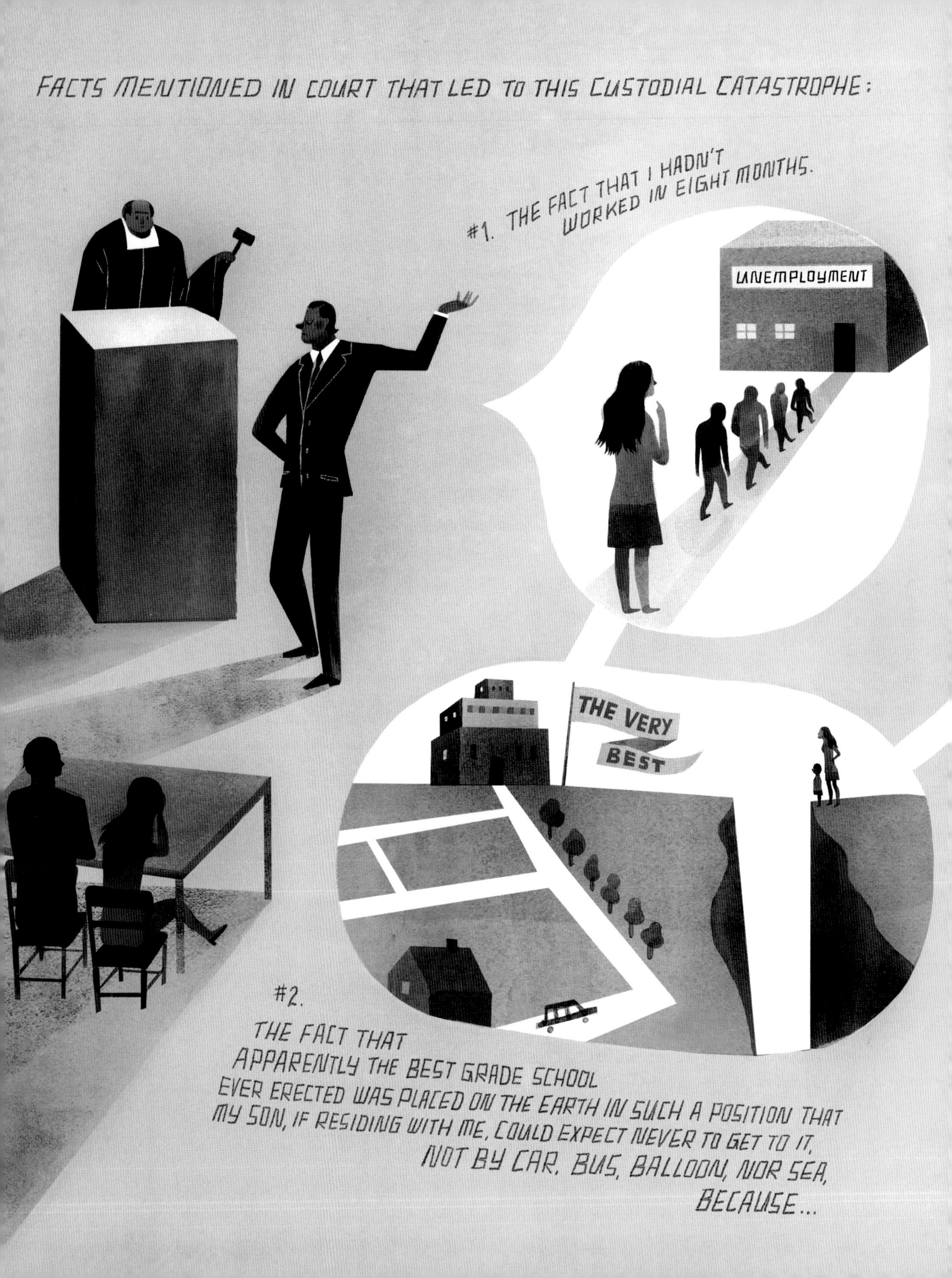
FACTS MENTIONED IN COURT THAT LED TO THIS CUSTODIAL CATASTROPHE:
#1. THE FACT THAT I HADN'T WORKED IN EIGHT MONTHS.
UNEMPLOYMENT
THE VERY BEST
#2.
THE FACT THAT
APPARENTLY THE BEST GRADE SCHOOL
EVER ERECTED WAS PLACED ON THE EARTH IN SUCH A POSITION THAT
MY SON, IF RESIDING WITH ME, COULD EXPECT NEVER TO GET TO IT,
NOT BY CAR, BUS, BALLOON, NOR SEA,
BECAUSE...

#2. CONTINUED... I WAS OBVIOUSLY NOT THE KIND OF WOMAN WHO COULD LIVE NEARBY THE BEST GRADE SCHOOL EVER ERECTED OR BE COUNTED ON TO GET HIM THERE.

FIG. A

FIG. B

MEANWHILE *
MY EX-HUSBAND
LIVED COINCIDENTALLY
AN EASY 3-BLOCK,
TREE-LINED WALK AWAY. †

#3. THE FACT THAT I HAD "INAPPROPRIATE" "ABUSIVE" "MEN" "LOITERING THE HOUSEHOLD."

THERE WERE SO MANY THINGS WRONG WITH THIS ONE, I DON'T KNOW WHERE TO BEGIN...

FOOTNOTES:

* YES, IT LOOKED LIKE HE WOULD ALWAYS BE MY EX-HUSBAND. THAT WORD "HUSBAND" WOULD BE PART OF WHAT HE WAS TO ME FOR ALL TIME, DESPITE STRENUOUS EFFORTS ON MY PART— INCLUDING ABANDONMENT AND DIVORCE—TO OUST HIM.

† WHAT, BTW, DOES A KID NEED TO GO TO THE BEST KINDERGARTEN IN EXISTENCE FOR? AND WHAT WAS SO GREAT ABOUT IT? DID THEY FINGERPAINT WITH GOLD?

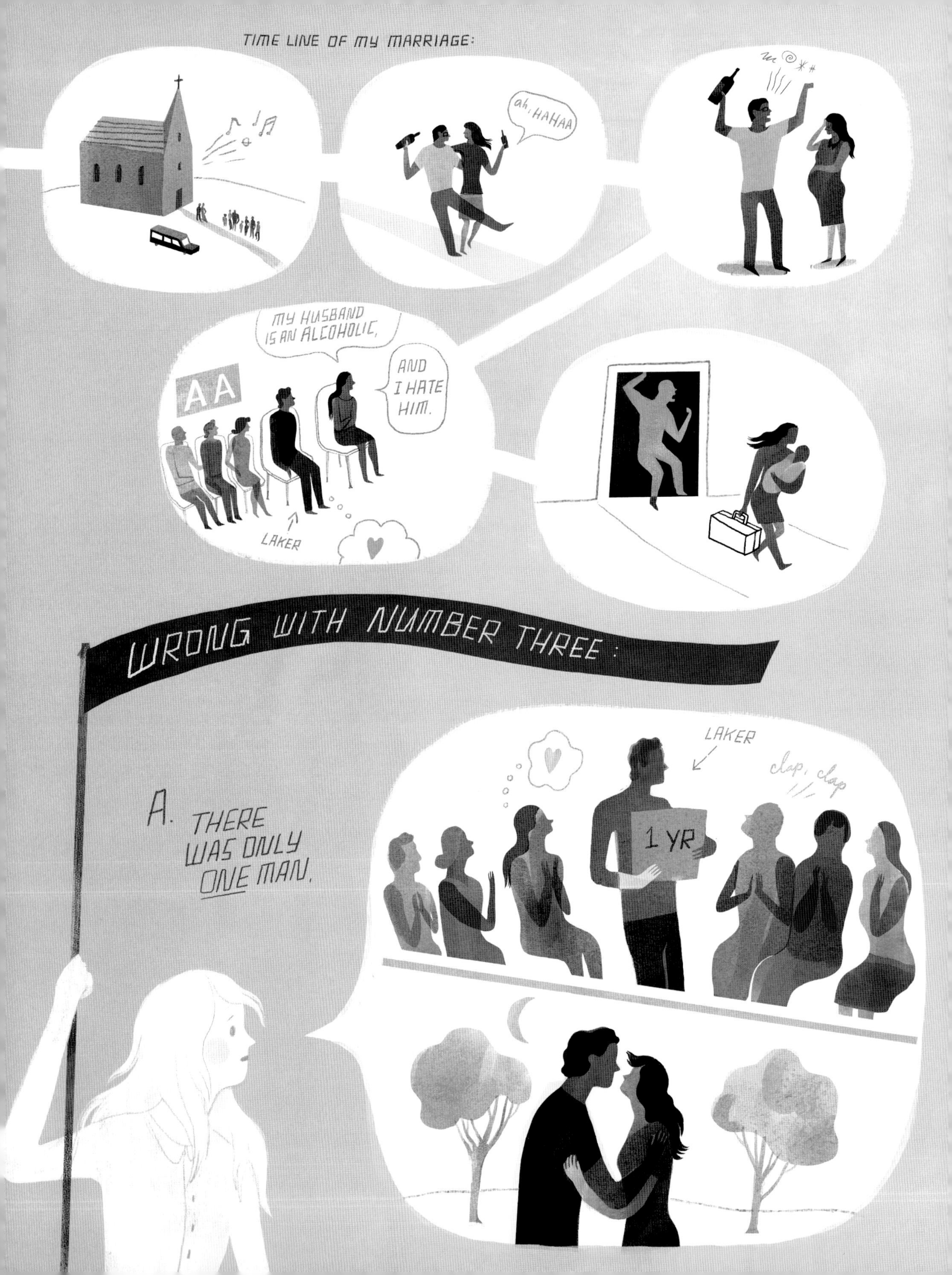

TIME LINE OF MY MARRIAGE:
ah, HAHAA
MY HUSBAND IS AN ALCOHOLIC,
AND I HATE HIM.
AA
LAKER
WRONG WITH NUMBER THREE:
A. THERE WAS ONLY ONE MAN.
LAKER
clap, clap
1 YR

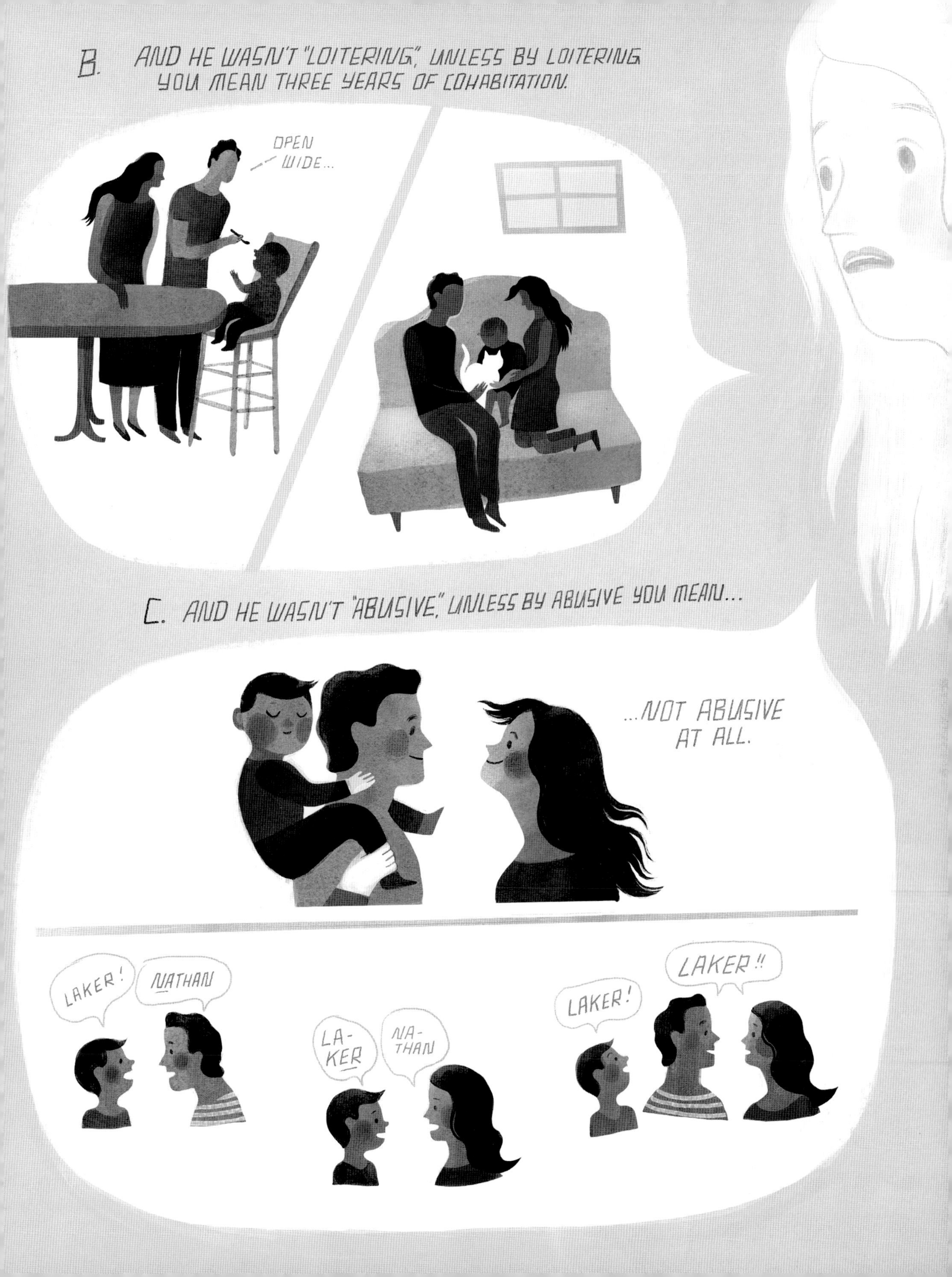

B. AND HE WASN'T "LOITERING," UNLESS BY LOITERING YOU MEAN THREE YEARS OF COHABITATION.
OPEN WIDE...
C. AND HE WASN'T "ABUSIVE," UNLESS BY ABUSIVE YOU MEAN...
...NOT ABUSIVE AT ALL.
LAKER!
NATHAN
LA-KER
NA-THAN
LAKER!
LAKER!!

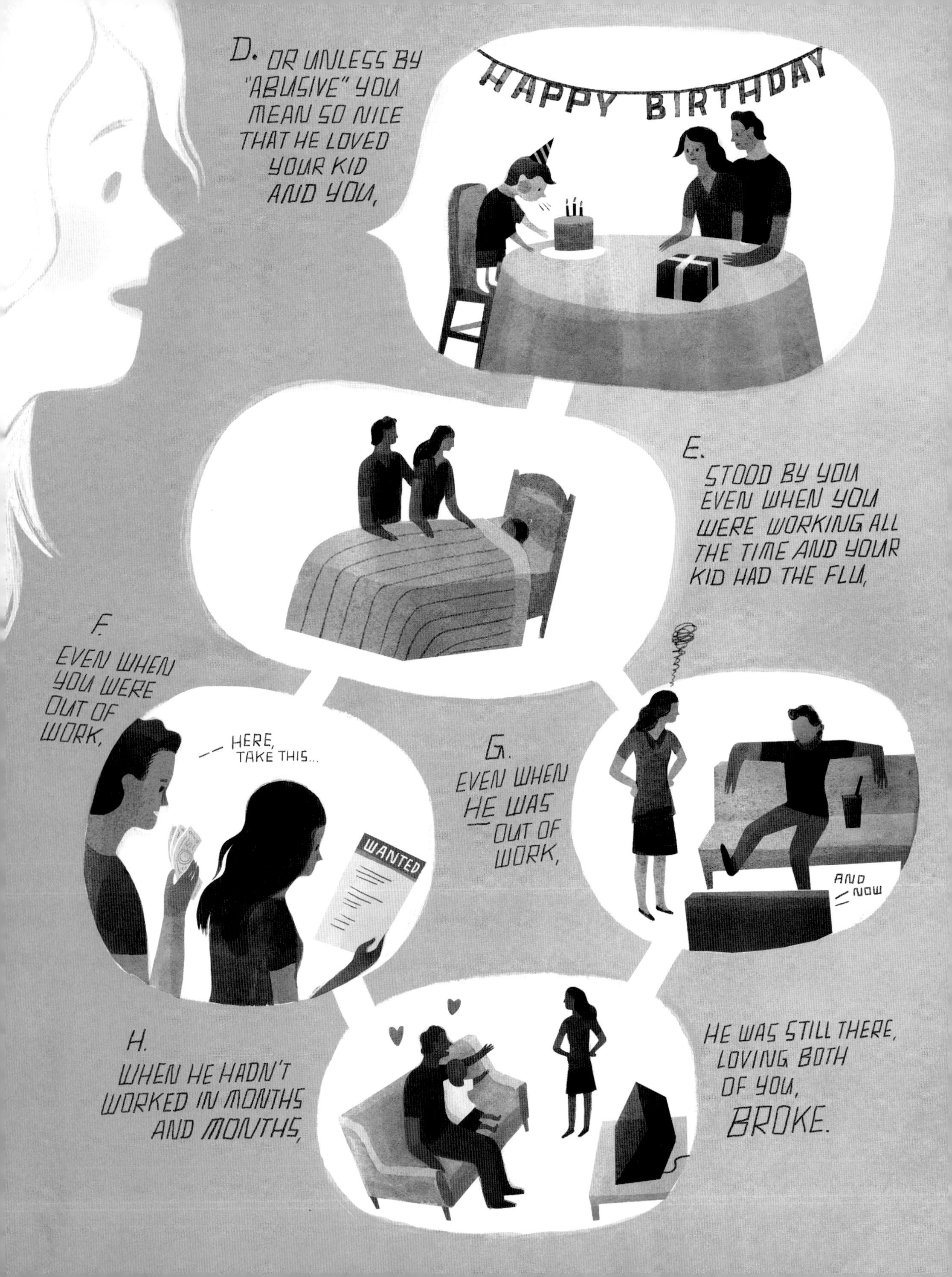
D. OR UNLESS BY "ABUSIVE" YOU MEAN SO NICE THAT HE LOVED YOUR KID AND YOU,
HAPPY BIRTHDAY
E. STOOD BY YOU EVEN WHEN YOU WERE WORKING ALL THE TIME AND YOUR KID HAD THE FLU,
F. EVEN WHEN YOU WERE OUT OF WORK,
-- HERE, TAKE THIS...
WANTED
G. EVEN WHEN HE WAS OUT OF WORK,
AND NOW
H. WHEN HE HADN'T WORKED IN MONTHS AND MONTHS,
HE WAS STILL THERE, LOVING BOTH OF YOU, BROKE.

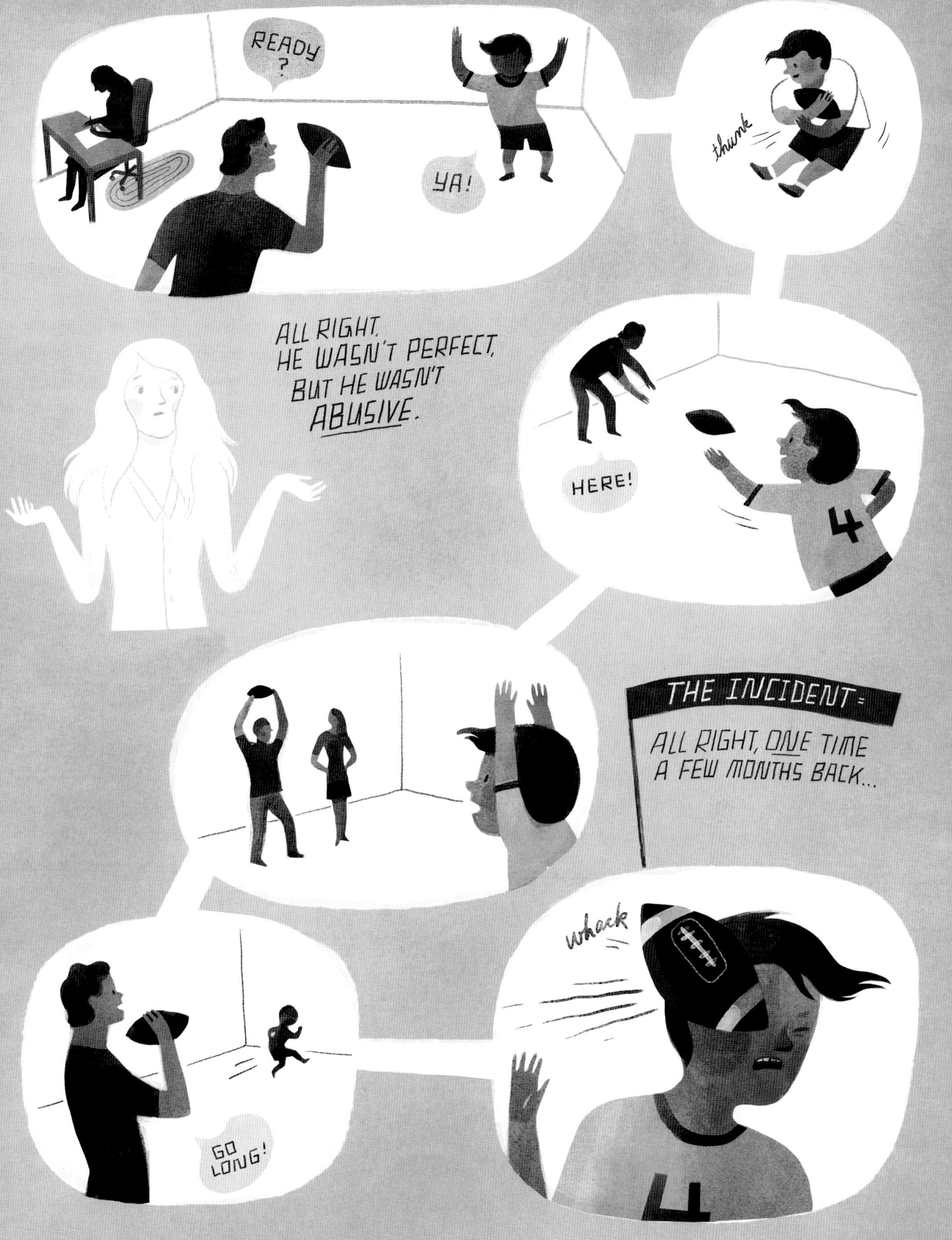
READY ?
YA!
thunk
ALL RIGHT, HE WASN'T PERFECT, BUT HE WASN'T ABUSIVE.
HERE!
THE INCIDENT:
ALL RIGHT, ONE TIME A FEW MONTHS BACK...
GO LONG!
whack

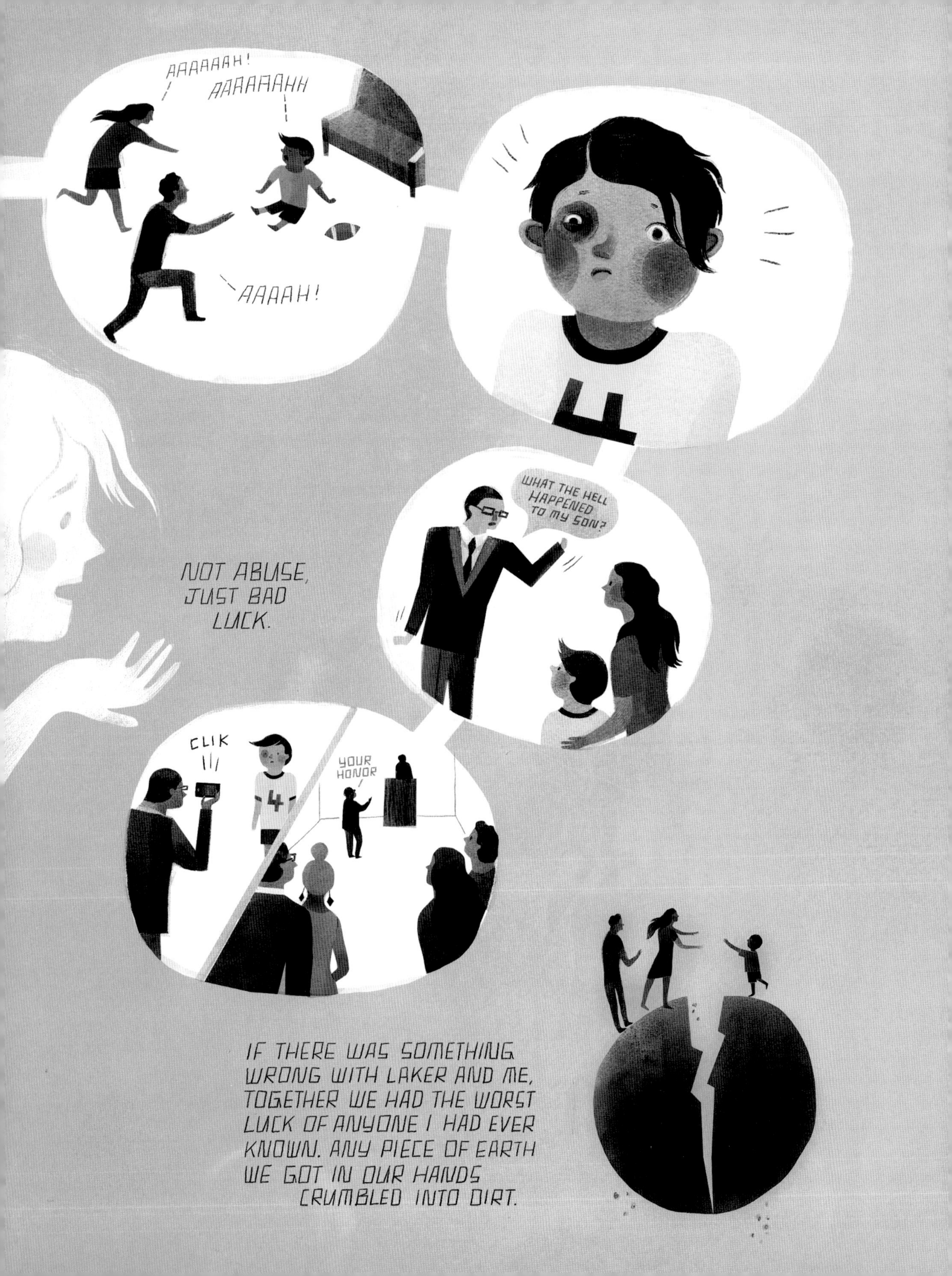
AAAAAAH!
AAAAAAHH
AAAAH!
WHAT THE HELL HAPPENED TO MY SON?
NOT ABUSE, JUST BAD LUCK.
CLIK
YOUR HONOR
IF THERE WAS SOMETHING WRONG WITH LAKER AND ME, TOGETHER WE HAD THE WORST LUCK OF ANYONE I HAD EVER KNOWN. ANY PIECE OF EARTH WE GOT IN OUR HANDS CRUMBLED INTO DIRT.

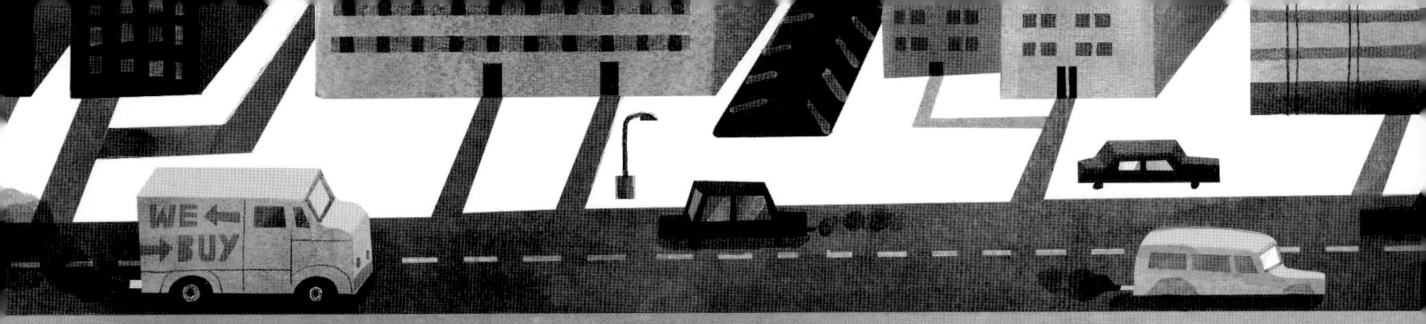
WE BUY

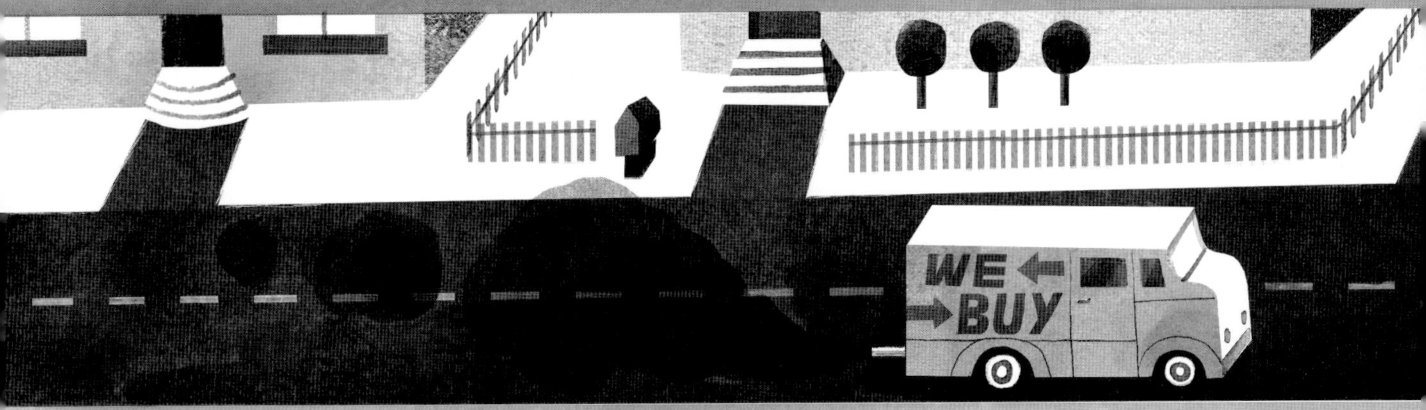
WE BUY

SO WAS I GOING TO INSIST LAKER AND I CHANGE ALL ASPECTS OF OUR LIVES IN ORDER THAT I MIGHT MORE SATISFACTORILY RESEMBLE AN ORGANIZED CITIZEN CAPABLE OF CARING FOR HER OWN SON?

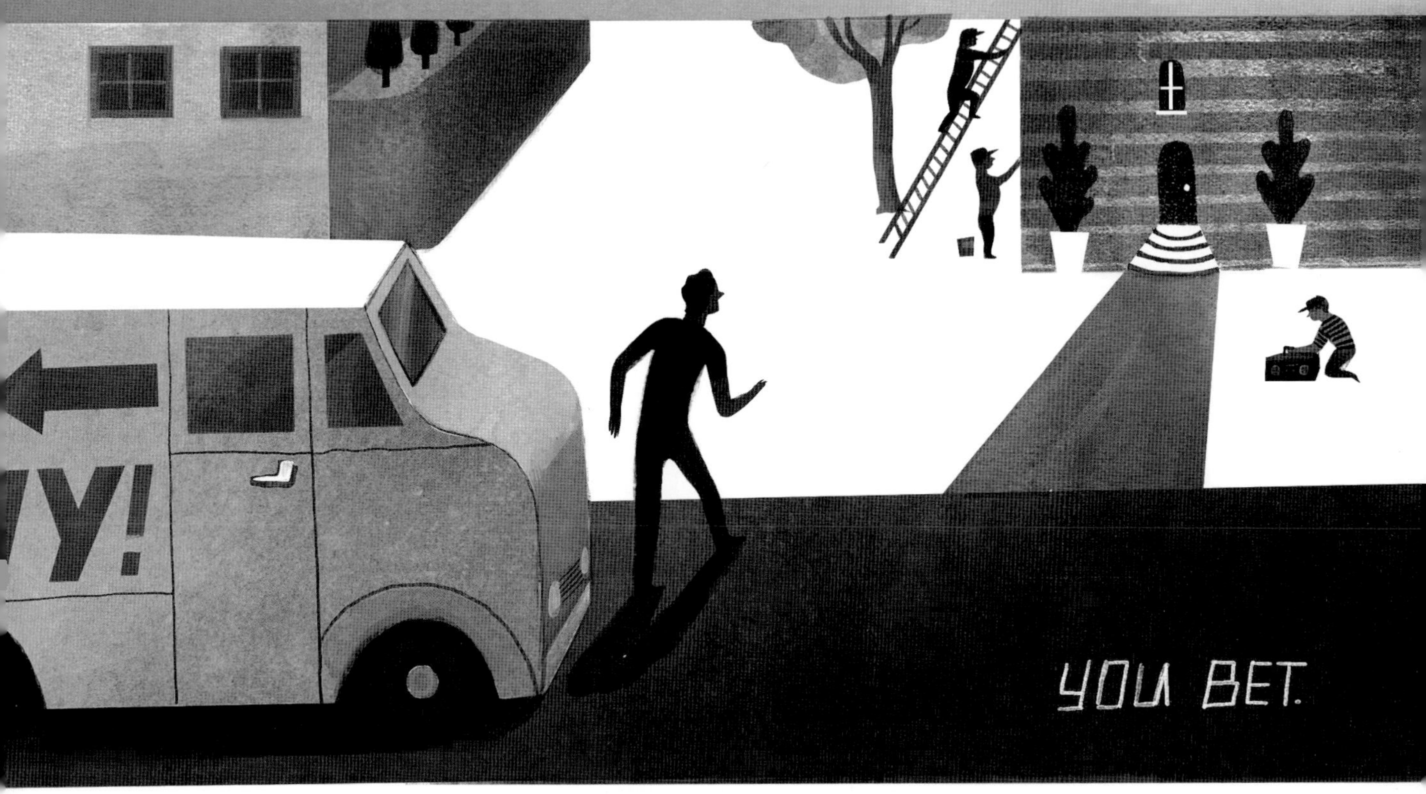
Y!
YOU BET.

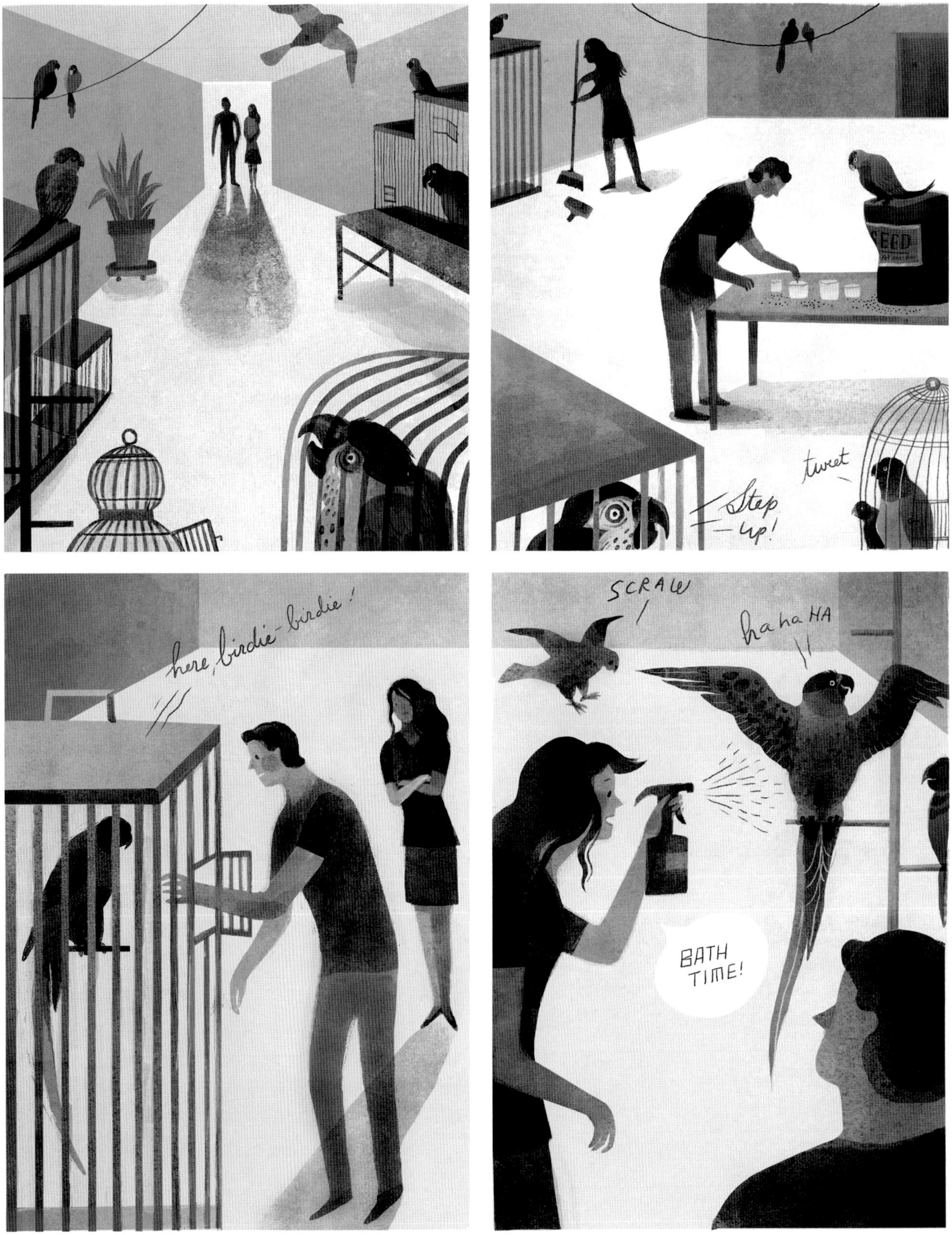
tweet
Step up!
here, birdie-birdie!
SCRAW
ha ha HA
BATH TIME!

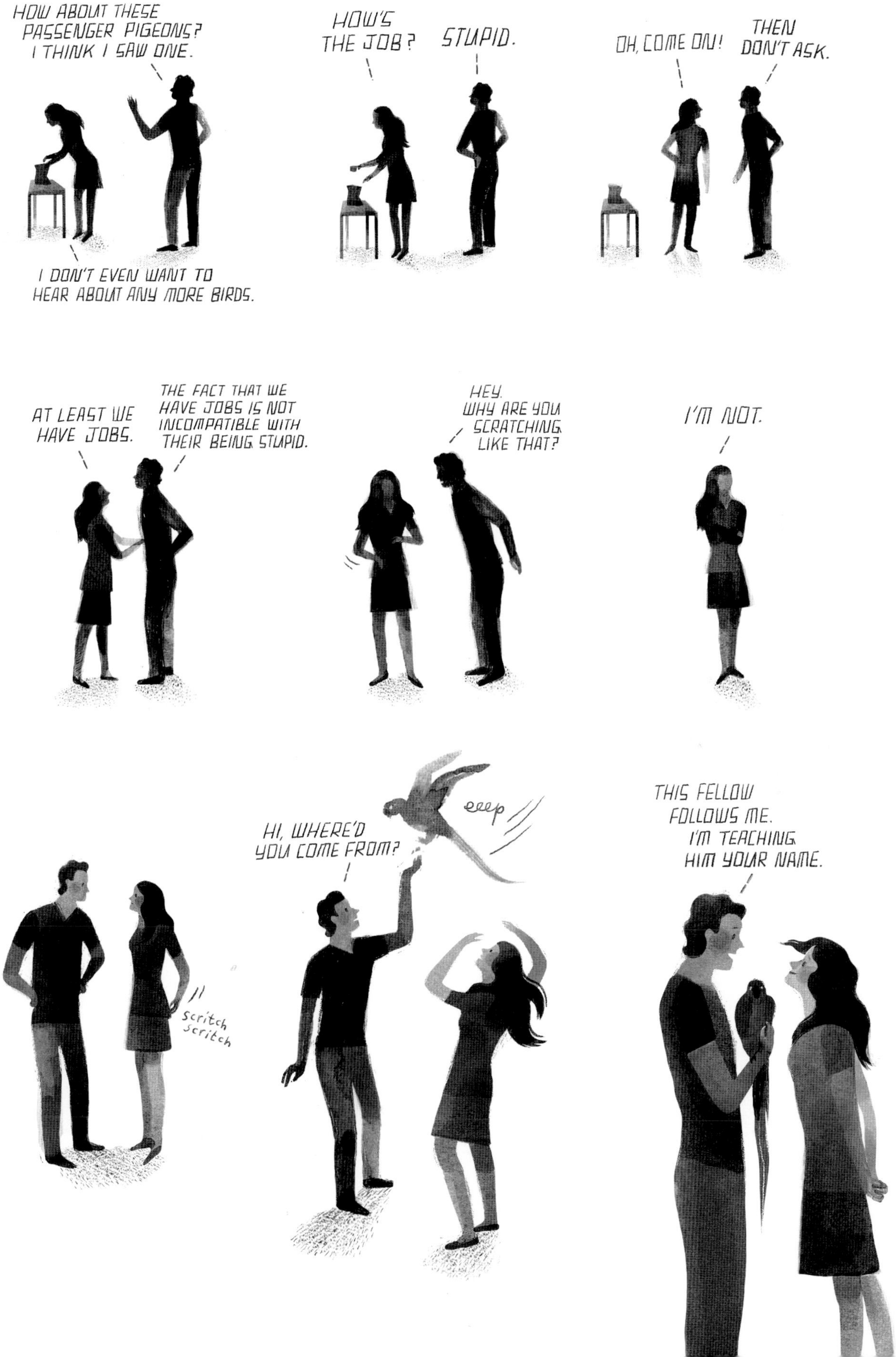
HOW ABOUT THESE PASSENGER PIGEONS? I THINK I SAW ONE.
I DON'T EVEN WANT TO HEAR ABOUT ANY MORE BIRDS.
HOW'S THE JOB?
STUPID.
OH, COME ON!
THEN DON'T ASK.
AT LEAST WE HAVE JOBS.
THE FACT THAT WE HAVE JOBS IS NOT INCOMPATIBLE WITH THEIR BEING STUPID.
HEY. WHY ARE YOU SCRATCHING LIKE THAT?
I'M NOT.
scritch scritch
HI, WHERE'D YOU COME FROM?
eeep
THIS FELLOW FOLLOWS ME. I'M TEACHING HIM YOUR NAME.

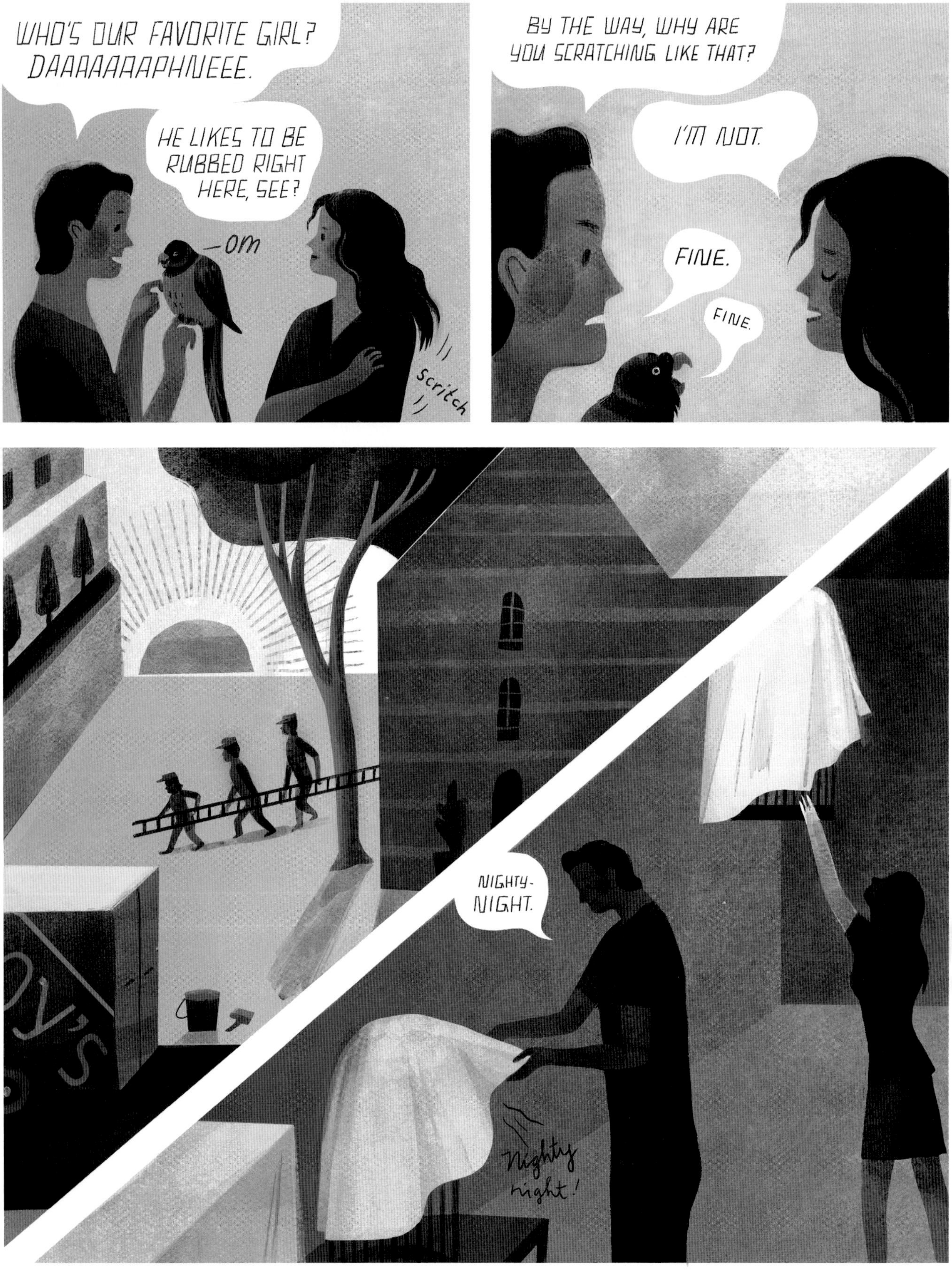
WHO'S OUR FAVORITE GIRL? DAAAAAAAPHNEEE.
HE LIKES TO BE RUBBED RIGHT HERE, SEE?
—om
scritch
BY THE WAY, WHY ARE YOU SCRATCHING LIKE THAT?
I'M NOT.
FINE.
FINE.
NIGHTY-NIGHT.
Nighty night!

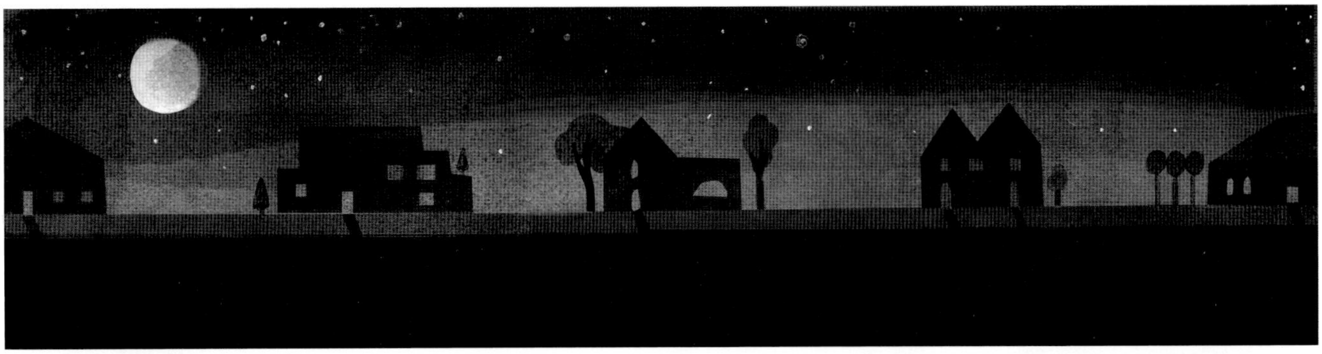

THE NEXT DAY I LIKE TO REMEMBER AS THE DAY I COULD SEE WHAT WAS POSSIBLE.

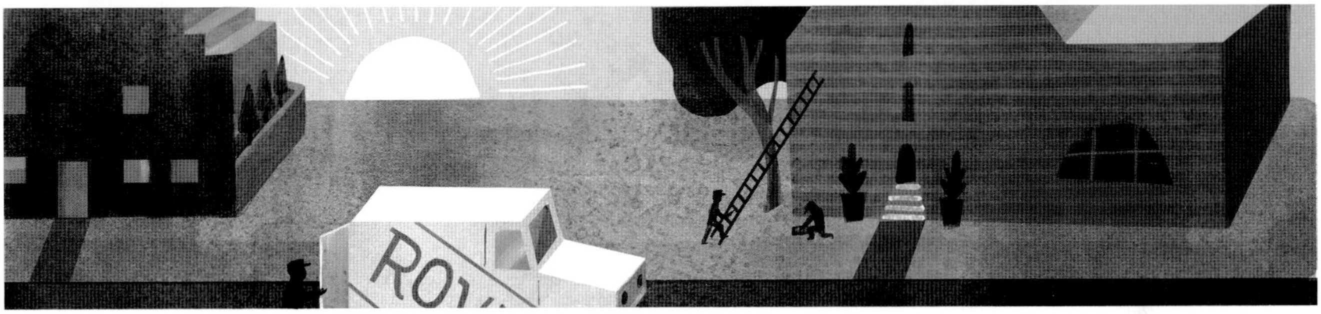

I COULD SEE US GETTING THROUGH THIS WITHOUT KILLING ANYONE OFF.

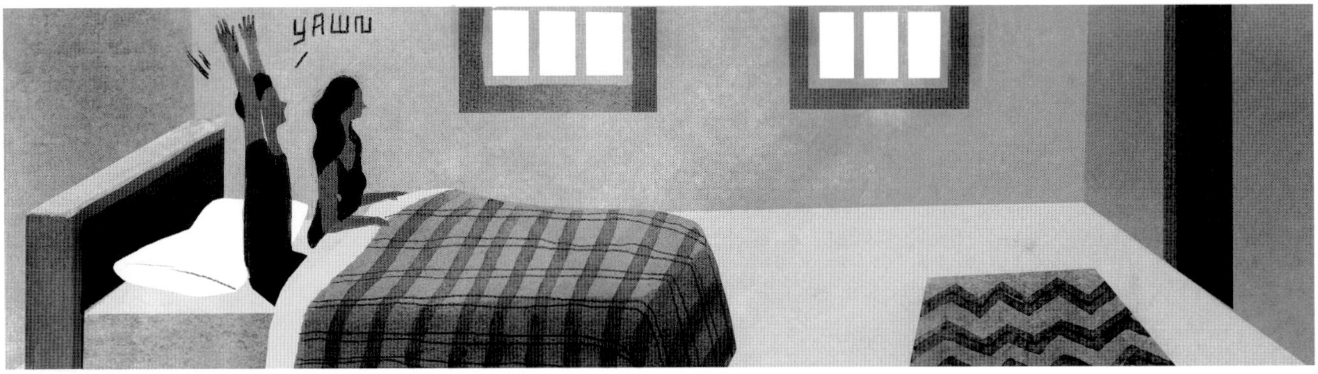
YAWN

MAYBE OUR LIVES HAD CHANGED. MAYBE JUST GETTING OUT OF OUR APARTMENT HAD DONE IT.

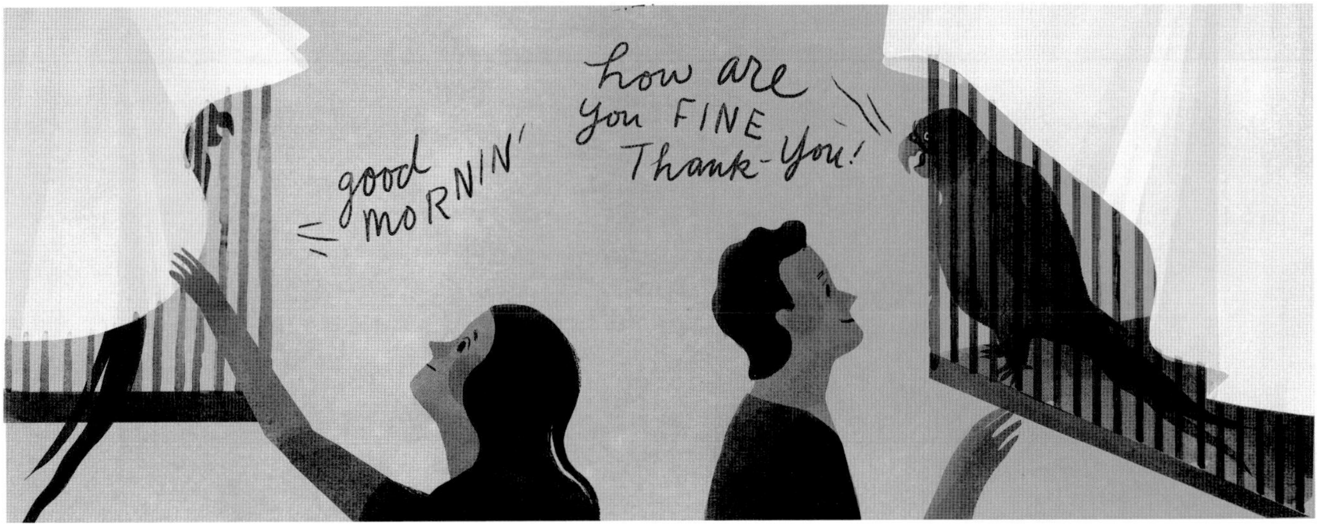
good MORNIN'
how are you FINE Thank-You!

THE BIRDS WERE BEAUTIFUL, WITH THEIR BIG, WILD PERSONALITIES.

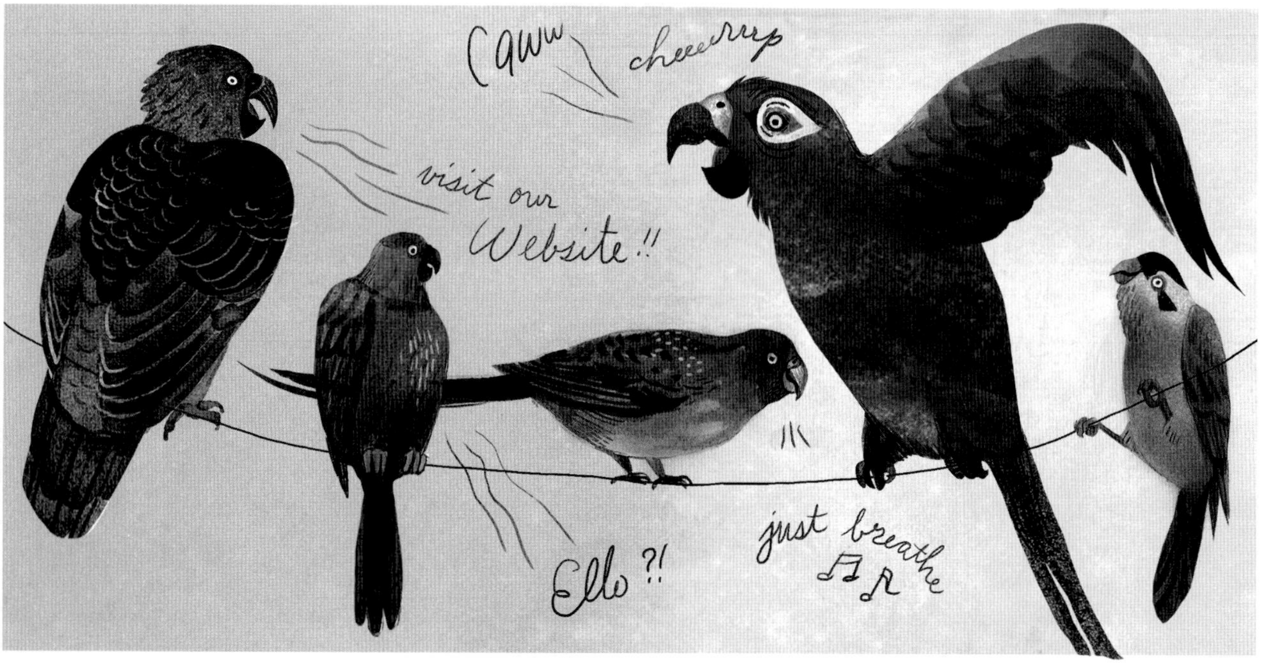
Caww
cheeerrup
visit our Website!!
Ello?!
just breathe

AND LAKER TOO, HIS BIG, WILD PERSONALITY, HE SEEMED TO KNOW JUST WHAT THEY NEEDED.

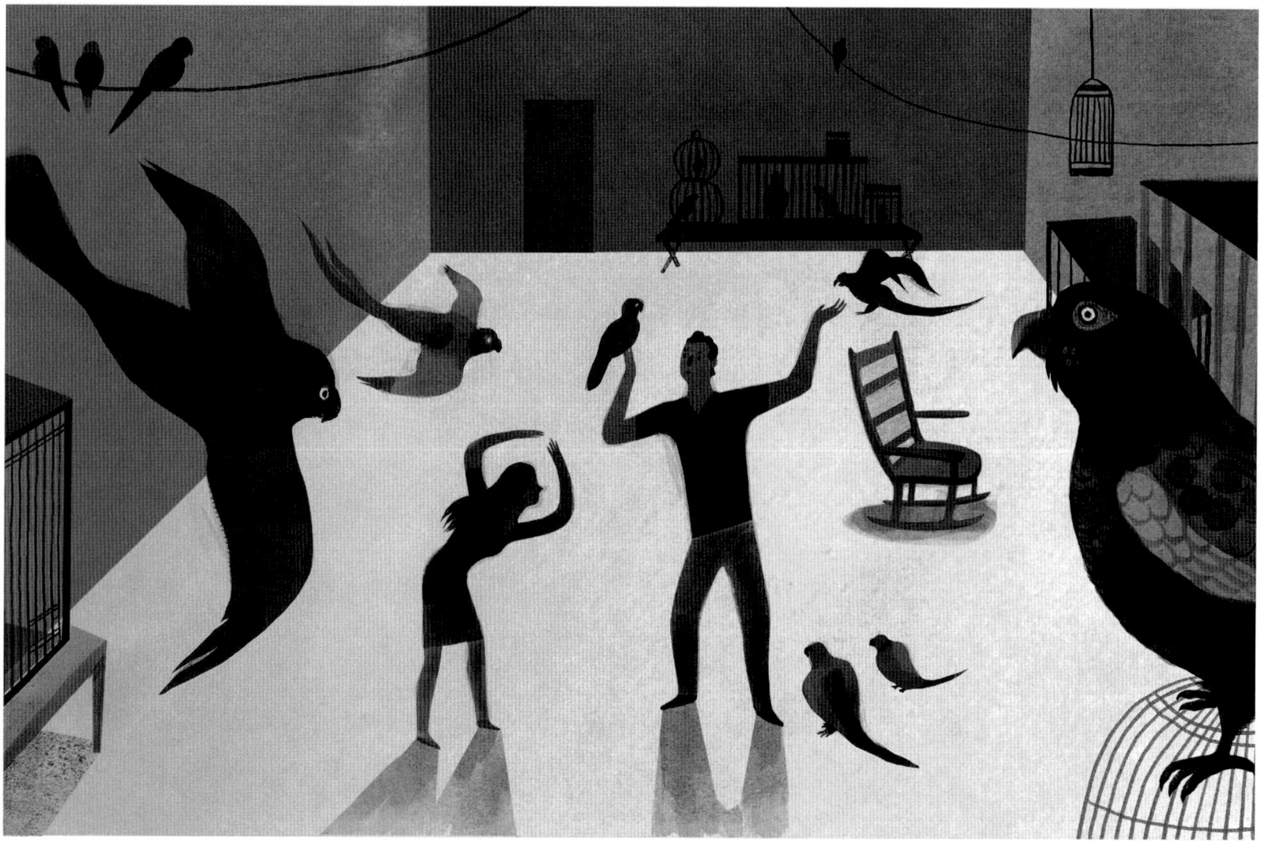

SHORT OF TREETOPS, RAIN, INFINITE SKY, LAKER WAS THE LEAST I COULD DO FOR THEM.

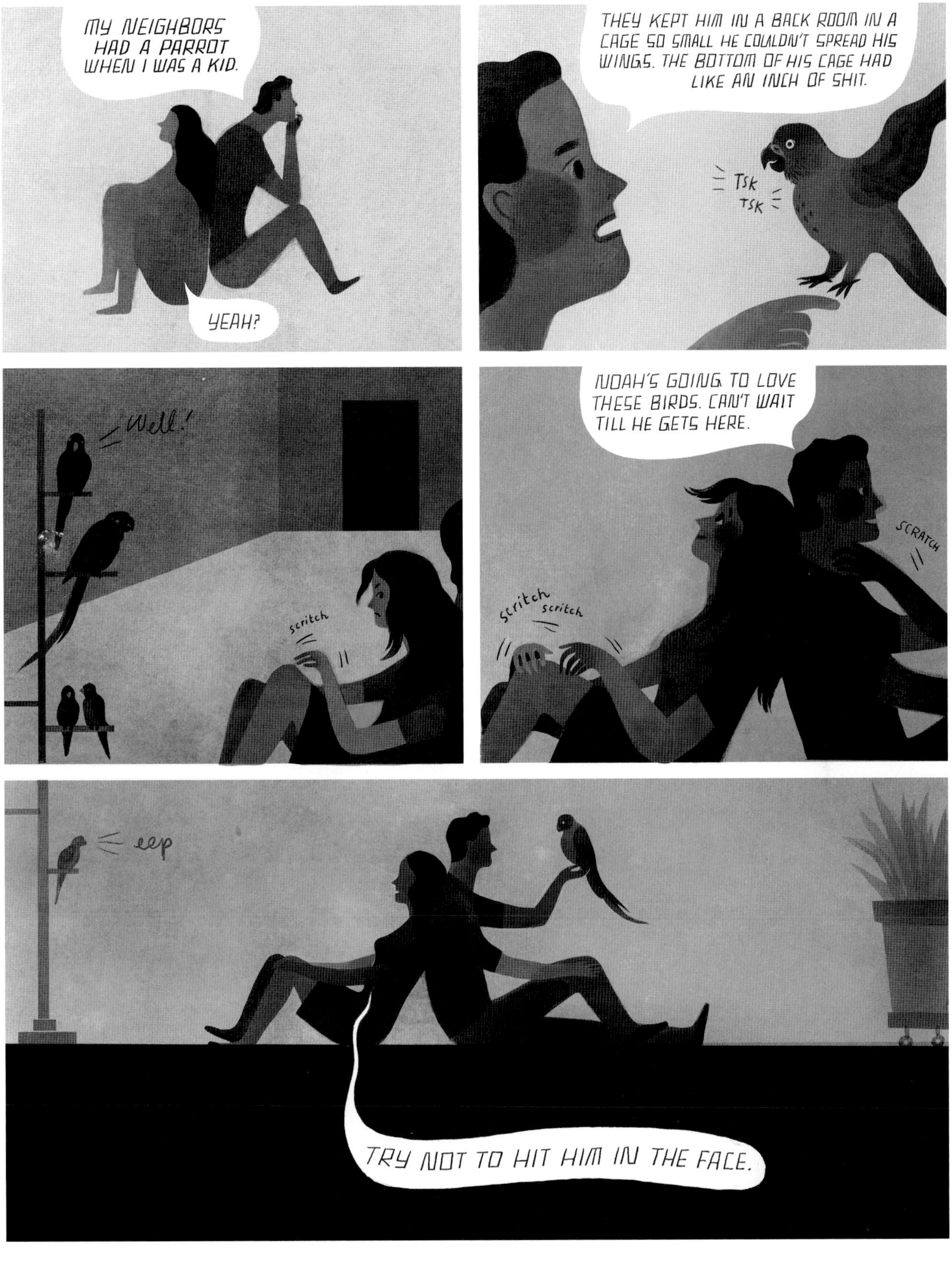
MY NEIGHBORS HAD A PARROT WHEN I WAS A KID.
YEAH?
THEY KEPT HIM IN A BACK ROOM IN A CAGE SO SMALL HE COULDN'T SPREAD HIS WINGS. THE BOTTOM OF HIS CAGE HAD LIKE AN INCH OF SHIT.
TSK TSK
Well!
scritch
NOAH'S GOING TO LOVE THESE BIRDS. CAN'T WAIT TILL HE GETS HERE.
SCRATCH
scritch scritch
eep
TRY NOT TO HIT HIM IN THE FACE.

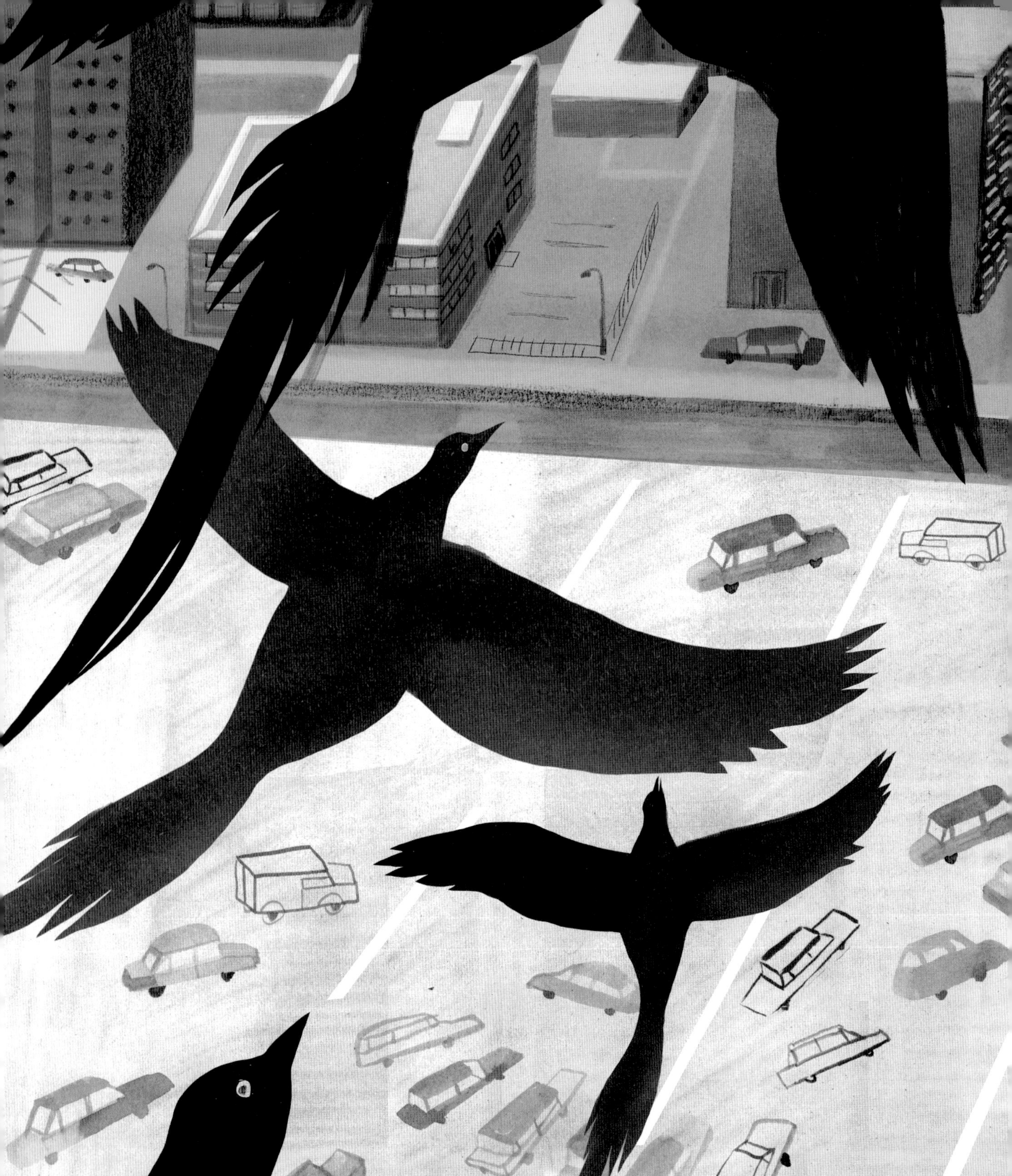

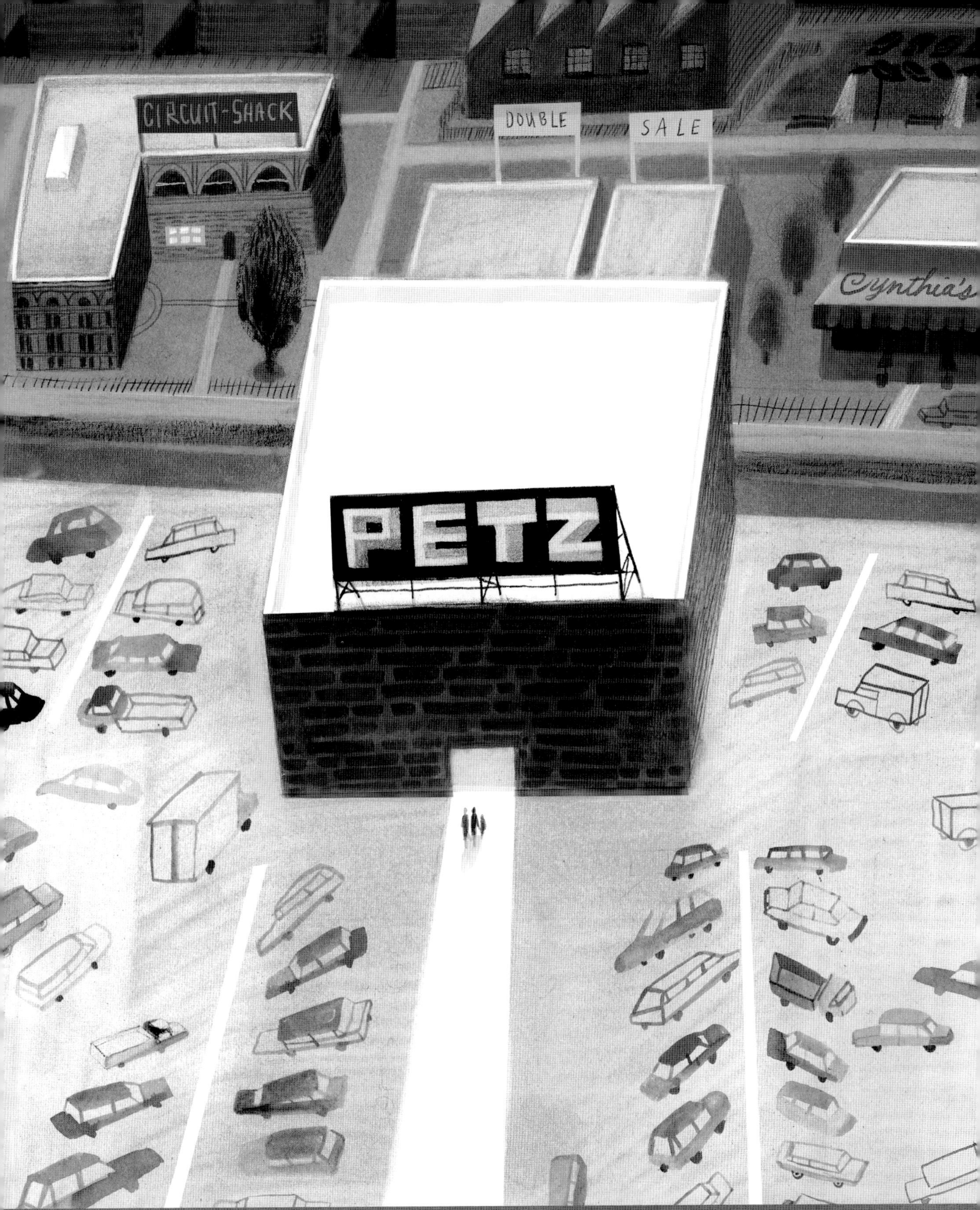
CIRCUIT-SHACK
DOUBLE
SALE
Cynthia's
PETZ

CHAPTER 3: INFESTED!

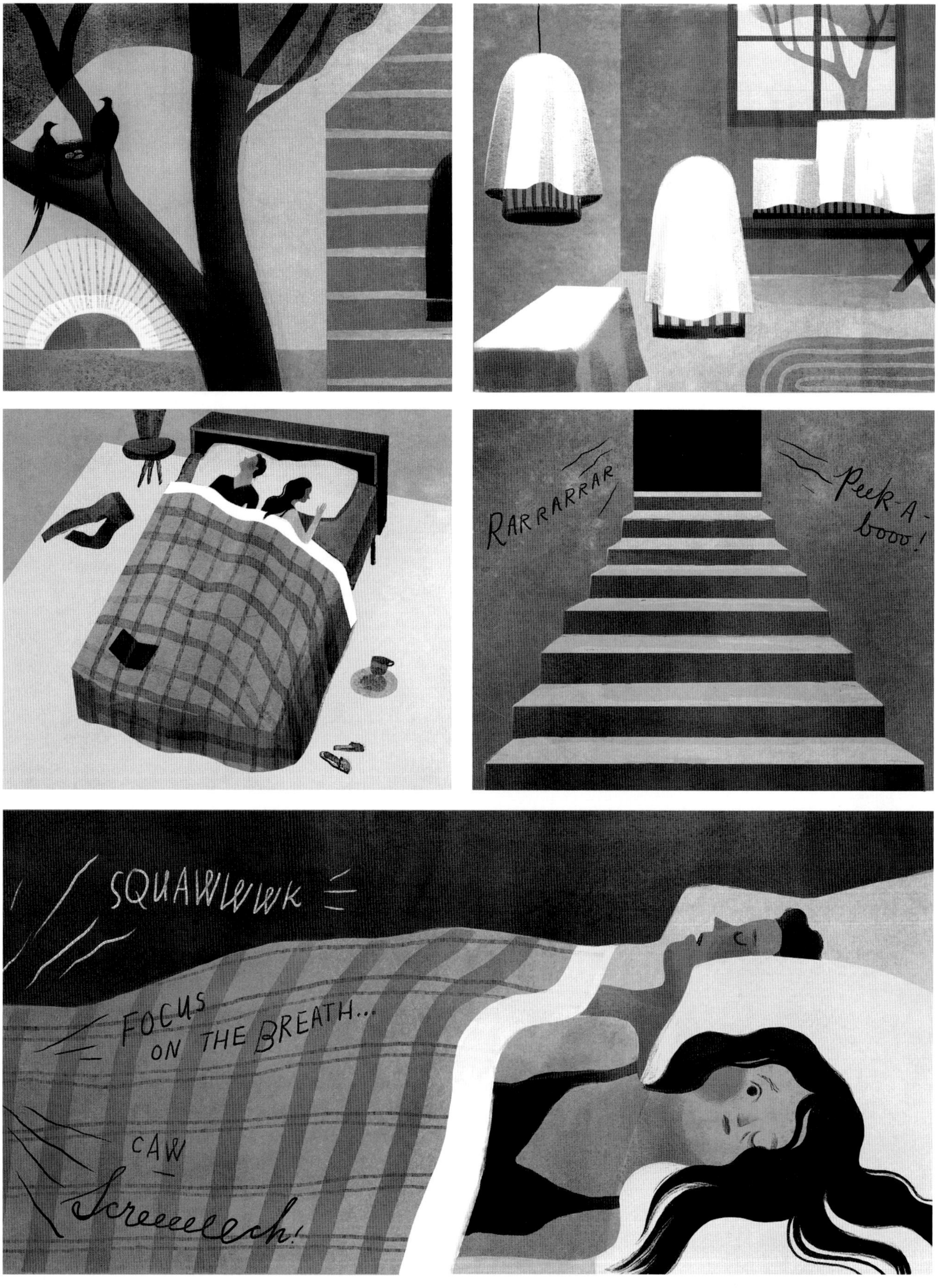
RARRARRAR
Peek-A-booo!
SQUAWWWK
FOCUS ON THE BREATH...
CAW
Screeeeech!

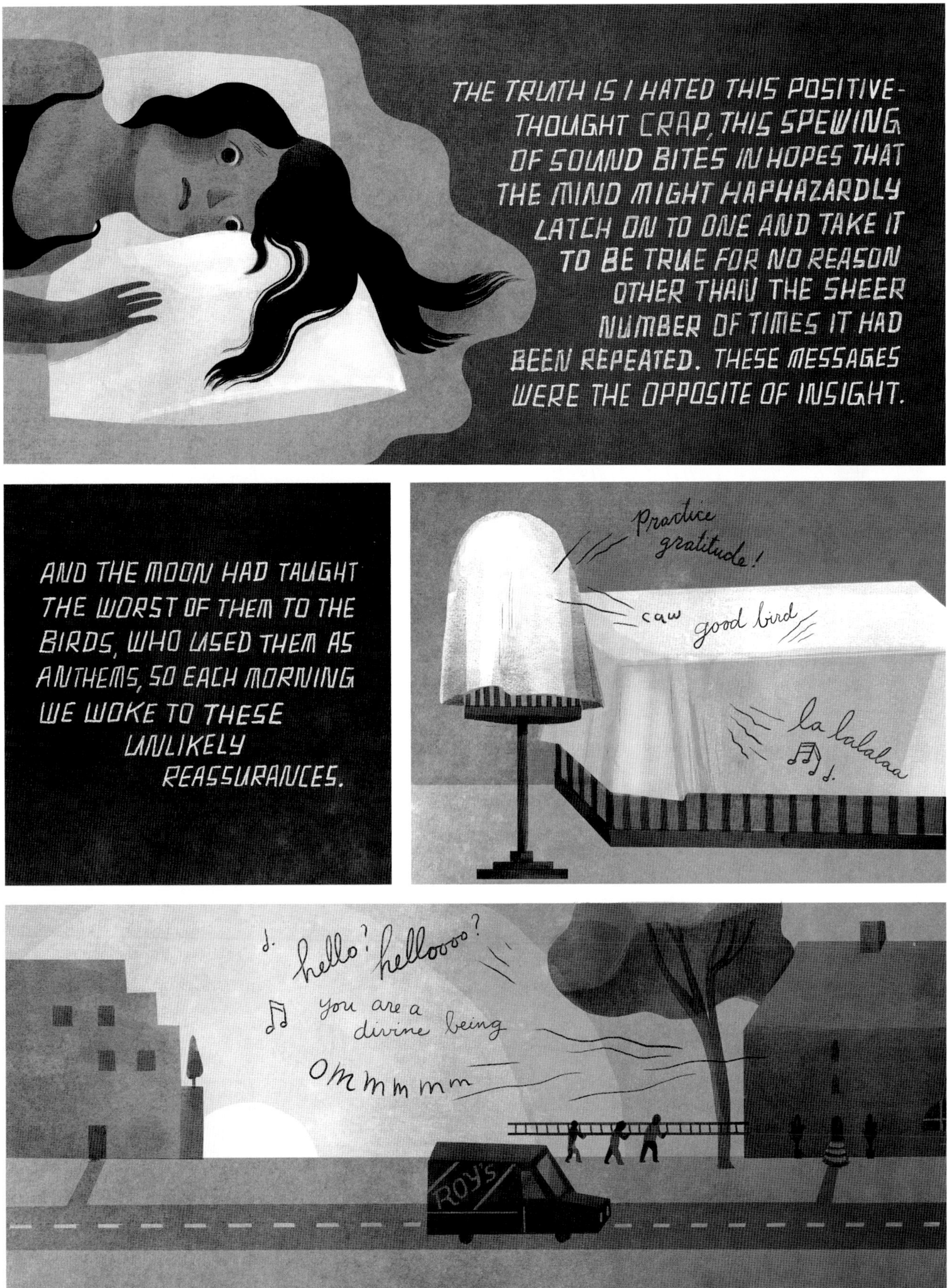
THE TRUTH IS I HATED THIS POSITIVE-THOUGHT CRAP, THIS SPEWING OF SOUND BITES IN HOPES THAT THE MIND MIGHT HAPHAZARDLY LATCH ON TO ONE AND TAKE IT TO BE TRUE FOR NO REASON OTHER THAN THE SHEER NUMBER OF TIMES IT HAD BEEN REPEATED. THESE MESSAGES WERE THE OPPOSITE OF INSIGHT.
AND THE MOON HAD TAUGHT THE WORST OF THEM TO THE BIRDS, WHO USED THEM AS ANTHEMS, SO EACH MORNING WE WOKE TO THESE UNLIKELY REASSURANCES.
Practice gratitude!
caw
good bird
la lalalaa
hello? hellooooo?
You are a divine being
Ommmmm
ROY'S

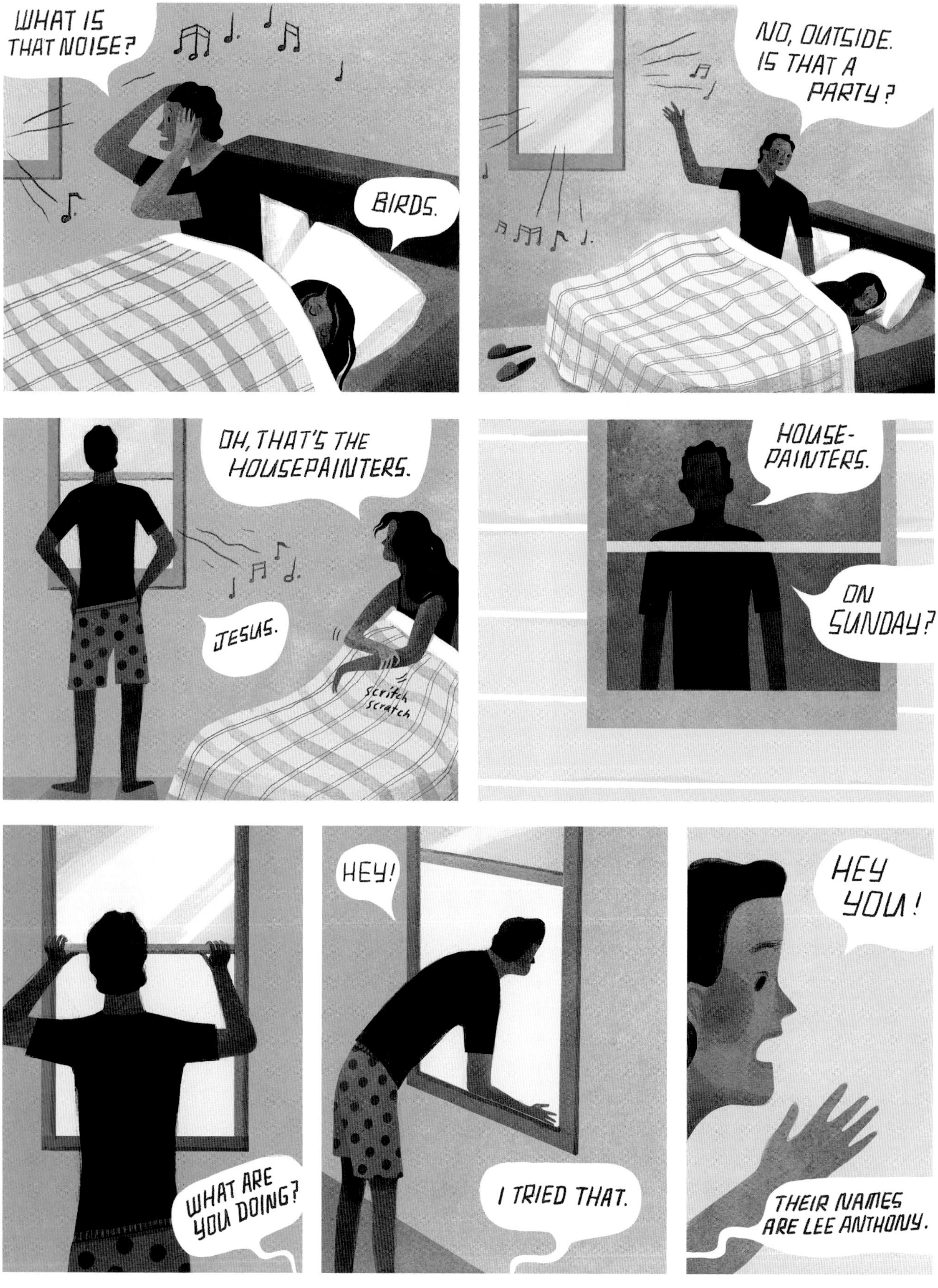
WHAT IS THAT NOISE?
BIRDS.
NO, OUTSIDE. IS THAT A PARTY?
OH, THAT'S THE HOUSEPAINTERS.
JESUS.
SCRITCH SCRATCH
HOUSE-PAINTERS.
ON SUNDAY?
WHAT ARE YOU DOING?
HEY!
I TRIED THAT.
HEY YOU!
THEIR NAMES ARE LEE ANTHONY.

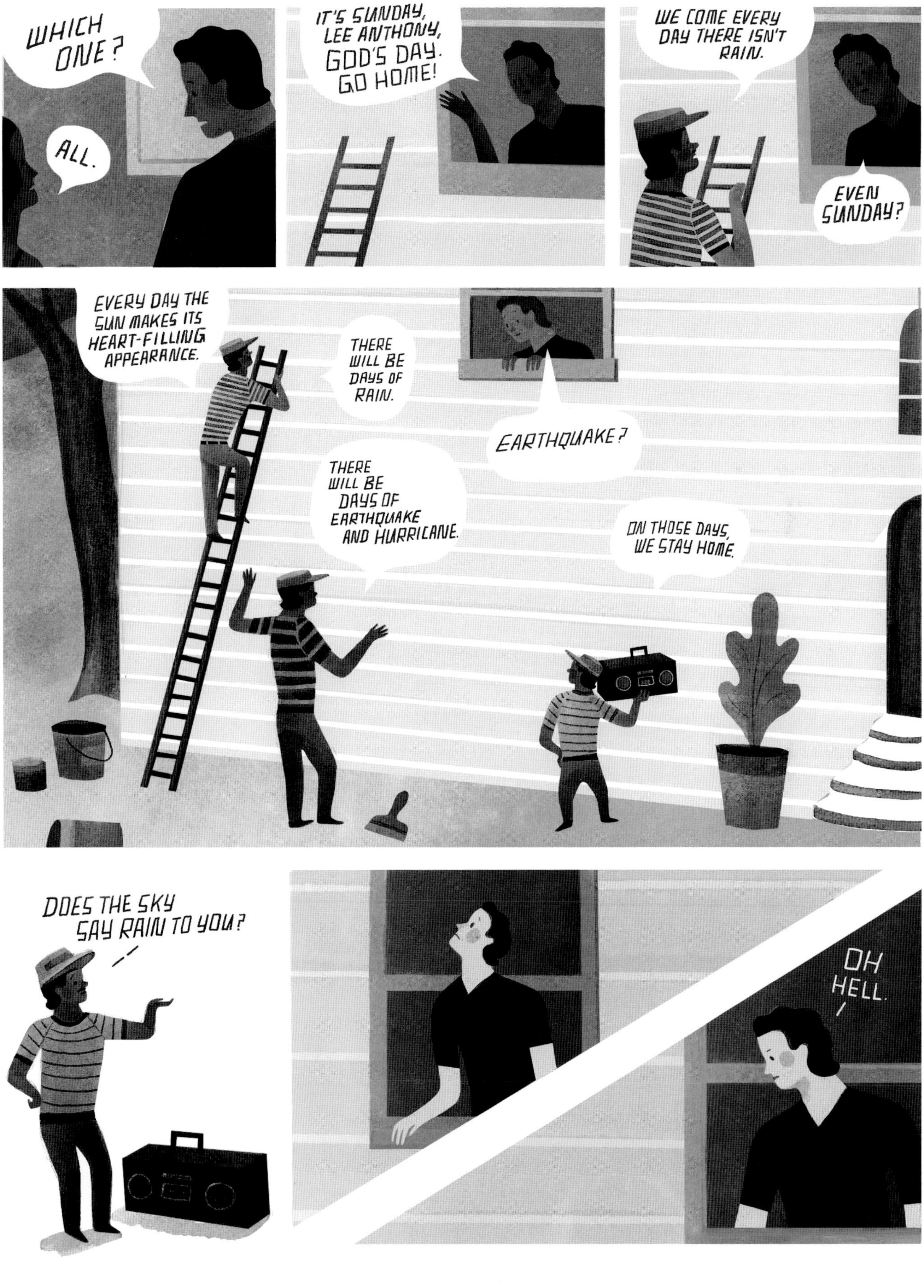
WHICH ONE?
ALL.
IT'S SUNDAY, LEE ANTHONY, GOD'S DAY. GO HOME!
WE COME EVERY DAY THERE ISN'T RAIN.
EVEN SUNDAY?
EVERY DAY THE SUN MAKES ITS HEART-FILLING APPEARANCE.
THERE WILL BE DAYS OF RAIN.
EARTHQUAKE?
THERE WILL BE DAYS OF EARTHQUAKE AND HURRICANE.
ON THOSE DAYS, WE STAY HOME.
DOES THE SKY SAY RAIN TO YOU?
OH HELL.

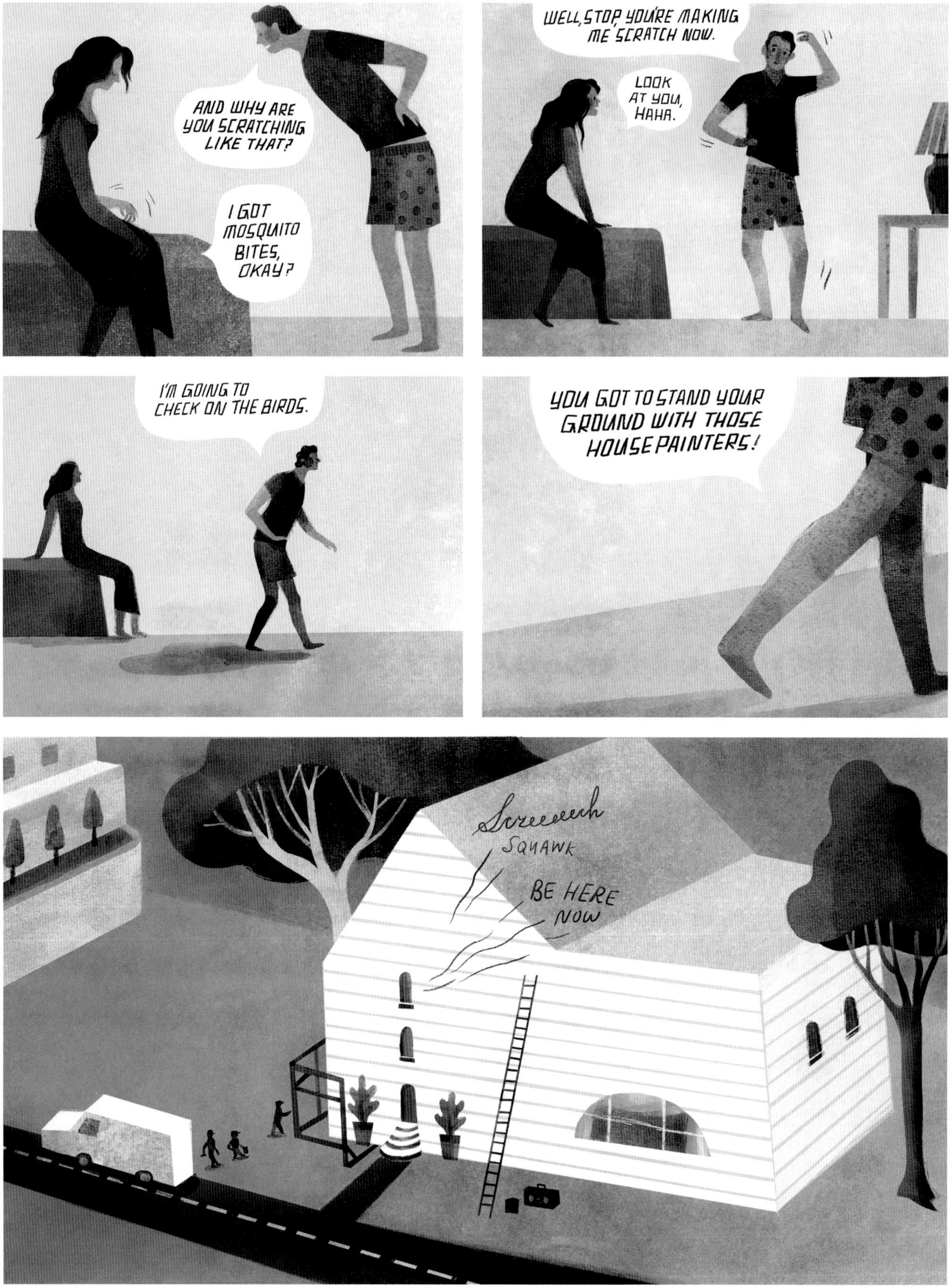
AND WHY ARE YOU SCRATCHING LIKE THAT?
I GOT MOSQUITO BITES, OKAY?
WELL, STOP, YOU'RE MAKING ME SCRATCH NOW.
LOOK AT YOU, HAHA.
I'M GOING TO CHECK ON THE BIRDS.
YOU GOT TO STAND YOUR GROUND WITH THOSE HOUSEPAINTERS!
Screeeeech
SQUAWK
BE HERE NOW

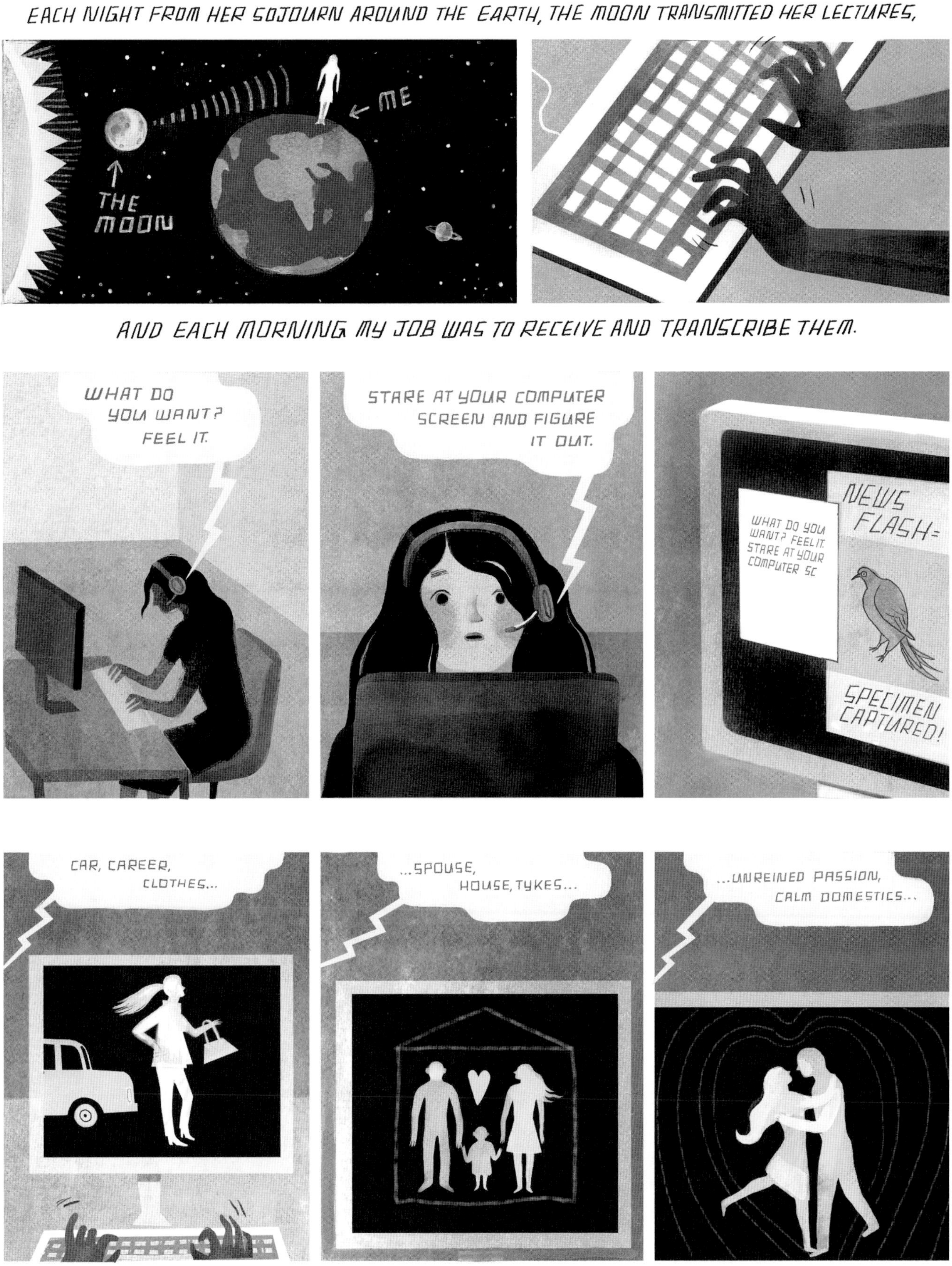
EACH NIGHT FROM HER SOJOURN AROUND THE EARTH, THE MOON TRANSMITTED HER LECTURES,
THE MOON
ME
AND EACH MORNING MY JOB WAS TO RECEIVE AND TRANSCRIBE THEM.
WHAT DO YOU WANT? FEEL IT.
STARE AT YOUR COMPUTER SCREEN AND FIGURE IT OUT.
WHAT DO YOU WANT? FEEL IT. STARE AT YOUR COMPUTER SC
NEWS FLASH=
SPECIMEN CAPTURED!
CAR, CAREER, CLOTHES...
...SPOUSE, HOUSE, TYKES...
...UNREINED PASSION, CALM DOMESTICS...

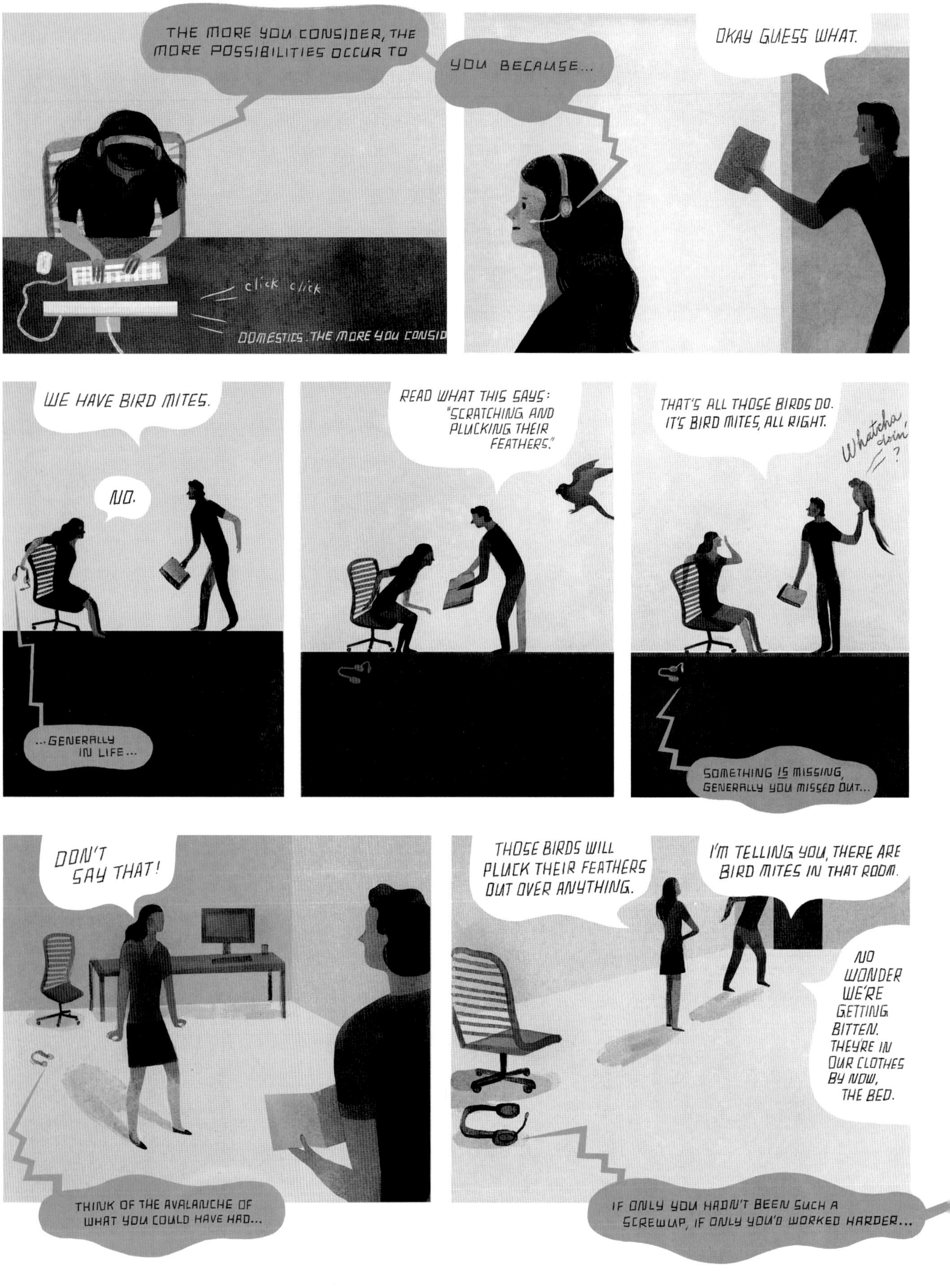
THE MORE YOU CONSIDER, THE MORE POSSIBILITIES OCCUR TO
click click
DOMESTICS. THE MORE YOU CONSID
YOU BECAUSE...
OKAY GUESS WHAT.
WE HAVE BIRD MITES.
NO.
...GENERALLY IN LIFE...
READ WHAT THIS SAYS: "SCRATCHING AND PLUCKING THEIR FEATHERS."
THAT'S ALL THOSE BIRDS DO. IT'S BIRD MITES, ALL RIGHT.
Whatcha doin'?
SOMETHING IS MISSING, GENERALLY YOU MISSED OUT...
DON'T SAY THAT!
THINK OF THE AVALANCHE OF WHAT YOU COULD HAVE HAD...
THOSE BIRDS WILL PLUCK THEIR FEATHERS OUT OVER ANYTHING.
I'M TELLING YOU, THERE ARE BIRD MITES IN THAT ROOM.
NO WONDER WE'RE GETTING BITTEN. THEY'RE IN OUR CLOTHES BY NOW, THE BED.
IF ONLY YOU HADN'T BEEN SUCH A SCREWUP, IF ONLY YOU'D WORKED HARDER...

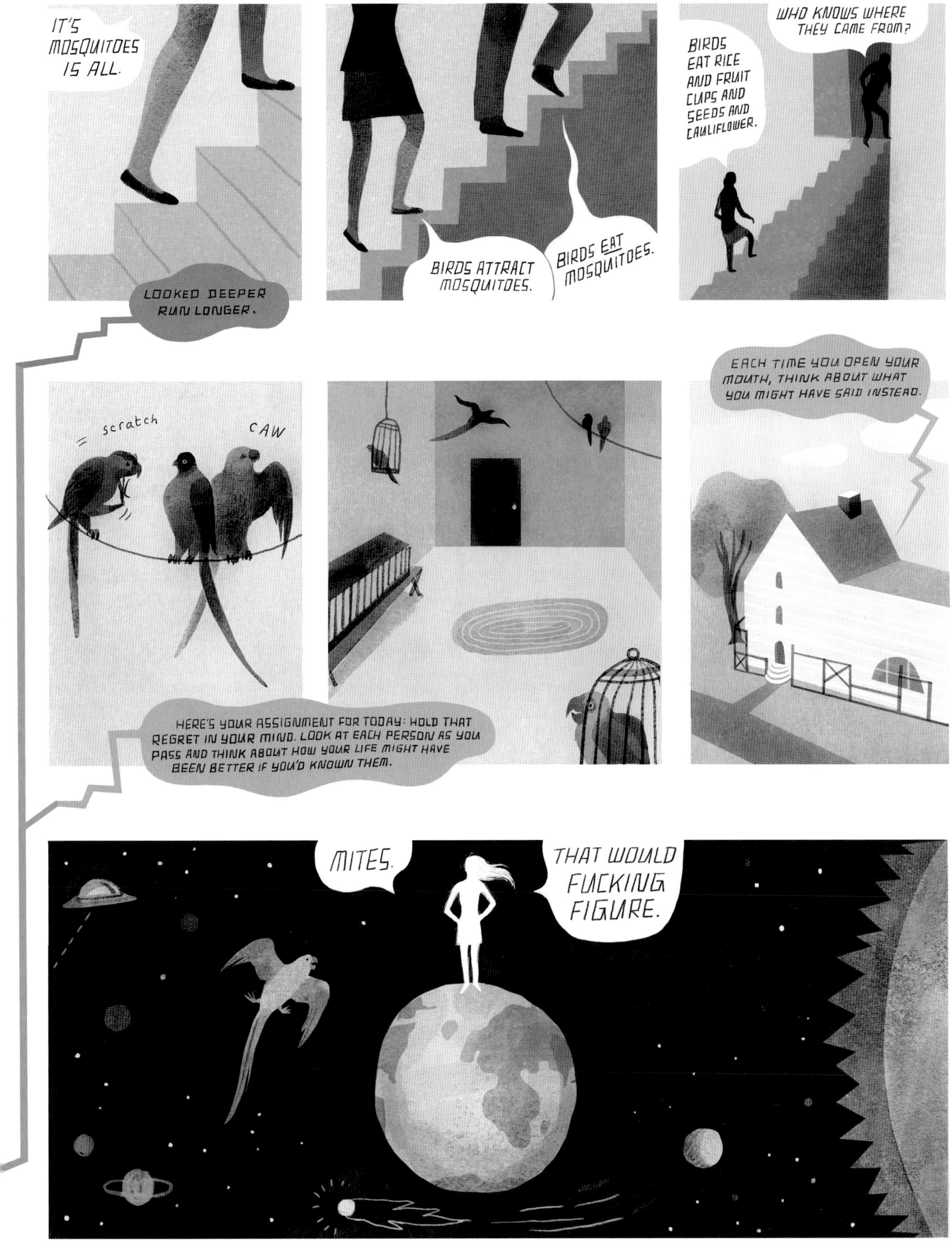
IT'S MOSQUITOES IS ALL.
BIRDS ATTRACT MOSQUITOES.
BIRDS EAT MOSQUITOES.
WHO KNOWS WHERE THEY CAME FROM?
BIRDS EAT RICE AND FRUIT CUPS AND SEEDS AND CAULIFLOWER.
LOOKED DEEPER RUN LONGER.
scratch
CAW
EACH TIME YOU OPEN YOUR MOUTH, THINK ABOUT WHAT YOU MIGHT HAVE SAID INSTEAD.
HERE'S YOUR ASSIGNMENT FOR TODAY: HOLD THAT REGRET IN YOUR MIND. LOOK AT EACH PERSON AS YOU PASS AND THINK ABOUT HOW YOUR LIFE MIGHT HAVE BEEN BETTER IF YOU'D KNOWN THEM.
MITES.
THAT WOULD FUCKING FIGURE.

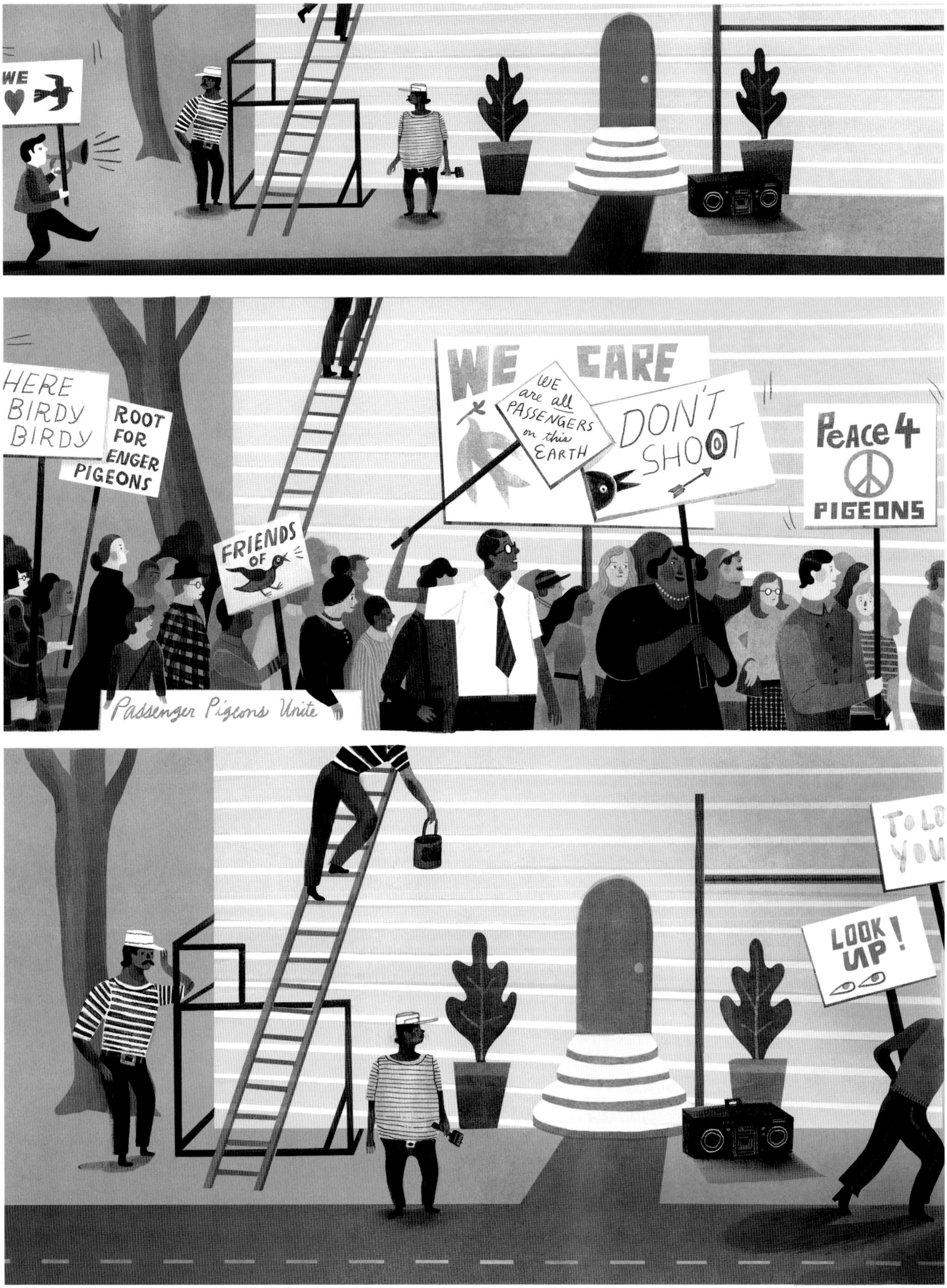
WE
HERE BIRDY BIRDY
ROOT FOR ENGER PIGEONS
FRIENDS OF
WE CARE
WE are all PASSENGERS on this EARTH
DON'T SHOOT
Peace 4 PIGEONS
Passenger Pigeons Unite
LOOK UP!

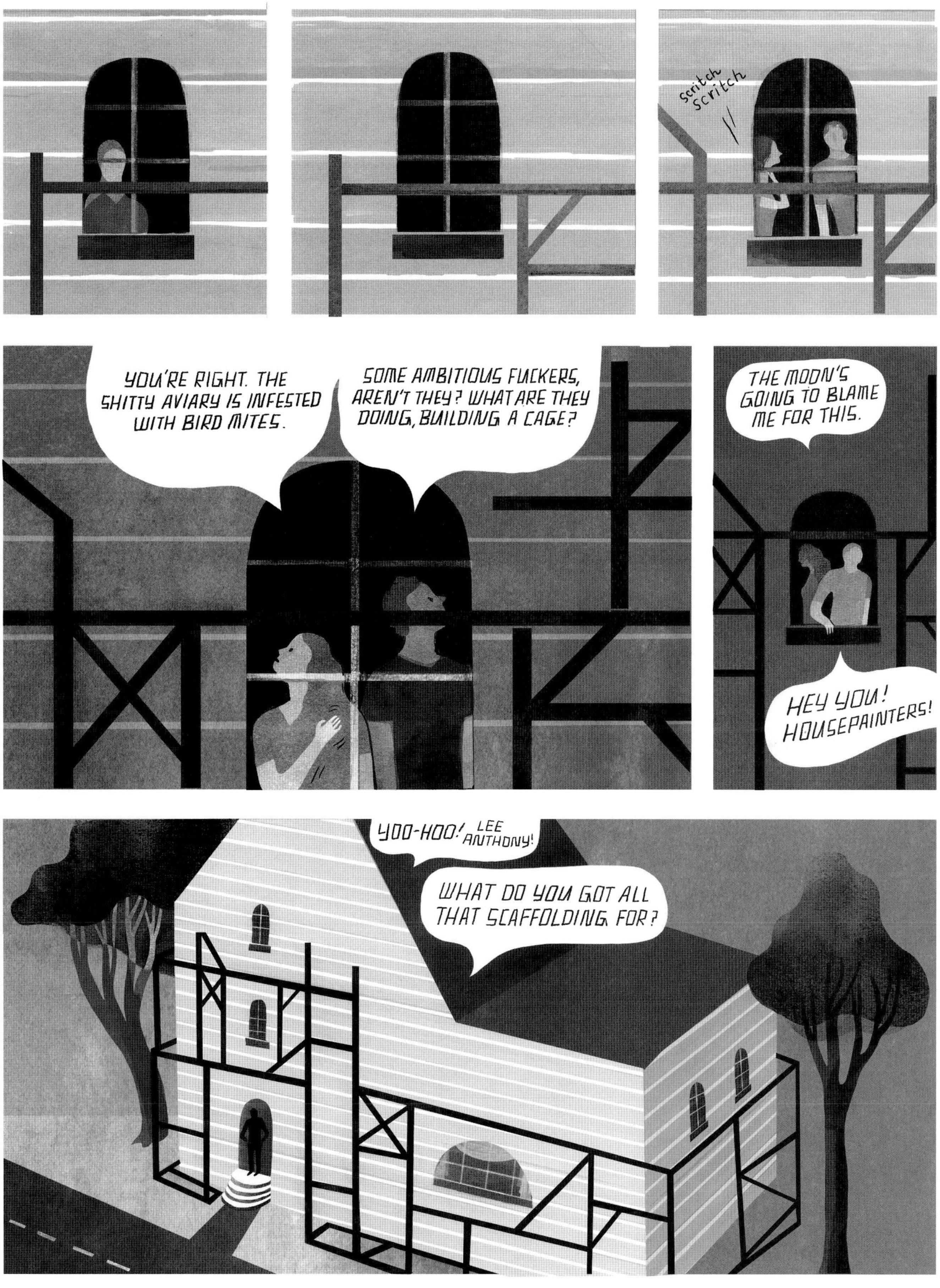

scritch
scritch
YOU'RE RIGHT. THE SHITTY AVIARY IS INFESTED WITH BIRD MITES.
SOME AMBITIOUS FUCKERS, AREN'T THEY? WHAT ARE THEY DOING, BUILDING A CAGE?
THE MOON'S GOING TO BLAME ME FOR THIS.
HEY YOU! HOUSEPAINTERS!
YOO-HOO! LEE ANTHONY!
WHAT DO YOU GOT ALL THAT SCAFFOLDING FOR?

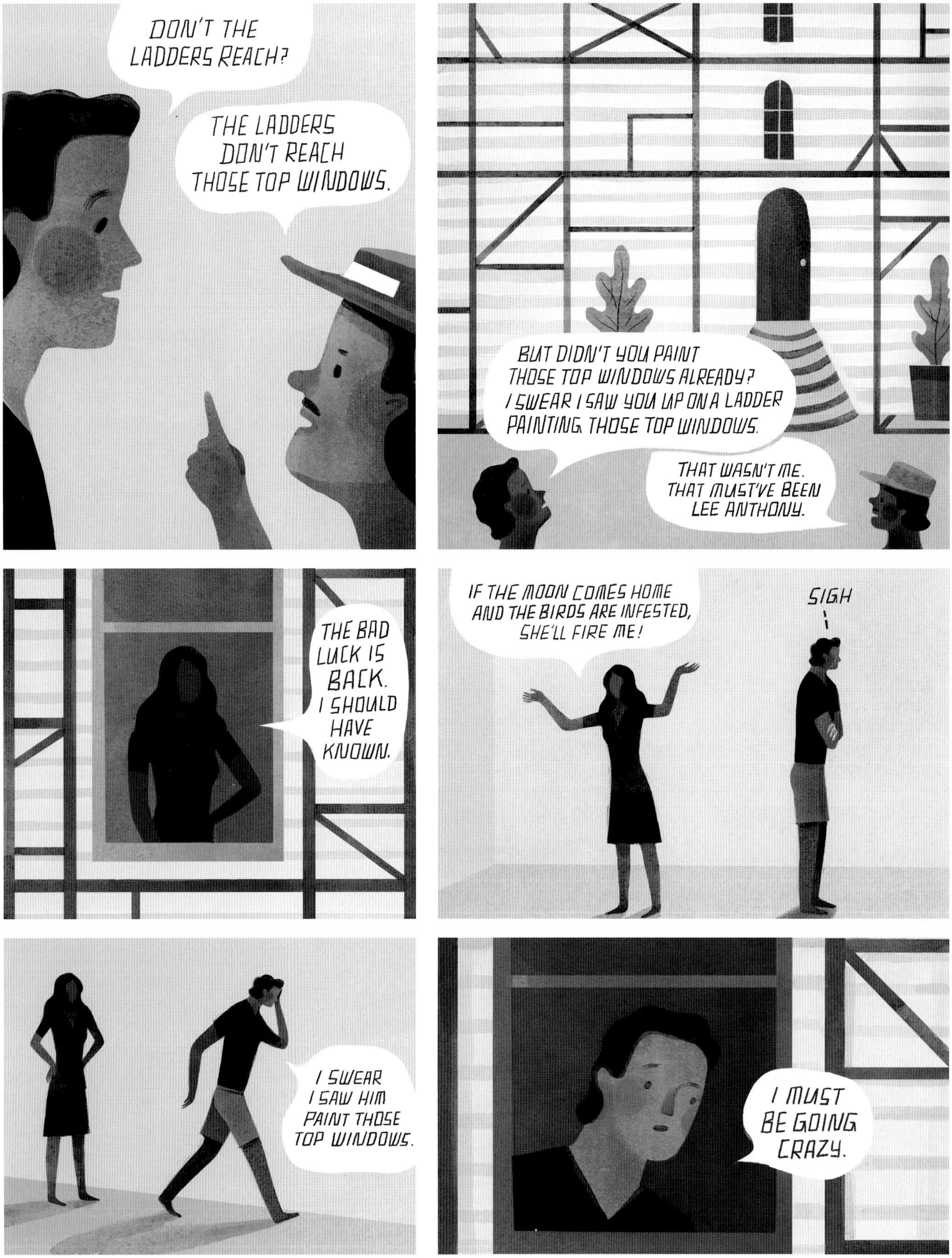
DON'T THE LADDERS REACH?
THE LADDERS DON'T REACH THOSE TOP WINDOWS.
BUT DIDN'T YOU PAINT THOSE TOP WINDOWS ALREADY? I SWEAR I SAW YOU UP ON A LADDER PAINTING THOSE TOP WINDOWS.
THAT WASN'T ME. THAT MUST'VE BEEN LEE ANTHONY.
THE BAD LUCK IS BACK. I SHOULD HAVE KNOWN.
IF THE MOON COMES HOME AND THE BIRDS ARE INFESTED, SHE'LL FIRE ME!
SIGH
I SWEAR I SAW HIM PAINT THOSE TOP WINDOWS.
I MUST BE GOING CRAZY.

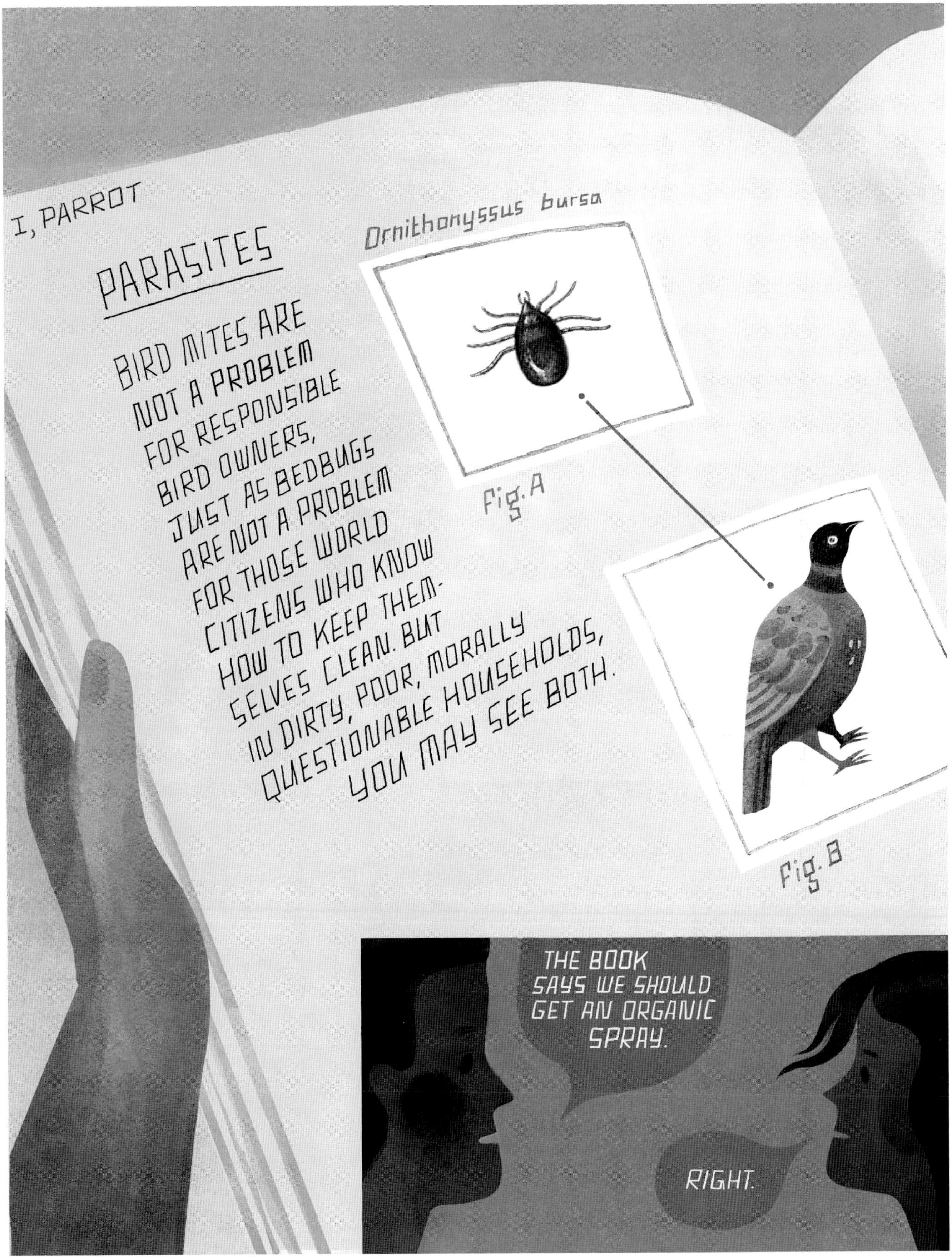
I, PARROT
PARASITES
BIRD MITES ARE NOT A PROBLEM FOR RESPONSIBLE BIRD OWNERS, JUST AS BEDBUGS ARE NOT A PROBLEM FOR THOSE WORLD CITIZENS WHO KNOW HOW TO KEEP THEMSELVES CLEAN. BUT IN DIRTY, POOR, MORALLY QUESTIONABLE HOUSEHOLDS, YOU MAY SEE BOTH.
Ornithonyssus bursa
Fig. A
Fig. B
THE BOOK SAYS WE SHOULD GET AN ORGANIC SPRAY.
RIGHT.

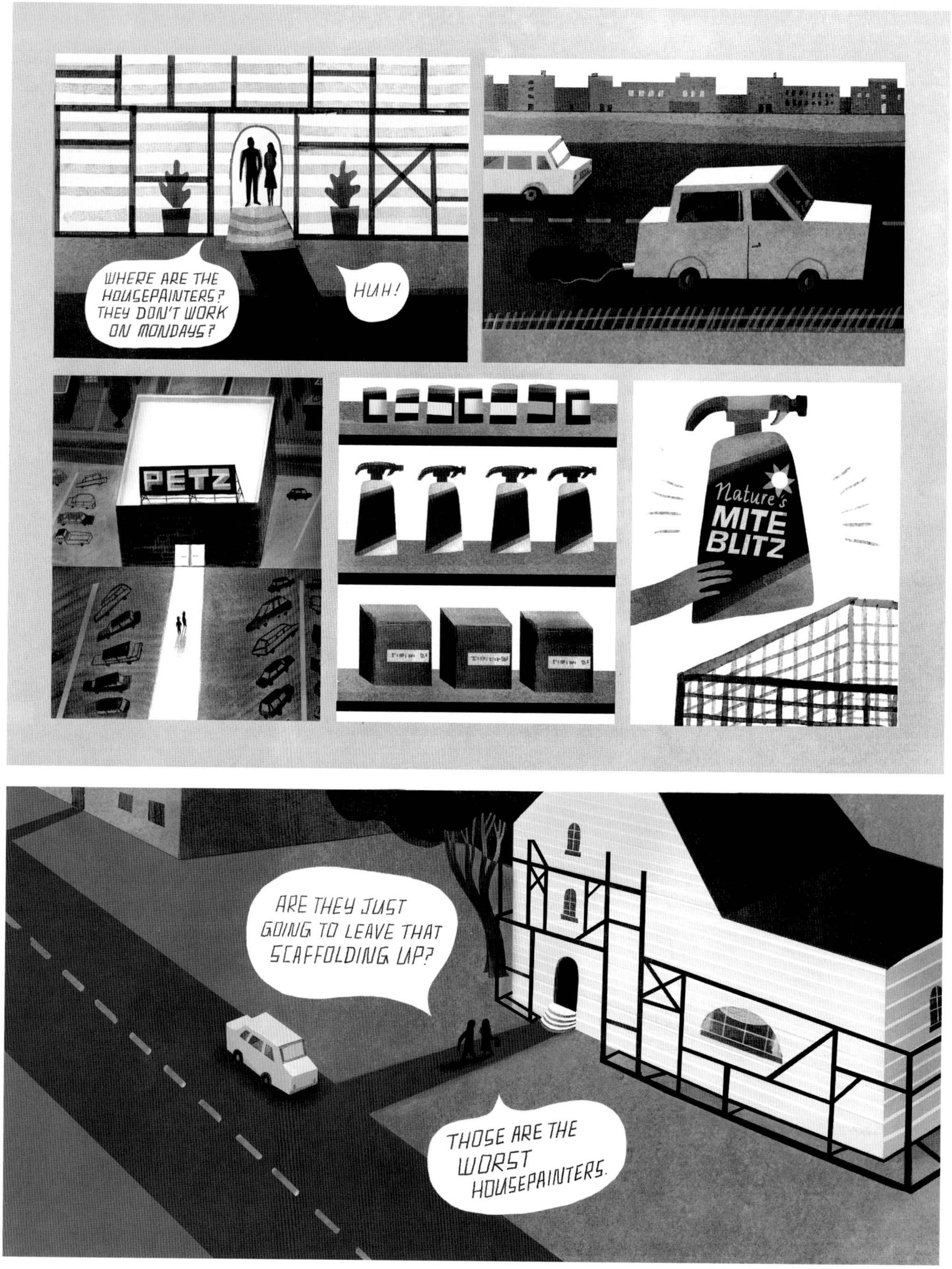
WHERE ARE THE HOUSEPAINTERS? THEY DON'T WORK ON MONDAYS?
HUH!
PETZ
Nature's
MITE BLITZ
ARE THEY JUST GOING TO LEAVE THAT SCAFFOLDING UP?
THOSE ARE THE WORST HOUSEPAINTERS.

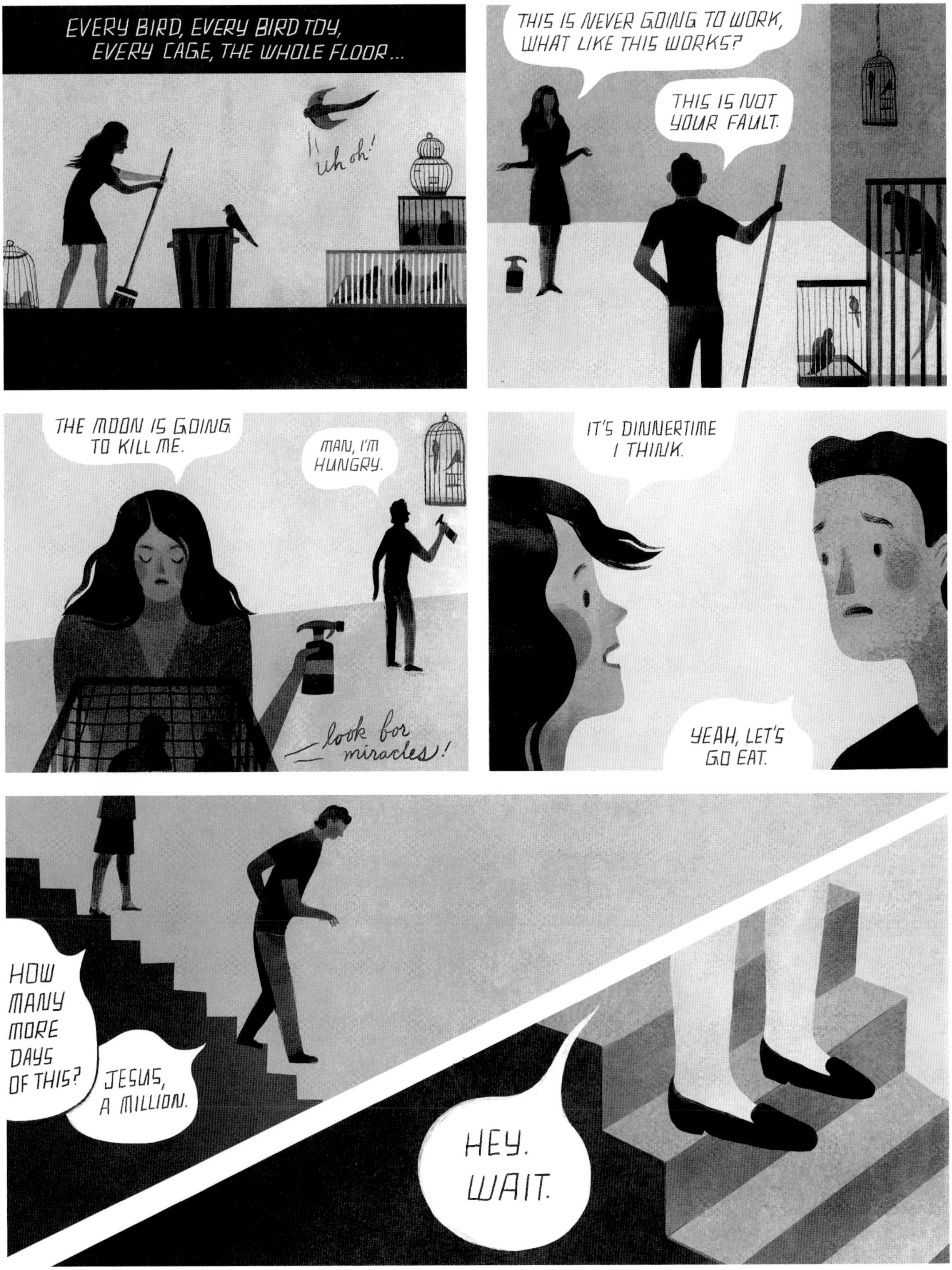
EVERY BIRD, EVERY BIRD TOY, EVERY CAGE, THE WHOLE FLOOR...
uh oh!
THIS IS NEVER GOING TO WORK, WHAT LIKE THIS WORKS?
THIS IS NOT YOUR FAULT.
THE MOON IS GOING TO KILL ME.
MAN, I'M HUNGRY.
look for miracles!
IT'S DINNERTIME I THINK.
YEAH, LET'S GO EAT.
HOW MANY MORE DAYS OF THIS?
JESUS, A MILLION.
HEY. WAIT.

IT'S MONDAY.

SHOULDN'T YOU'VE
BEEN OUT TODAY DRIVING
THAT STUPID VAN IN CIRCLES?

DON'T TELL ME.

IT WASN'T
MY FAULT.

IT'S INCREDIBLE.

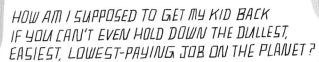

HOW AM I SUPPOSED TO GET MY KID BACK
IF YOU CAN'T EVEN HOLD DOWN THE DULLEST,
EASIEST, LOWEST-PAYING JOB ON THE PLANET?

YOU'RE GOING TO MAKE ME CHOOSE
BETWEEN YOUR BUM ASS AND MY KID?

hang in there

YES

YOU KNOW WHAT?
FINE. I'LL MAKE IT
EASY ON YOU.

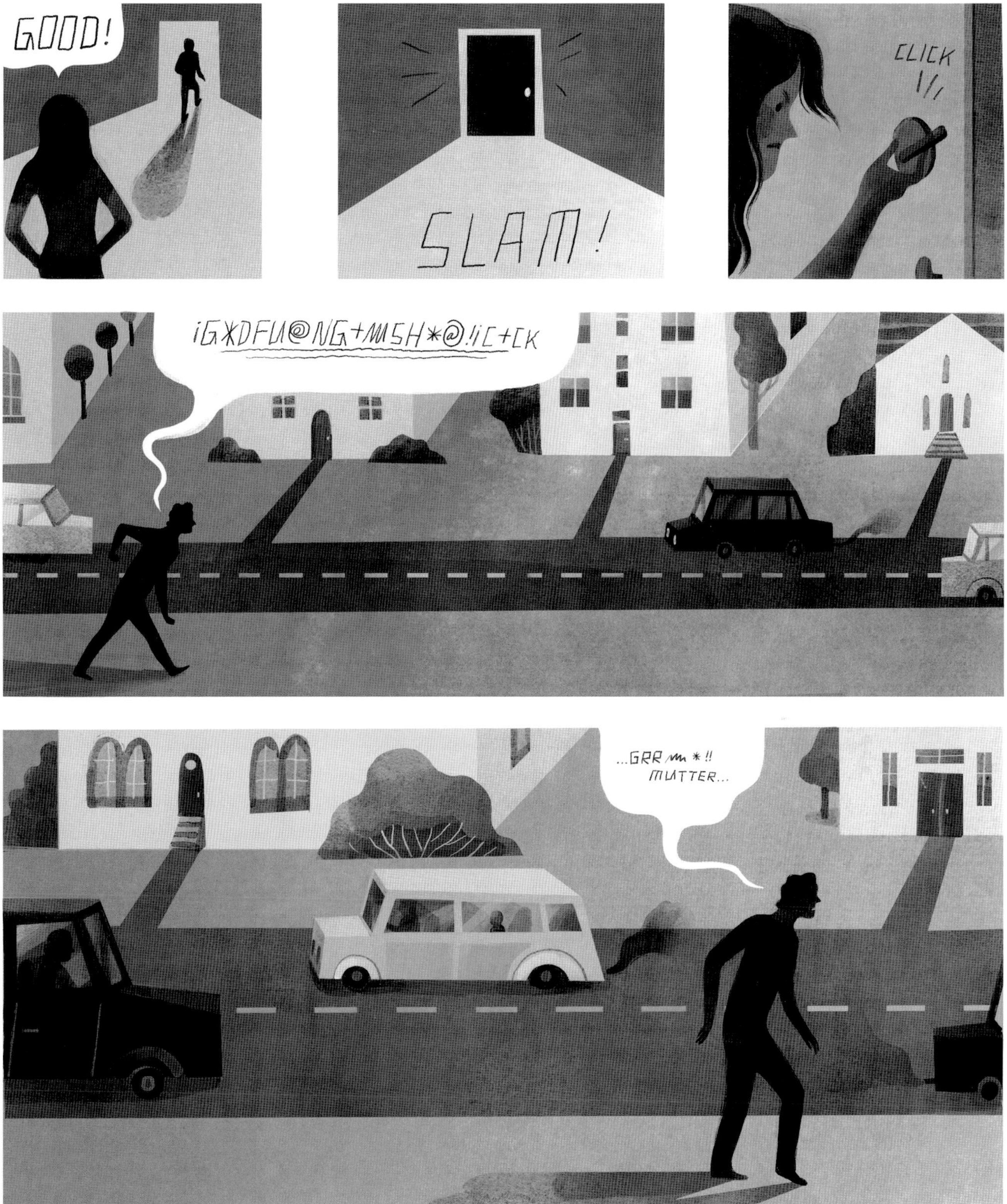
GOOD!
SLAM!
CLICK
iG*DFU@NG+MSH*@!iC+CK
...GRR *!!
MUTTER...

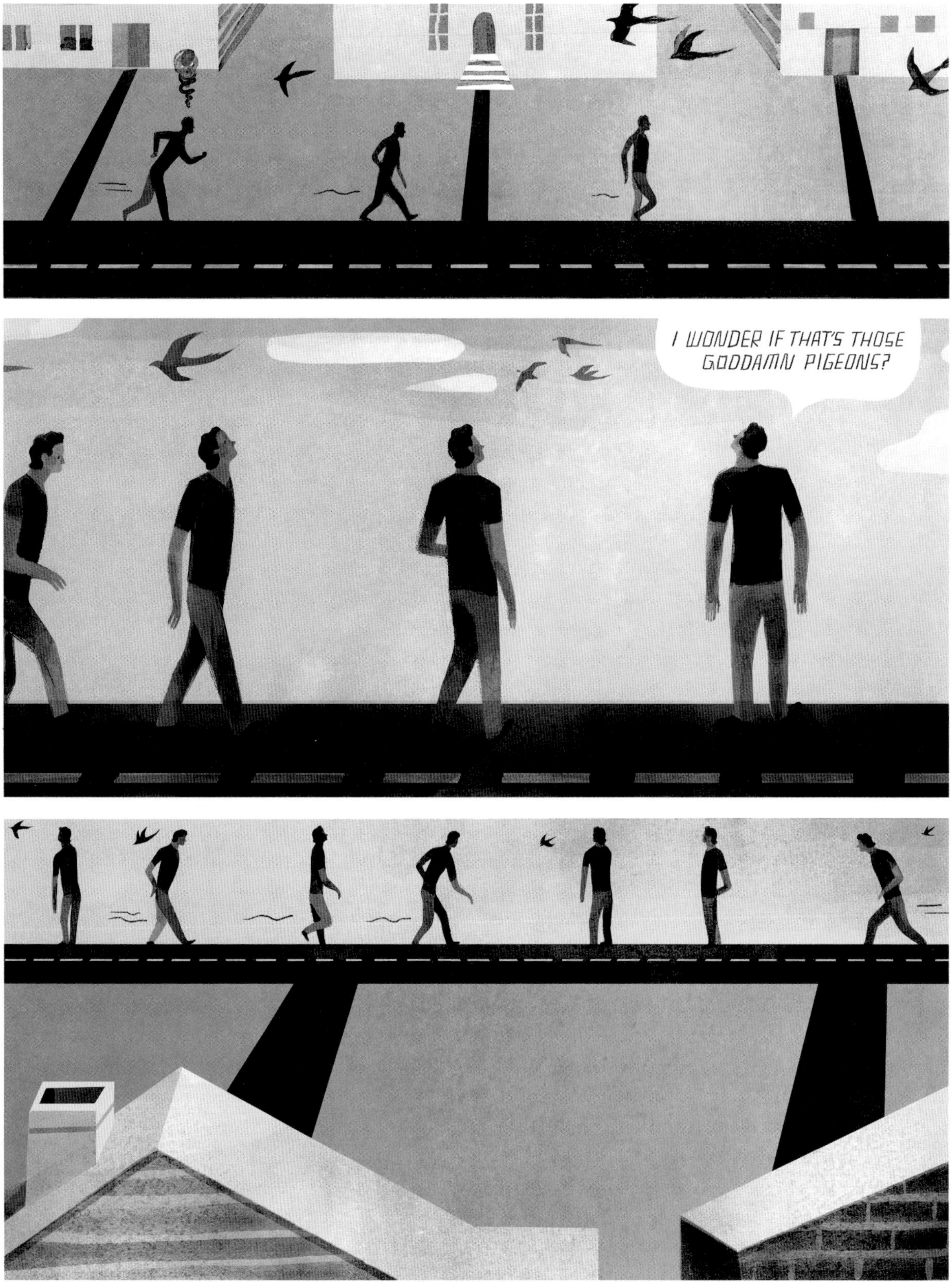
I WONDER IF THAT'S THOSE GODDAMN PIGEONS?

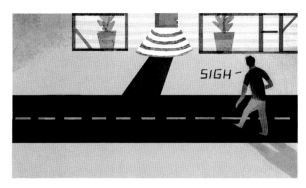

SIGH—

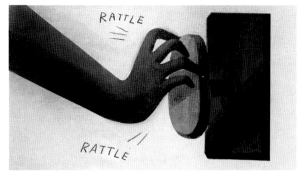

RATTLE

RATTLE

HEY, LET ME IN.

NO.

LET ME IN RIGHT NOW!

GO AWAY, LAKER!

AHEM.

WHAT ARE YOU DOING HERE?

HEE HEE, LITTLE ARGUMENT!

GO AWAY, LAKER, I'LL CALL THE POLICE!

ISN'T IT A BIT LATE FOR YOU GUYS? IT'S SEVEN O'CLOCK.

WHAT'D YOU DO TO HER?

WHAT'D I DO?

NOTHING.

IN FACT I CAN TELL YOU A YEAR AGO SHE WAS SHOUTING A DIFFERENT SLOGAN.

A YEAR AGO SHE TOLD ME SHE WAS THE HAPPIEST SHE'D EVER BEEN.

HAPPIER THAN SHE EVER DREAMED SHE WOULD BE.

AND THAT HAD TO BE PRETTY FUCKING HAPPY BECAUSE HUMANS HAVE BIG DREAMS.

HUMANS ARE AMAZINGLY GOOD AT IMAGINING HOW HAPPY THEY COULD BE IF ONLY THINGS WERE DIFFERENT.

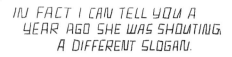

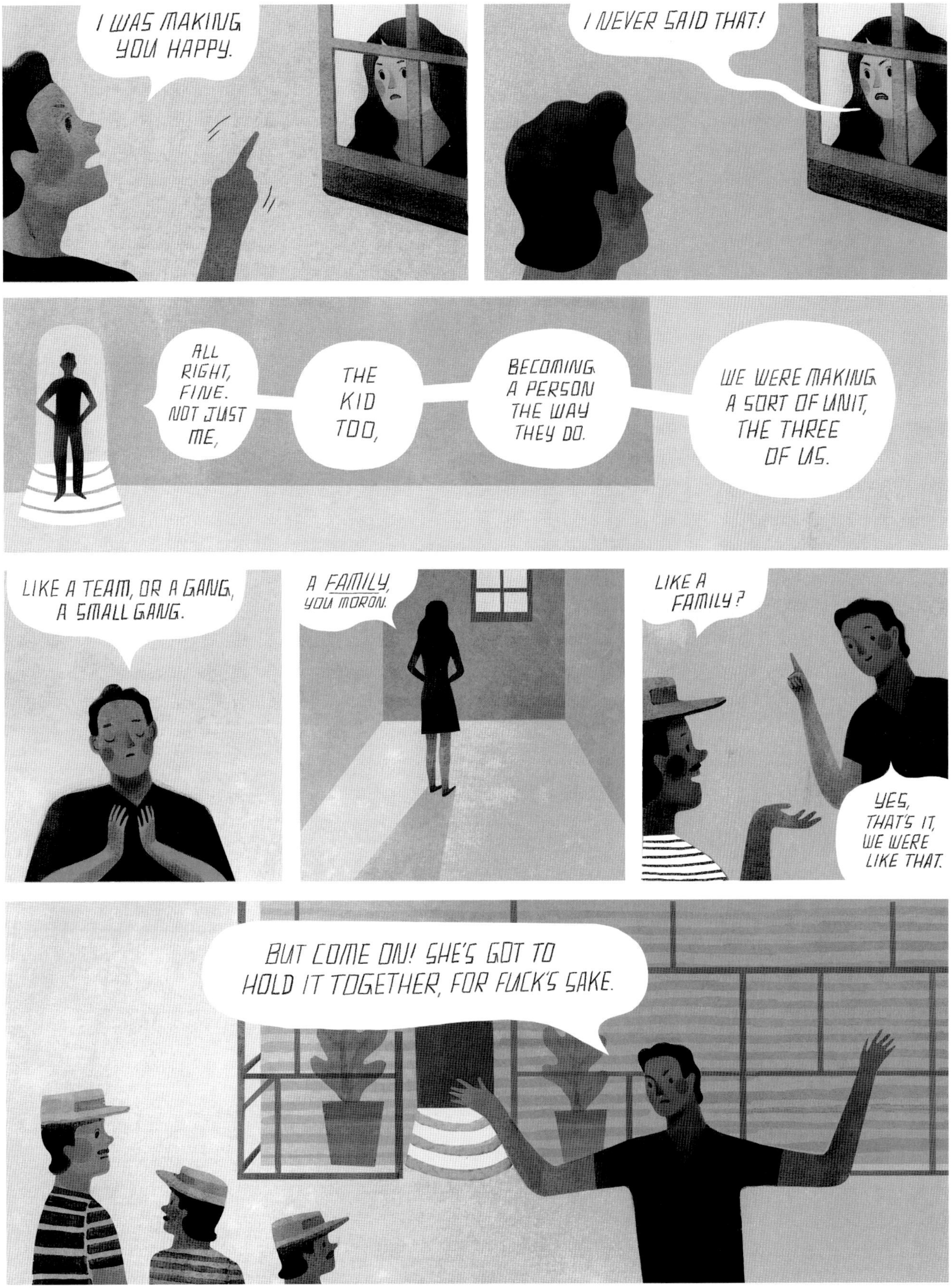
I WAS MAKING YOU HAPPY.
I NEVER SAID THAT!
ALL RIGHT, FINE. NOT JUST ME,
THE KID TOO,
BECOMING A PERSON THE WAY THEY DO.
WE WERE MAKING A SORT OF UNIT, THE THREE OF US.
LIKE A TEAM, OR A GANG, A SMALL GANG.
A FAMILY, YOU MORON.
LIKE A FAMILY?
YES, THAT'S IT, WE WERE LIKE THAT.
BUT COME ON! SHE'S GOT TO HOLD IT TOGETHER, FOR FUCK'S SAKE.

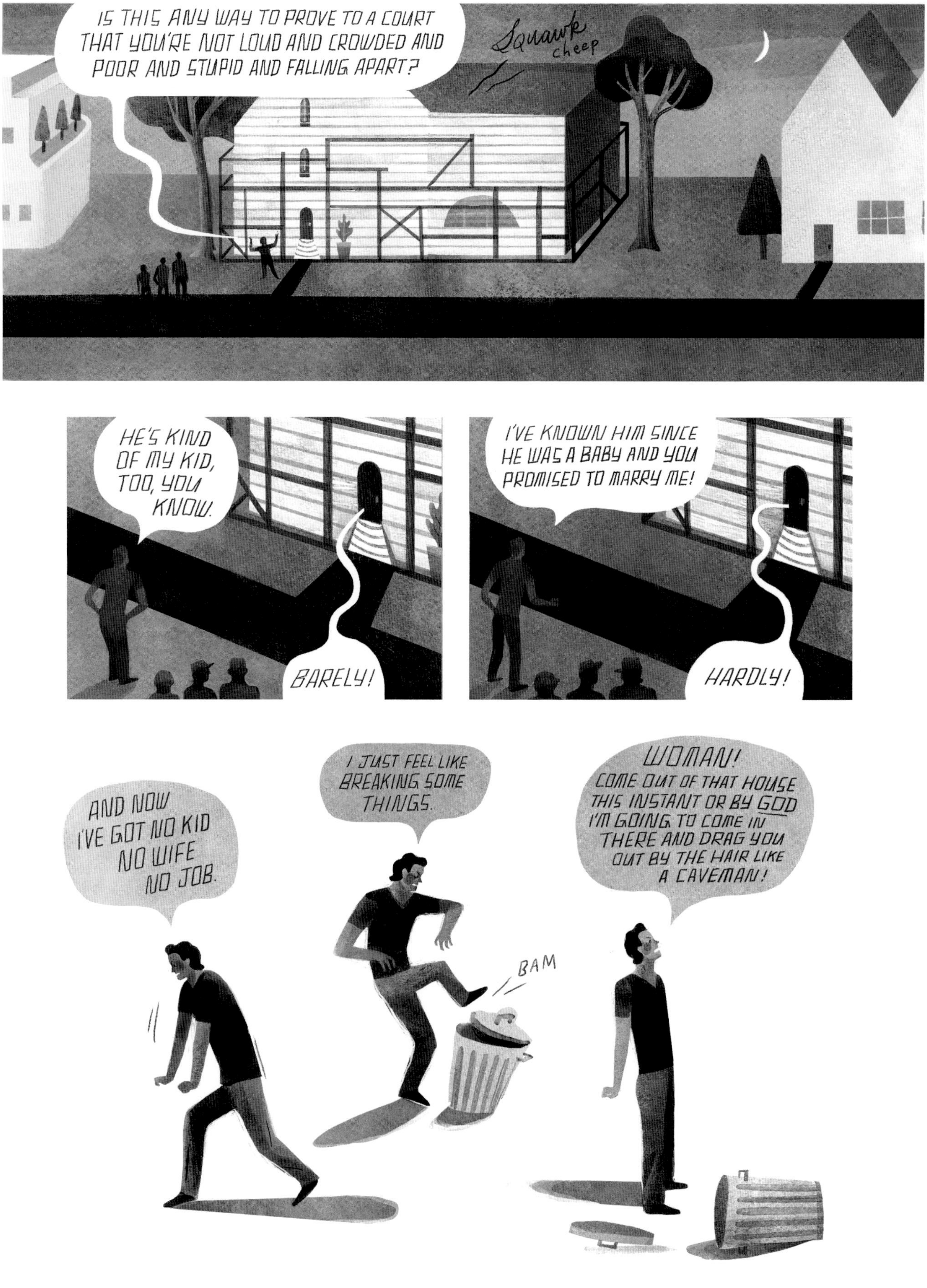
IS THIS ANY WAY TO PROVE TO A COURT THAT YOU'RE NOT LOUD AND CROWDED AND POOR AND STUPID AND FALLING APART?
Squawk
cheep
HE'S KIND OF MY KID, TOO, YOU KNOW.
BARELY!
I'VE KNOWN HIM SINCE HE WAS A BABY AND YOU PROMISED TO MARRY ME!
HARDLY!
AND NOW I'VE GOT NO KID NO WIFE NO JOB.
I JUST FEEL LIKE BREAKING SOME THINGS.
BAM
WOMAN! COME OUT OF THAT HOUSE THIS INSTANT OR BY GOD I'M GOING TO COME IN THERE AND DRAG YOU OUT BY THE HAIR LIKE A CAVEMAN!

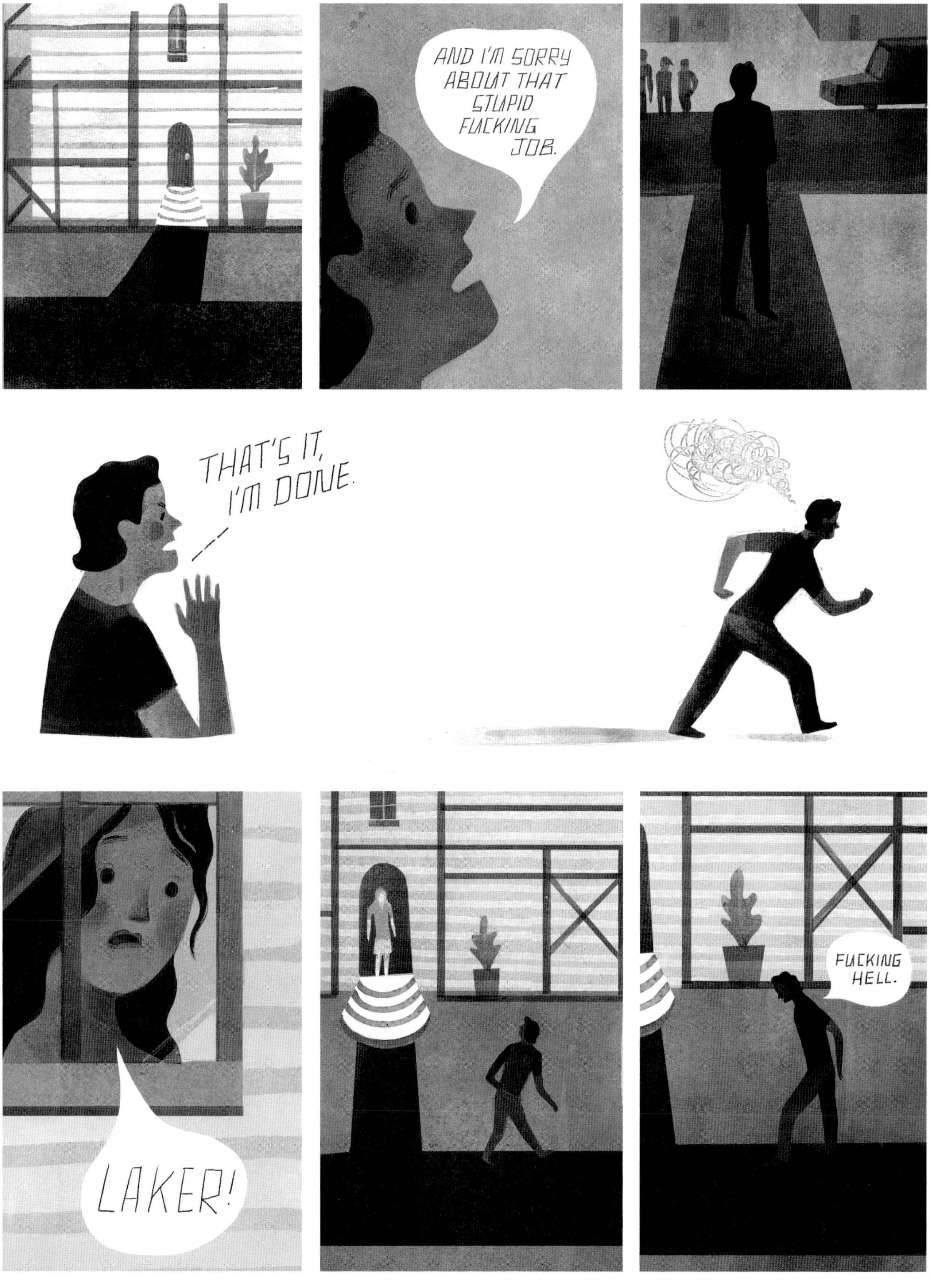
AND I'M SORRY ABOUT THAT STUPID FUCKING JOB.
THAT'S IT, I'M DONE.
LAKER!
FUCKING HELL.

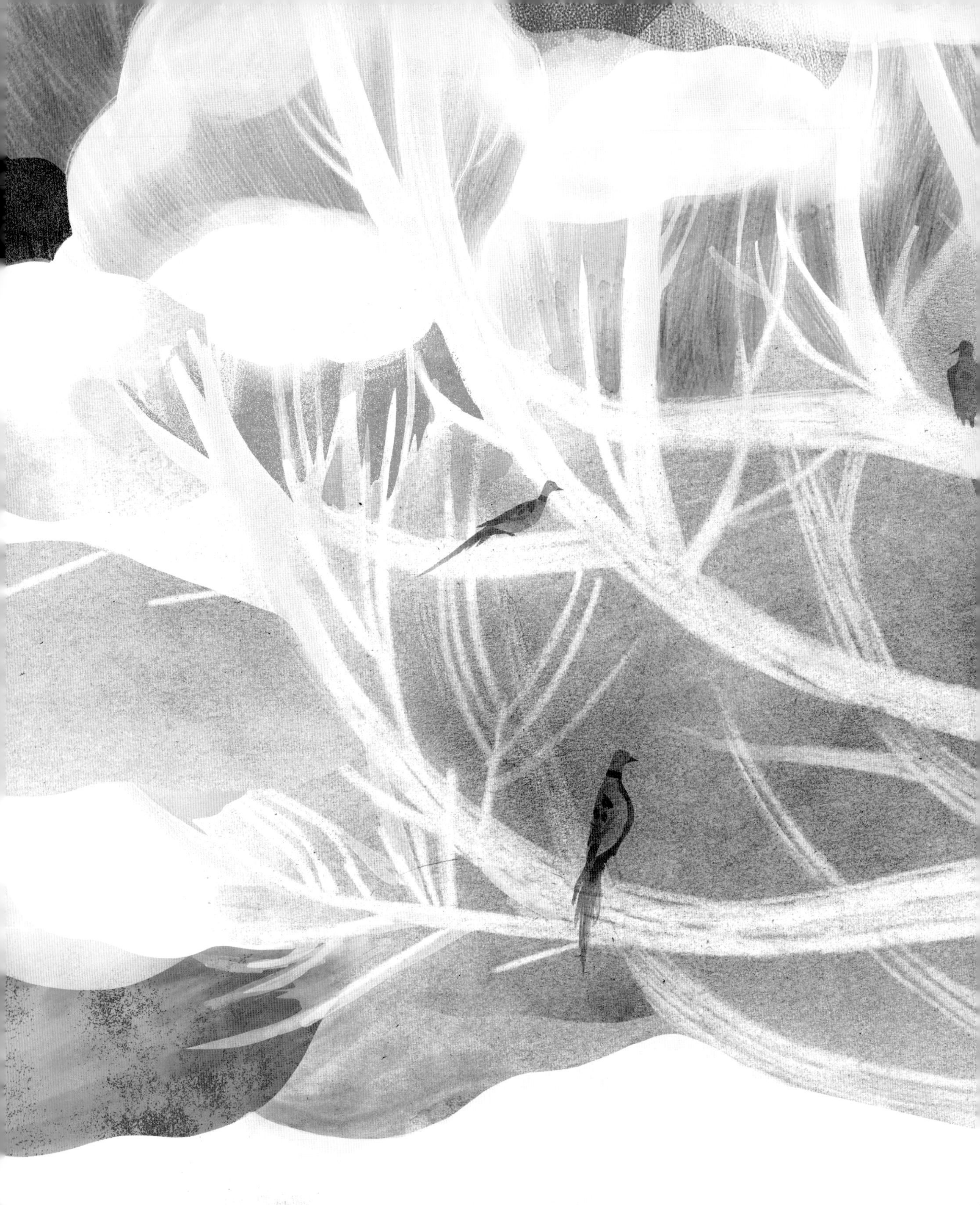

CHAPTER 4: YOUR MOTHER'S HERE

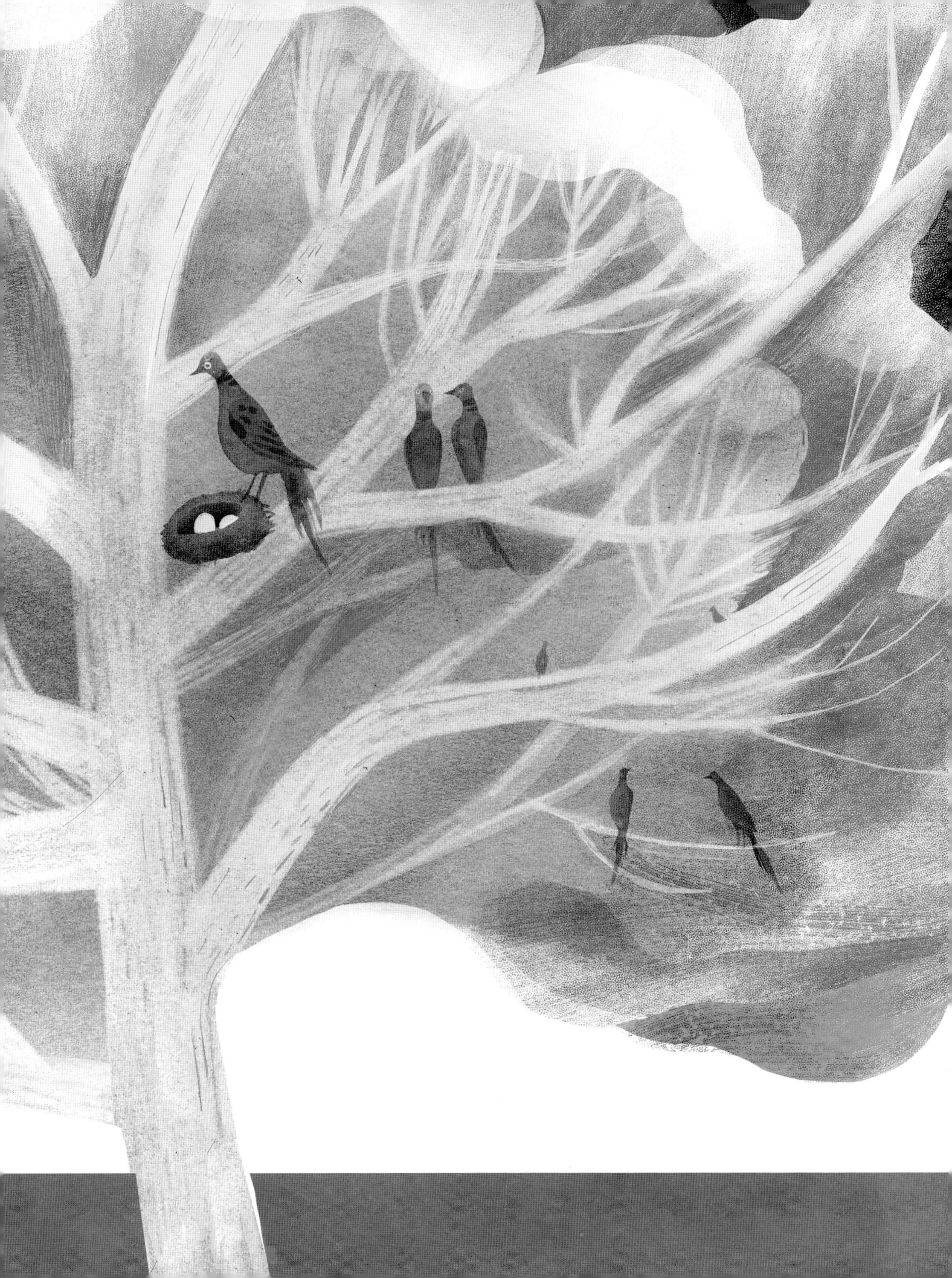

FINALLY FRIDAY ARRIVED.

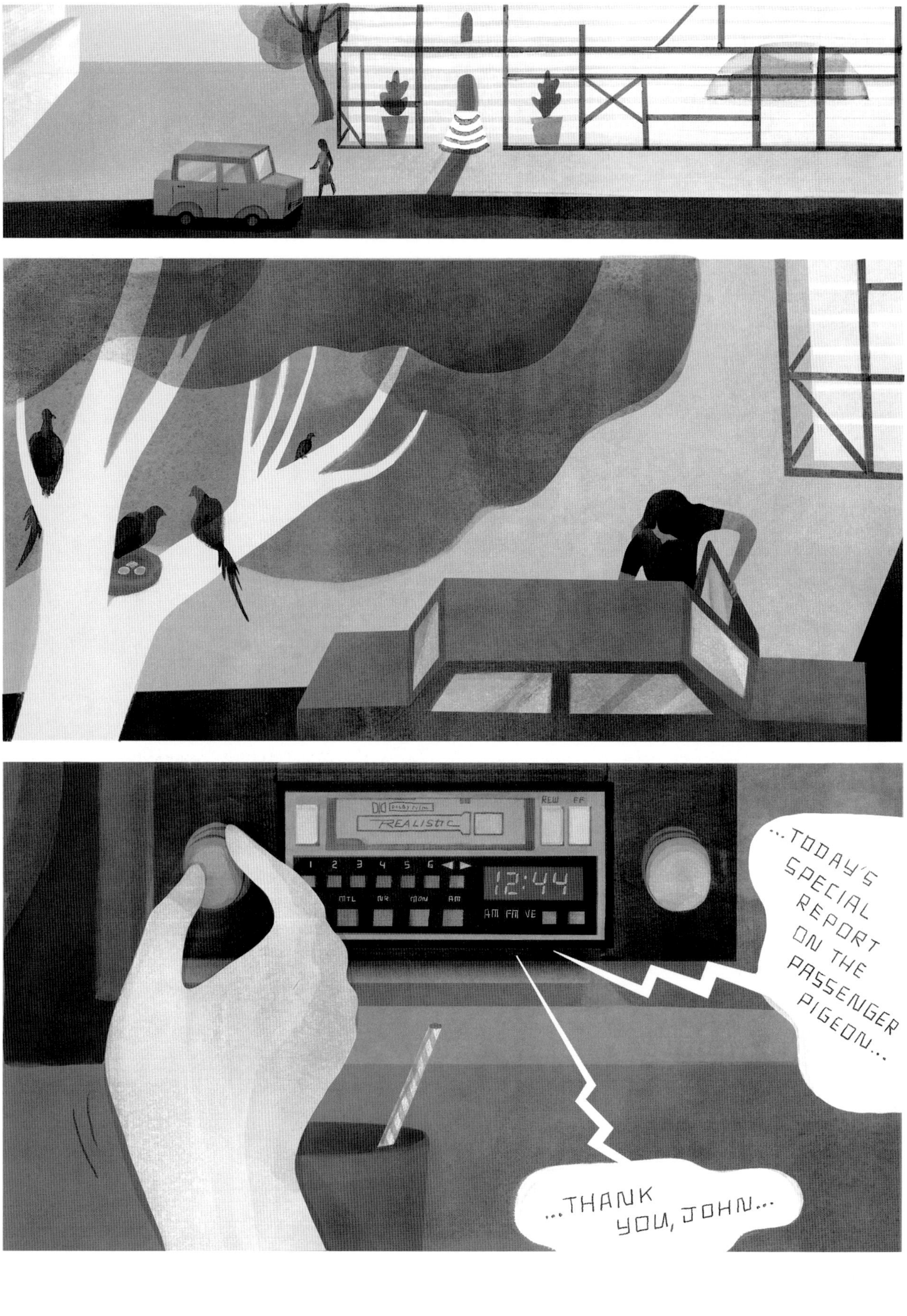
REALISTIC
12:44
...TODAY'S SPECIAL REPORT ON THE PASSENGER PIGEON...
...THANK YOU, JOHN...

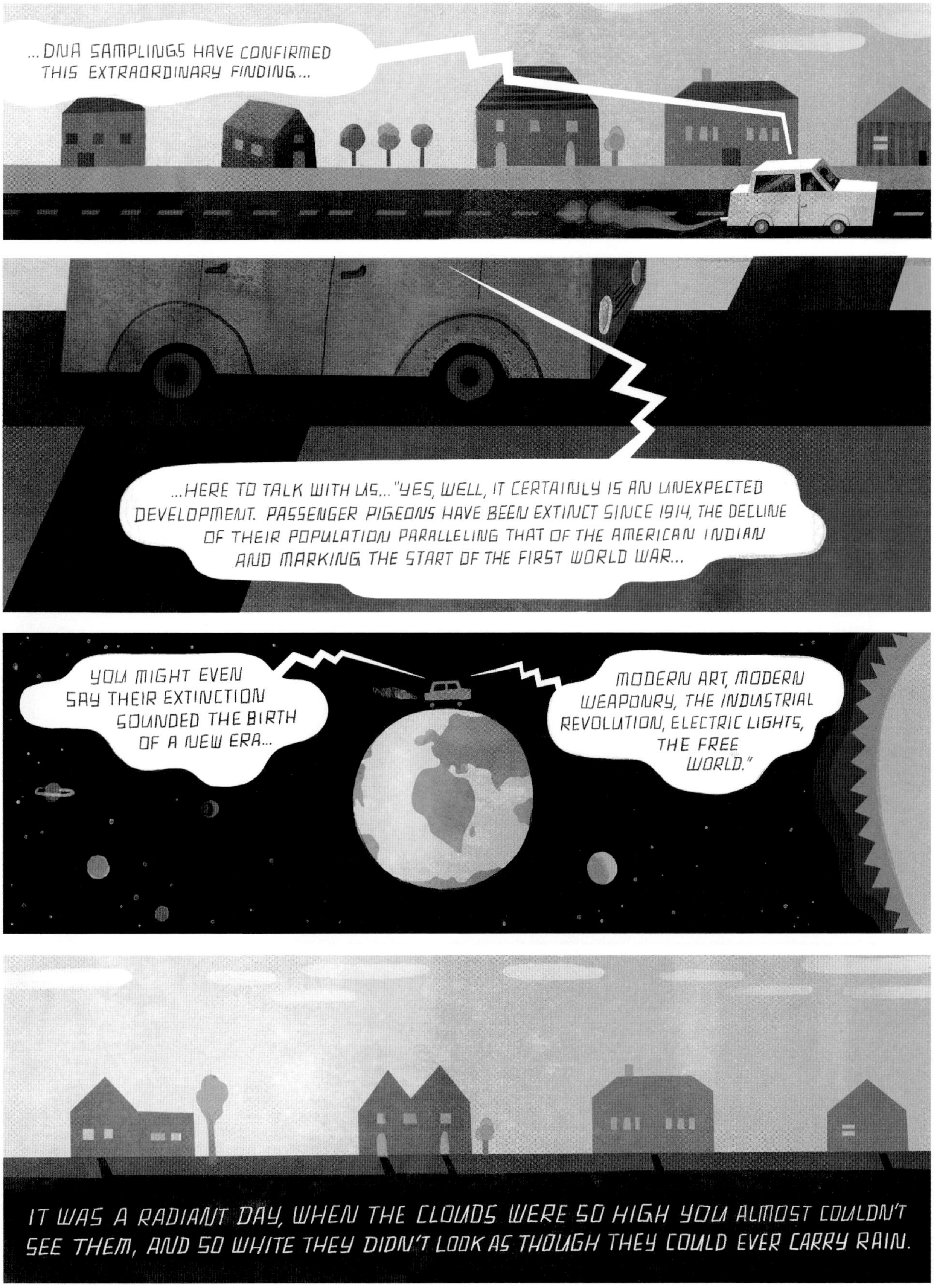
...DNA SAMPLINGS HAVE CONFIRMED THIS EXTRAORDINARY FINDING...
...HERE TO TALK WITH US..."YES, WELL, IT CERTAINLY IS AN UNEXPECTED DEVELOPMENT. PASSENGER PIGEONS HAVE BEEN EXTINCT SINCE 1914, THE DECLINE OF THEIR POPULATION PARALLELING THAT OF THE AMERICAN INDIAN AND MARKING THE START OF THE FIRST WORLD WAR...
YOU MIGHT EVEN SAY THEIR EXTINCTION SOUNDED THE BIRTH OF A NEW ERA...
MODERN ART, MODERN WEAPONRY, THE INDUSTRIAL REVOLUTION, ELECTRIC LIGHTS, THE FREE WORLD."
IT WAS A RADIANT DAY, WHEN THE CLOUDS WERE SO HIGH YOU ALMOST COULDN'T SEE THEM, AND SO WHITE THEY DIDN'T LOOK AS THOUGH THEY COULD EVER CARRY RAIN.

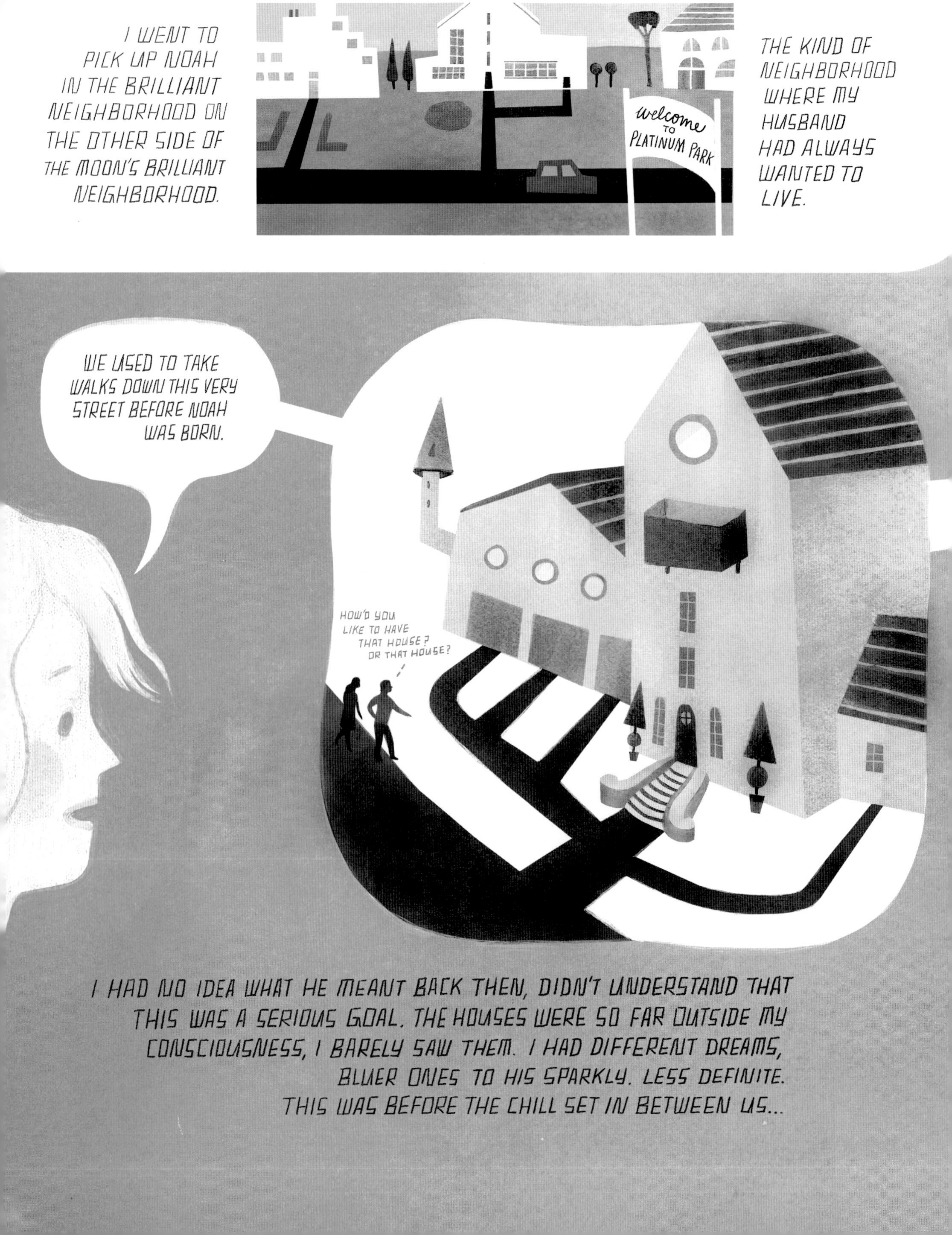
I WENT TO PICK UP NOAH IN THE BRILLIANT NEIGHBORHOOD ON THE OTHER SIDE OF THE MOON'S BRILLIANT NEIGHBORHOOD.
Welcome TO PLATINUM PARK
THE KIND OF NEIGHBORHOOD WHERE MY HUSBAND HAD ALWAYS WANTED TO LIVE.
WE USED TO TAKE WALKS DOWN THIS VERY STREET BEFORE NOAH WAS BORN.
HOW'D YOU LIKE TO HAVE THAT HOUSE? OR THAT HOUSE?
I HAD NO IDEA WHAT HE MEANT BACK THEN, DIDN'T UNDERSTAND THAT THIS WAS A SERIOUS GOAL. THE HOUSES WERE SO FAR OUTSIDE MY CONSCIOUSNESS, I BARELY SAW THEM. I HAD DIFFERENT DREAMS, BLUER ONES TO HIS SPARKLY. LESS DEFINITE. THIS WAS BEFORE THE CHILL SET IN BETWEEN US...

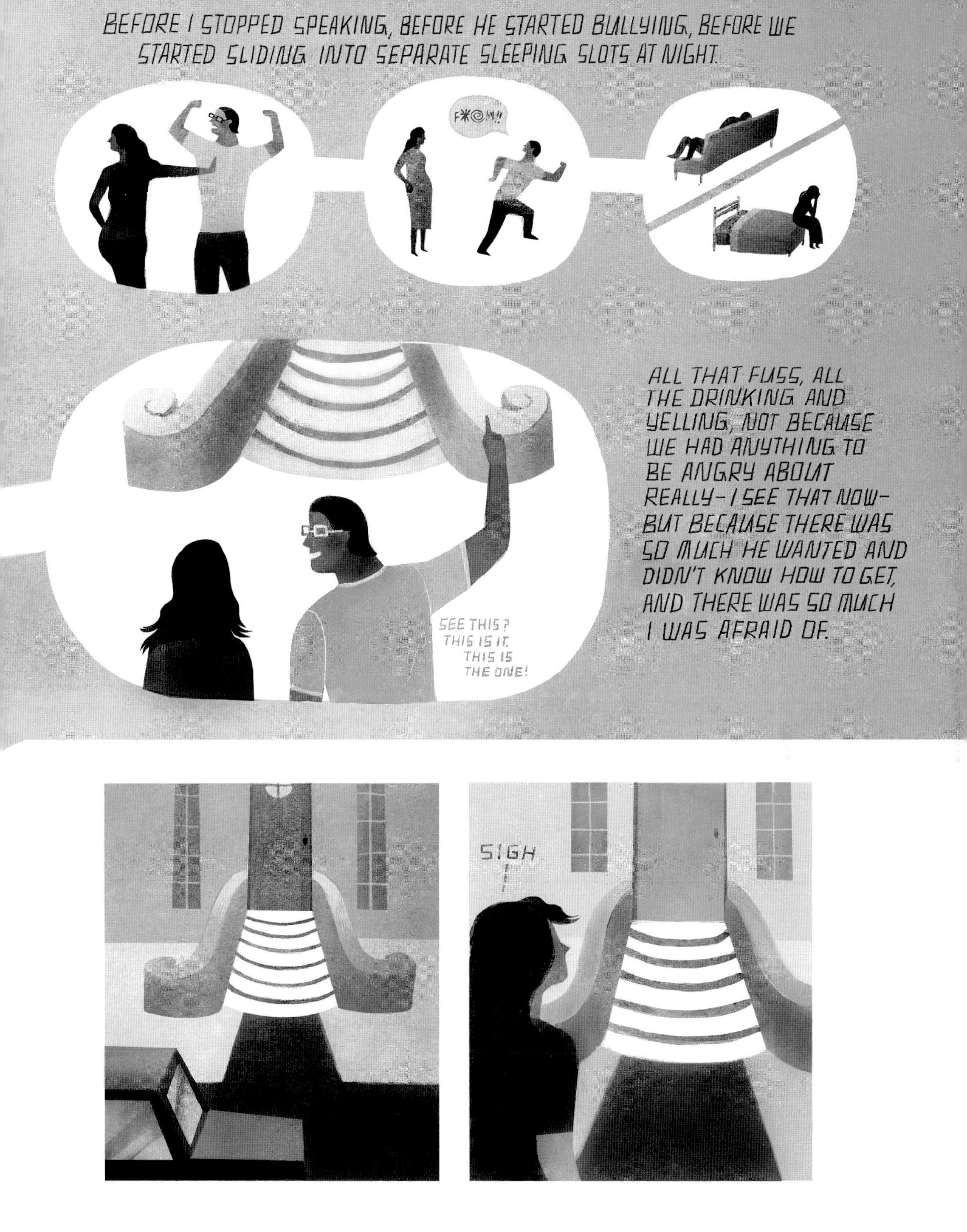
BEFORE I STOPPED SPEAKING, BEFORE HE STARTED BULLYING, BEFORE WE STARTED SLIDING INTO SEPARATE SLEEPING SLOTS AT NIGHT.
F*@M!!
ALL THAT FUSS, ALL THE DRINKING AND YELLING, NOT BECAUSE WE HAD ANYTHING TO BE ANGRY ABOUT REALLY– I SEE THAT NOW– BUT BECAUSE THERE WAS SO MUCH HE WANTED AND DIDN'T KNOW HOW TO GET, AND THERE WAS SO MUCH I WAS AFRAID OF.
SEE THIS? THIS IS IT. THIS IS THE ONE!
SIGH

DID IT SEEM THIS NEW WIFE DIDN'T CARE MUCH FOR NOAH? SHE PUT UP A GOOD FRONT, OF COURSE. SHE LAID ON A NICE FACE, KNOCKED OUT OF HER VOICE ANY ANNOYANCE, BUT I SAW UNDERNEATH A THIN LAYER OF SYNTHETIC PATIENCE.

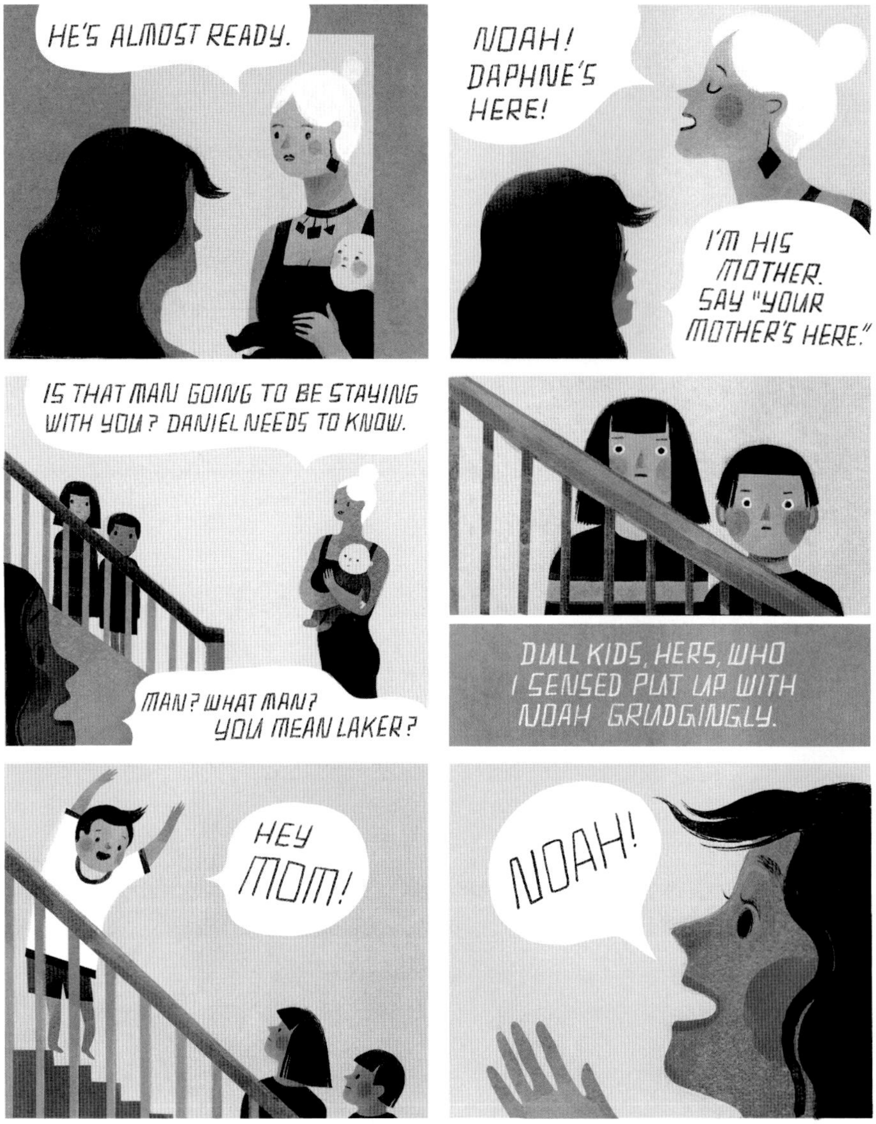
HE'S ALMOST READY.
NOAH! DAPHNE'S HERE!
I'M HIS MOTHER. SAY "YOUR MOTHER'S HERE."
IS THAT MAN GOING TO BE STAYING WITH YOU? DANIEL NEEDS TO KNOW.
MAN? WHAT MAN? YOU MEAN LAKER?
DULL KIDS, HERS, WHO I SENSED PUT UP WITH NOAH GRUDGINGLY.
HEY MOM!
NOAH!

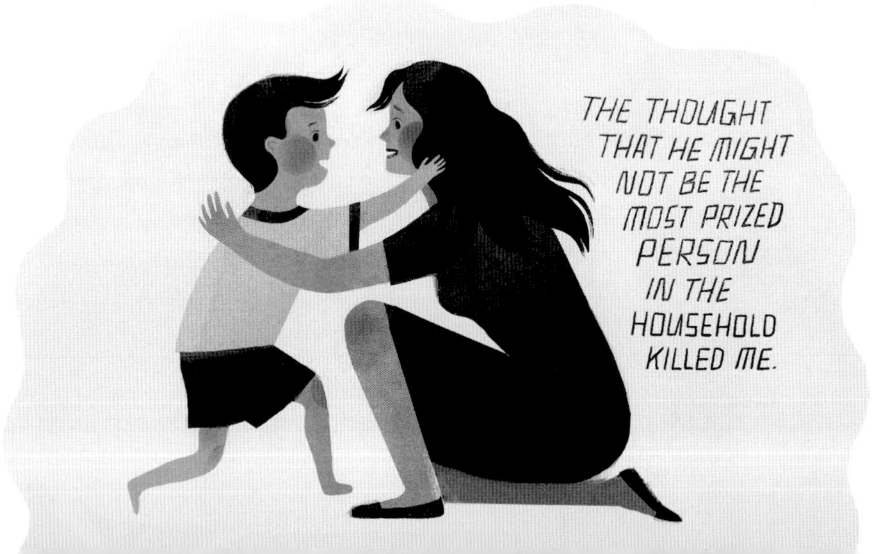
THE THOUGHT THAT HE MIGHT NOT BE THE MOST PRIZED PERSON IN THE HOUSEHOLD KILLED ME.

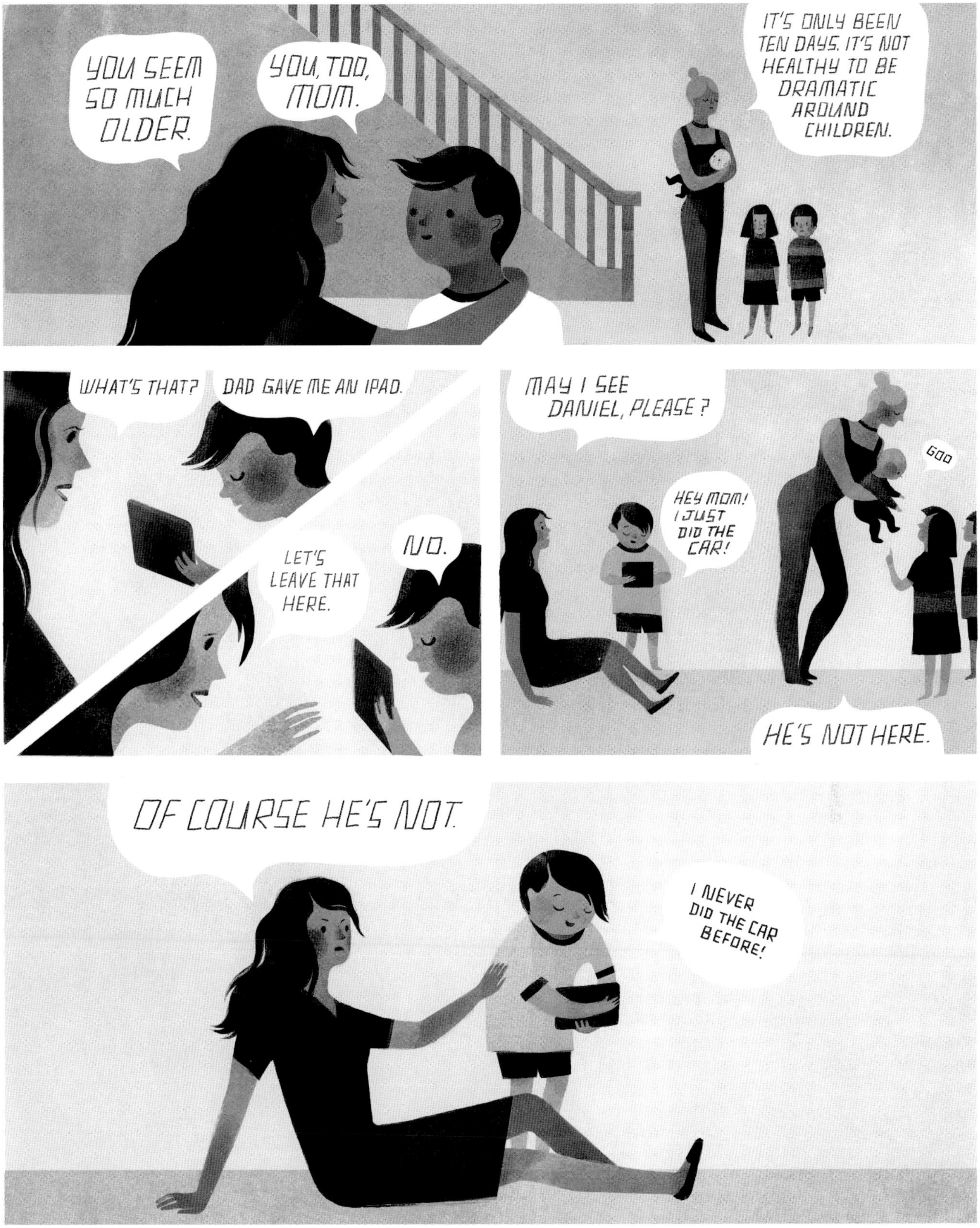
YOU SEEM SO MUCH OLDER.
YOU, TOO, MOM.
IT'S ONLY BEEN TEN DAYS. IT'S NOT HEALTHY TO BE DRAMATIC AROUND CHILDREN.
WHAT'S THAT?
DAD GAVE ME AN IPAD.
LET'S LEAVE THAT HERE.
NO.
MAY I SEE DANIEL, PLEASE?
HEY MOM! I JUST DID THE CAR!
GOO
HE'S NOT HERE.
OF COURSE HE'S NOT.
I NEVER DID THE CAR BEFORE!

DANIEL WORKED WITHOUT END NOW,
WHILE THIS STRANGER-LADY RAISED MY SON.

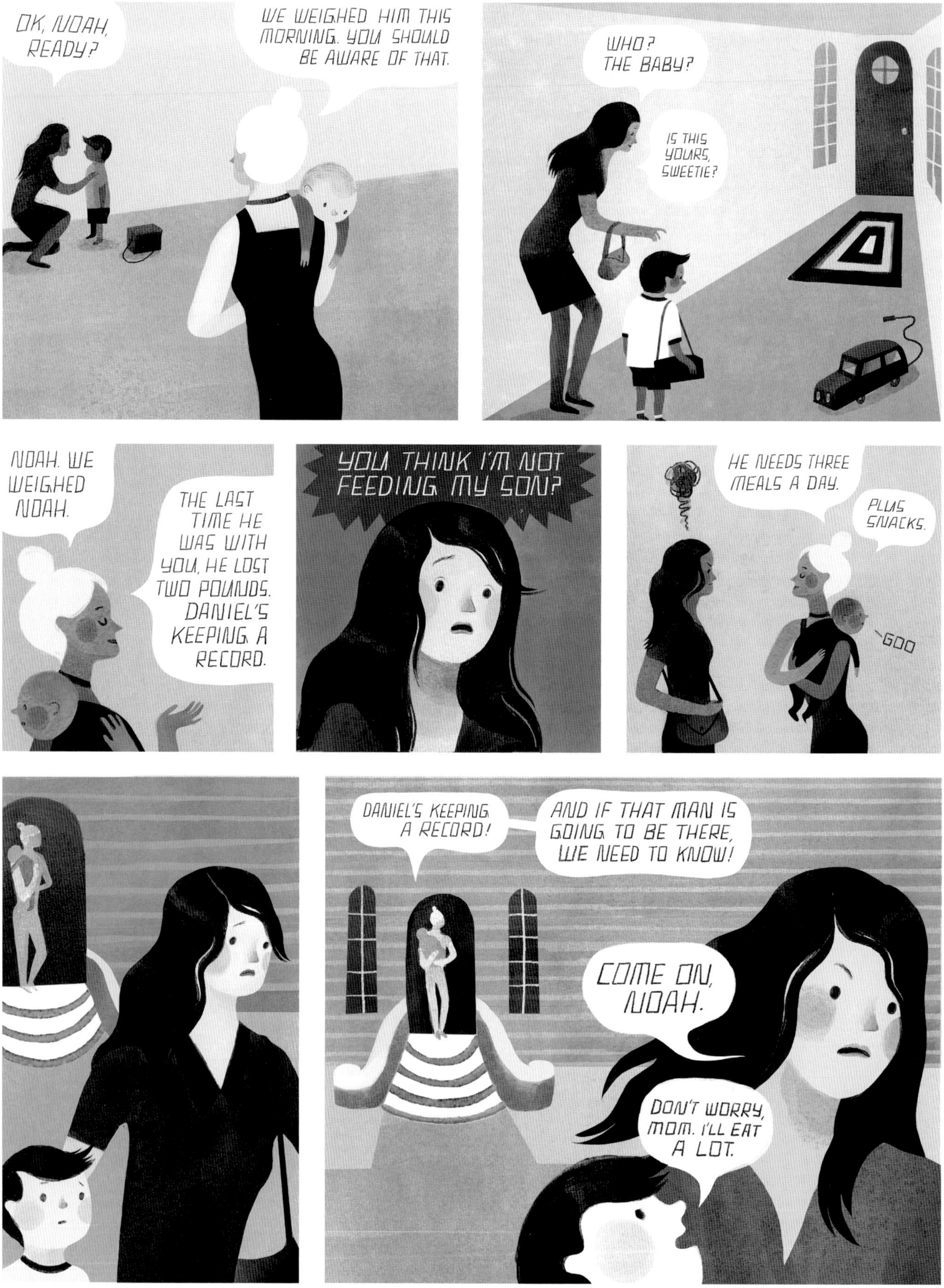
OK, NOAH, READY?
WE WEIGHED HIM THIS MORNING. YOU SHOULD BE AWARE OF THAT.
WHO? THE BABY?
IS THIS YOURS, SWEETIE?
NOAH. WE WEIGHED NOAH.
THE LAST TIME HE WAS WITH YOU, HE LOST TWO POUNDS. DANIEL'S KEEPING A RECORD.
YOU THINK I'M NOT FEEDING MY SON?
HE NEEDS THREE MEALS A DAY.
PLUS SNACKS.
GOO
DANIEL'S KEEPING A RECORD!
AND IF THAT MAN IS GOING TO BE THERE, WE NEED TO KNOW!
COME ON, NOAH.
DON'T WORRY, MOM. I'LL EAT A LOT.

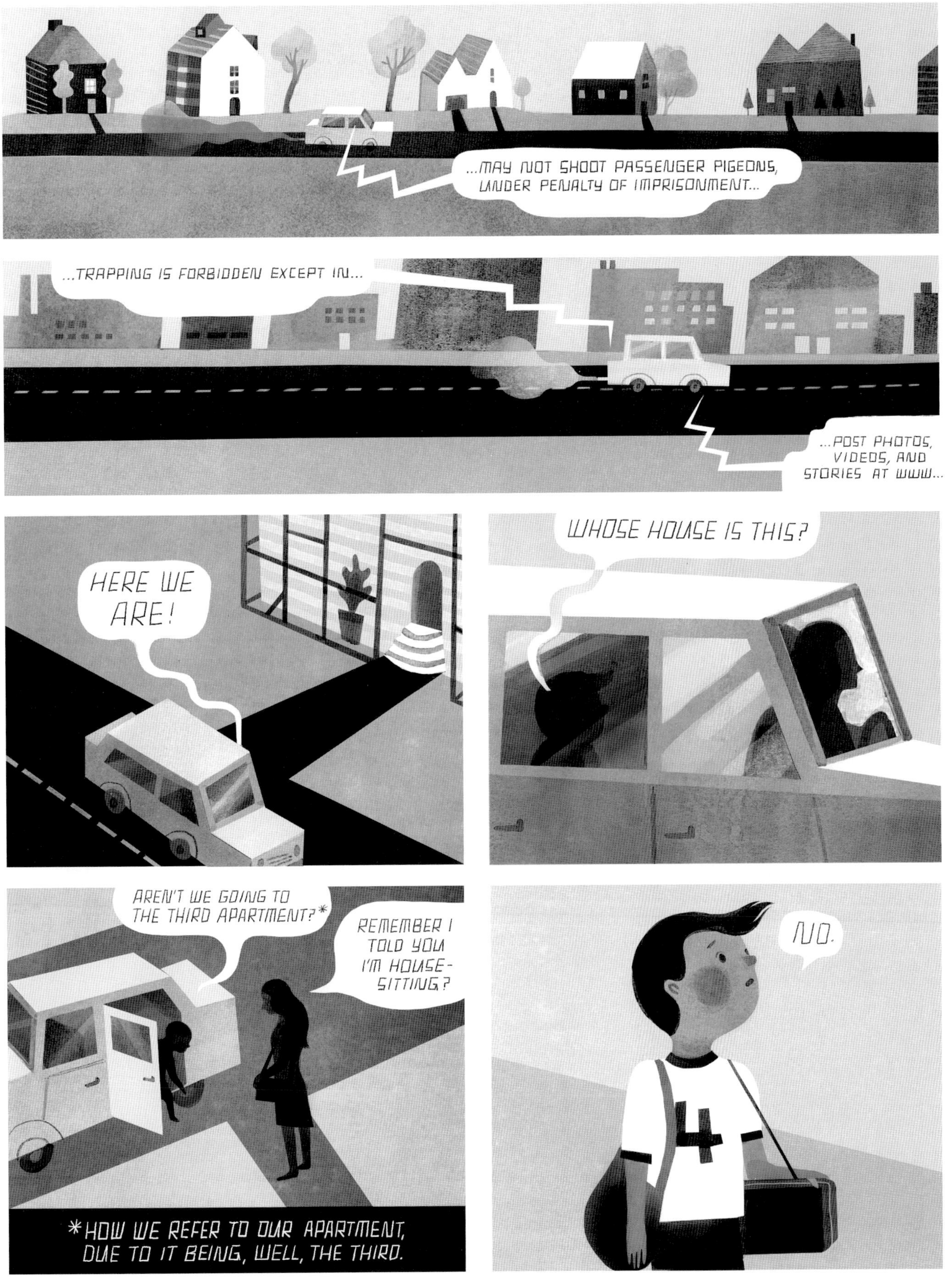

...MAY NOT SHOOT PASSENGER PIGEONS, UNDER PENALTY OF IMPRISONMENT...
...TRAPPING IS FORBIDDEN EXCEPT IN...
...POST PHOTOS, VIDEOS, AND STORIES AT WWW...
HERE WE ARE!
WHOSE HOUSE IS THIS?
AREN'T WE GOING TO THE THIRD APARTMENT?*
REMEMBER I TOLD YOU I'M HOUSE-SITTING?
*HOW WE REFER TO OUR APARTMENT, DUE TO IT BEING, WELL, THE THIRD.
NO.

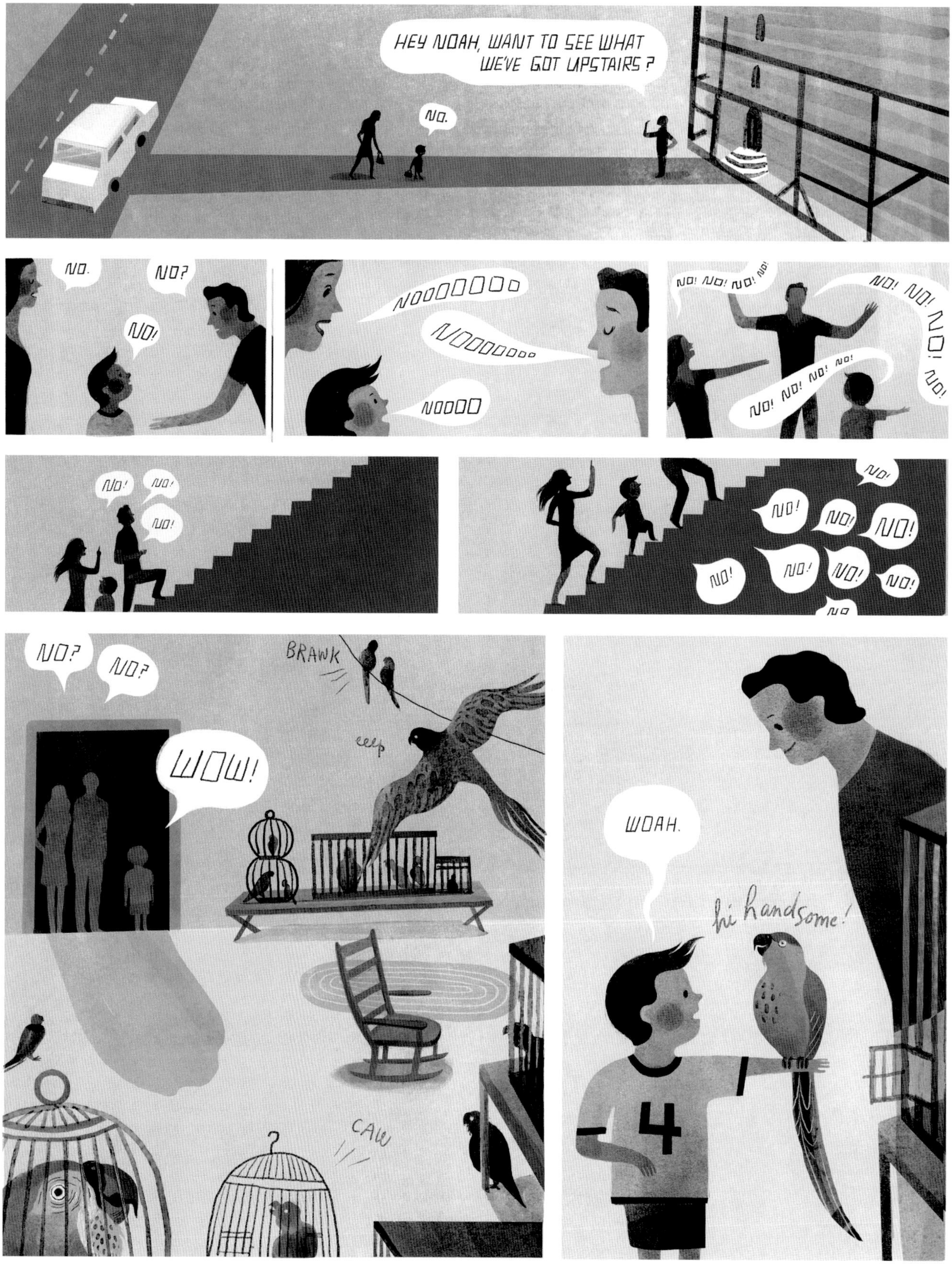
HEY NOAH, WANT TO SEE WHAT WE'VE GOT UPSTAIRS?
NO.
NO.
NO?
NO!
NOOOOOOOo
NOOOOOooo
NOOOO
NO! NO! NO! NO!
NO! NO! NO!
NO!
NO! NO! NO! NO!
NO!
NO!
NO!
NO!
NO!
NO!
NO!
NO!
NO!
NO!
NO!
NO!
NO?
NO?
BRAWK
WOW!
eeep
CAW
WOAH.
hi handsome!

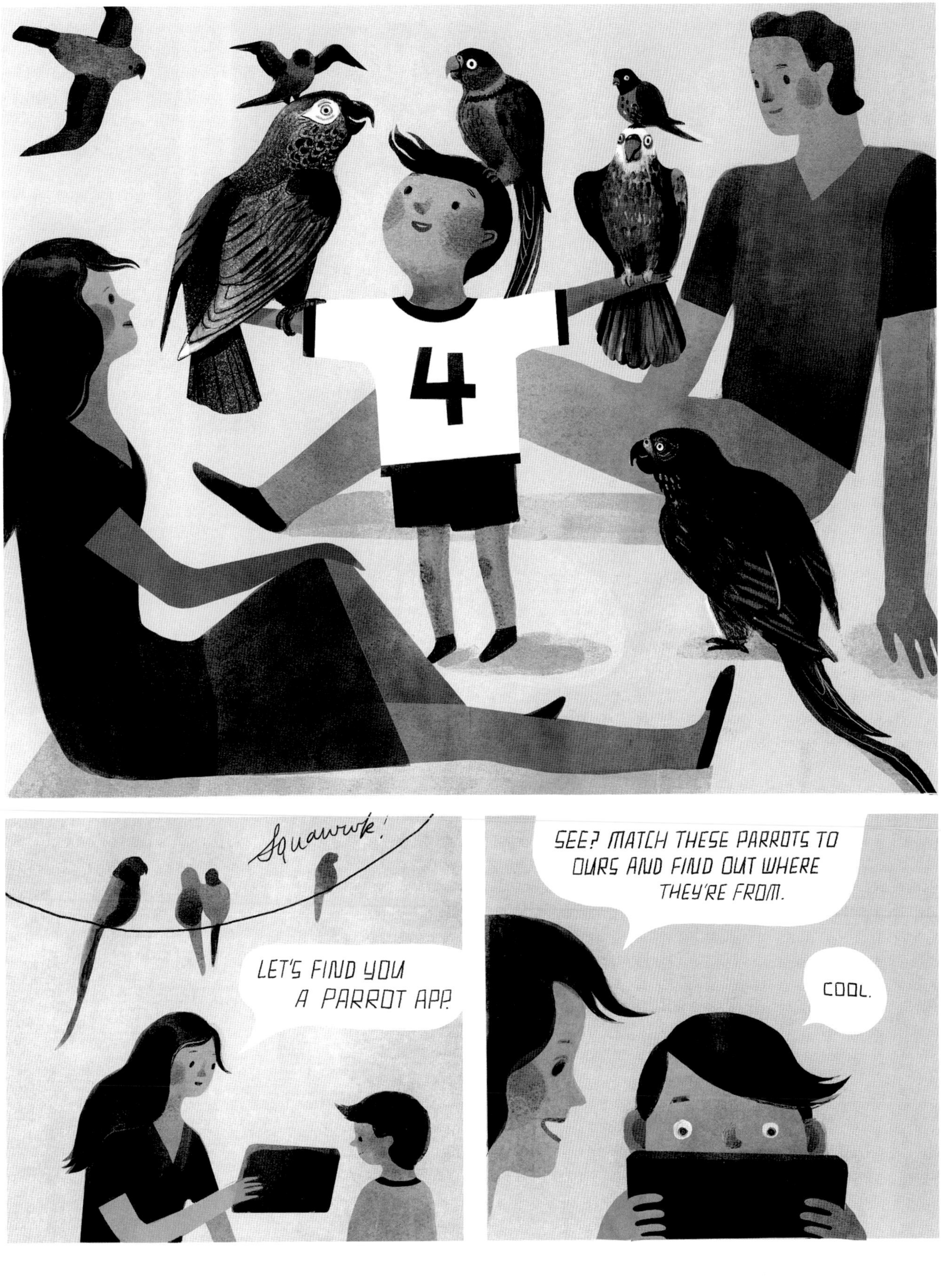
Squawwk!
LET'S FIND YOU A PARROT APP.
SEE? MATCH THESE PARROTS TO OURS AND FIND OUT WHERE THEY'RE FROM.
COOL.

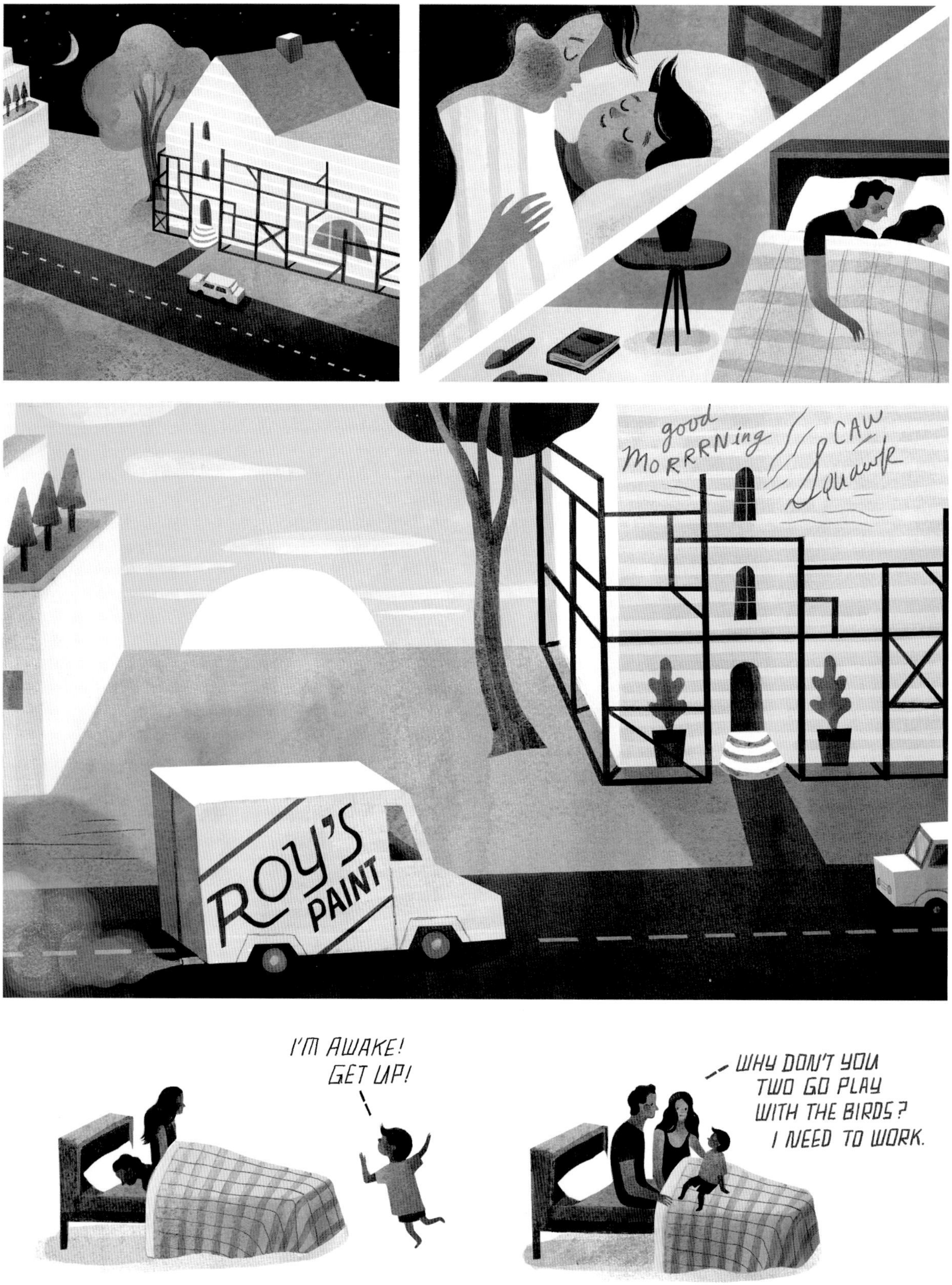
good MORRRNing
CAW
Squawk
ROY'S PAINT
I'M AWAKE! GET UP!
WHY DON'T YOU TWO GO PLAY WITH THE BIRDS? I NEED TO WORK.

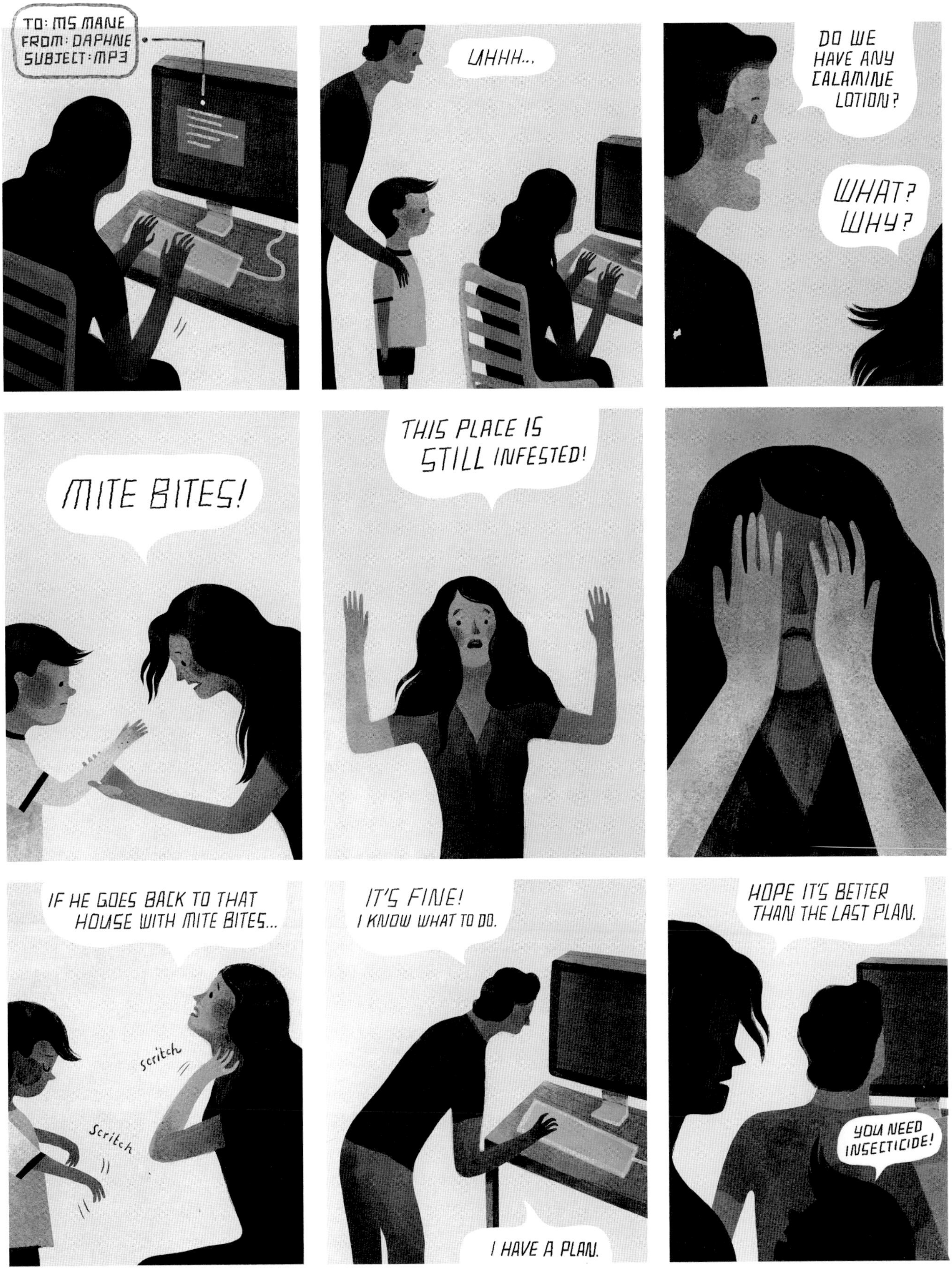
TO: MS MANE
FROM: DAPHNE
SUBJECT: MP3
UHHH...
DO WE HAVE ANY CALAMINE LOTION?
WHAT? WHY?
MITE BITES!
THIS PLACE IS STILL INFESTED!
IF HE GOES BACK TO THAT HOUSE WITH MITE BITES...
scritch
scritch
IT'S FINE! I KNOW WHAT TO DO.
I HAVE A PLAN.
HOPE IT'S BETTER THAN THE LAST PLAN.
YOU NEED INSECTICIDE!

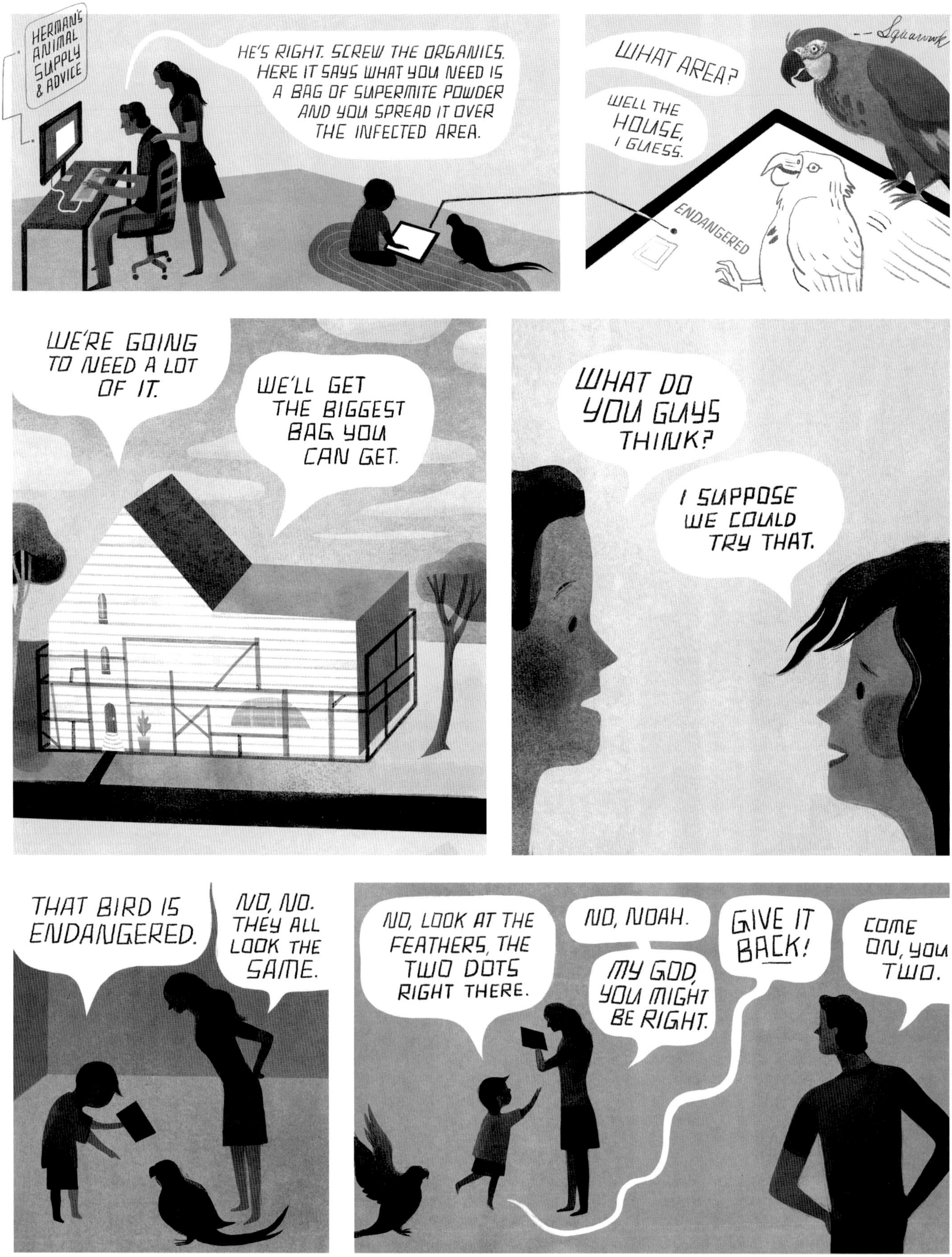
HERMAN'S ANIMAL SUPPLY & ADVICE
HE'S RIGHT. SCREW THE ORGANICS. HERE IT SAYS WHAT YOU NEED IS A BAG OF SUPERMITE POWDER AND YOU SPREAD IT OVER THE INFECTED AREA.
WHAT AREA?
WELL THE HOUSE, I GUESS.
--Squawk
ENDANGERED
WE'RE GOING TO NEED A LOT OF IT.
WE'LL GET THE BIGGEST BAG YOU CAN GET.
WHAT DO YOU GUYS THINK?
I SUPPOSE WE COULD TRY THAT.
THAT BIRD IS ENDANGERED.
NO, NO. THEY ALL LOOK THE SAME.
NO, LOOK AT THE FEATHERS, THE TWO DOTS RIGHT THERE.
NO, NOAH.
MY GOD, YOU MIGHT BE RIGHT.
GIVE IT BACK!
COME ON, YOU TWO.

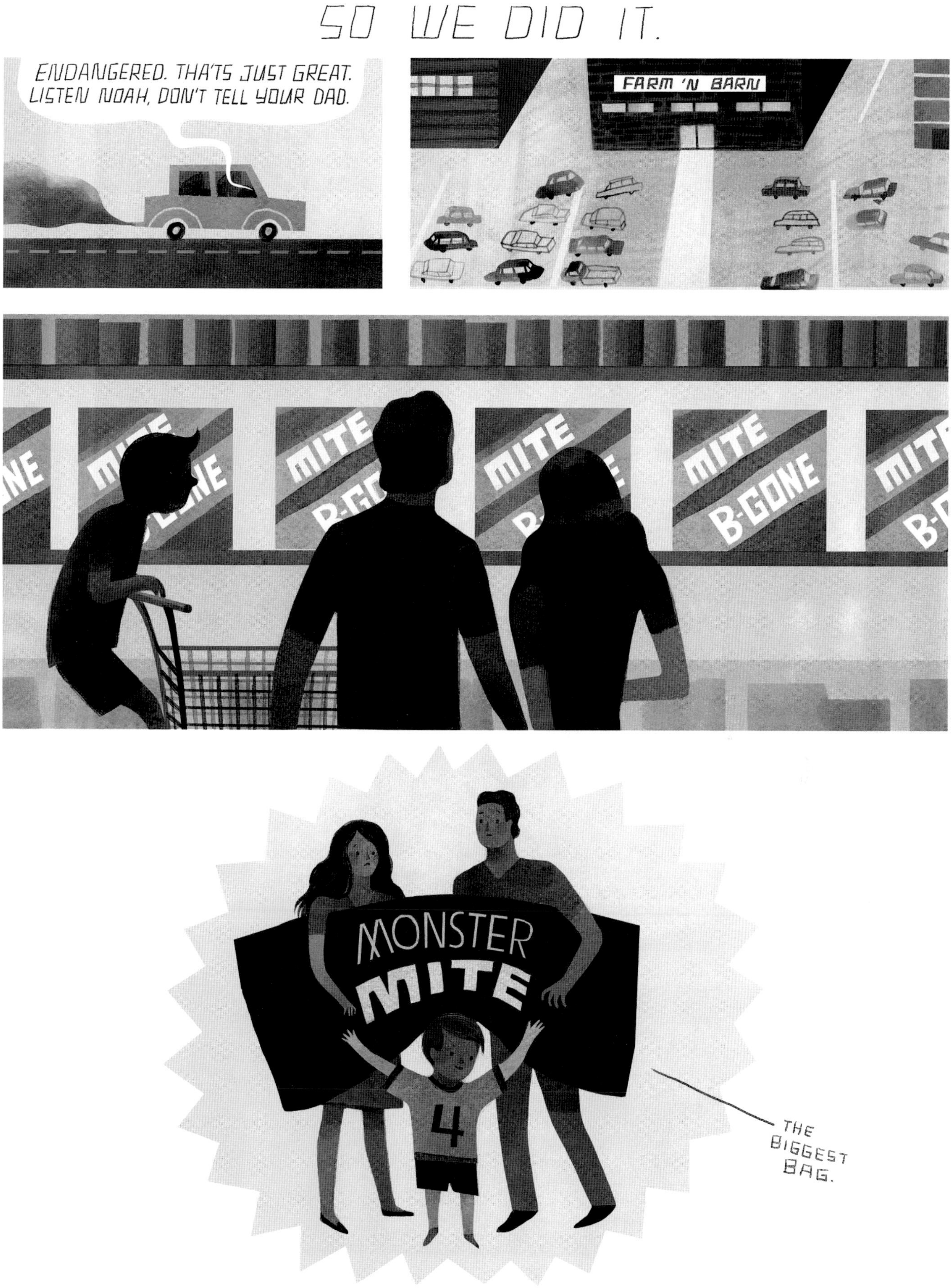
SO WE DID IT.
ENDANGERED. THAT'S JUST GREAT. LISTEN NOAH, DON'T TELL YOUR DAD.
FARM 'N BARN
MITE B-GONE
MONSTER MITE
4
THE BIGGEST BAG.

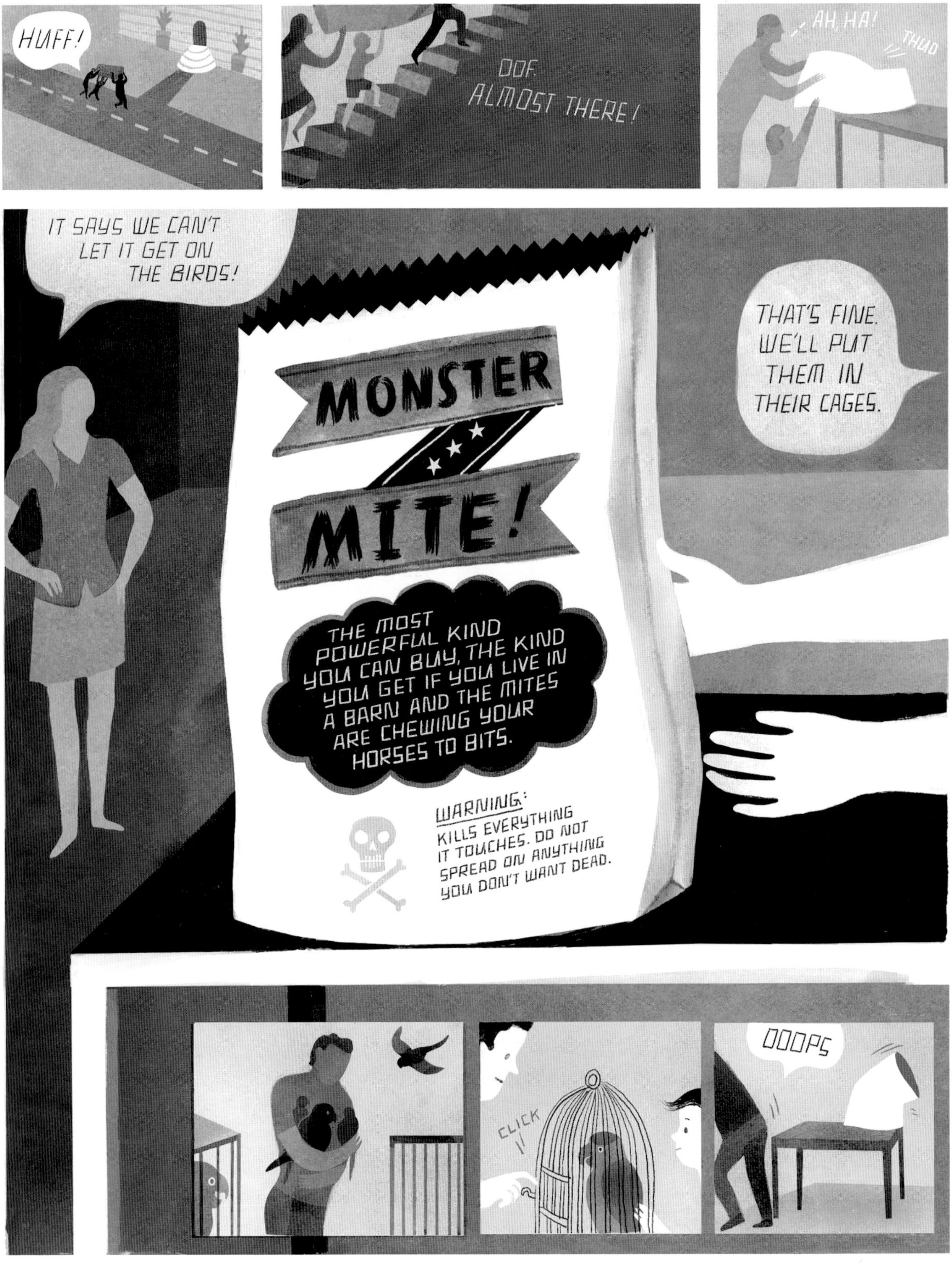
HUFF!
OOF. ALMOST THERE!
AH, HA!
THUD
IT SAYS WE CAN'T LET IT GET ON THE BIRDS!
MONSTER MITE!
THE MOST POWERFUL KIND YOU CAN BUY, THE KIND YOU GET IF YOU LIVE IN A BARN AND THE MITES ARE CHEWING YOUR HORSES TO BITS.
WARNING: KILLS EVERYTHING IT TOUCHES. DO NOT SPREAD ON ANYTHING YOU DON'T WANT DEAD.
THAT'S FINE. WE'LL PUT THEM IN THEIR CAGES.
CLICK
OOOPS

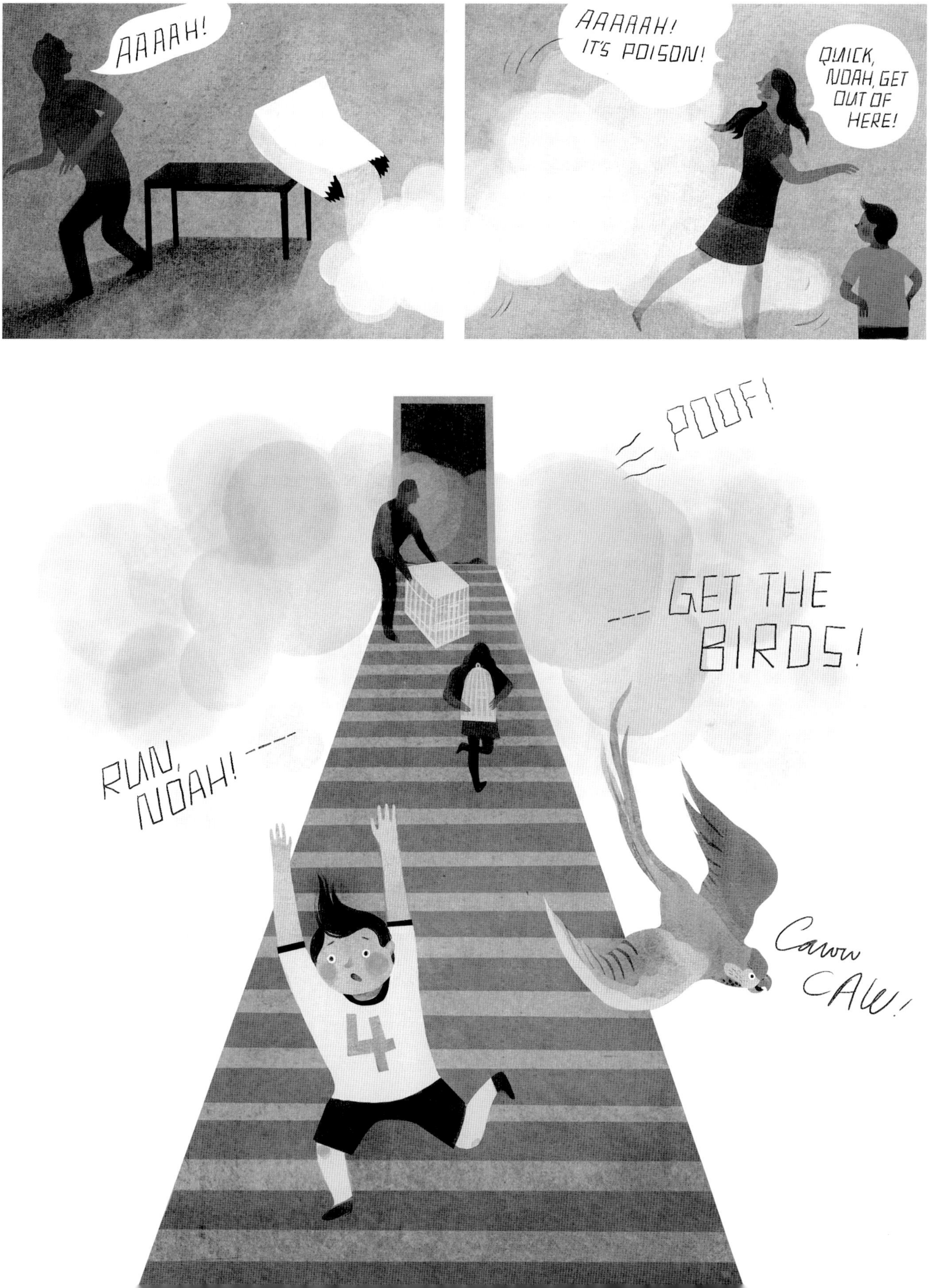
AAAAH!
AAAAAH! IT'S POISON!
QUICK, NOAH, GET OUT OF HERE!
POOF!
--- GET THE BIRDS!
RUN, NOAH! ---
Caww CAW!

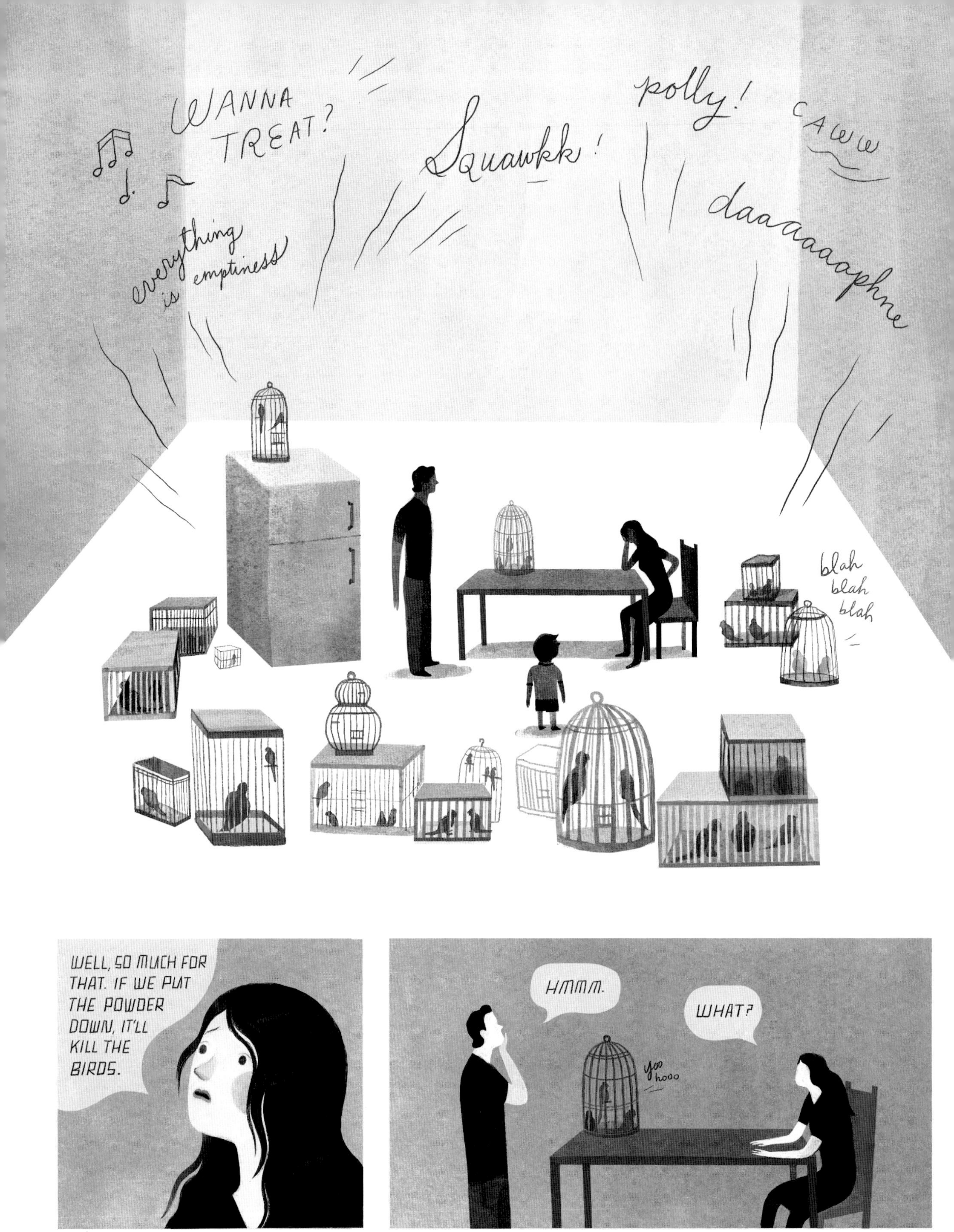
WANNA TREAT?
everything is emptiness
Squawkk!
polly!
CAWW
daaaaaaaphne
blah blah blah
WELL, SO MUCH FOR THAT. IF WE PUT THE POWDER DOWN, IT'LL KILL THE BIRDS.
HMMM.
yoo hooo
WHAT?

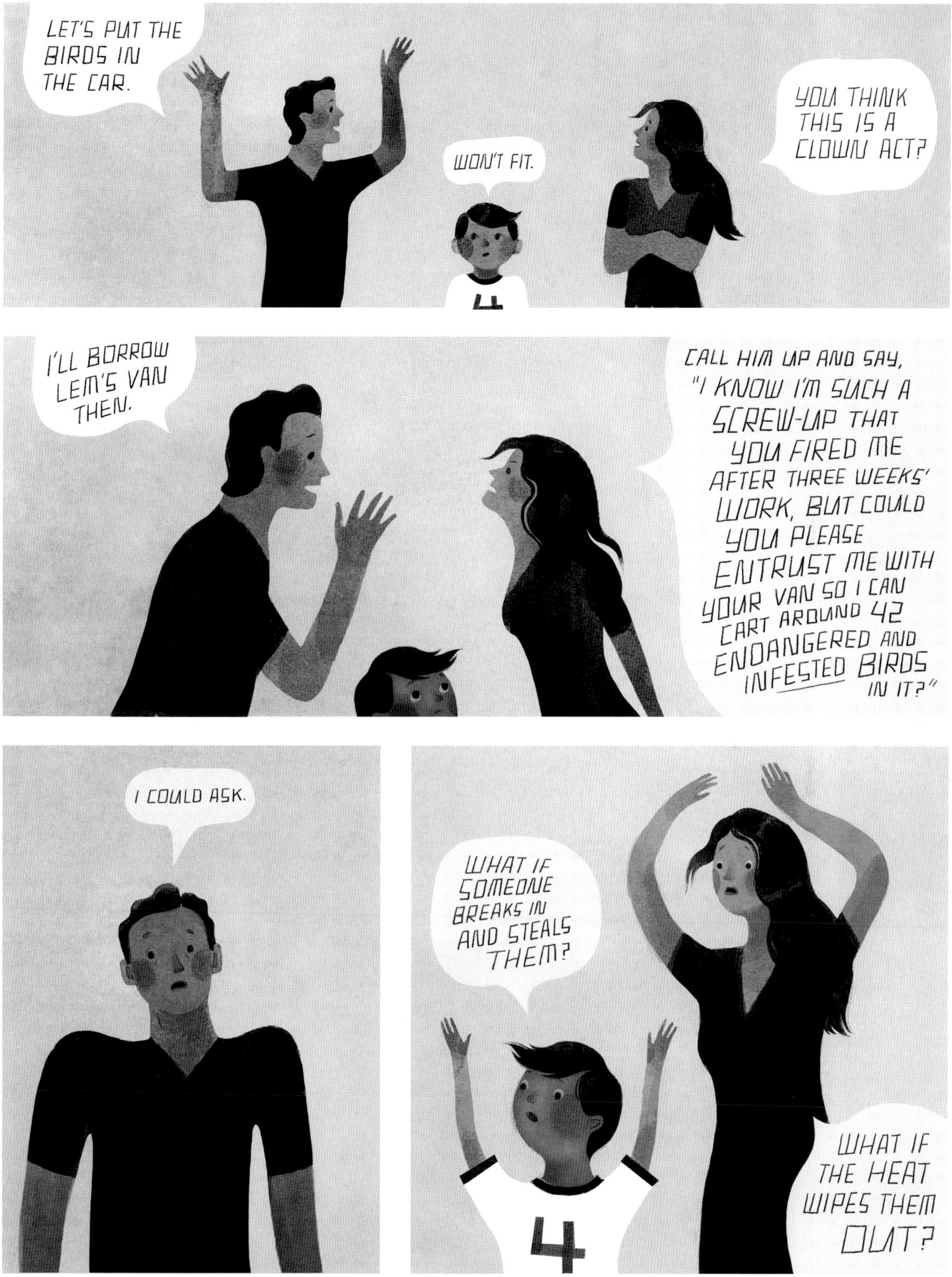
LET'S PUT THE BIRDS IN THE CAR.
WON'T FIT.
YOU THINK THIS IS A CLOWN ACT?
I'LL BORROW LEM'S VAN THEN.
CALL HIM UP AND SAY, "I KNOW I'M SUCH A SCREW-UP THAT YOU FIRED ME AFTER THREE WEEKS' WORK, BUT COULD YOU PLEASE ENTRUST ME WITH YOUR VAN SO I CAN CART AROUND 42 ENDANGERED AND INFESTED BIRDS IN IT?"
I COULD ASK.
WHAT IF SOMEONE BREAKS IN AND STEALS THEM?
WHAT IF THE HEAT WIPES THEM OUT?

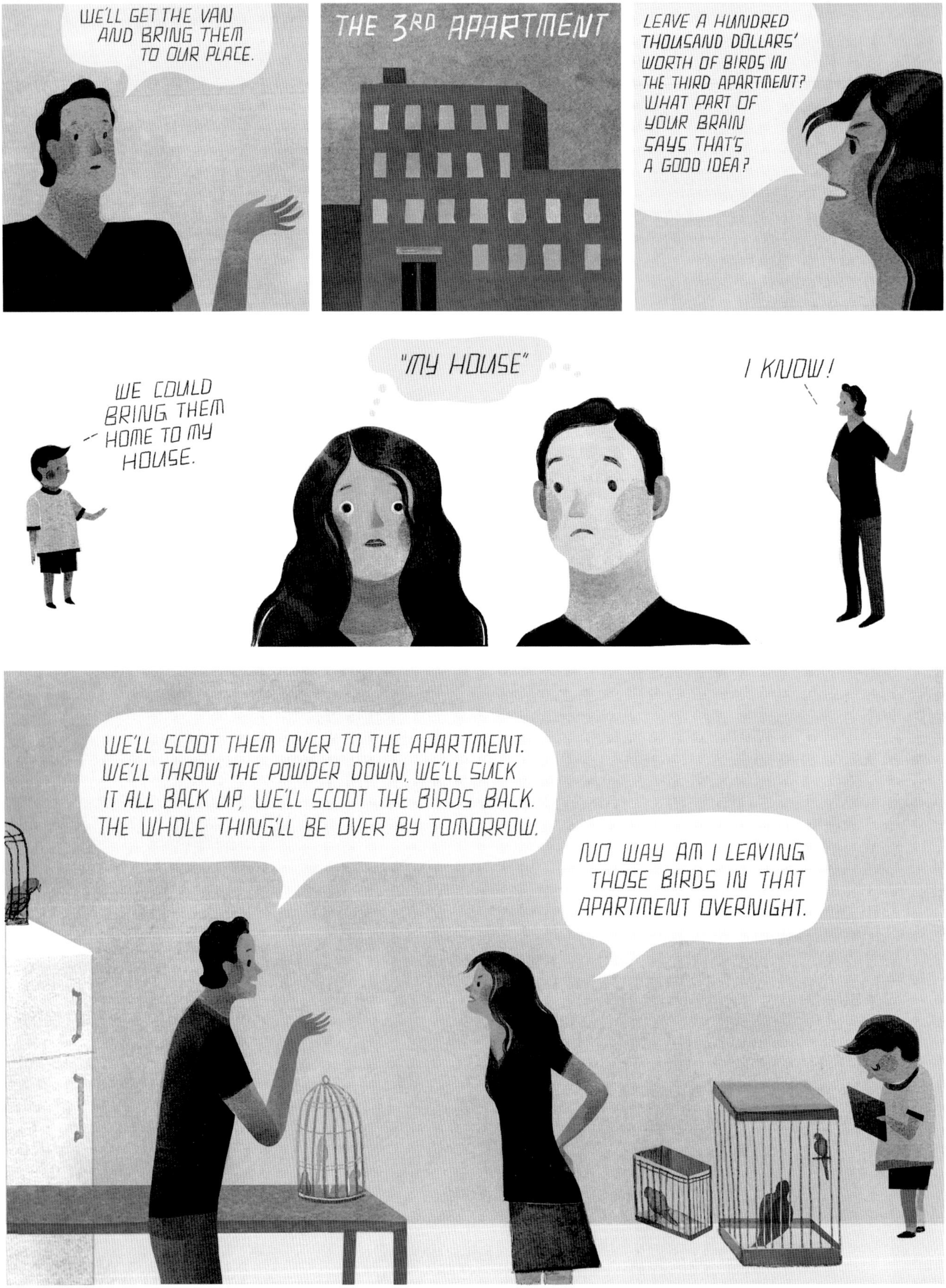
WE'LL GET THE VAN AND BRING THEM TO OUR PLACE.
THE 3RD APARTMENT
LEAVE A HUNDRED THOUSAND DOLLARS' WORTH OF BIRDS IN THE THIRD APARTMENT? WHAT PART OF YOUR BRAIN SAYS THAT'S A GOOD IDEA?
WE COULD BRING THEM HOME TO MY HOUSE.
"MY HOUSE"
I KNOW!
WE'LL SCOOT THEM OVER TO THE APARTMENT. WE'LL THROW THE POWDER DOWN, WE'LL SUCK IT ALL BACK UP, WE'LL SCOOT THE BIRDS BACK. THE WHOLE THING'LL BE OVER BY TOMORROW.
NO WAY AM I LEAVING THOSE BIRDS IN THAT APARTMENT OVERNIGHT.

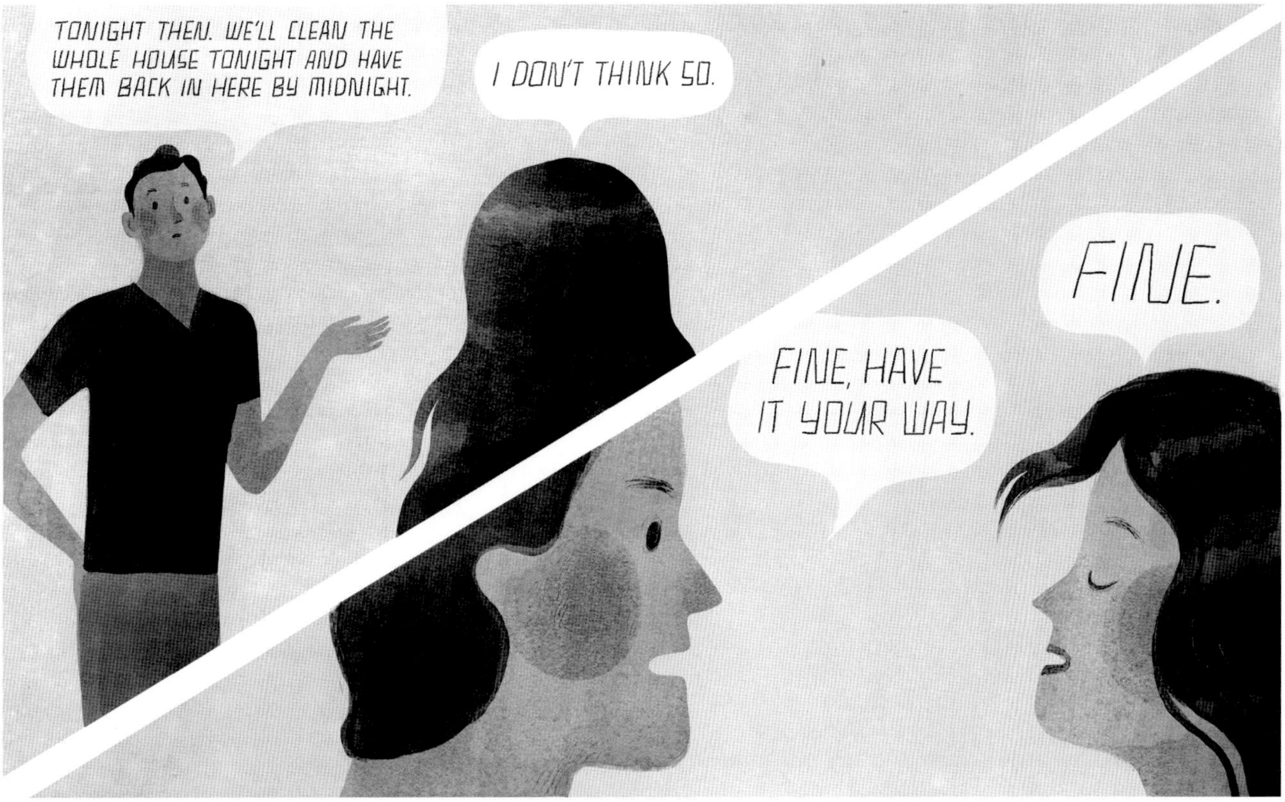
TONIGHT THEN. WE'LL CLEAN THE WHOLE HOUSE TONIGHT AND HAVE THEM BACK IN HERE BY MIDNIGHT.
I DON'T THINK SO.
FINE, HAVE IT YOUR WAY.
FINE.

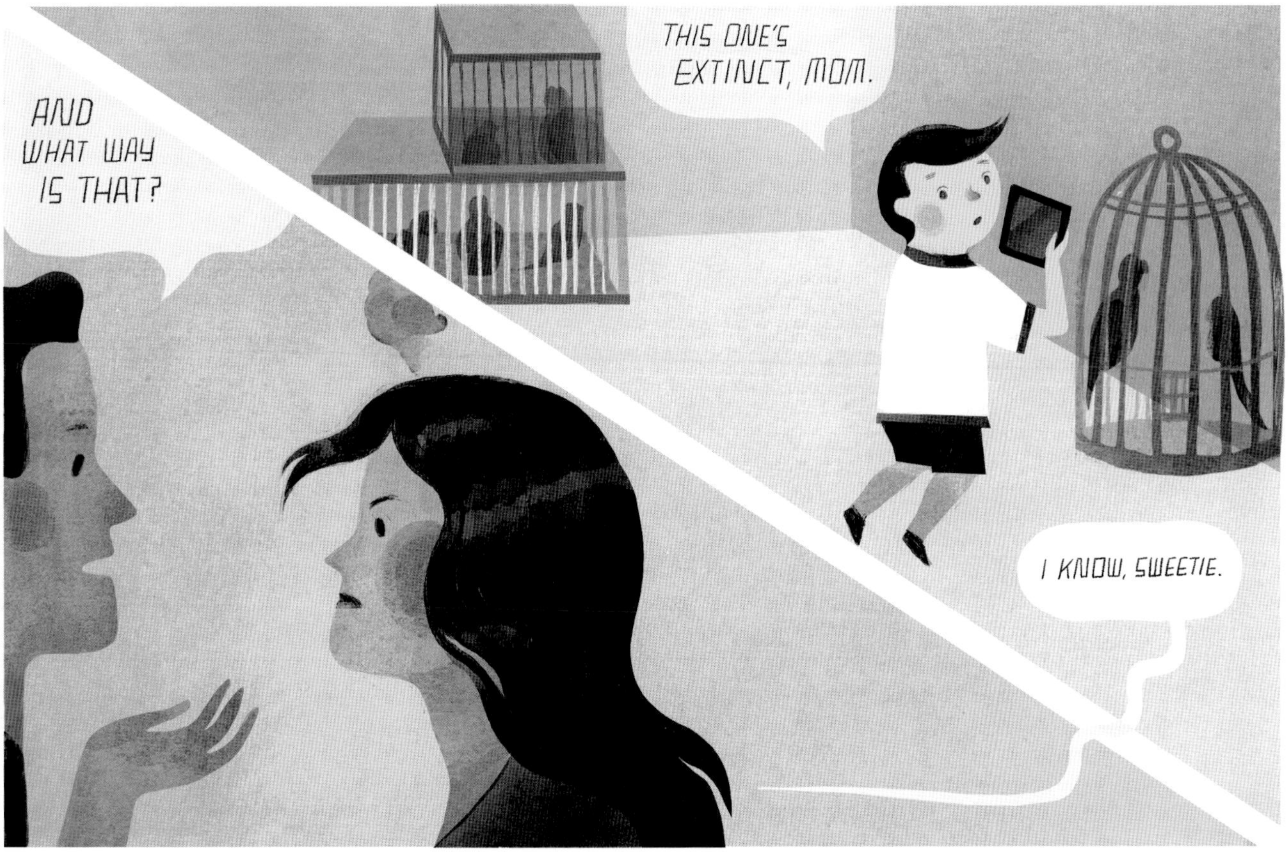
AND WHAT WAY IS THAT?
THIS ONE'S EXTINCT, MOM.
I KNOW, SWEETIE.

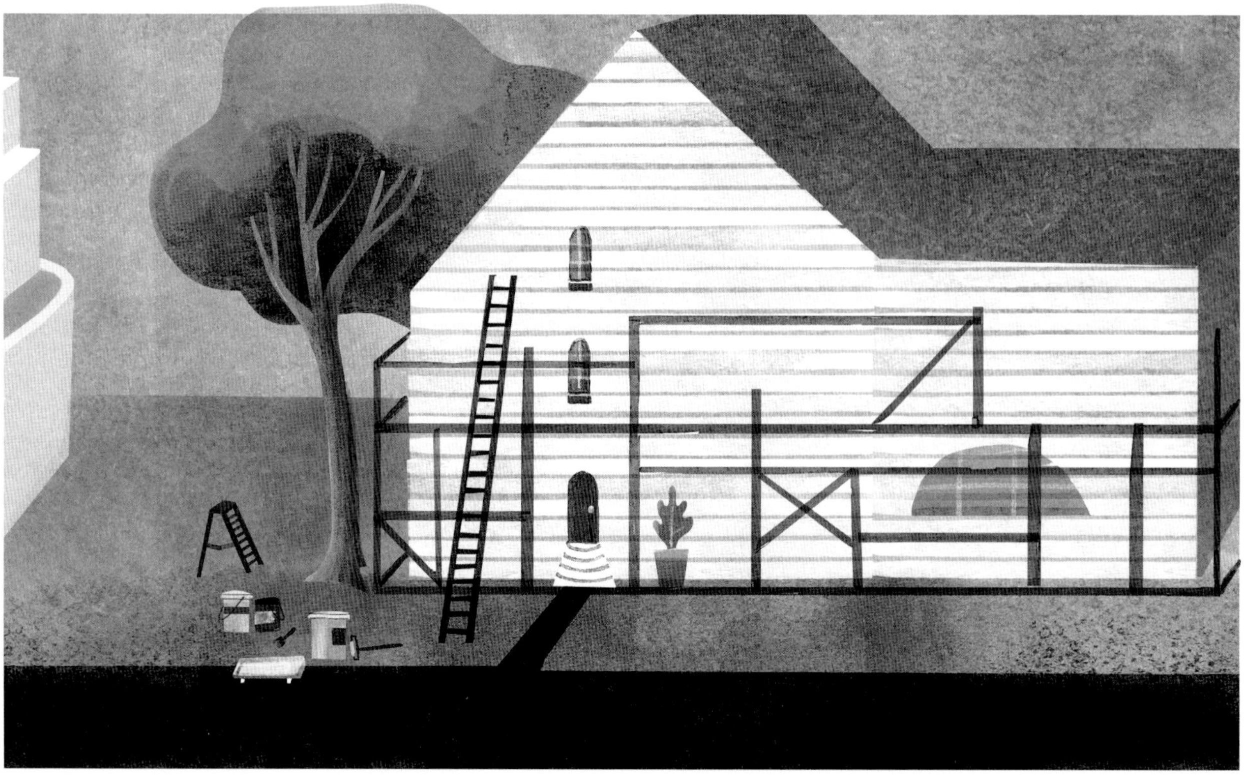

SO WE DID IT.

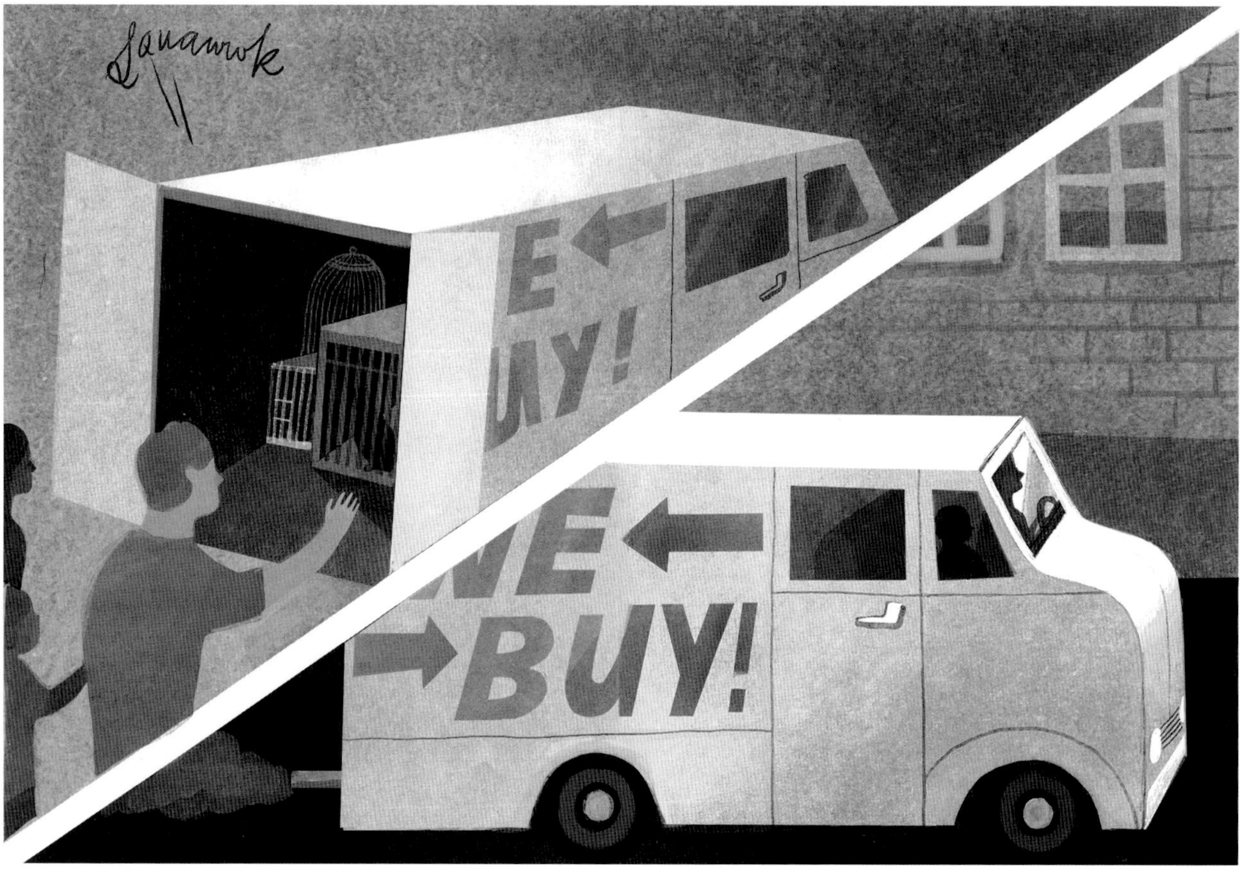
Squawk
BUY!

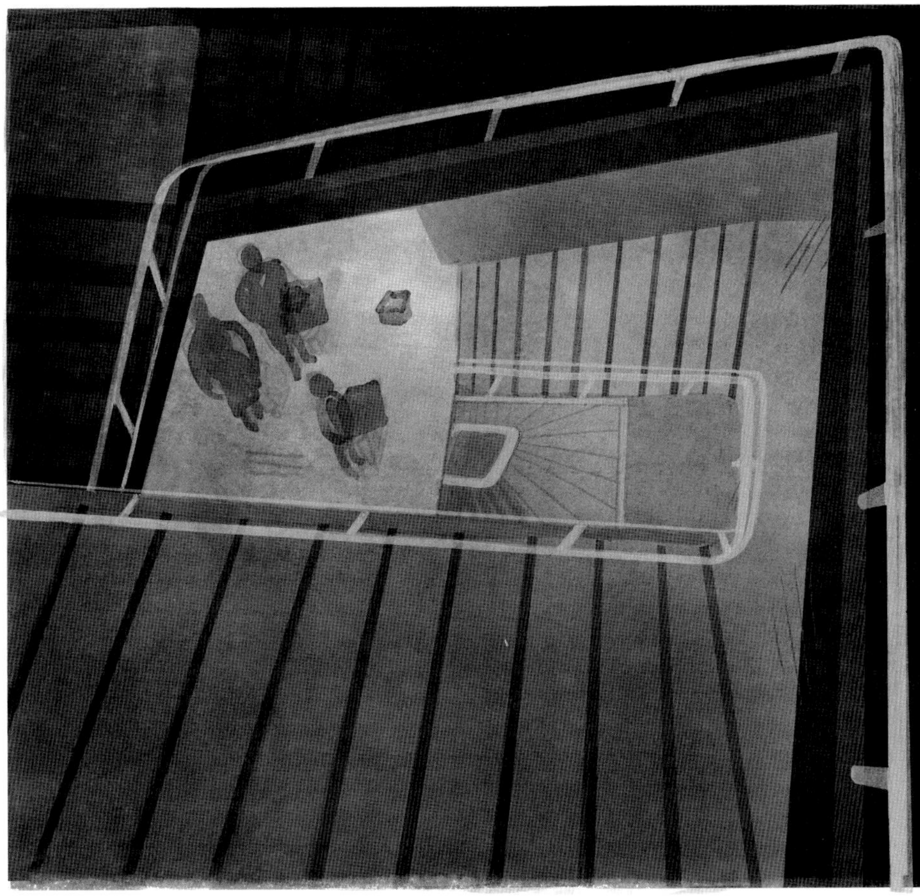

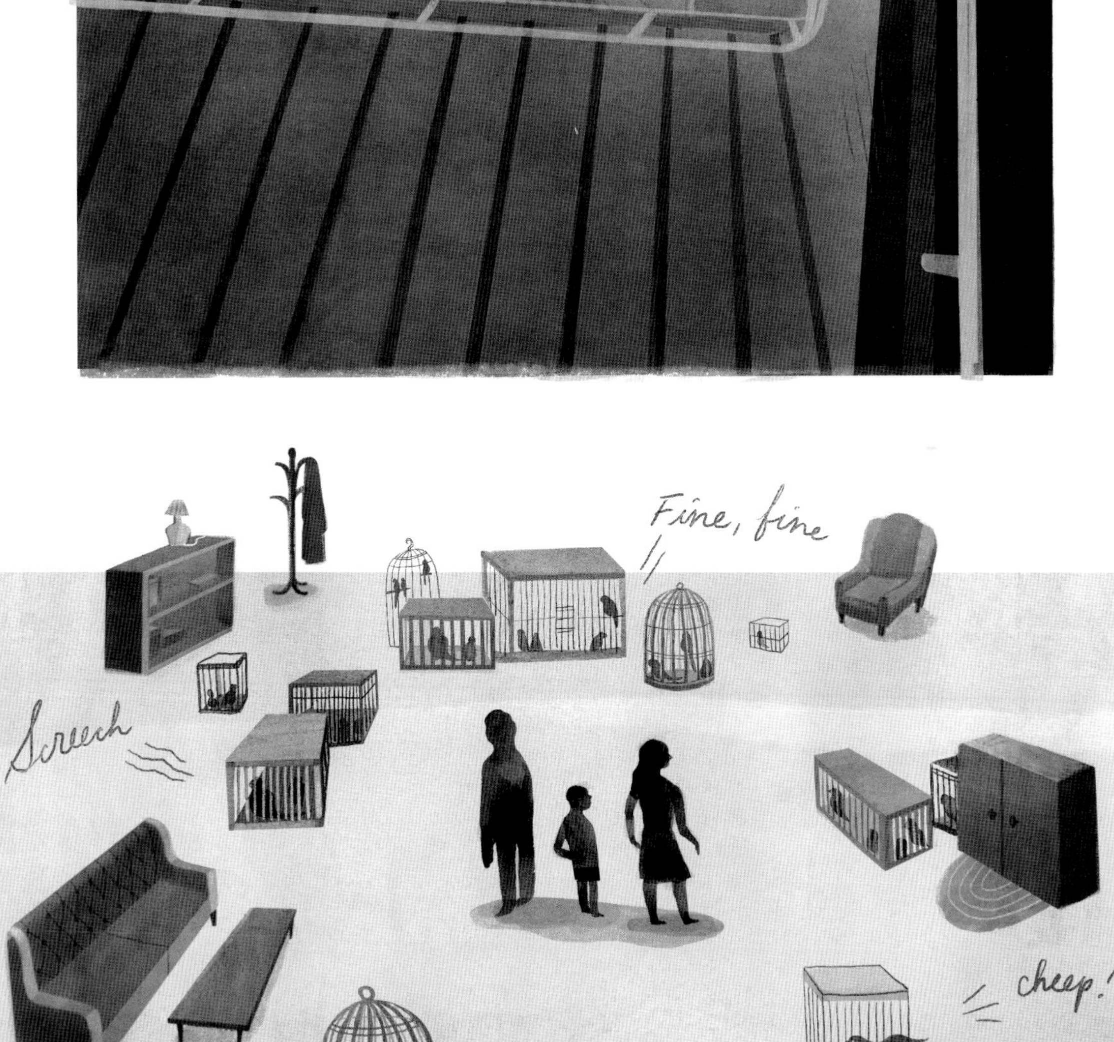
Fine, fine
Screech
cheep!

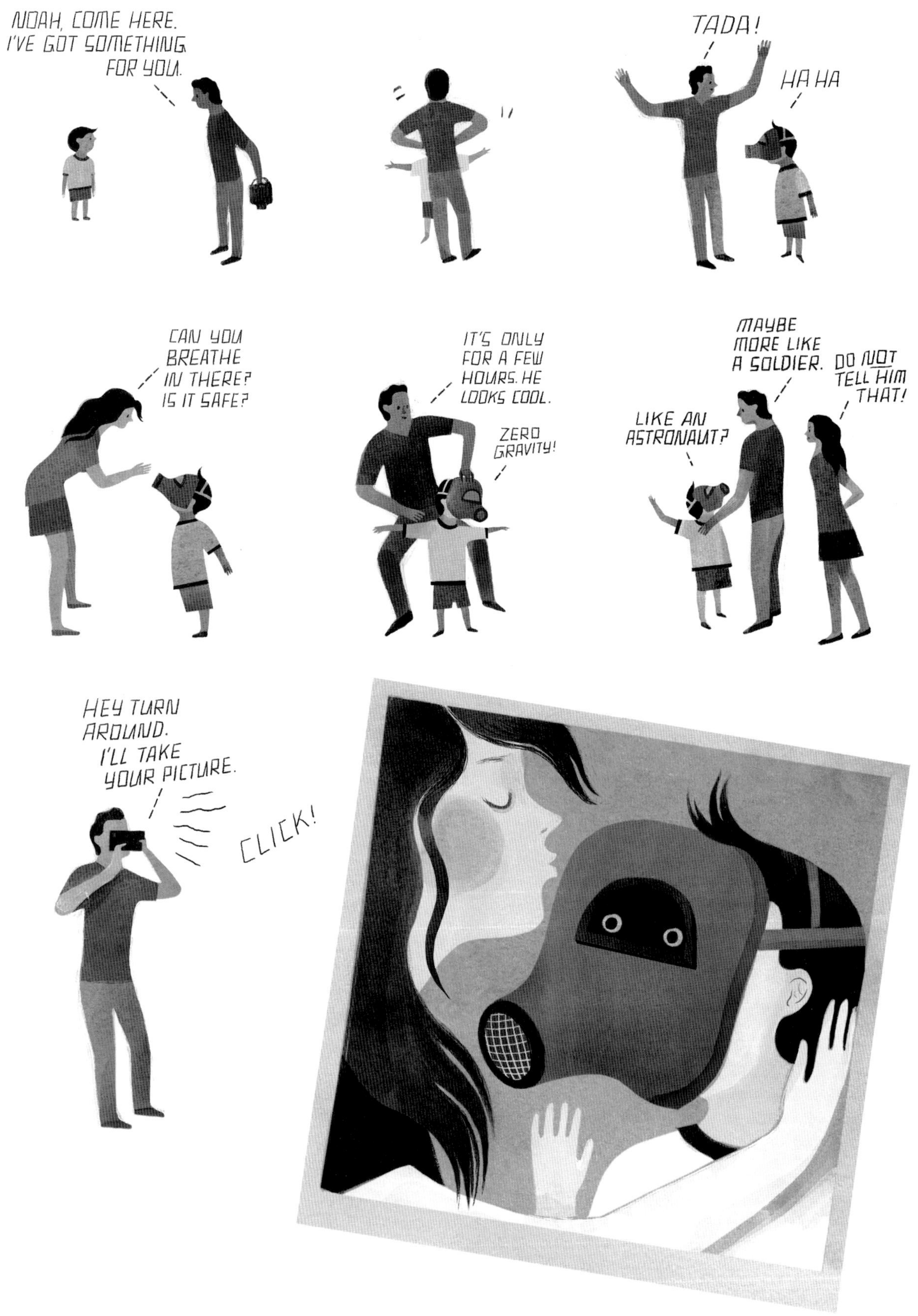
NOAH, COME HERE. I'VE GOT SOMETHING FOR YOU.
TADA!
HA HA
CAN YOU BREATHE IN THERE? IS IT SAFE?
IT'S ONLY FOR A FEW HOURS. HE LOOKS COOL.
ZERO GRAVITY!
LIKE AN ASTRONAUT?
MAYBE MORE LIKE A SOLDIER.
DO NOT TELL HIM THAT!
HEY TURN AROUND. I'LL TAKE YOUR PICTURE.
CLICK!

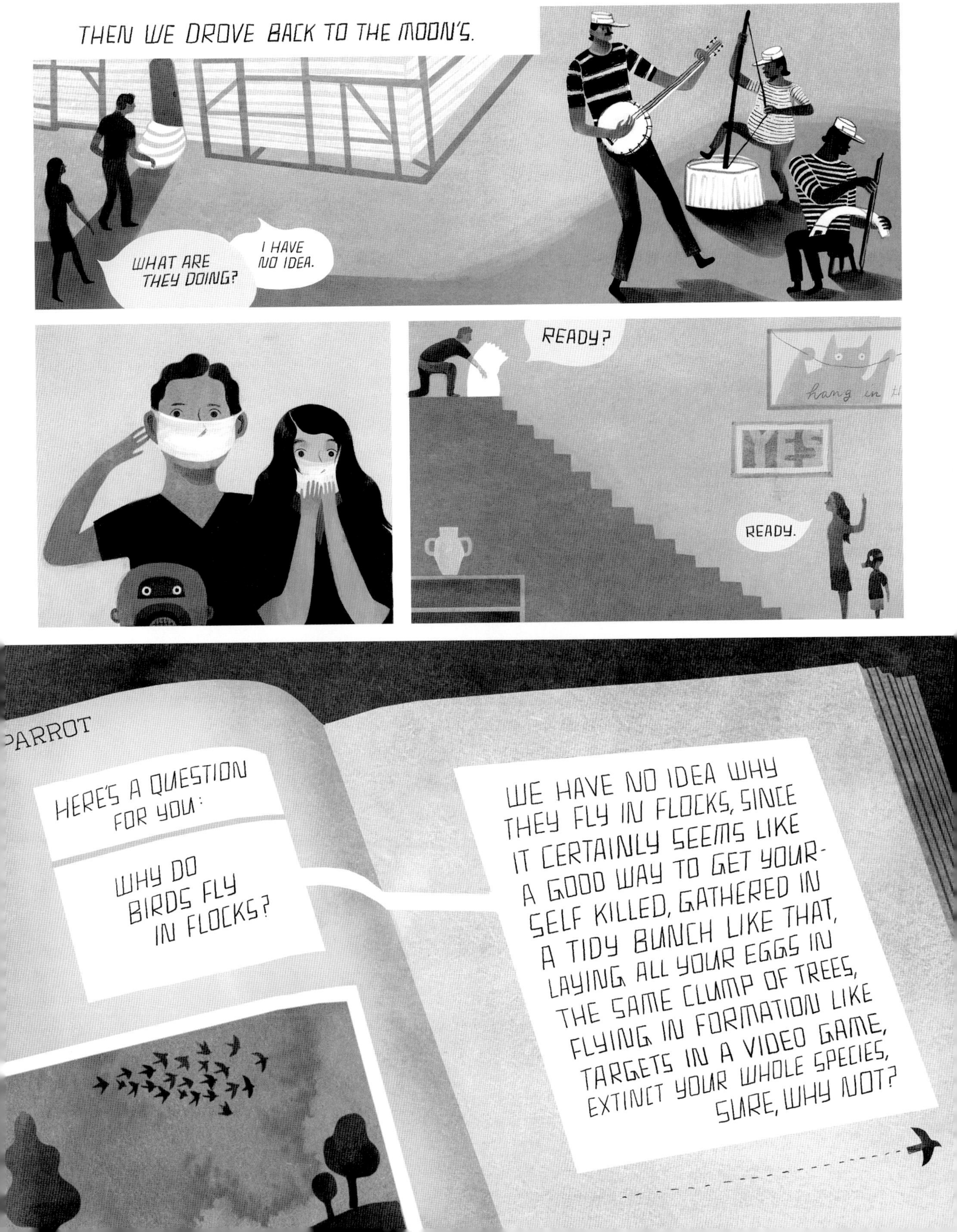

THEN WE DROVE BACK TO THE MOON'S.
WHAT ARE THEY DOING?
I HAVE NO IDEA.
READY?
READY.
PARROT
HERE'S A QUESTION FOR YOU:
WHY DO BIRDS FLY IN FLOCKS?
WE HAVE NO IDEA WHY THEY FLY IN FLOCKS, SINCE IT CERTAINLY SEEMS LIKE A GOOD WAY TO GET YOURSELF KILLED, GATHERED IN A TIDY BUNCH LIKE THAT, LAYING ALL YOUR EGGS IN THE SAME CLUMP OF TREES, FLYING IN FORMATION LIKE TARGETS IN A VIDEO GAME, EXTINCT YOUR WHOLE SPECIES, SURE, WHY NOT?

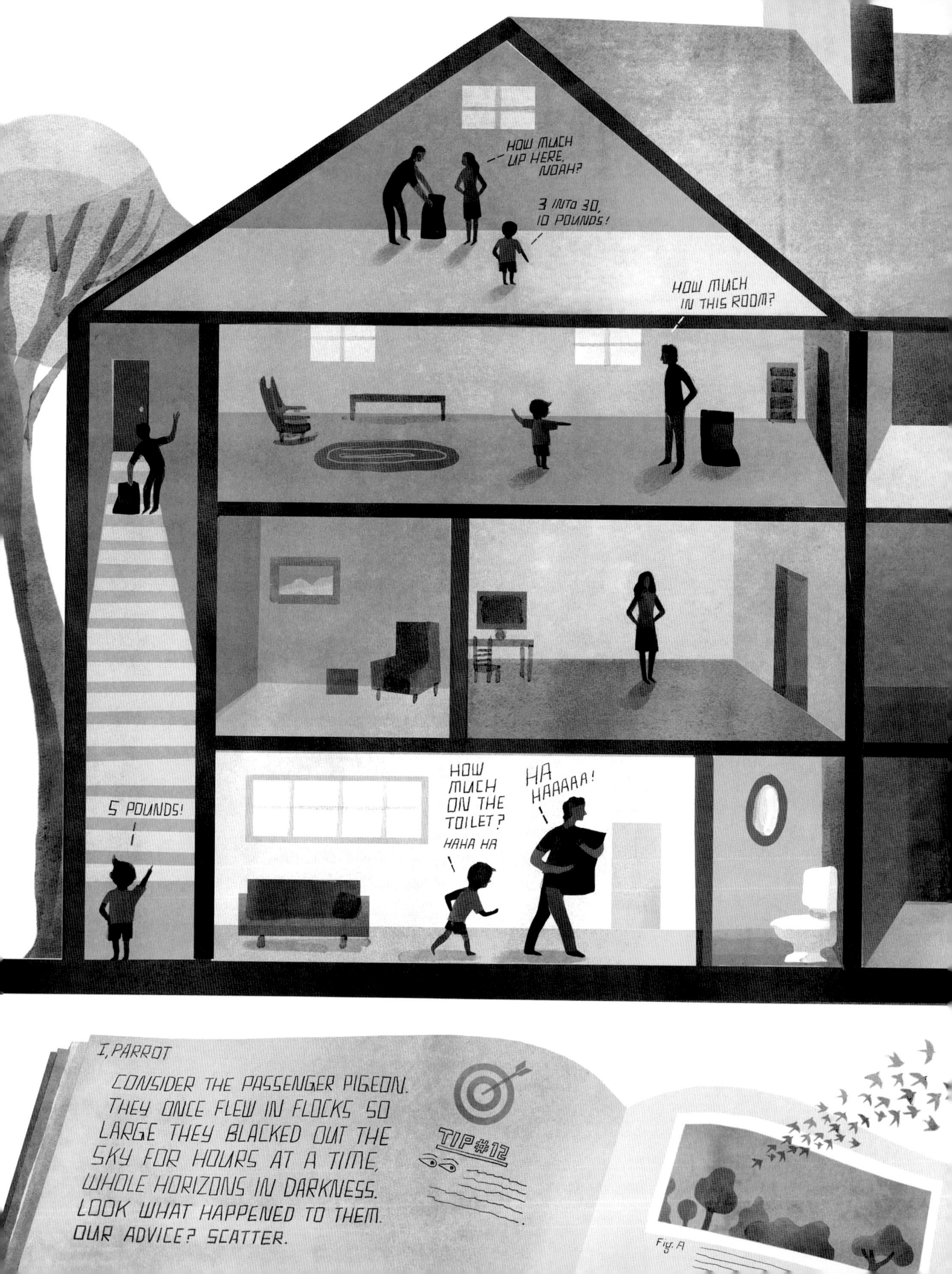
HOW MUCH UP HERE, NOAH?
3 INTO 30, 10 POUNDS!
HOW MUCH IN THIS ROOM?
5 POUNDS!
HOW MUCH ON THE TOILET?
HAHA HA
HA HAAAAA!
I, PARROT
CONSIDER THE PASSENGER PIGEON. THEY ONCE FLEW IN FLOCKS SO LARGE THEY BLACKED OUT THE SKY FOR HOURS AT A TIME, WHOLE HORIZONS IN DARKNESS. LOOK WHAT HAPPENED TO THEM. OUR ADVICE? SCATTER.
TIP #12
Fig. A

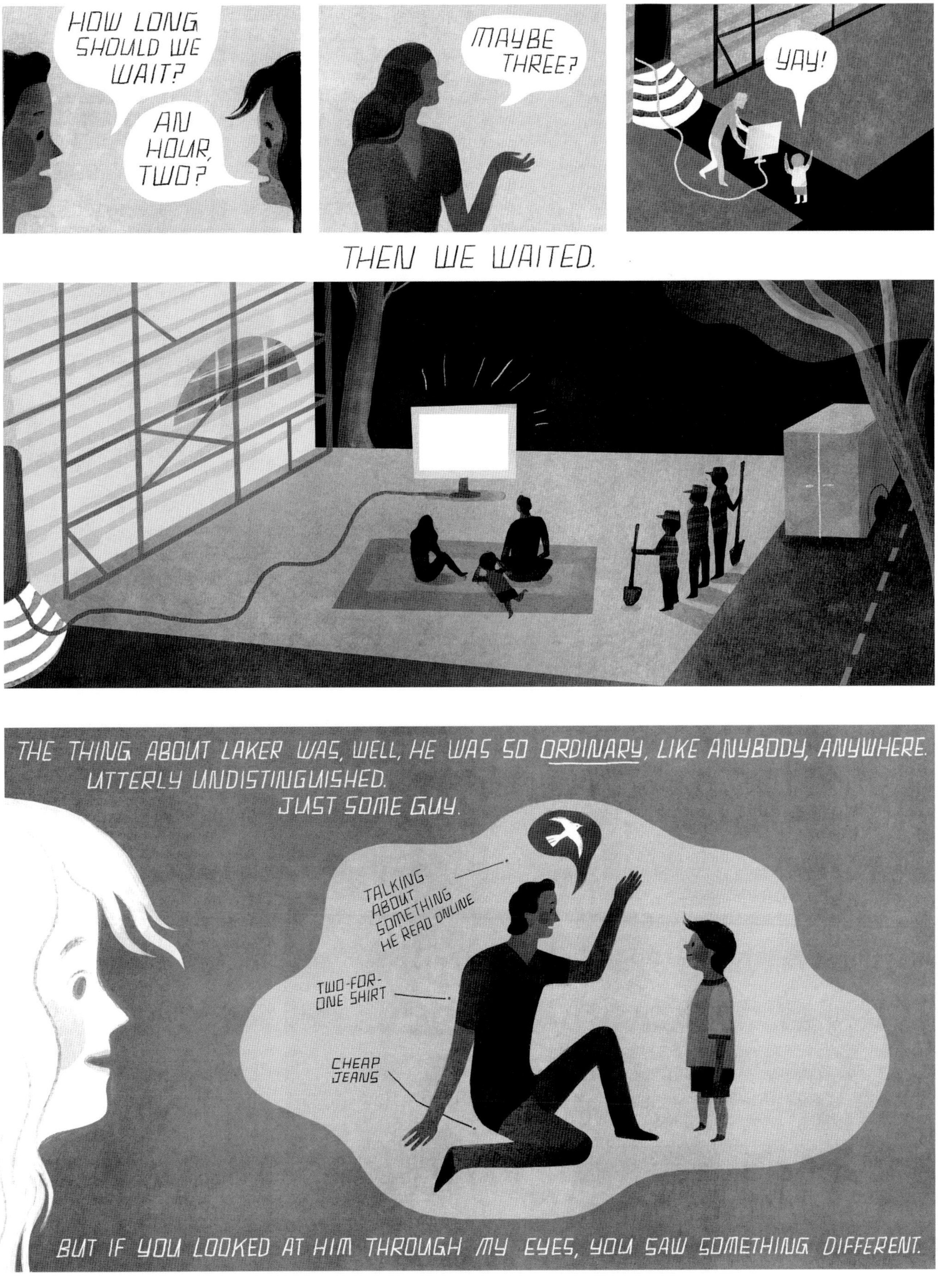
HOW LONG SHOULD WE WAIT?
AN HOUR, TWO?
MAYBE THREE?
YAY!
THEN WE WAITED.
THE THING ABOUT LAKER WAS, WELL, HE WAS SO ORDINARY, LIKE ANYBODY, ANYWHERE.
UTTERLY UNDISTINGUISHED.
JUST SOME GUY.
TALKING ABOUT SOMETHING HE READ ONLINE
TWO-FOR-ONE SHIRT
CHEAP JEANS
BUT IF YOU LOOKED AT HIM THROUGH MY EYES, YOU SAW SOMETHING DIFFERENT.

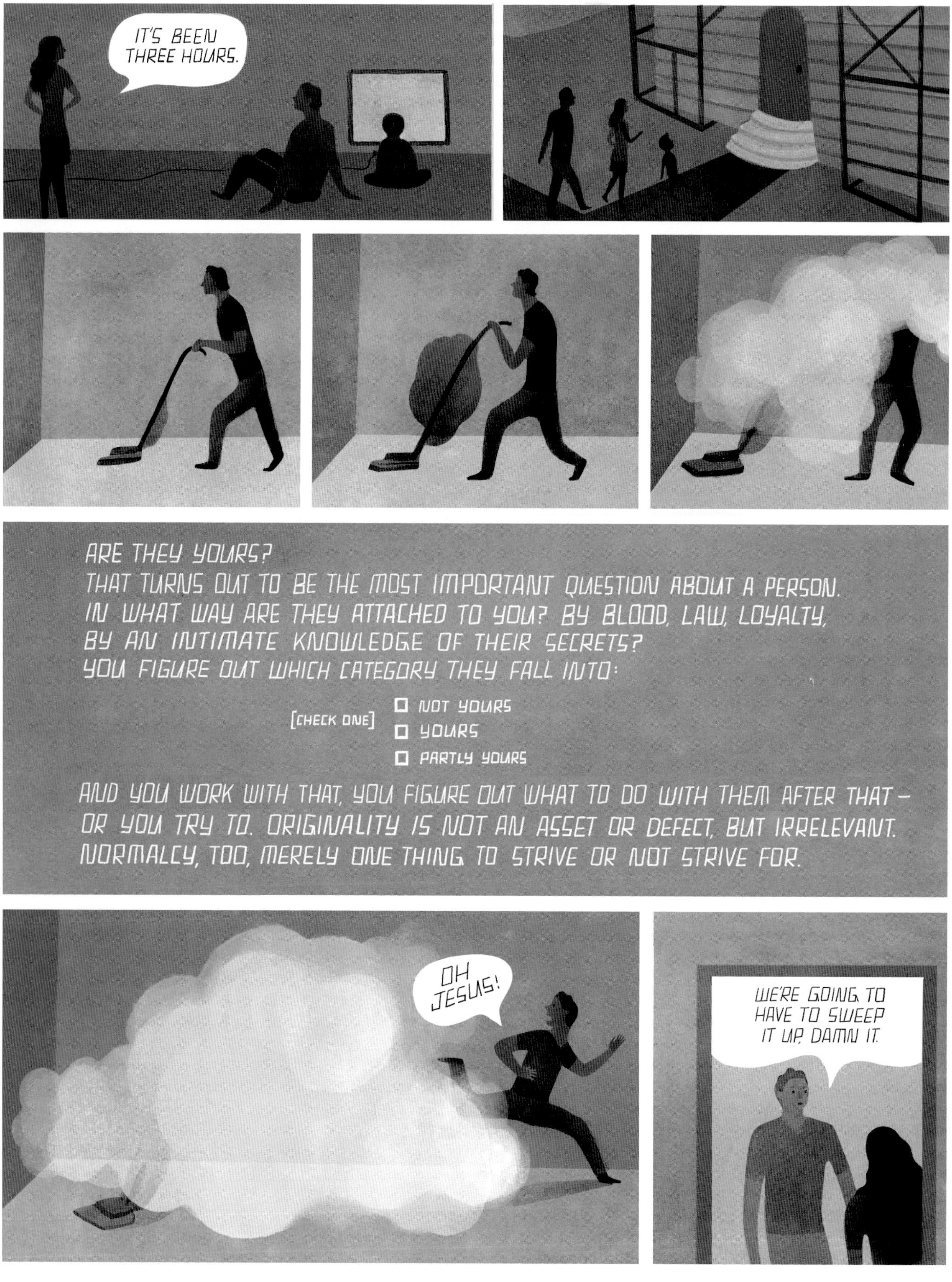
IT'S BEEN THREE HOURS.
ARE THEY YOURS?
THAT TURNS OUT TO BE THE MOST IMPORTANT QUESTION ABOUT A PERSON.
IN WHAT WAY ARE THEY ATTACHED TO YOU? BY BLOOD, LAW, LOYALTY,
BY AN INTIMATE KNOWLEDGE OF THEIR SECRETS?
YOU FIGURE OUT WHICH CATEGORY THEY FALL INTO:
[CHECK ONE] ☐ NOT YOURS ☐ YOURS ☐ PARTLY YOURS
AND YOU WORK WITH THAT, YOU FIGURE OUT WHAT TO DO WITH THEM AFTER THAT – OR YOU TRY TO. ORIGINALITY IS NOT AN ASSET OR DEFECT, BUT IRRELEVANT. NORMALCY, TOO, MERELY ONE THING TO STRIVE OR NOT STRIVE FOR.
OH JESUS!
WE'RE GOING TO HAVE TO SWEEP IT UP, DAMN IT.

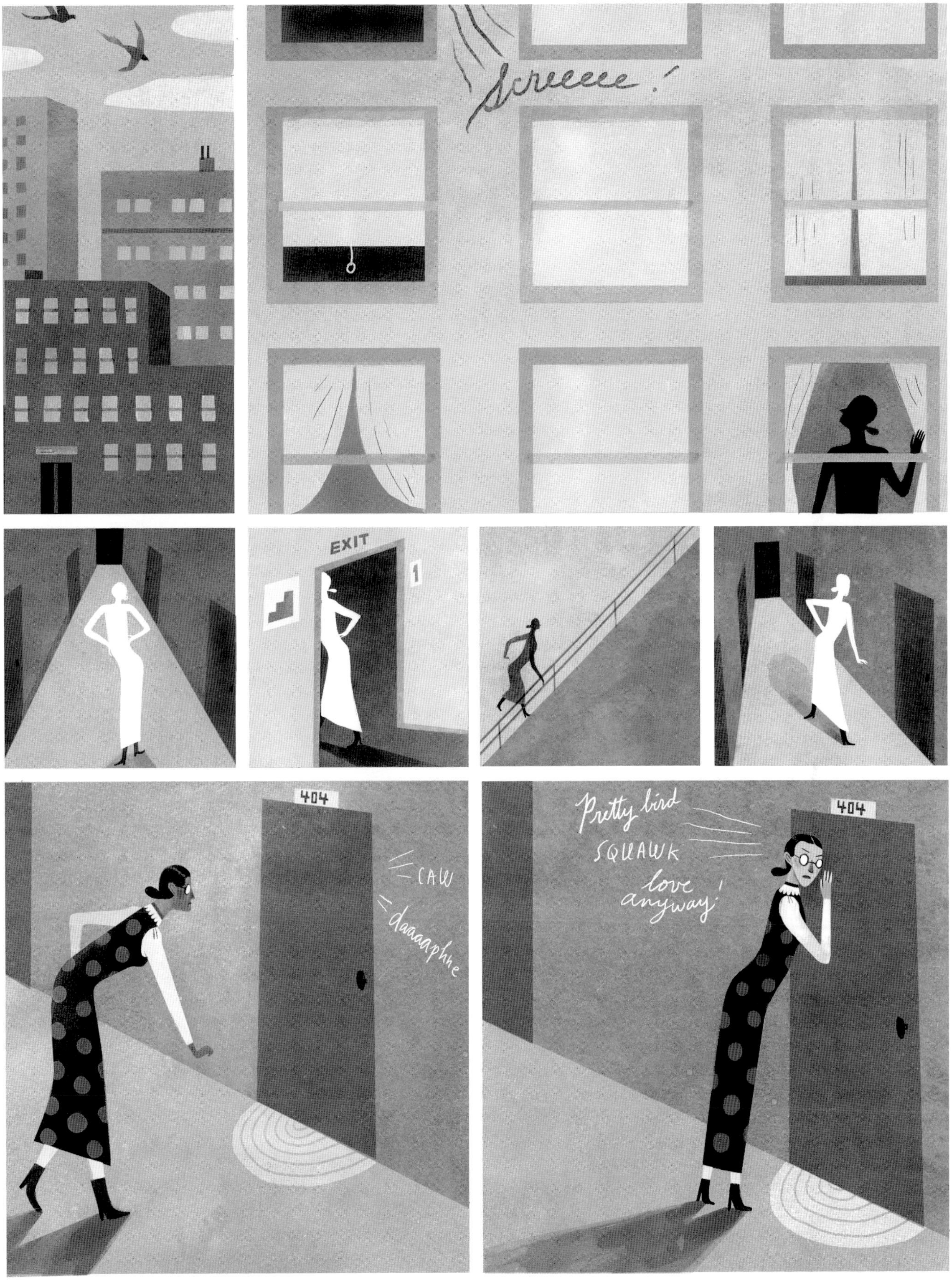
Screeeee!
EXIT
1
404
CAW
daaaaphne
404
Pretty bird
SQUAWK
love anyway!

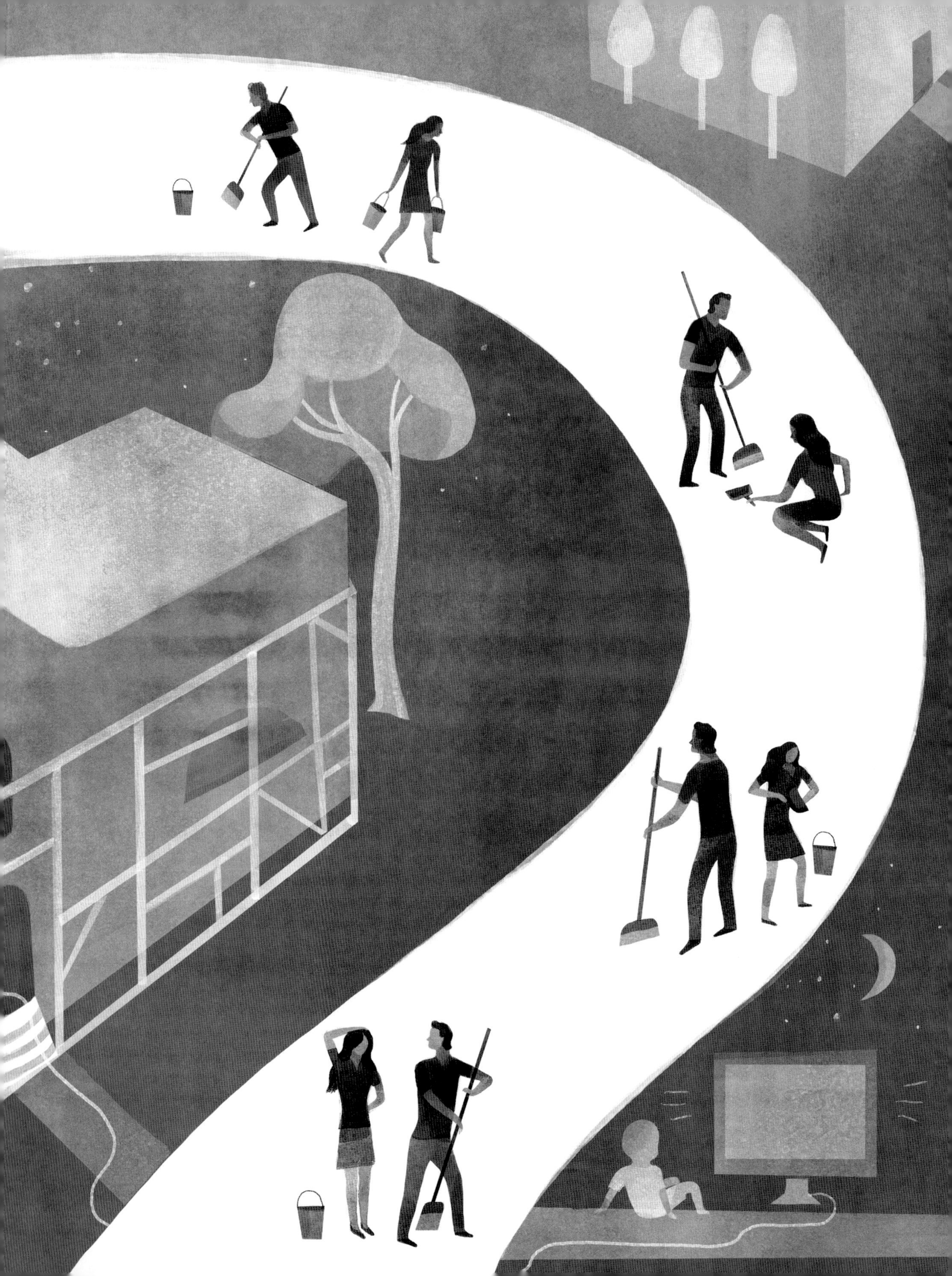

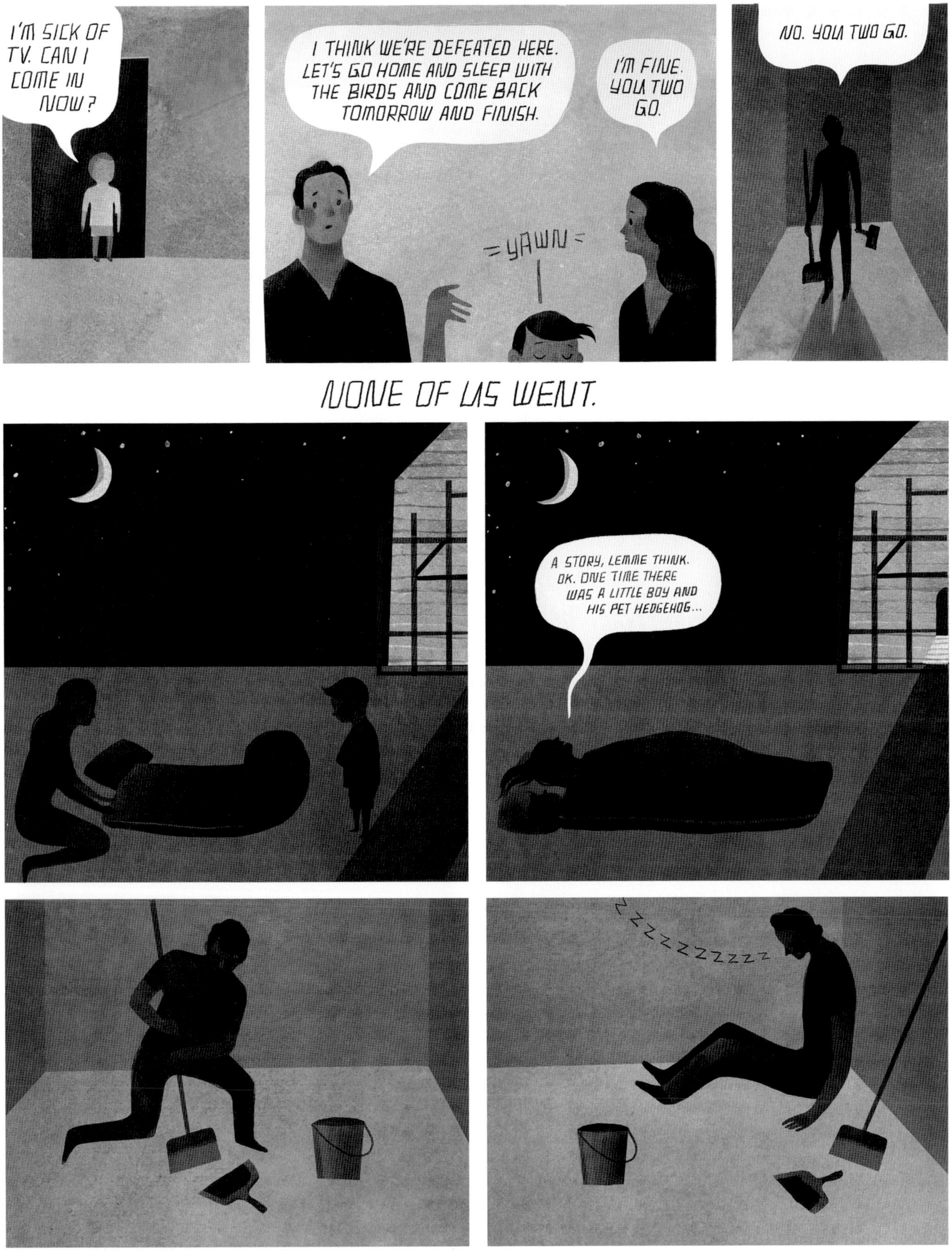
I'M SICK OF TV. CAN I COME IN NOW?
I THINK WE'RE DEFEATED HERE. LET'S GO HOME AND SLEEP WITH THE BIRDS AND COME BACK TOMORROW AND FINISH.
I'M FINE. YOU TWO GO.
=YAWN=
NO. YOU TWO GO.
NONE OF US WENT.
A STORY, LEMME THINK. OK. ONE TIME THERE WAS A LITTLE BOY AND HIS PET HEDGEHOG...
ZZZZZZZZZZZ

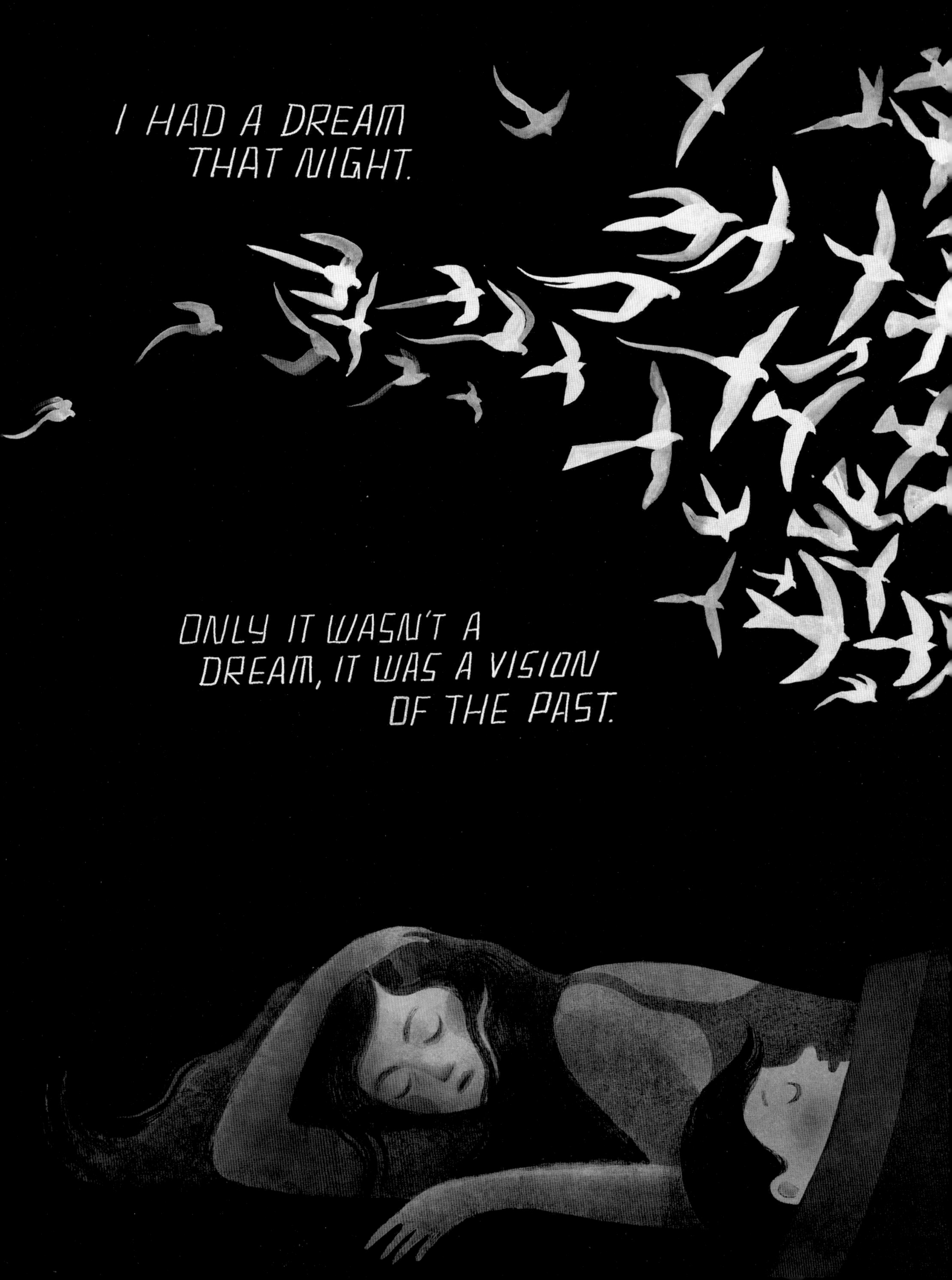
I HAD A DREAM THAT NIGHT.
ONLY IT WASN'T A DREAM, IT WAS A VISION OF THE PAST.

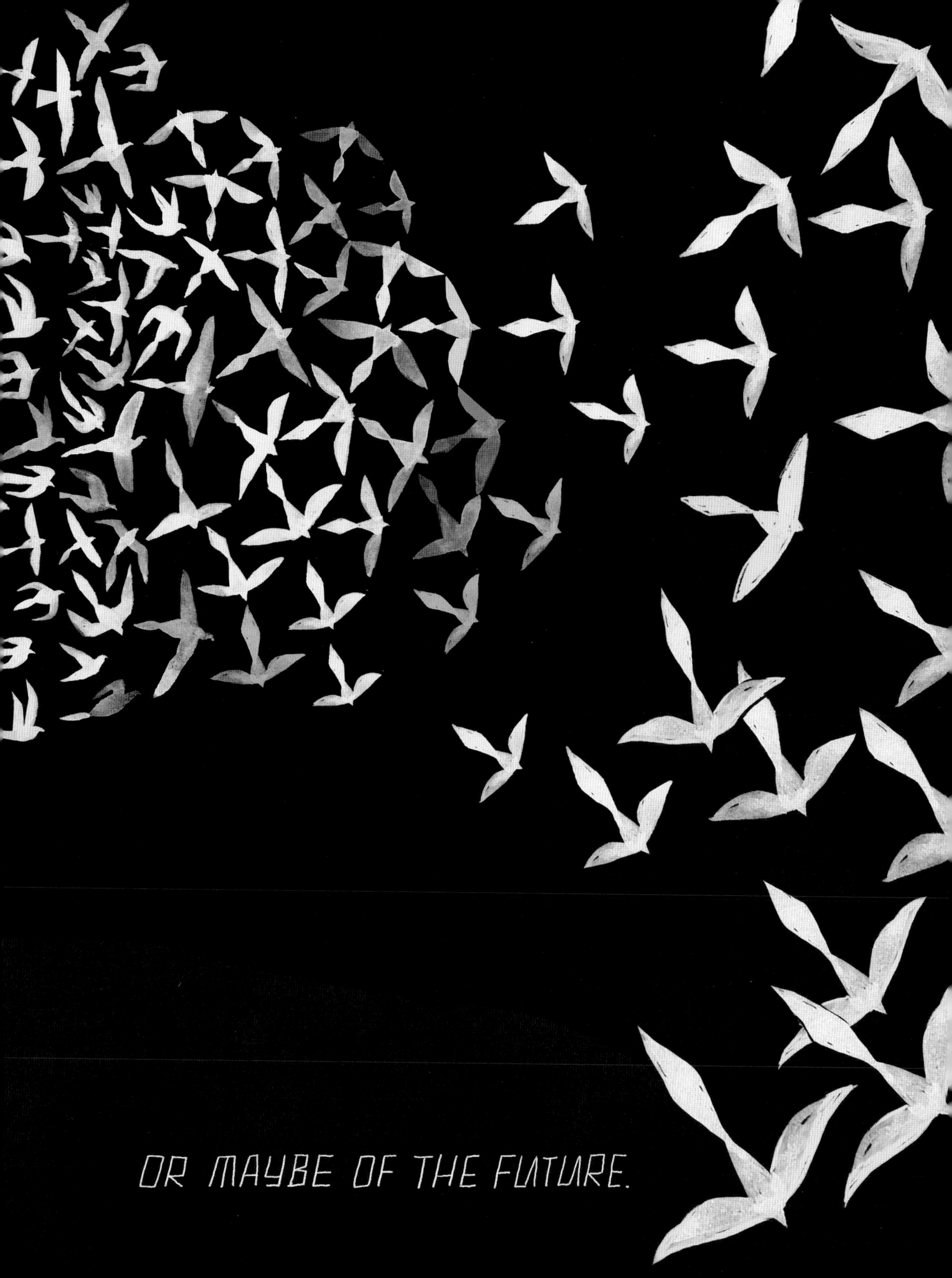
OR MAYBE OF THE FUTURE.

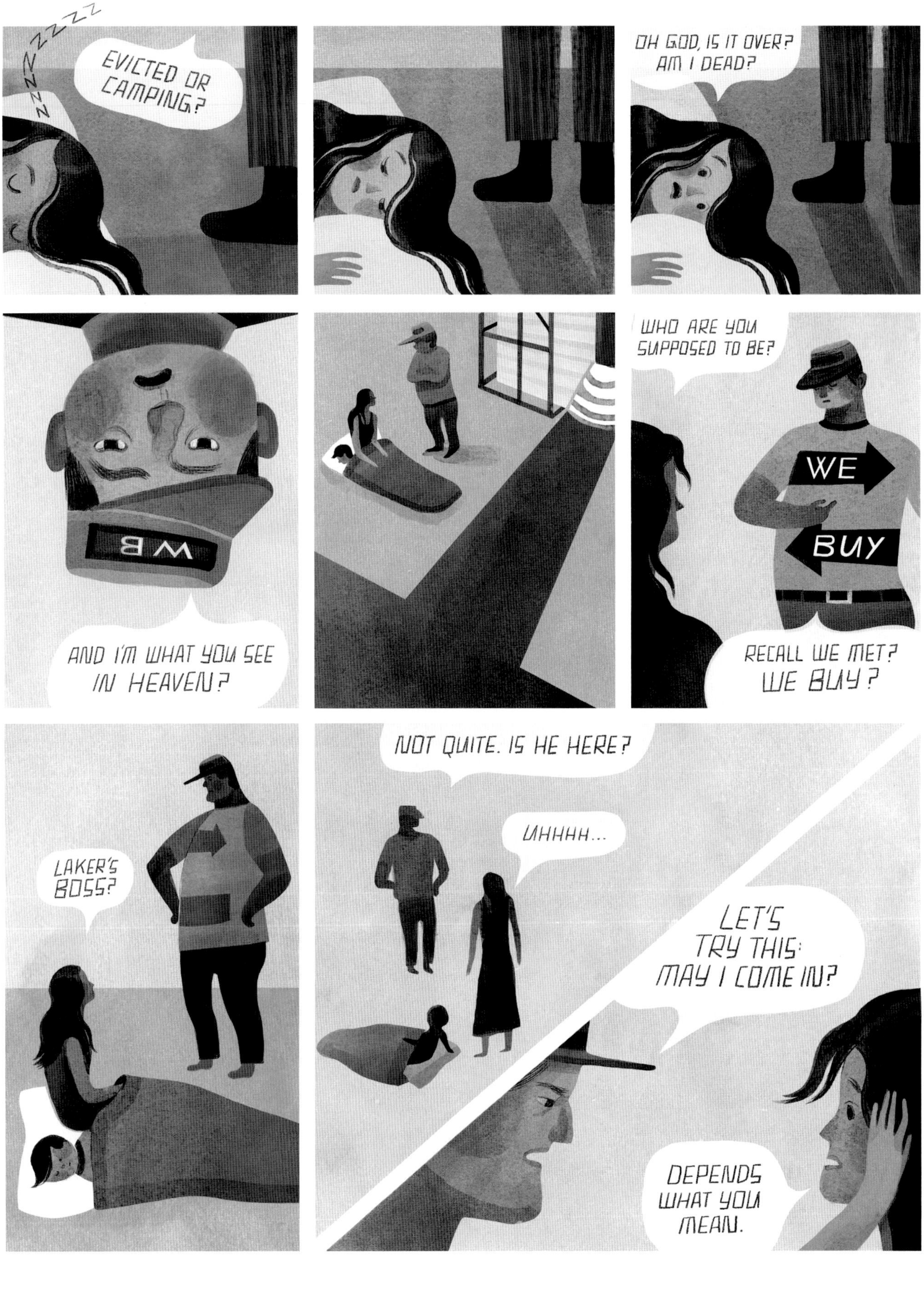
ZZZZZZZZZZ
EVICTED OR CAMPING?
OH GOD, IS IT OVER? AM I DEAD?
WB
AND I'M WHAT YOU SEE IN HEAVEN?
WHO ARE YOU SUPPOSED TO BE?
WE
BUY
RECALL WE MET? WE BUY?
LAKER'S BOSS?
NOT QUITE. IS HE HERE?
UHHHH...
LET'S TRY THIS: MAY I COME IN?
DEPENDS WHAT YOU MEAN.

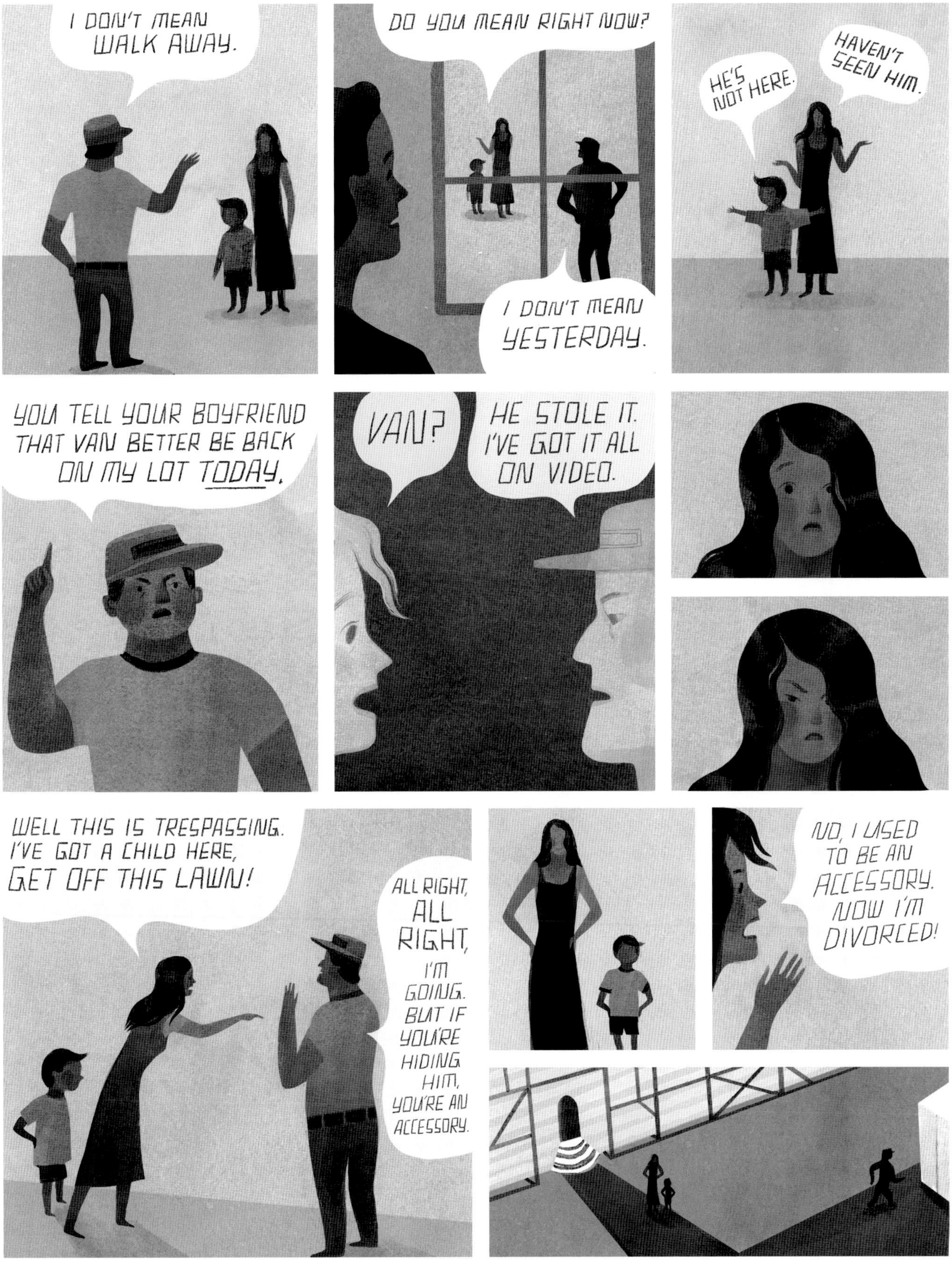

I DON'T MEAN WALK AWAY.
DO YOU MEAN RIGHT NOW?
I DON'T MEAN YESTERDAY.
HE'S NOT HERE.
HAVEN'T SEEN HIM.
YOU TELL YOUR BOYFRIEND THAT VAN BETTER BE BACK ON MY LOT TODAY.
VAN?
HE STOLE IT. I'VE GOT IT ALL ON VIDEO.
WELL THIS IS TRESPASSING. I'VE GOT A CHILD HERE, GET OFF THIS LAWN!
ALL RIGHT, ALL RIGHT, I'M GOING. BUT IF YOU'RE HIDING HIM, YOU'RE AN ACCESSORY.
NO, I USED TO BE AN ACCESSORY. NOW I'M DIVORCED!

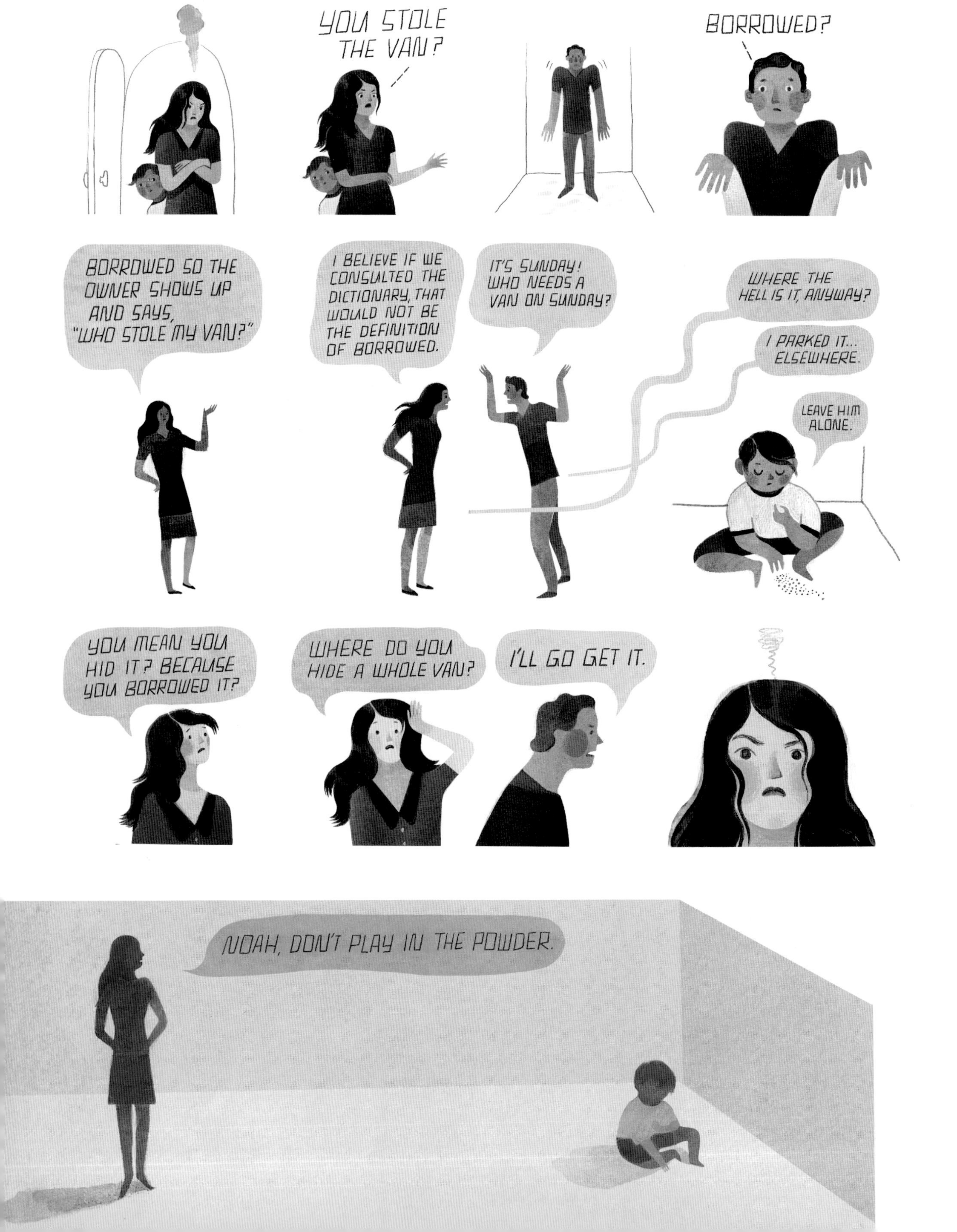
YOU STOLE THE VAN?
BORROWED?
BORROWED SO THE OWNER SHOWS UP AND SAYS, "WHO STOLE MY VAN?"
I BELIEVE IF WE CONSULTED THE DICTIONARY, THAT WOULD NOT BE THE DEFINITION OF BORROWED.
IT'S SUNDAY! WHO NEEDS A VAN ON SUNDAY?
WHERE THE HELL IS IT, ANYWAY?
I PARKED IT... ELSEWHERE.
LEAVE HIM ALONE.
YOU MEAN YOU HID IT? BECAUSE YOU BORROWED IT?
WHERE DO YOU HIDE A WHOLE VAN?
I'LL GO GET IT.
NOAH, DON'T PLAY IN THE POWDER.

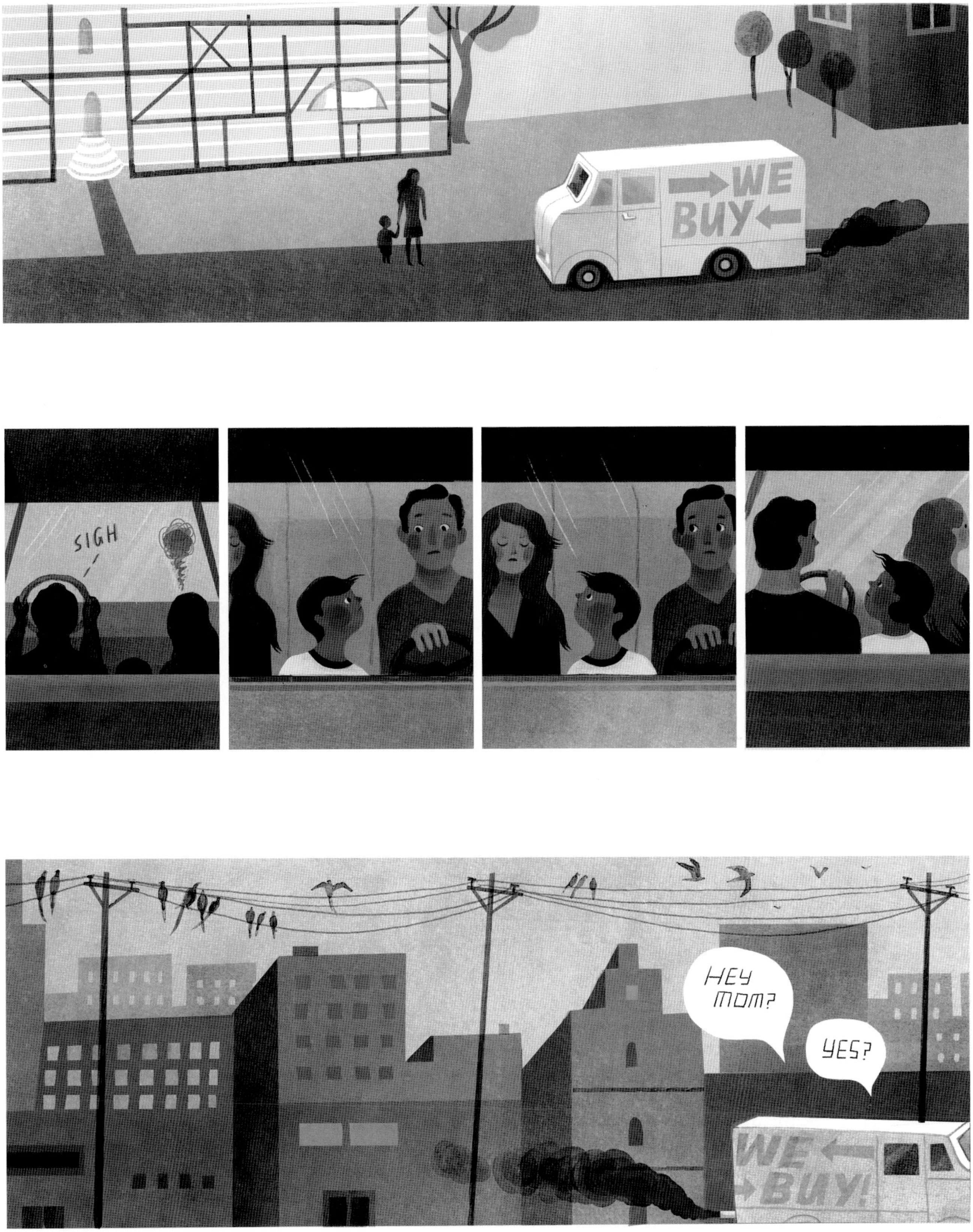
WE BUY
SIGH
HEY MOM?
YES?
WE BUY!

WAS IT SO MUCH TO ASK? NOT COMMITTING FELONIES MOST DAYS OF THE WEEK SO THAT I COULD SPEND A FEW HOURS WITH MY SON? WHOM I BORE, NURSED, AND LOVED, AND WHO WAS STILL SO SMALL AND NEEDED ME?

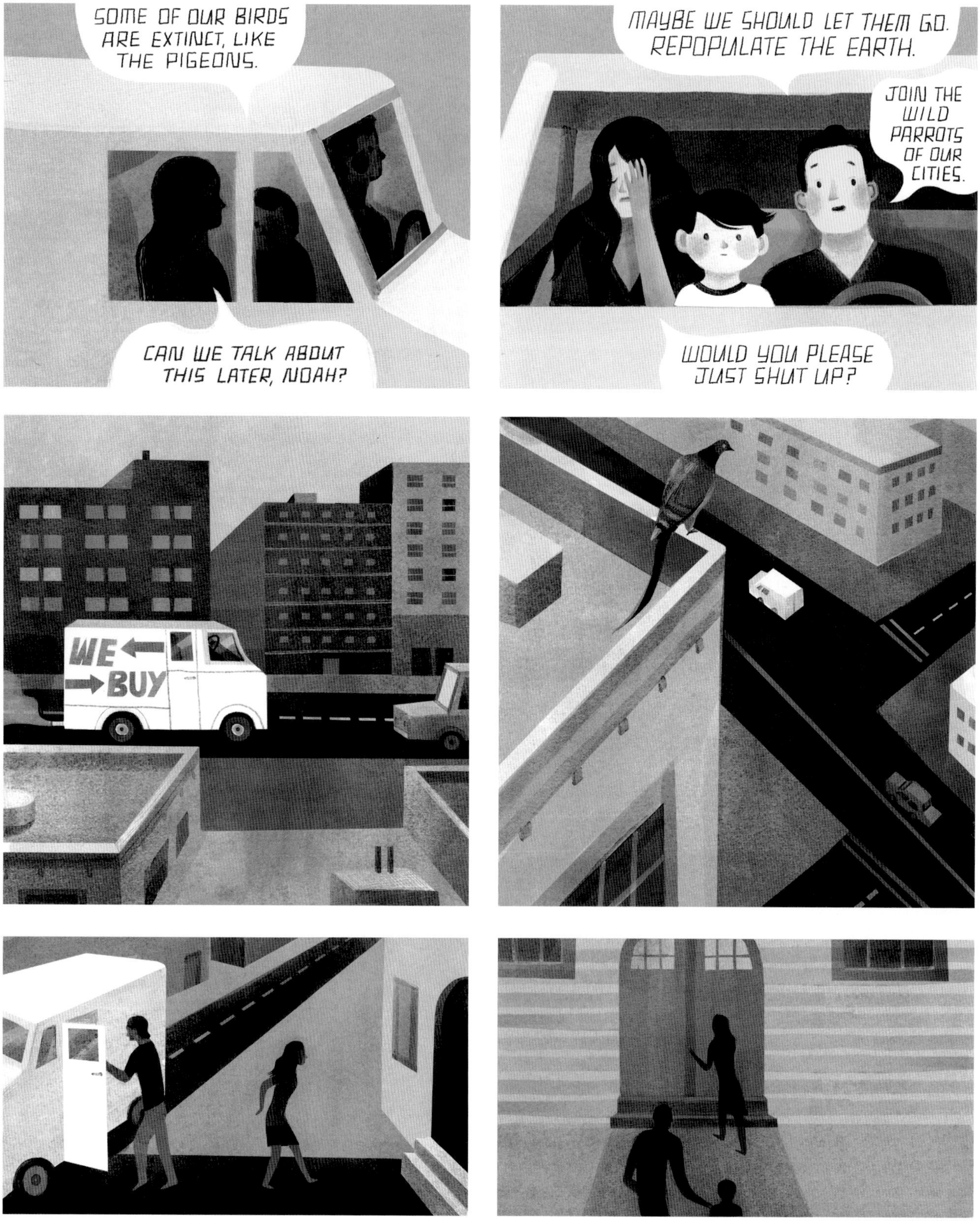
SOME OF OUR BIRDS ARE EXTINCT, LIKE THE PIGEONS.
CAN WE TALK ABOUT THIS LATER, NOAH?
MAYBE WE SHOULD LET THEM GO. REPOPULATE THE EARTH.
JOIN THE WILD PARROTS OF OUR CITIES.
WOULD YOU PLEASE JUST SHUT UP?
WE BUY

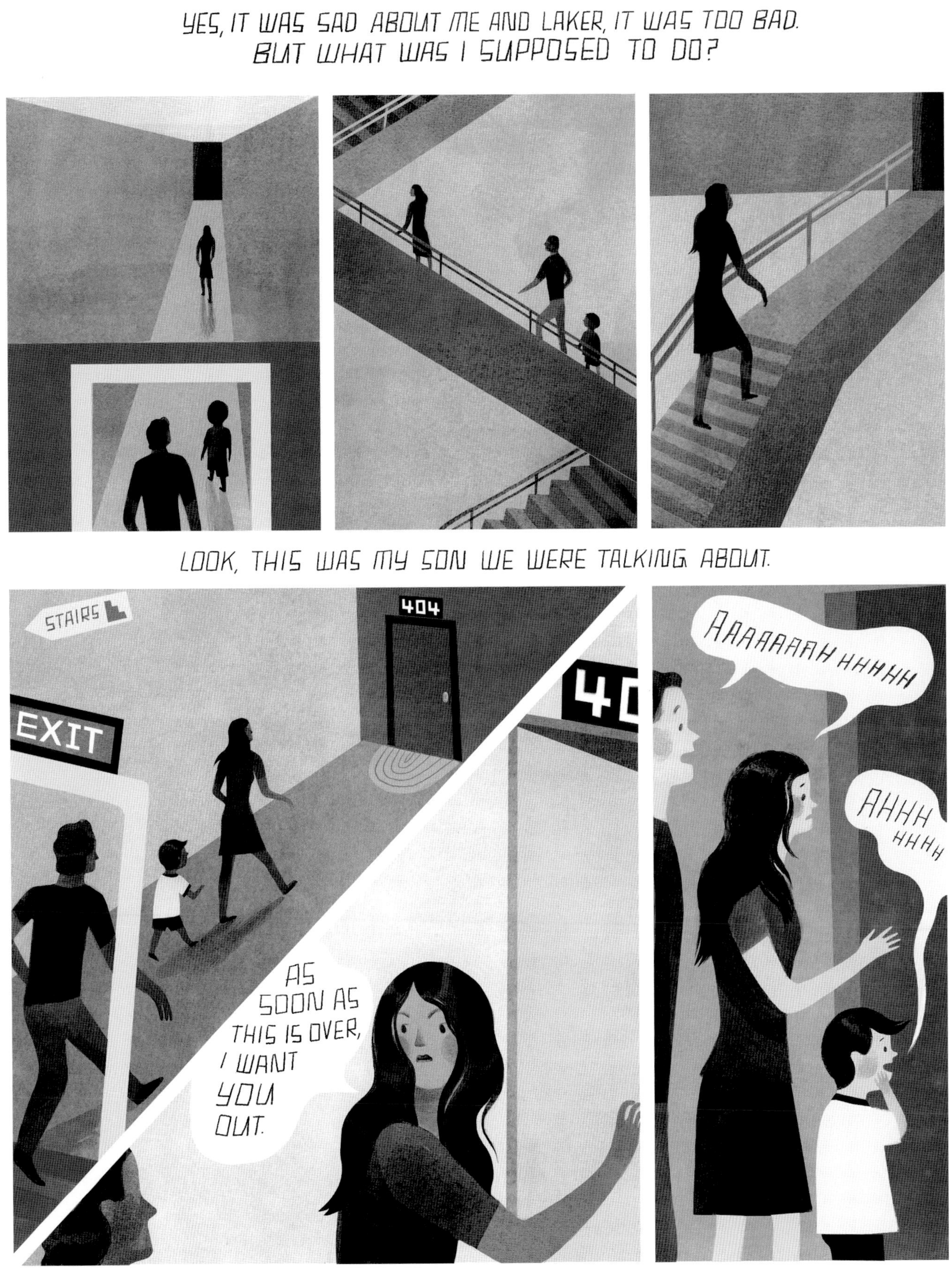

YES, IT WAS SAD ABOUT ME AND LAKER, IT WAS TOO BAD.
BUT WHAT WAS I SUPPOSED TO DO?
LOOK, THIS WAS MY SON WE WERE TALKING ABOUT.
STAIRS
404
EXIT
AS SOON AS THIS IS OVER, I WANT YOU OUT.
AAAAAAAHHHHHH
AHHHHHHH

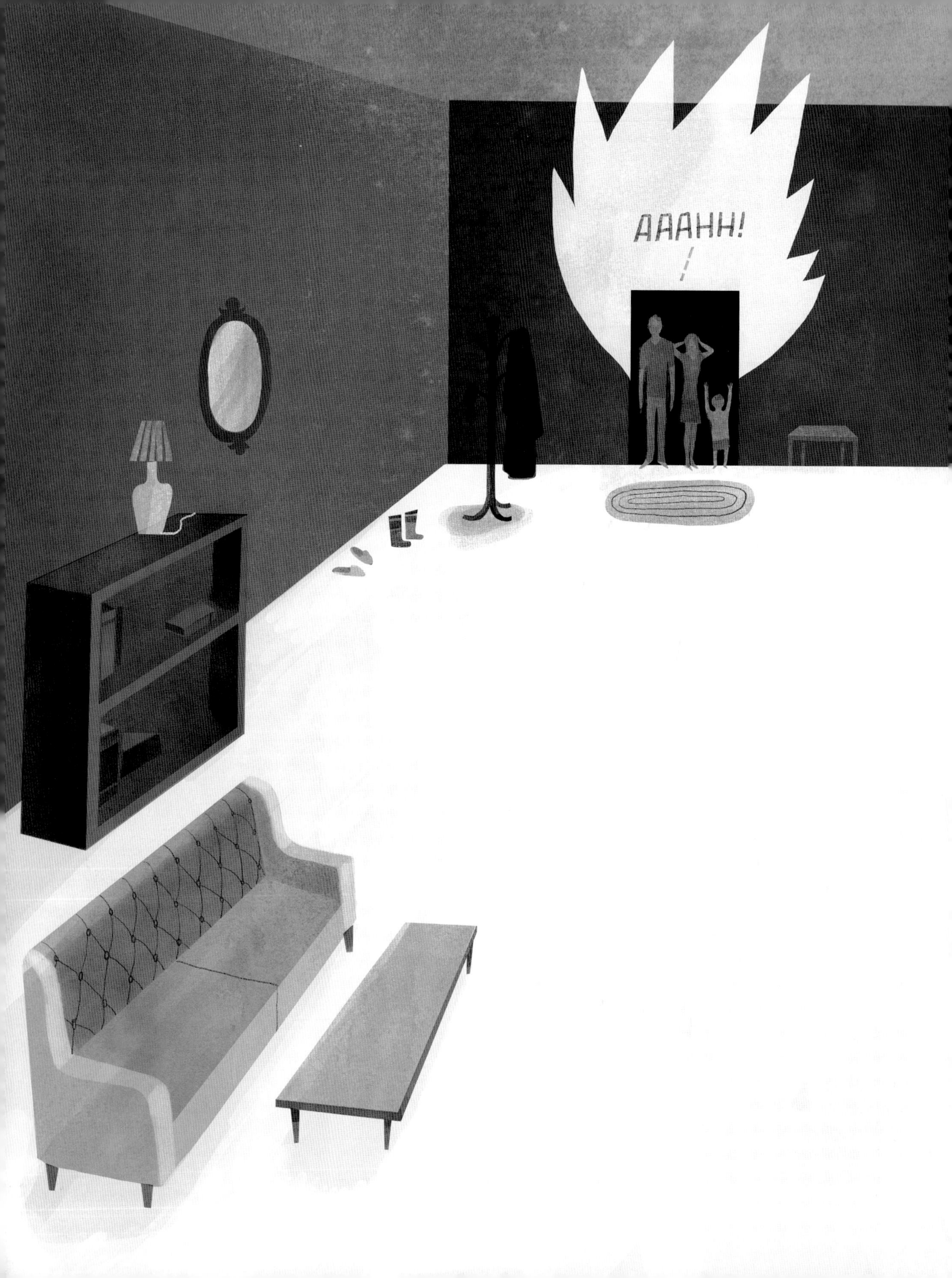
AAAHH!

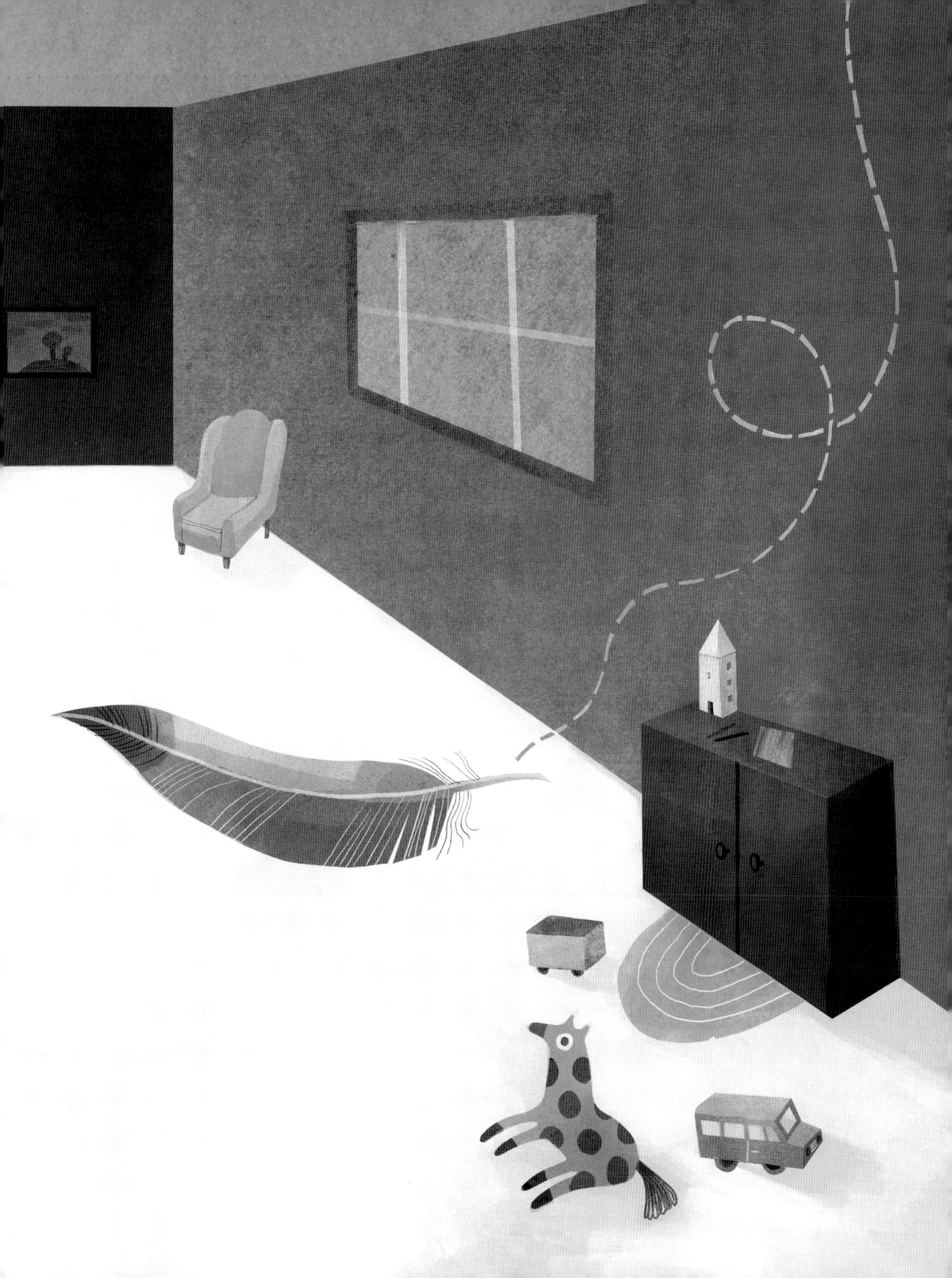

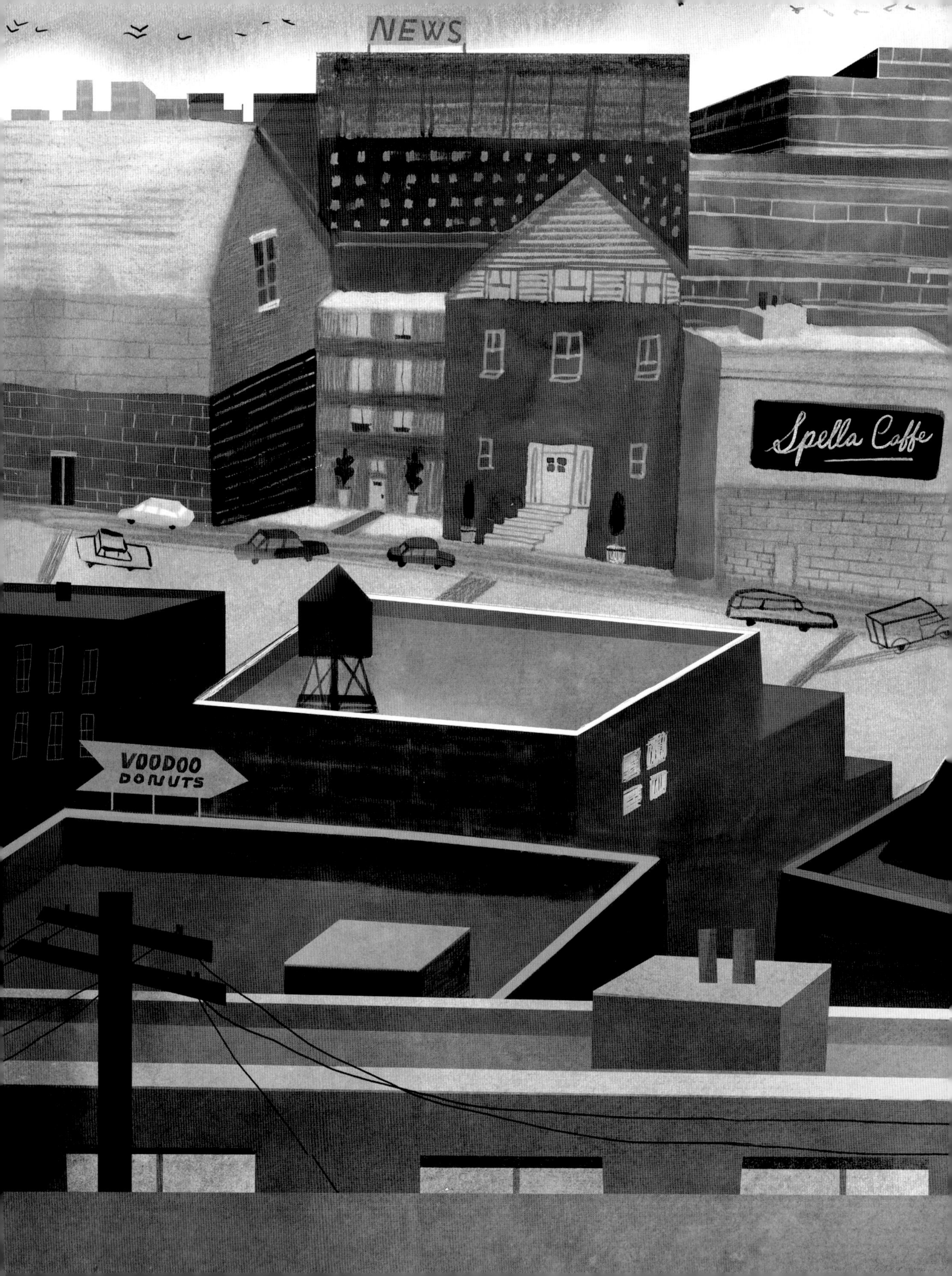
NEWS
Spella Caffe
VOODOO DONUTS

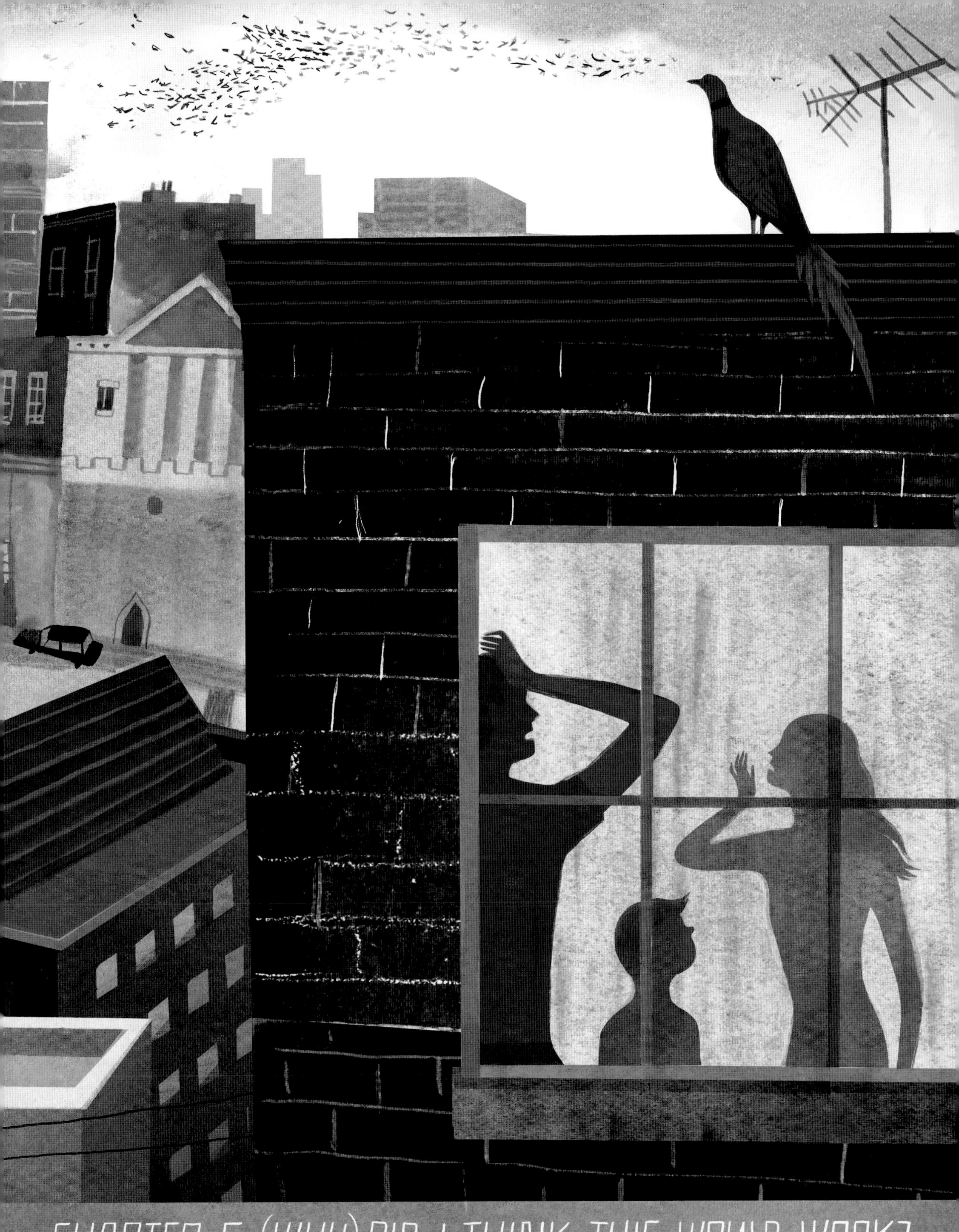

CHAPTER 5: (WHY) DID I THINK THIS WOULD WORK?

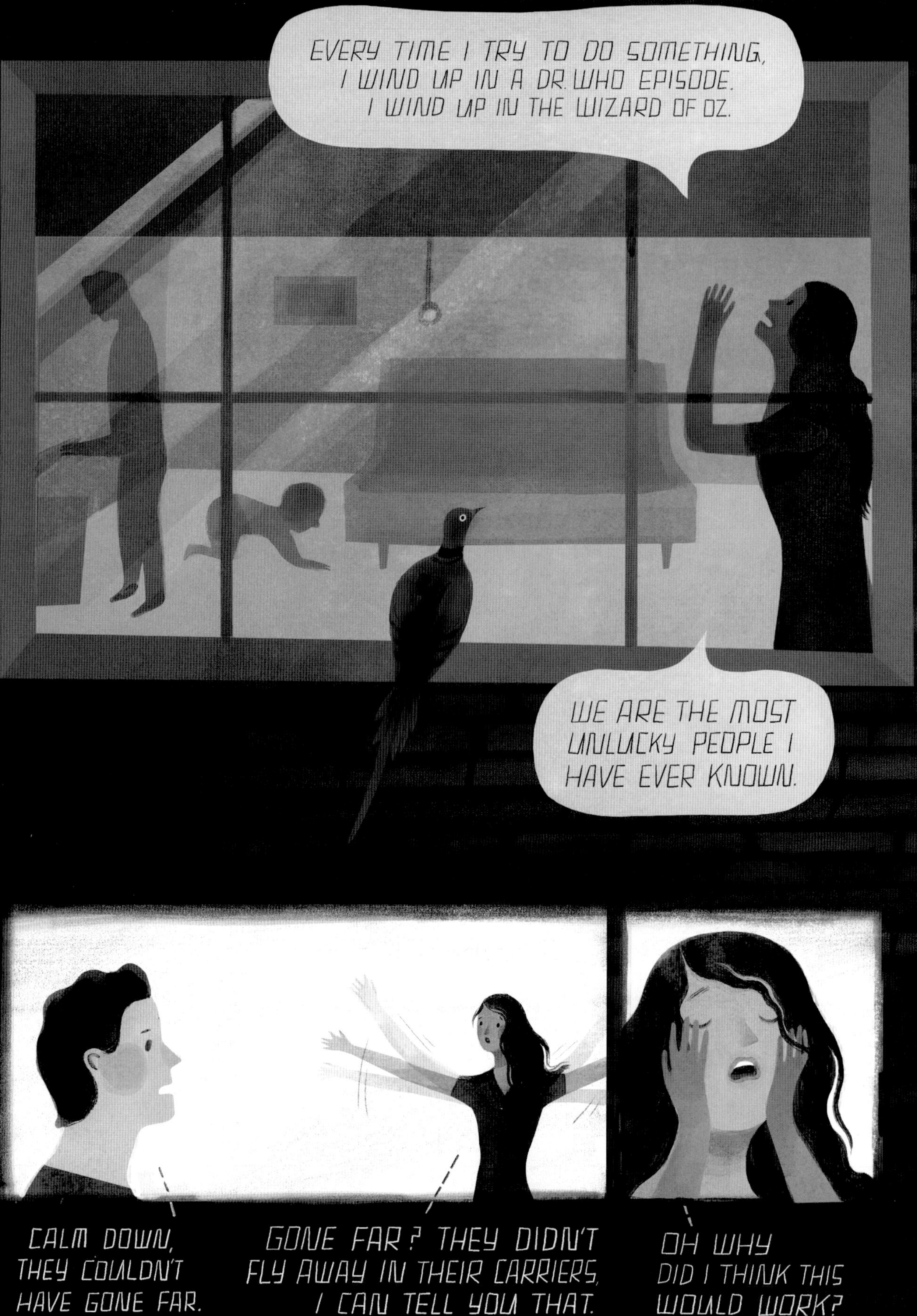
EVERY TIME I TRY TO DO SOMETHING, I WIND UP IN A DR. WHO EPISODE. I WIND UP IN THE WIZARD OF OZ.
WE ARE THE MOST UNLUCKY PEOPLE I HAVE EVER KNOWN.
CALM DOWN, THEY COULDN'T HAVE GONE FAR.
GONE FAR? THEY DIDN'T FLY AWAY IN THEIR CARRIERS, I CAN TELL YOU THAT.
OH WHY DID I THINK THIS WOULD WORK?

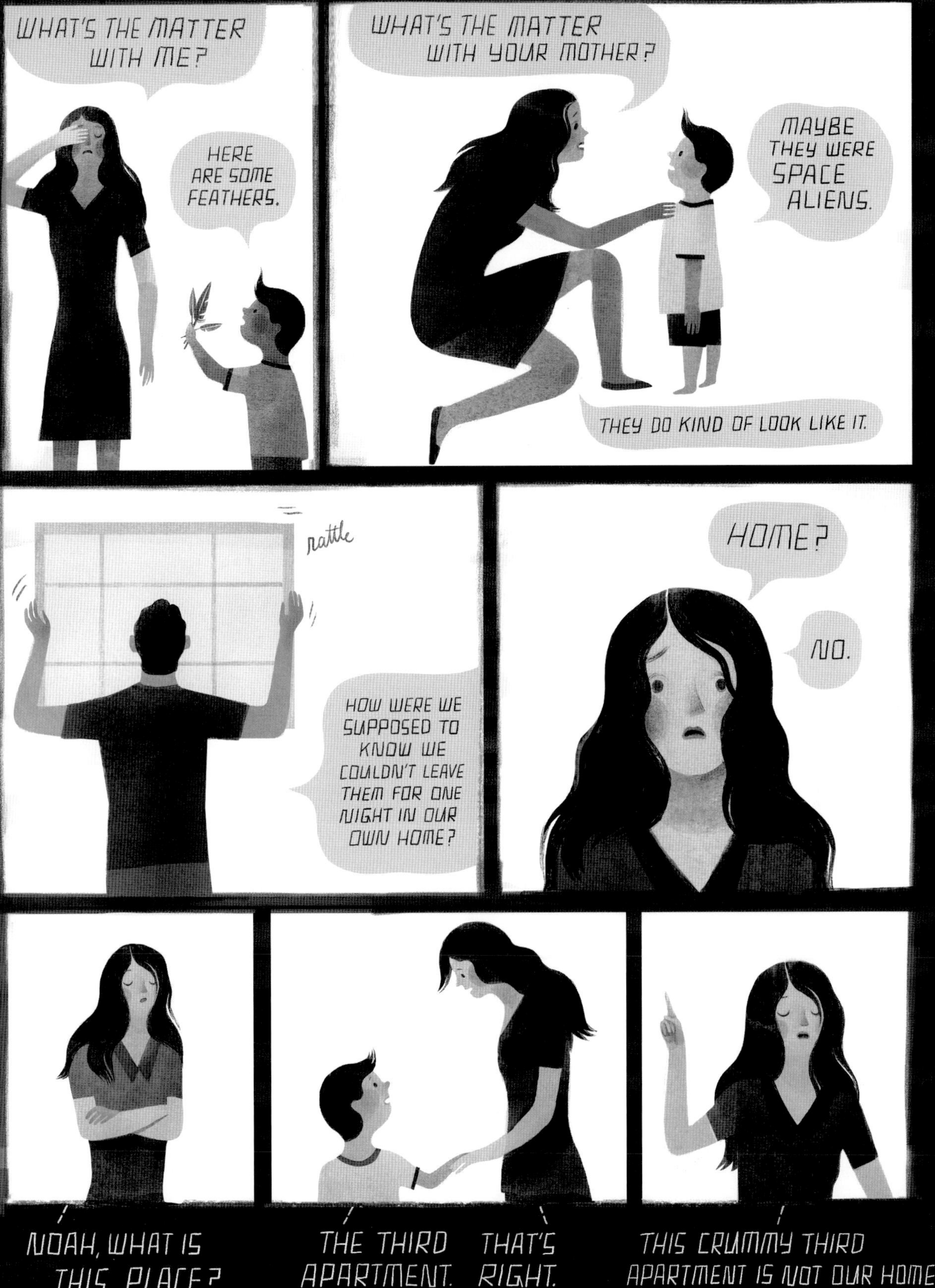
WHAT'S THE MATTER WITH ME?
HERE ARE SOME FEATHERS.
WHAT'S THE MATTER WITH YOUR MOTHER?
MAYBE THEY WERE SPACE ALIENS.
THEY DO KIND OF LOOK LIKE IT.
rattle
HOW WERE WE SUPPOSED TO KNOW WE COULDN'T LEAVE THEM FOR ONE NIGHT IN OUR OWN HOME?
HOME?
NO.
NOAH, WHAT IS THIS PLACE?
THE THIRD APARTMENT.
THAT'S RIGHT.
THIS CRUMMY THIRD APARTMENT IS NOT OUR HOME.

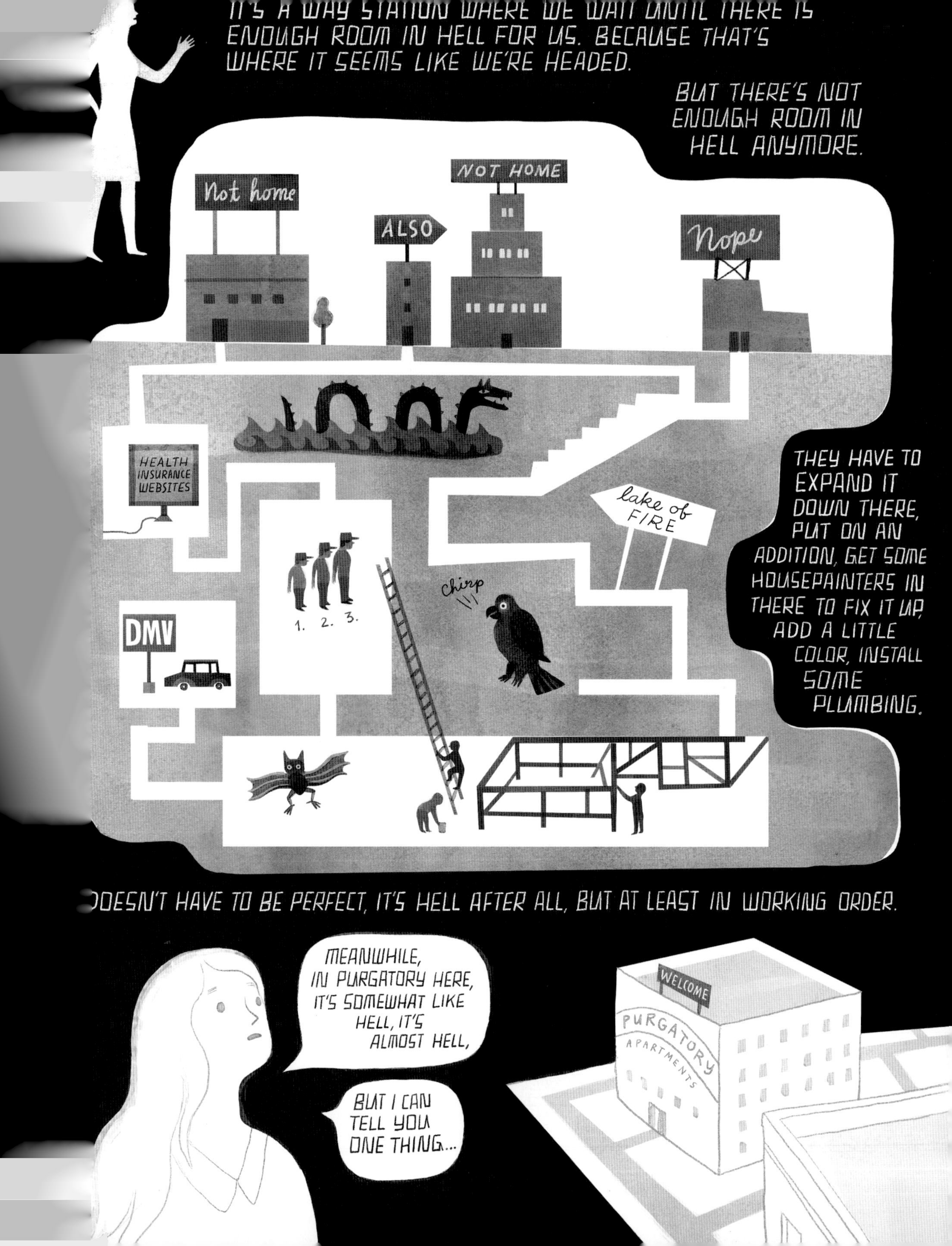

IT'S A WAY STATION WHERE WE WAIT UNTIL THERE IS ENOUGH ROOM IN HELL FOR US. BECAUSE THAT'S WHERE IT SEEMS LIKE WE'RE HEADED.
BUT THERE'S NOT ENOUGH ROOM IN HELL ANYMORE.
Not home
ALSO
NOT HOME
Nope
HEALTH INSURANCE WEBSITES
lake of FIRE
Chirp
1. 2. 3.
DMV
THEY HAVE TO EXPAND IT DOWN THERE, PUT ON AN ADDITION, GET SOME HOUSEPAINTERS IN THERE TO FIX IT UP, ADD A LITTLE COLOR, INSTALL SOME PLUMBING.
DOESN'T HAVE TO BE PERFECT, IT'S HELL AFTER ALL, BUT AT LEAST IN WORKING ORDER.
MEANWHILE, IN PURGATORY HERE, IT'S SOMEWHAT LIKE HELL, IT'S ALMOST HELL,
BUT I CAN TELL YOU ONE THING...
WELCOME
PURGATORY APARTMENTS

THIS IS NOT A HOME.

THIS IS NOT WHERE WE WILL BE REMAINING.

ESPECIALLY NOT WHERE YOU WILL BE REMAINING, BECAUSE I WANT YOU OUT.

COMMITTING FELONIES...

NOAH, WHERE ARE YOU GOING?

TO ASK BERTHA IF SHE SAW THE BIRDS.

GOOD IDEA, SWEETIE.

LET'S GO HAVE THE LANDLADY YELL AT US BECAUSE WE OWE HER SO MUCH MONEY.

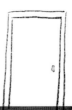

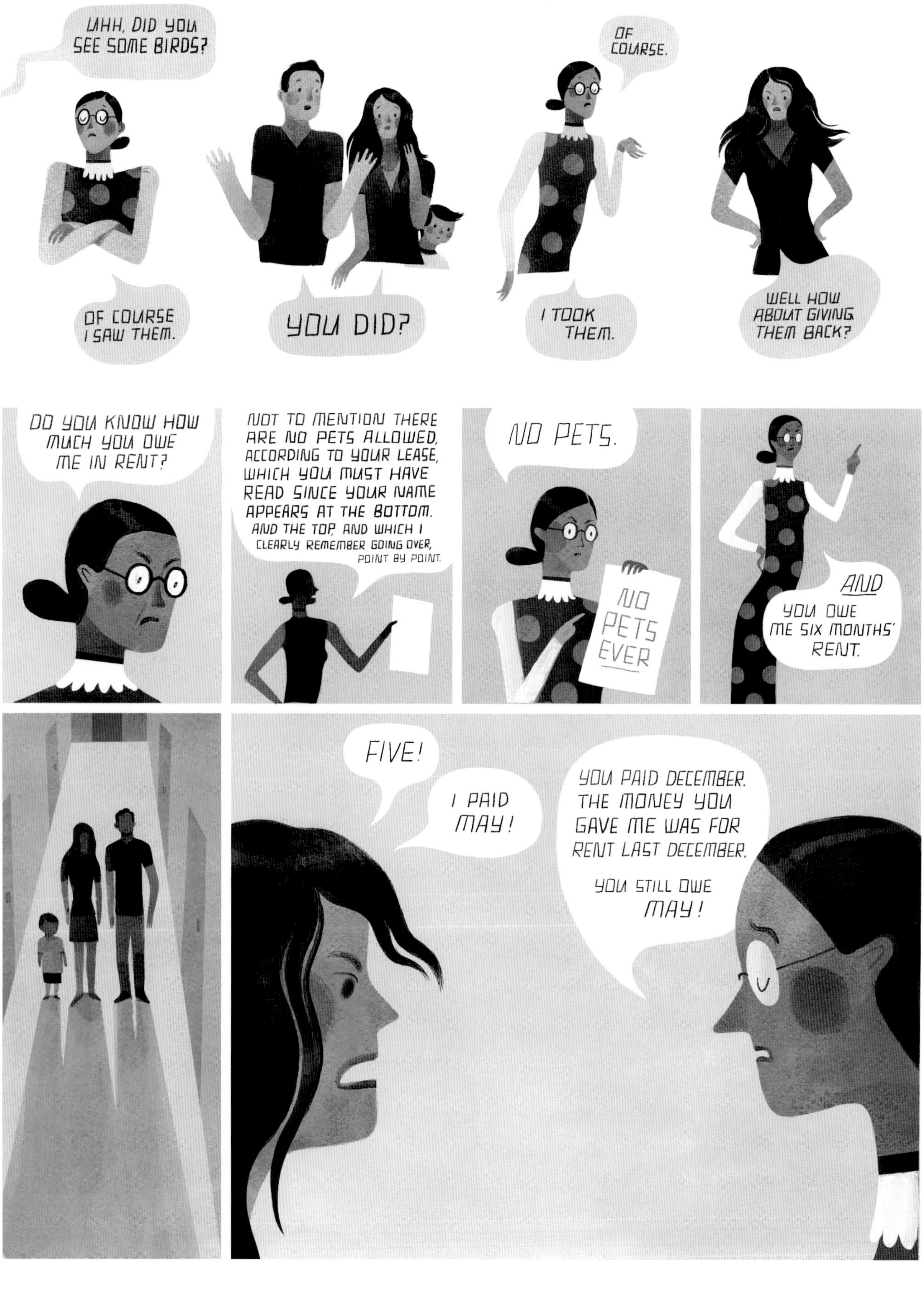
UHH, DID YOU SEE SOME BIRDS?
OF COURSE I SAW THEM.
YOU DID?
OF COURSE.
I TOOK THEM.
WELL HOW ABOUT GIVING THEM BACK?
DO YOU KNOW HOW MUCH YOU OWE ME IN RENT?
NOT TO MENTION THERE ARE NO PETS ALLOWED, ACCORDING TO YOUR LEASE, WHICH YOU MUST HAVE READ SINCE YOUR NAME APPEARS AT THE BOTTOM. AND THE TOP, AND WHICH I CLEARLY REMEMBER GOING OVER, POINT BY POINT.
NO PETS.
NO PETS EVER
AND YOU OWE ME SIX MONTHS' RENT.
FIVE!
I PAID MAY!
YOU PAID DECEMBER. THE MONEY YOU GAVE ME WAS FOR RENT LAST DECEMBER.
YOU STILL OWE MAY!

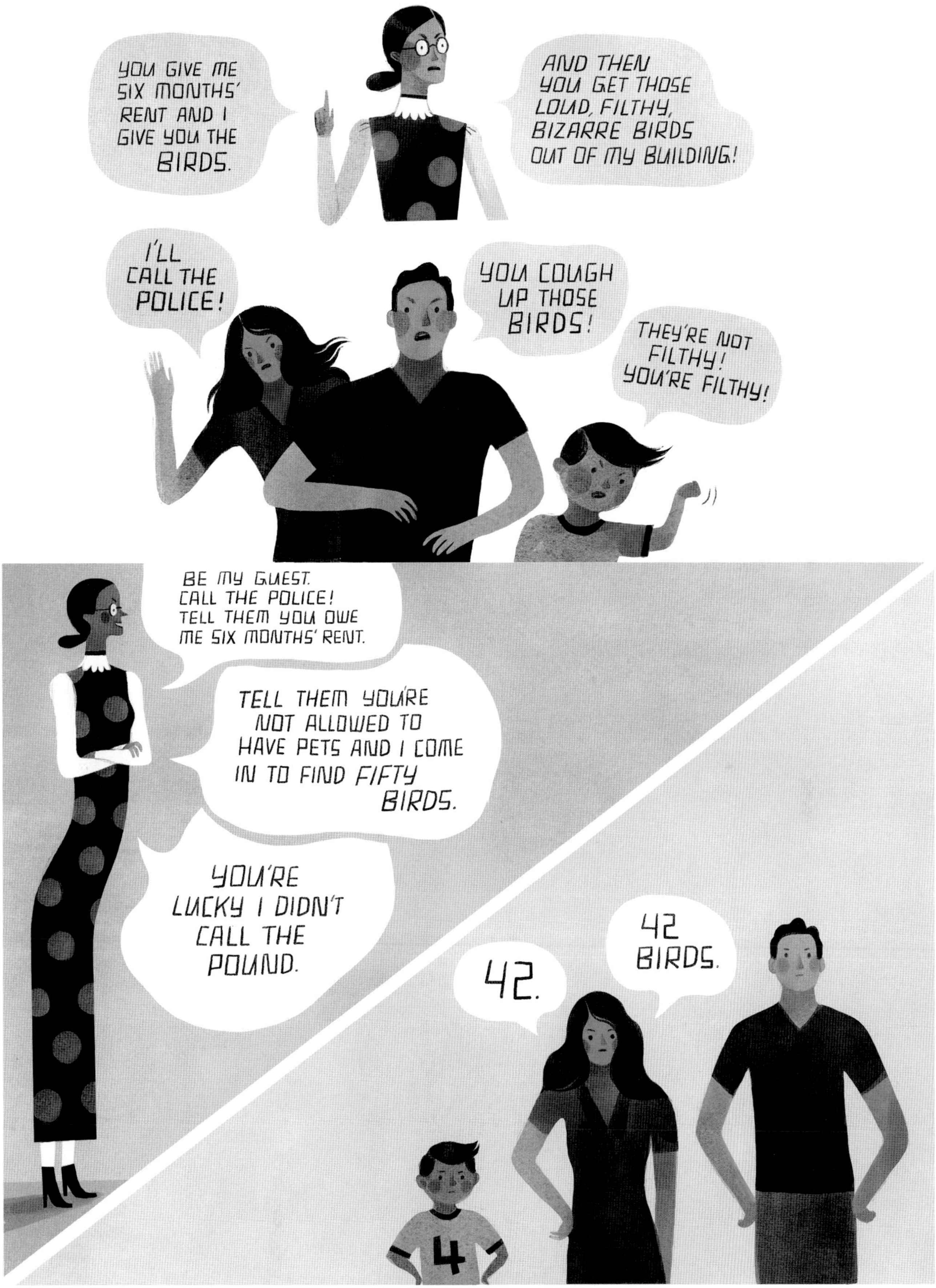

YOU GIVE ME SIX MONTHS' RENT AND I GIVE YOU THE BIRDS.
AND THEN YOU GET THOSE LOUD, FILTHY, BIZARRE BIRDS OUT OF MY BUILDING!
I'LL CALL THE POLICE!
YOU COUGH UP THOSE BIRDS!
THEY'RE NOT FILTHY! YOU'RE FILTHY!
BE MY GUEST. CALL THE POLICE! TELL THEM YOU OWE ME SIX MONTHS' RENT.
TELL THEM YOU'RE NOT ALLOWED TO HAVE PETS AND I COME IN TO FIND FIFTY BIRDS.
YOU'RE LUCKY I DIDN'T CALL THE POUND.
42.
42 BIRDS.
4

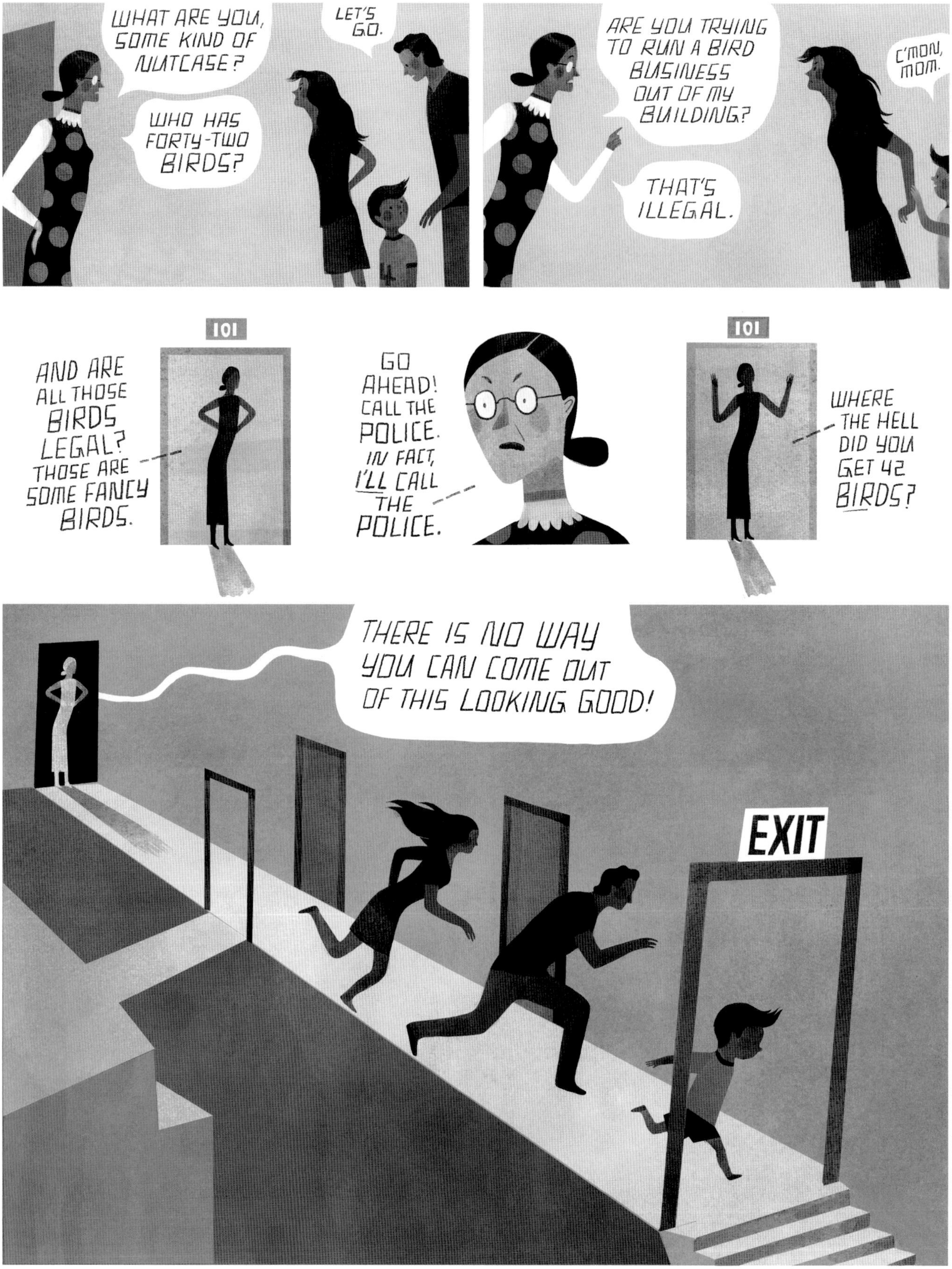
WHAT ARE YOU, SOME KIND OF NUTCASE?
WHO HAS FORTY-TWO BIRDS?
LET'S GO.
ARE YOU TRYING TO RUN A BIRD BUSINESS OUT OF MY BUILDING?
THAT'S ILLEGAL.
C'MON, MOM.
AND ARE ALL THOSE BIRDS LEGAL? THOSE ARE SOME FANCY BIRDS.
101
GO AHEAD! CALL THE POLICE. IN FACT, I'LL CALL THE POLICE.
101
WHERE THE HELL DID YOU GET 42 BIRDS?
THERE IS NO WAY YOU CAN COME OUT OF THIS LOOKING GOOD!
EXIT

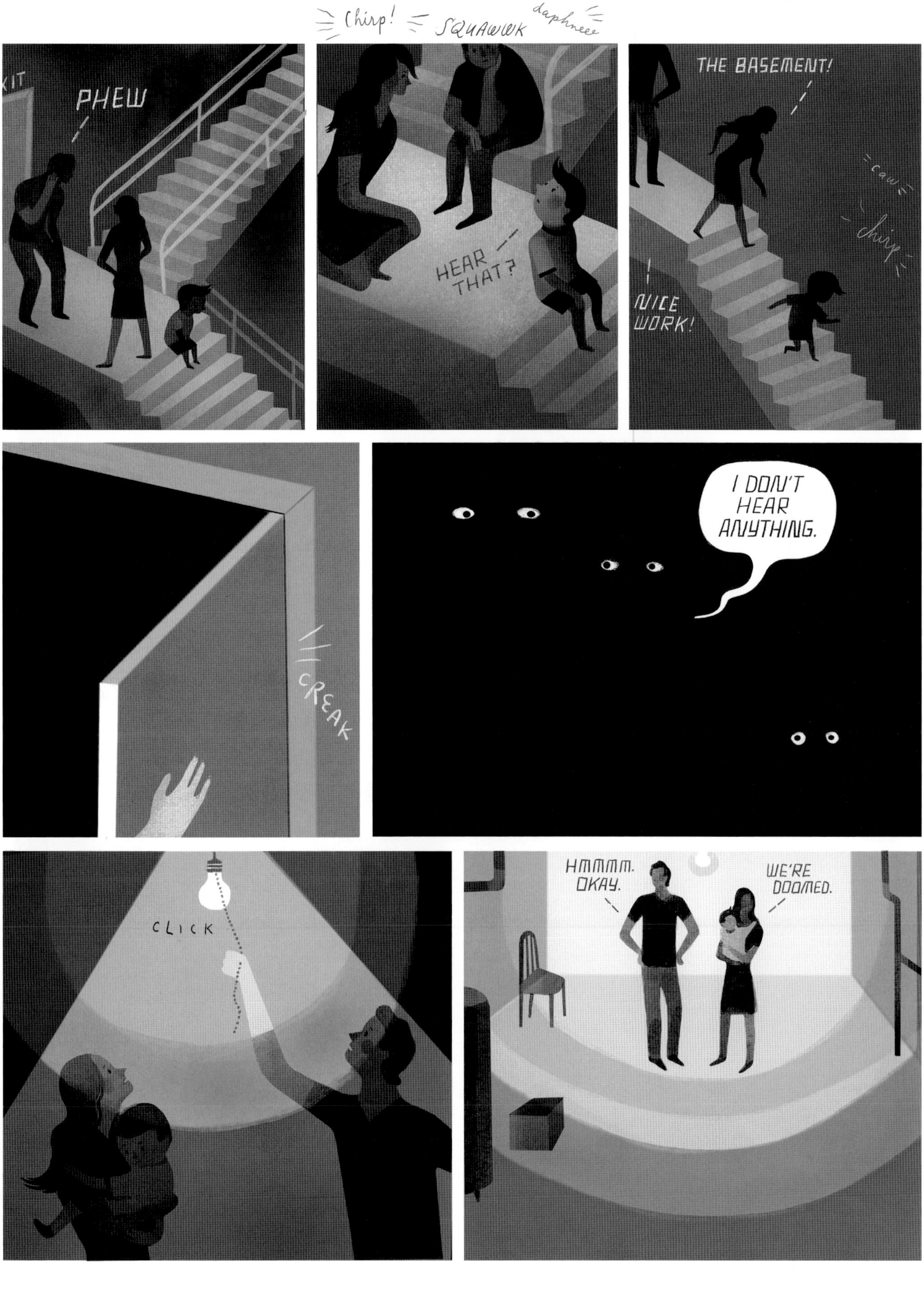
Chirp!
SQUAWWK
daphneee
XIT
PHEW
HEAR THAT?
THE BASEMENT!
caw
chirp
NICE WORK!
CREAK
I DON'T HEAR ANYTHING.
CLICK
HMMMM. OKAY.
WE'RE DOOMED.

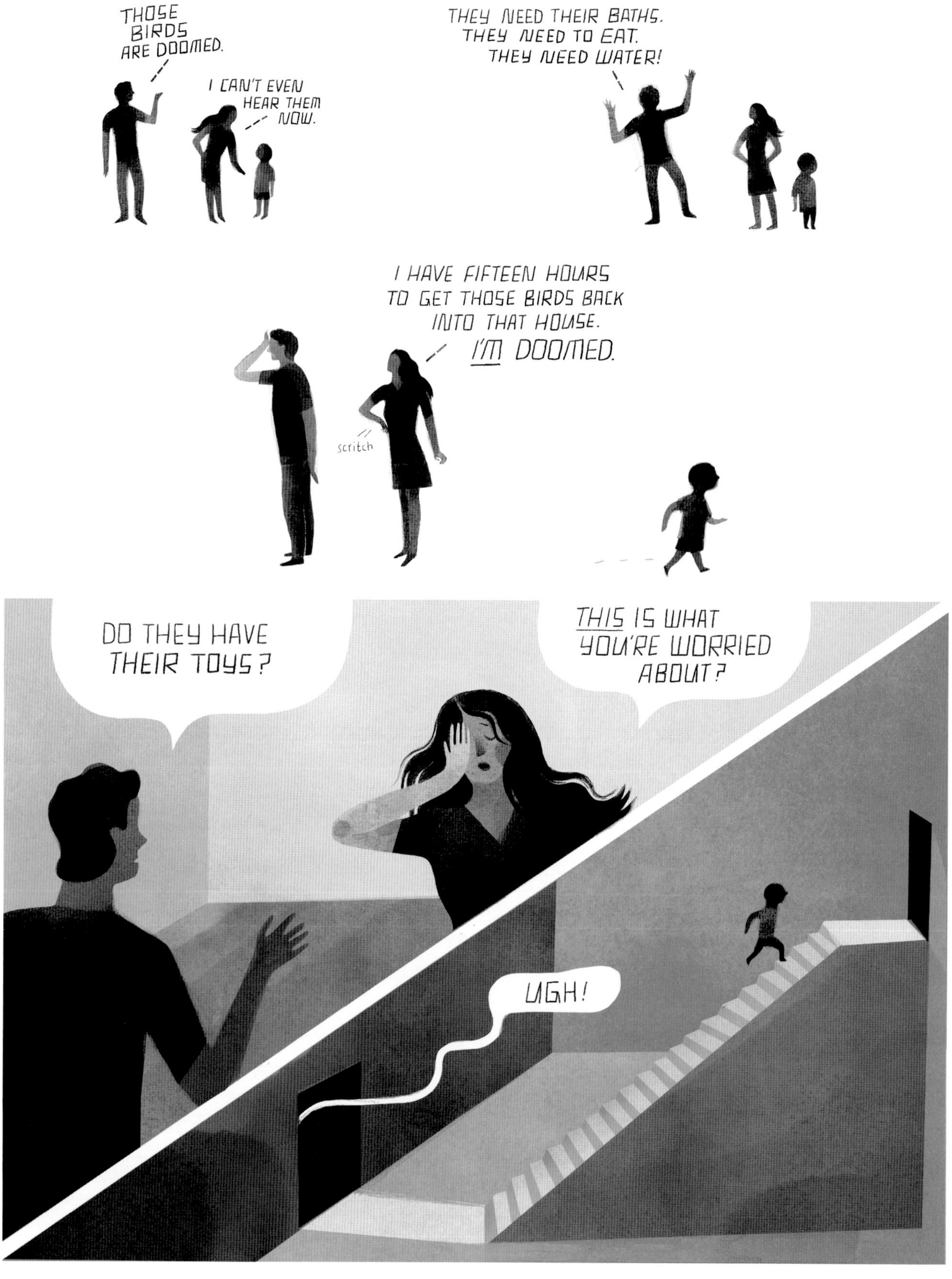
THOSE BIRDS ARE DOOMED.
I CAN'T EVEN HEAR THEM NOW.
THEY NEED THEIR BATHS. THEY NEED TO EAT. THEY NEED WATER!
I HAVE FIFTEEN HOURS TO GET THOSE BIRDS BACK INTO THAT HOUSE.
I'M DOOMED.
scritch
DO THEY HAVE THEIR TOYS?
THIS IS WHAT YOU'RE WORRIED ABOUT?
UGH!

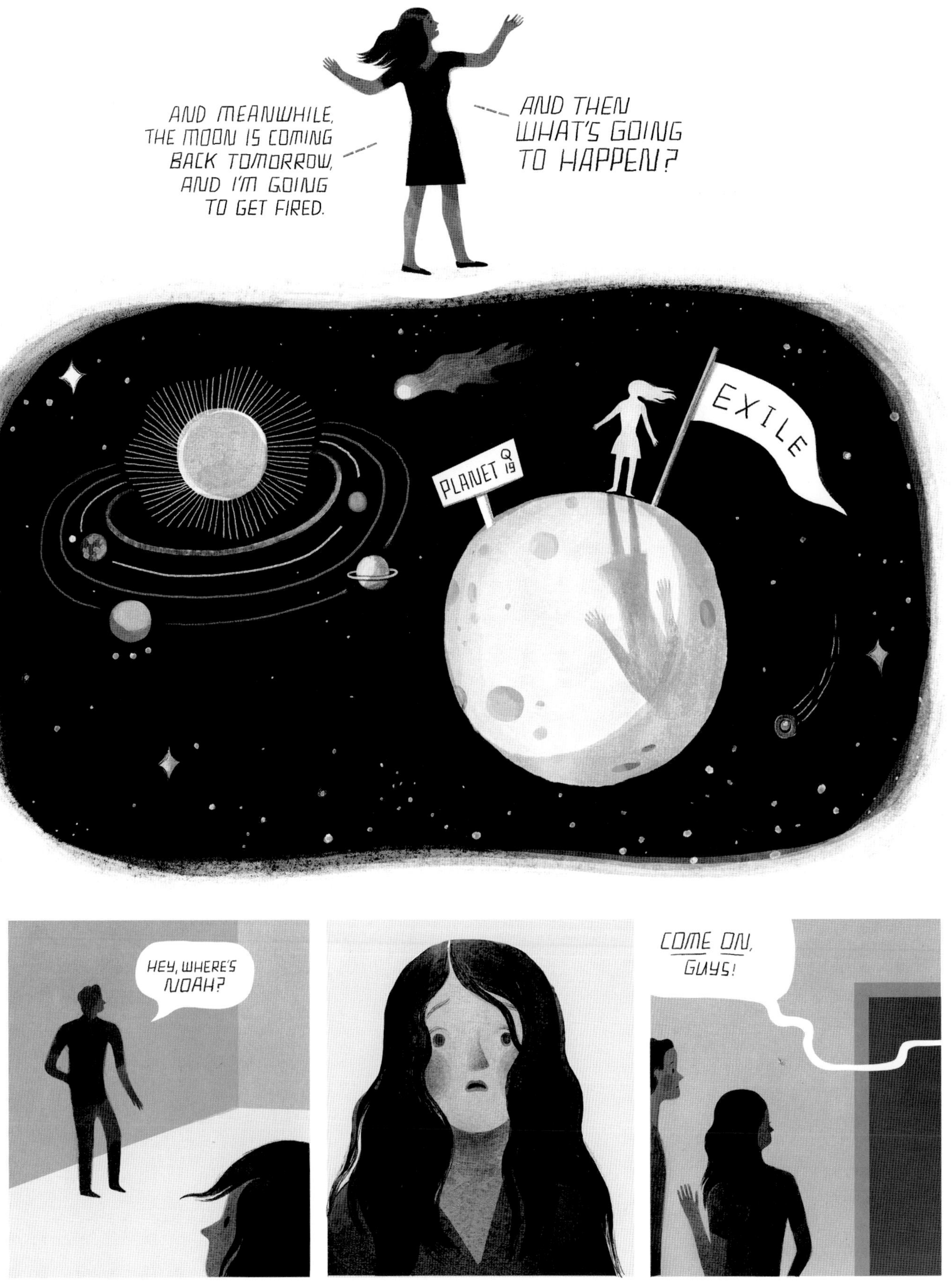
AND MEANWHILE, THE MOON IS COMING BACK TOMORROW, AND I'M GOING TO GET FIRED.
AND THEN WHAT'S GOING TO HAPPEN?
PLANET Q19
EXILE
HEY, WHERE'S NOAH?
COME ON, GUYS!

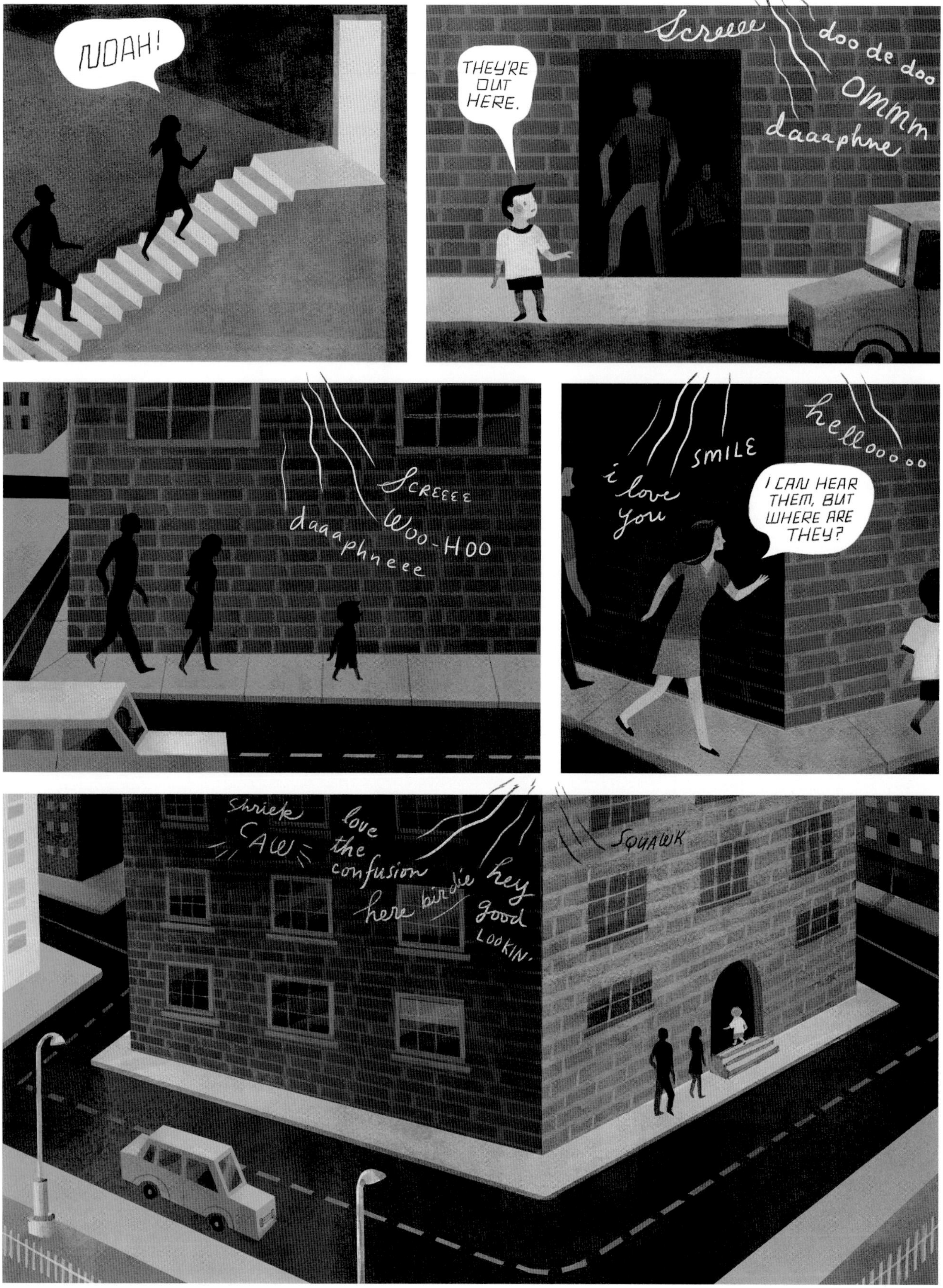
NOAH!
THEY'RE OUT HERE.
Screeee
doo de doo
OMMM
daaaphne
SCREEEE
WOO-HOO
daaaphneee
i love you
SMILE
hellooooo
I CAN HEAR THEM, BUT WHERE ARE THEY?
Shriek
CAW
love the confusion
here birdie
hey good LOOKIN'
SQUAWK

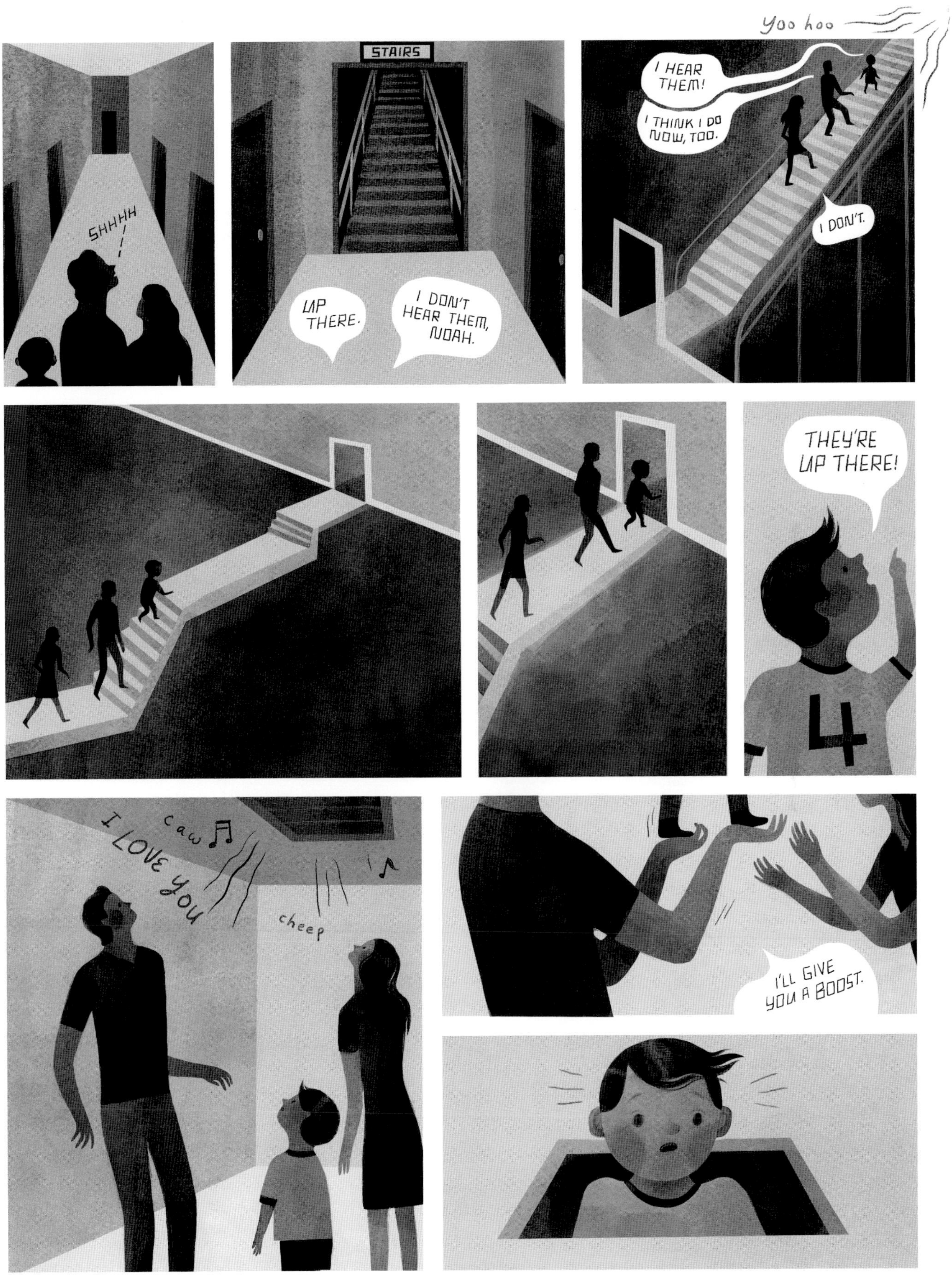
yoo hoo
SHHHH
STAIRS
UP THERE.
I DON'T HEAR THEM, NOAH.
I HEAR THEM!
I THINK I DO NOW, TOO.
I DON'T.
THEY'RE UP THERE!
4
caw
I LOVE YOU
cheep
I'LL GIVE YOU A BOOST.

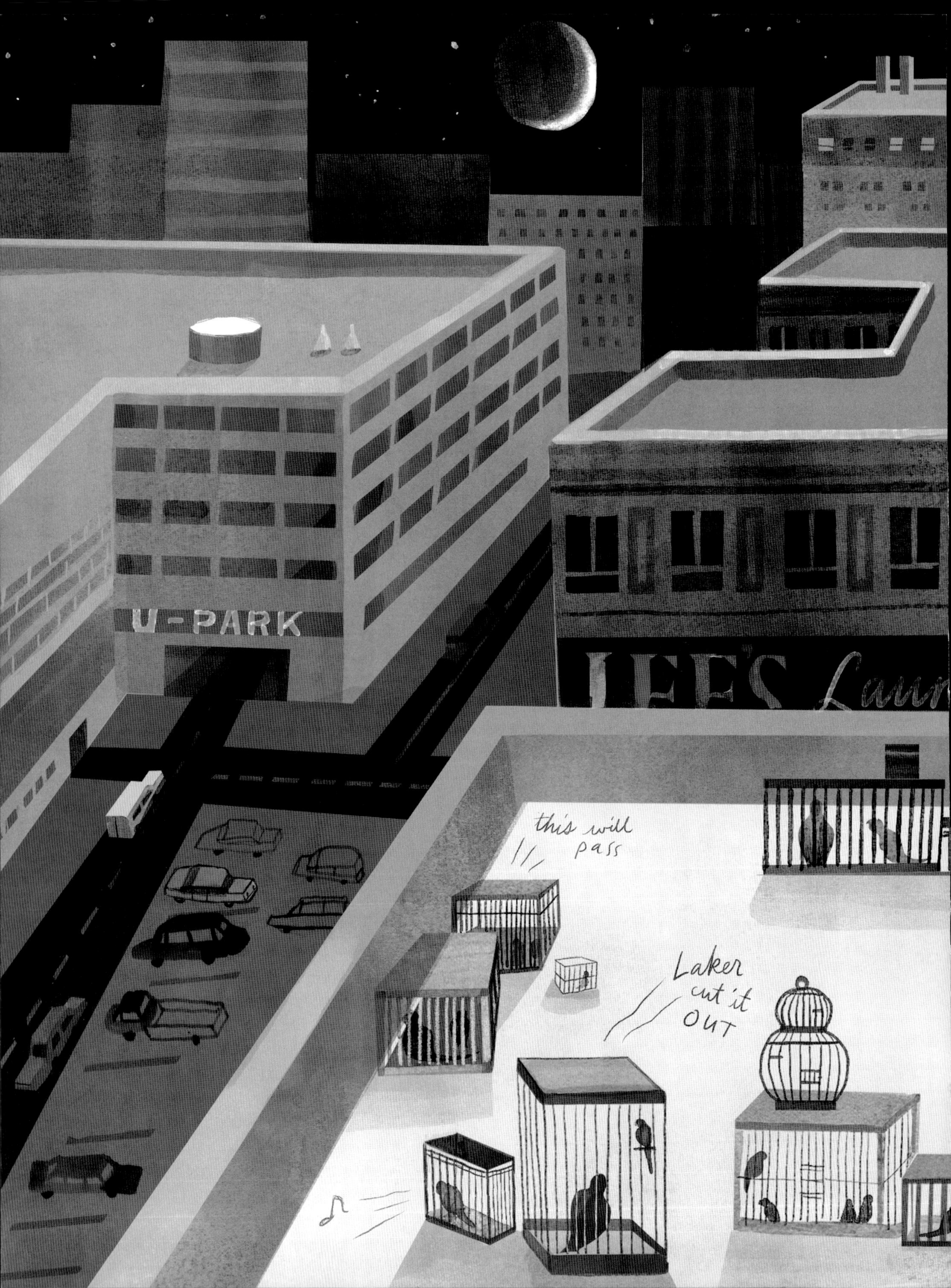
U-PARK
this will pass
Laker cut it OUT

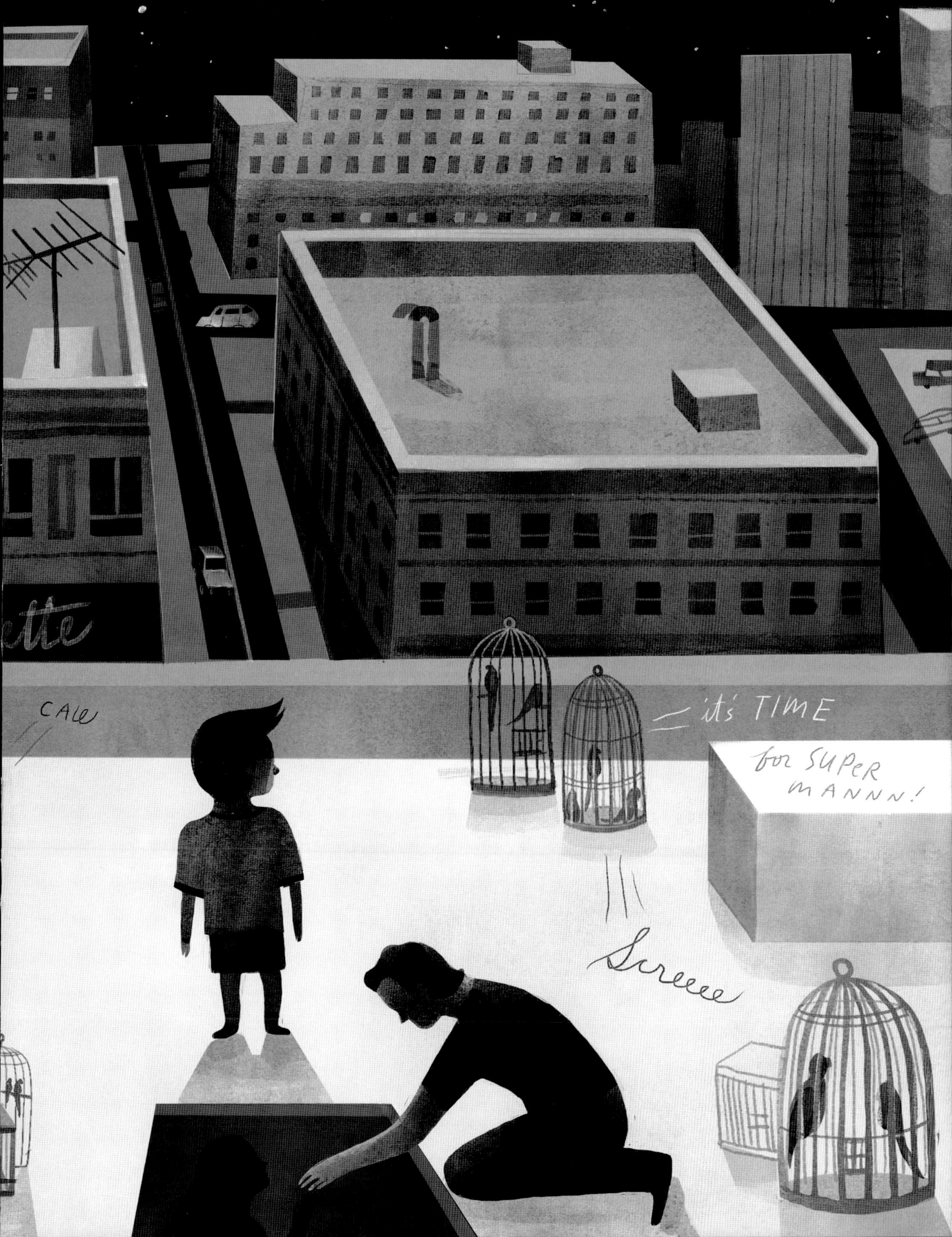
ette
CAW
it's TIME
for SUPER MANNN!
Screeee

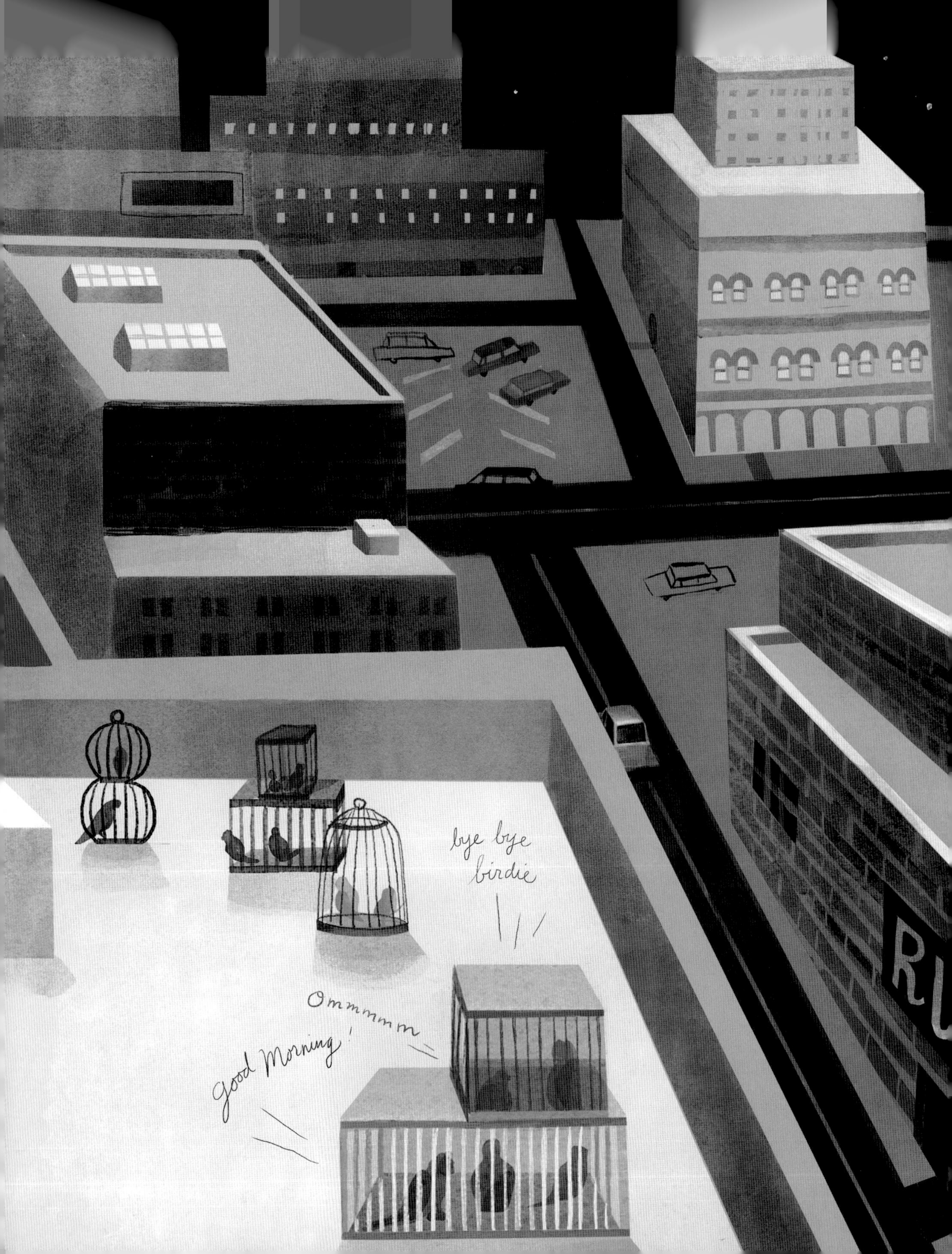
bye bye birdie
Ommmmm
Good Morning!

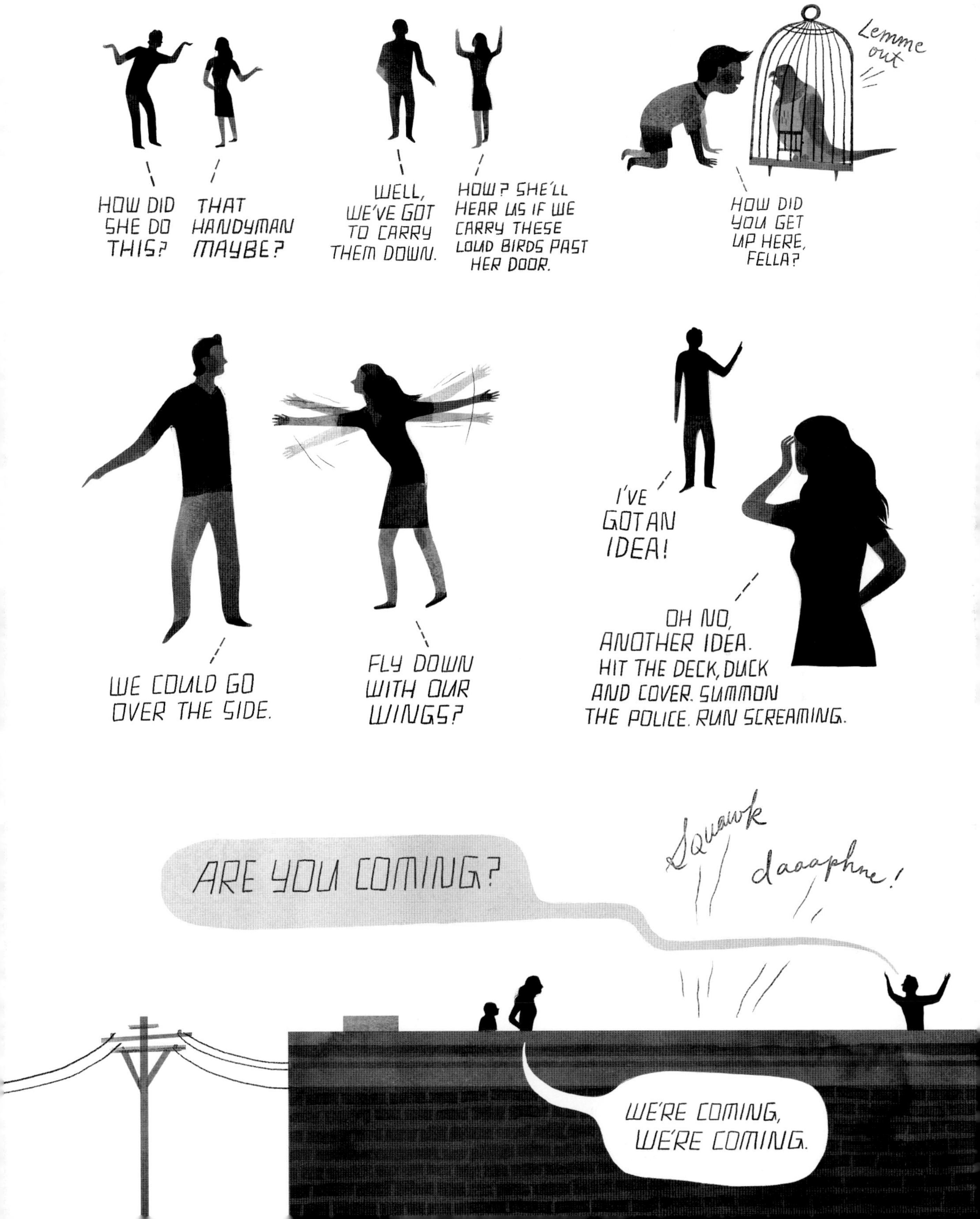
Lemme out
HOW DID SHE DO THIS?
THAT HANDYMAN MAYBE?
WELL, WE'VE GOT TO CARRY THEM DOWN.
HOW? SHE'LL HEAR US IF WE CARRY THESE LOUD BIRDS PAST HER DOOR.
HOW DID YOU GET UP HERE, FELLA?
WE COULD GO OVER THE SIDE.
FLY DOWN WITH OUR WINGS?
I'VE GOT AN IDEA!
OH NO, ANOTHER IDEA. HIT THE DECK, DUCK AND COVER. SUMMON THE POLICE. RUN SCREAMING.
ARE YOU COMING?
Squawk
daaaphne!
WE'RE COMING, WE'RE COMING.

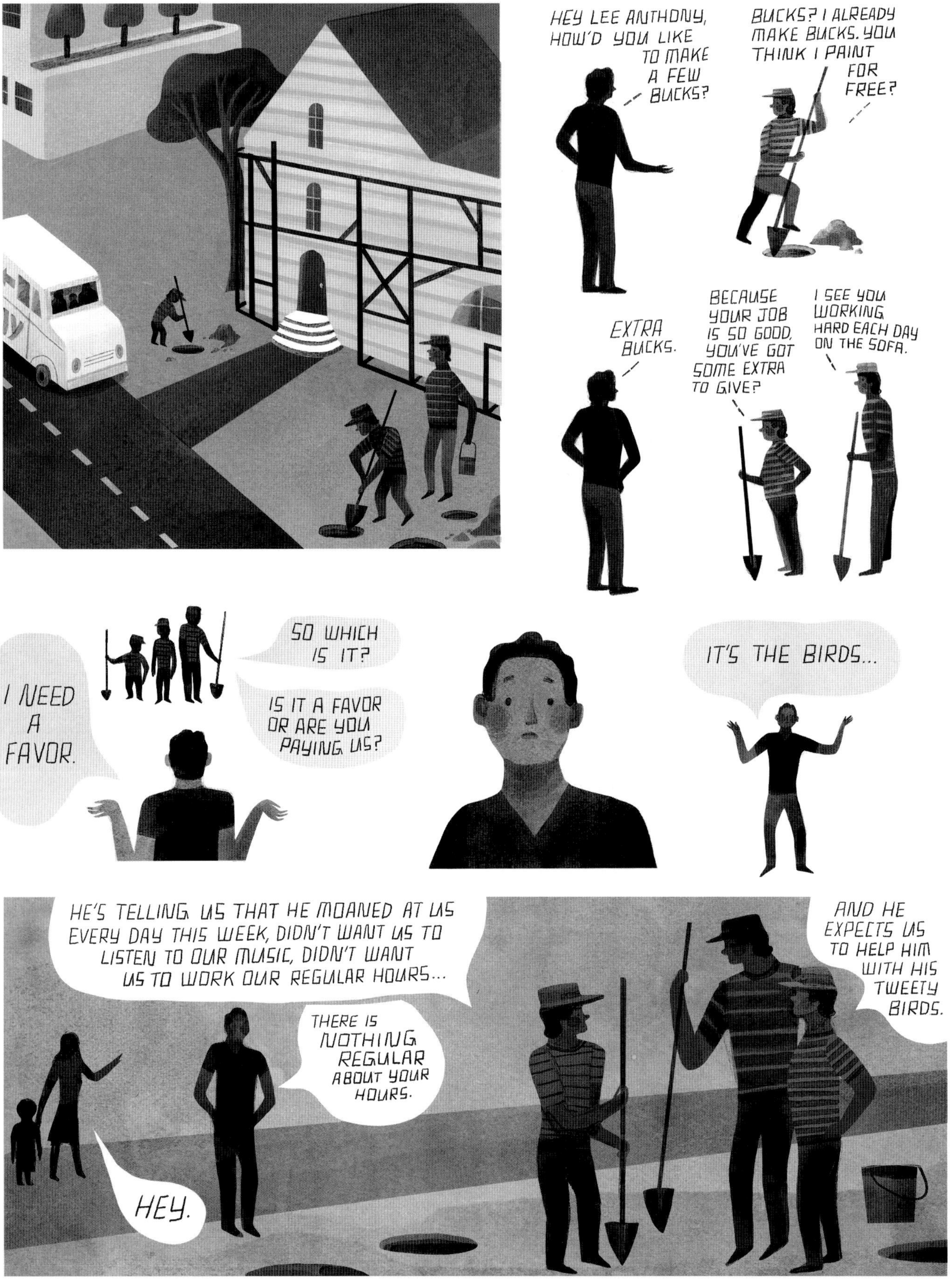
HEY LEE ANTHONY, HOW'D YOU LIKE TO MAKE A FEW BUCKS?
BUCKS? I ALREADY MAKE BUCKS. YOU THINK I PAINT FOR FREE?
EXTRA BUCKS.
BECAUSE YOUR JOB IS SO GOOD, YOU'VE GOT SOME EXTRA TO GIVE?
I SEE YOU WORKING HARD EACH DAY ON THE SOFA.
I NEED A FAVOR.
SO WHICH IS IT?
IS IT A FAVOR OR ARE YOU PAYING US?
IT'S THE BIRDS...
HE'S TELLING US THAT HE MOANED AT US EVERY DAY THIS WEEK, DIDN'T WANT US TO LISTEN TO OUR MUSIC, DIDN'T WANT US TO WORK OUR REGULAR HOURS...
AND HE EXPECTS US TO HELP HIM WITH HIS TWEETY BIRDS.
THERE IS NOTHING REGULAR ABOUT YOUR HOURS.
HEY.

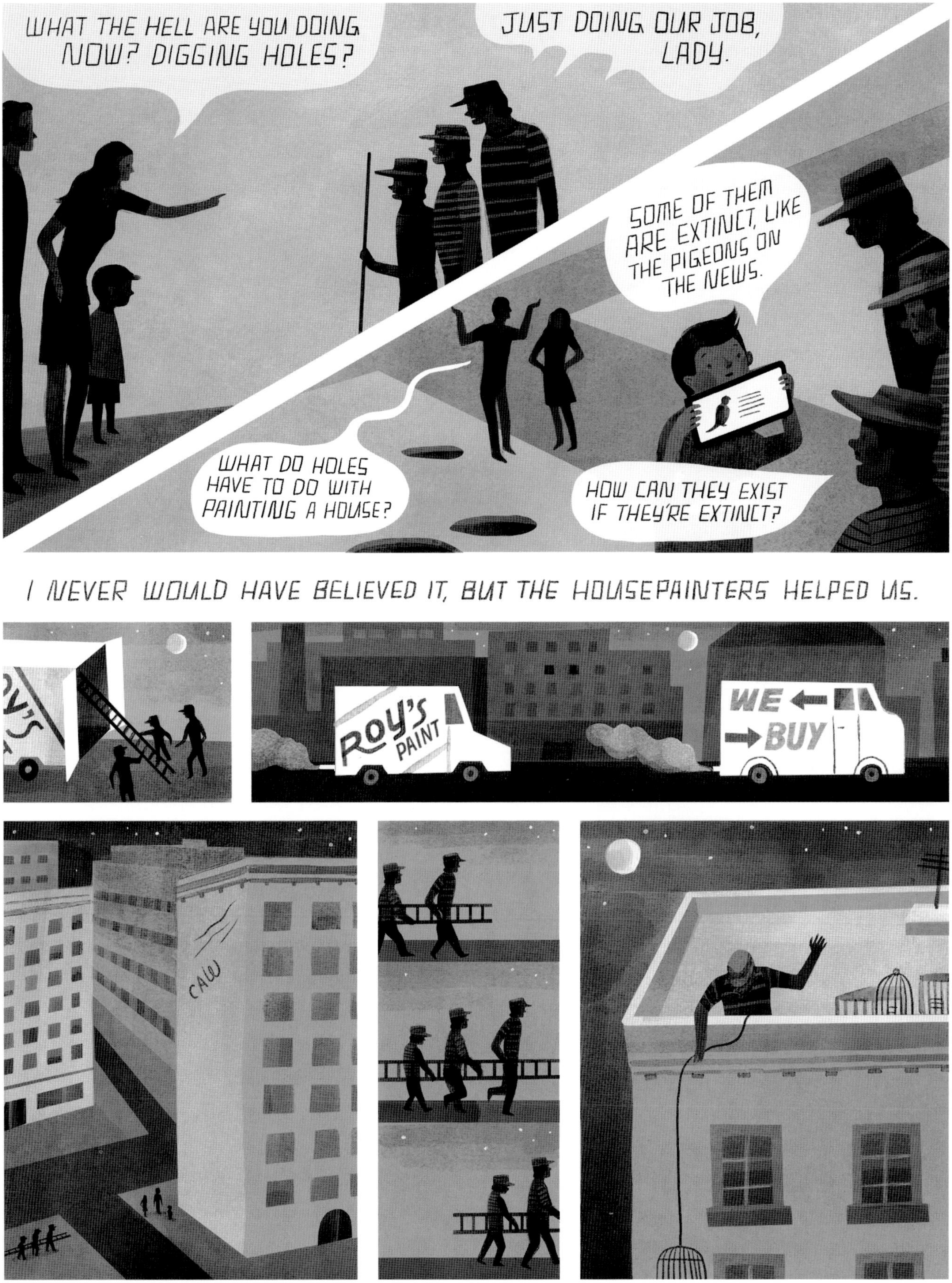
WHAT THE HELL ARE YOU DOING NOW? DIGGING HOLES?
JUST DOING OUR JOB, LADY.
WHAT DO HOLES HAVE TO DO WITH PAINTING A HOUSE?
SOME OF THEM ARE EXTINCT, LIKE THE PIGEONS ON THE NEWS.
HOW CAN THEY EXIST IF THEY'RE EXTINCT?
I NEVER WOULD HAVE BELIEVED IT, BUT THE HOUSEPAINTERS HELPED US.
ROY'S PAINT
WE ← → BUY
CAW

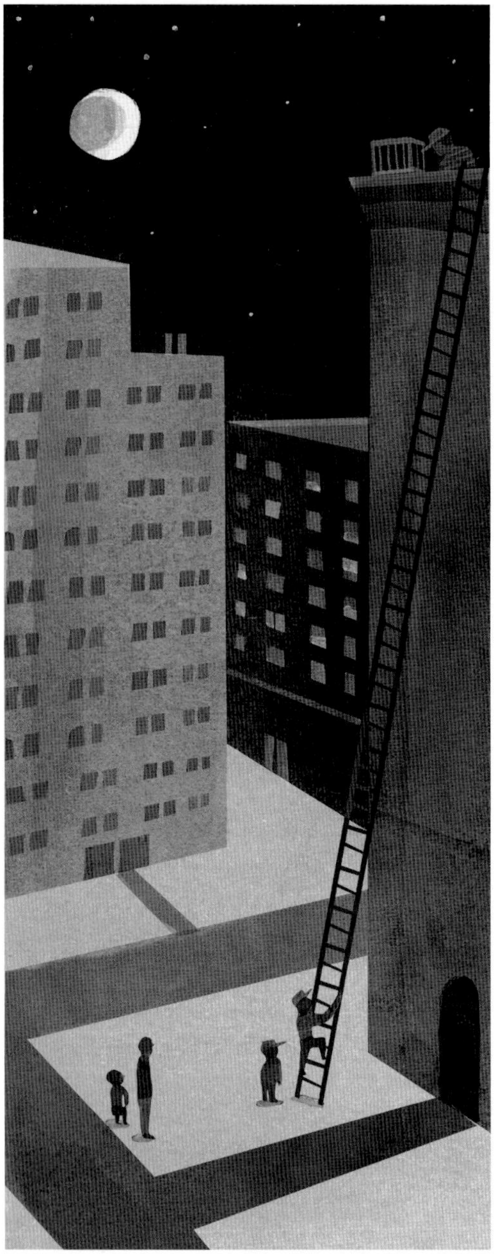

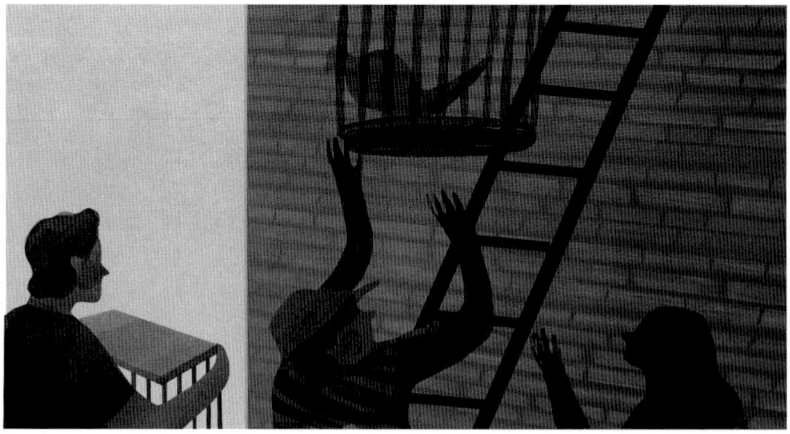

I WISH YOU COULD HAVE SEEN THOSE BIRDS THE WAY I SAW THEM, COMING OVER THE BUILDING IN THE NIGHT. WHOSE BIRDS WERE THEY? NO ONE'S BIRDS? THEY WERE REFUGEES, THAT'S WHAT THEY WERE.

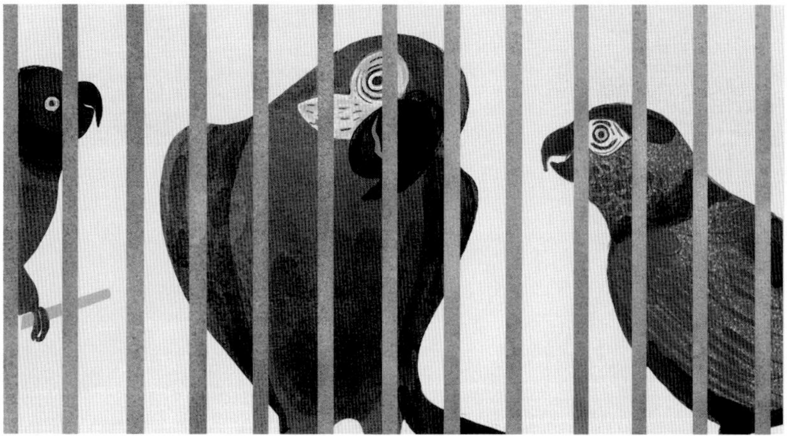

I'D READ ABOUT THE CITIES THAT HAD PARROT POPULATIONS, PARROTS ESCAPED FROM CAGES, FINDING ONE ANOTHER, AND MAKING A HOME.

IF BIRDS COULD DO THAT,

AGAINST SO MANY ODDS...

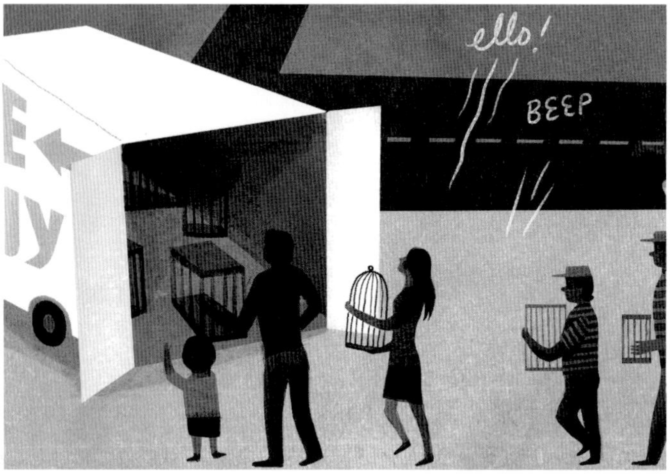
ello!
BEEP

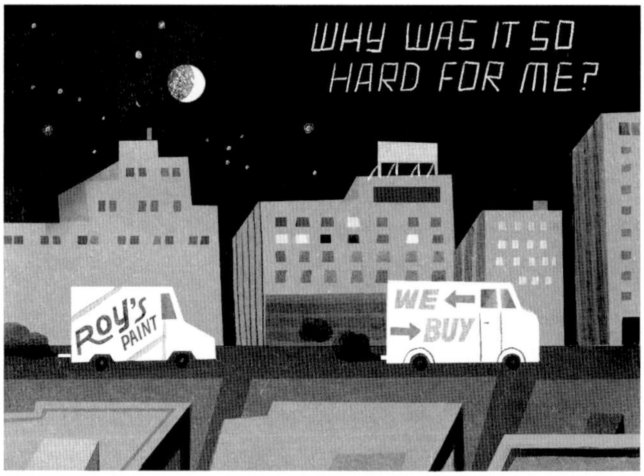
WHY WAS IT SO HARD FOR ME?
ROY'S PAINT
WE ← BUY

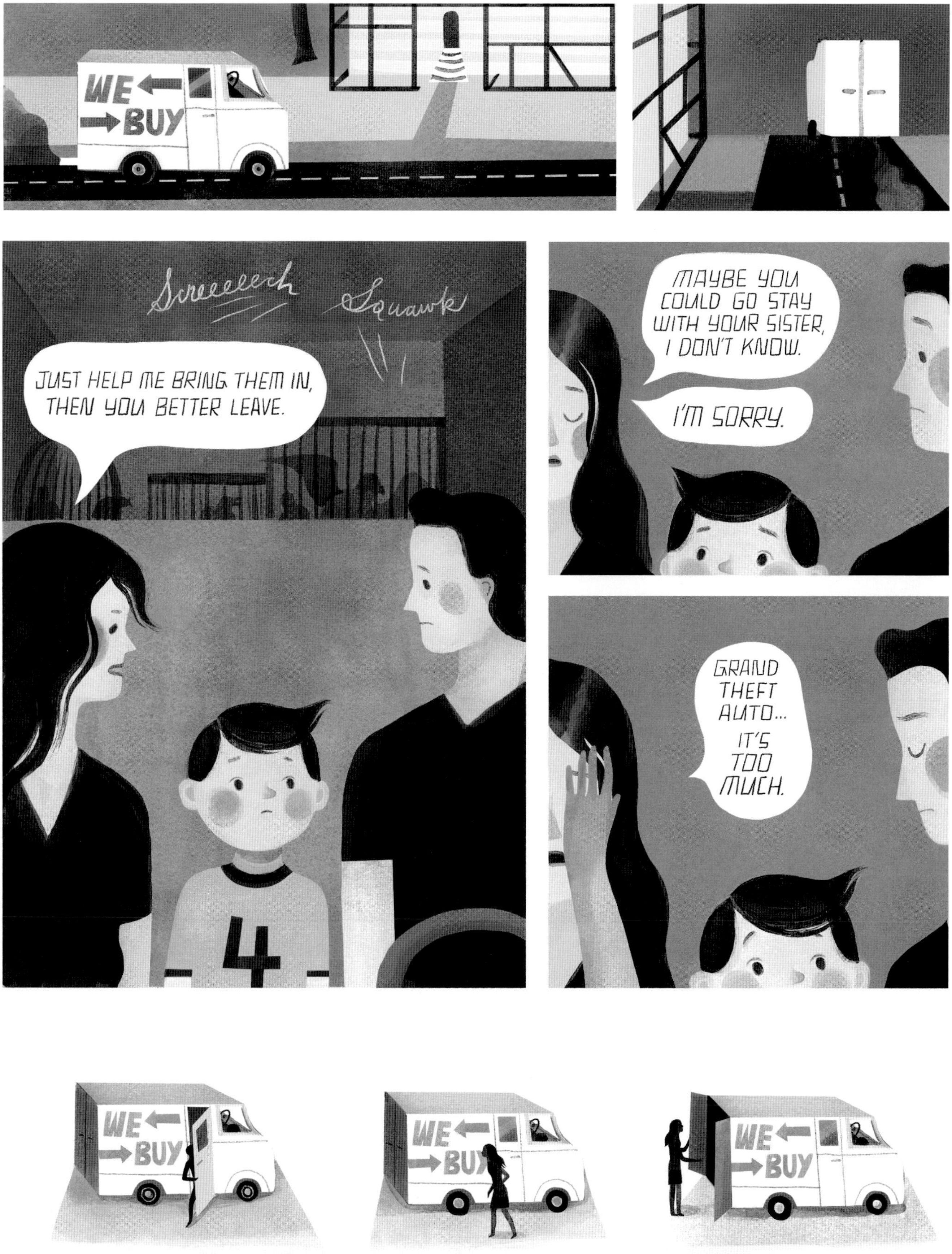
WE BUY
Screeeech
Squawk
JUST HELP ME BRING THEM IN, THEN YOU BETTER LEAVE.
MAYBE YOU COULD GO STAY WITH YOUR SISTER, I DON'T KNOW.
I'M SORRY.
GRAND THEFT AUTO... IT'S TOO MUCH.
WE BUY
WE BUY
WE BUY

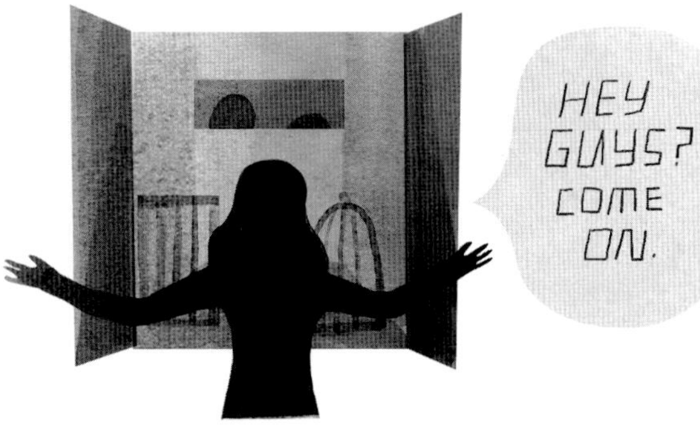
HEY GUYS? COME ON.

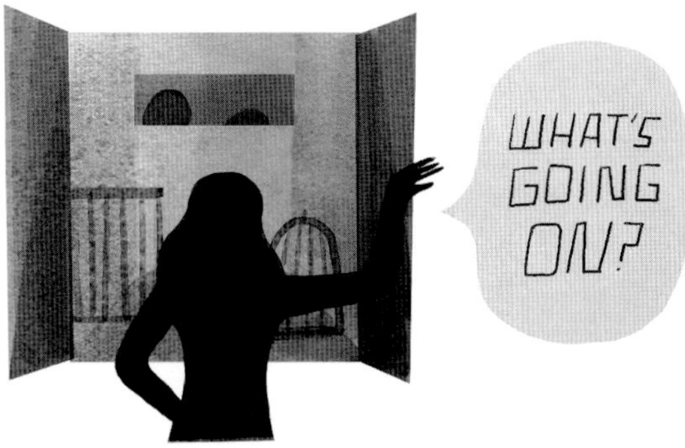
WHAT'S GOING ON?

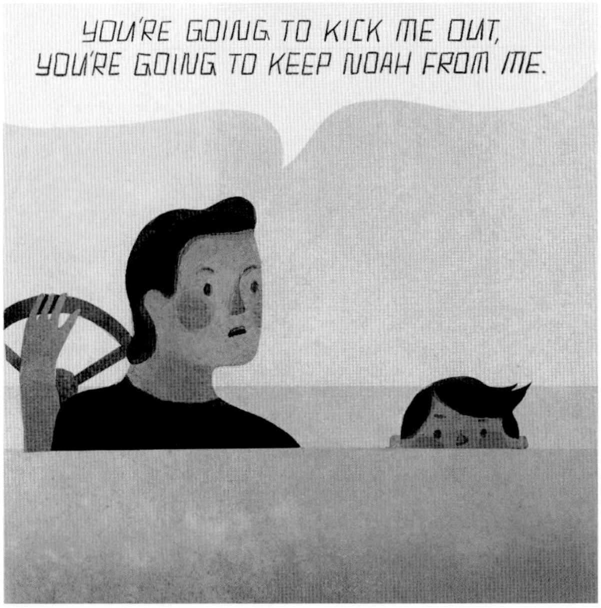
YOU'RE GOING TO KICK ME OUT, YOU'RE GOING TO KEEP NOAH FROM ME.

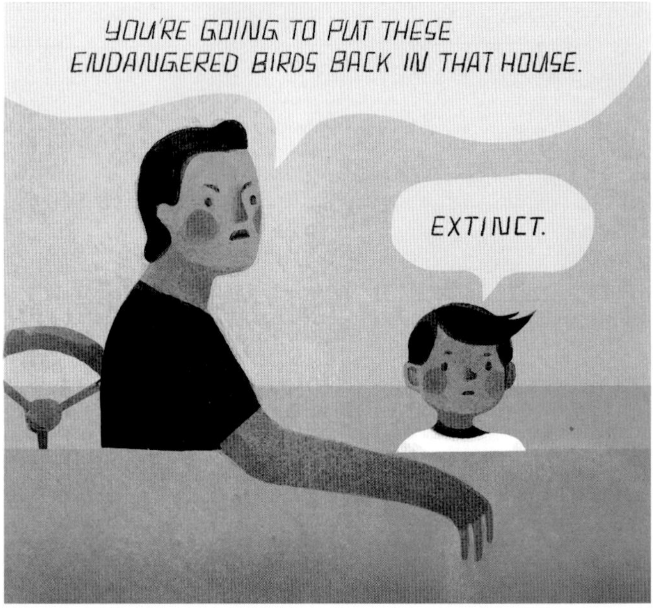
YOU'RE GOING TO PUT THESE ENDANGERED BIRDS BACK IN THAT HOUSE.
EXTINCT.

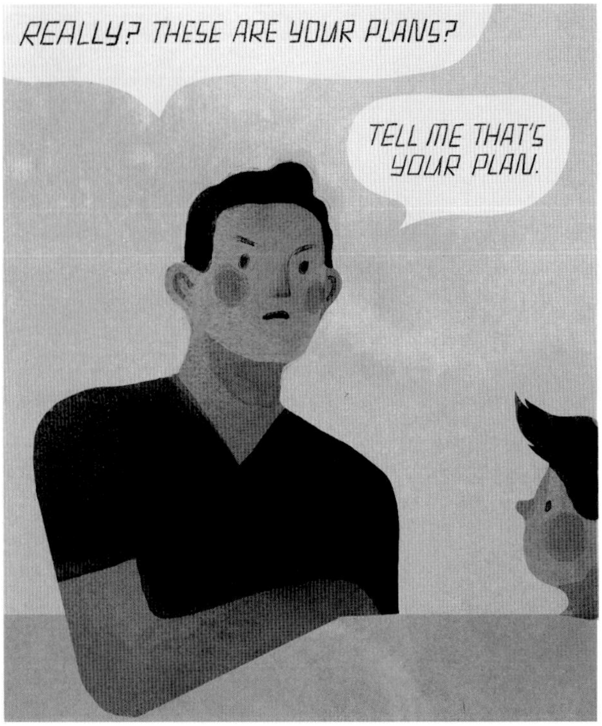
REALLY? THESE ARE YOUR PLANS?
TELL ME THAT'S YOUR PLAN.

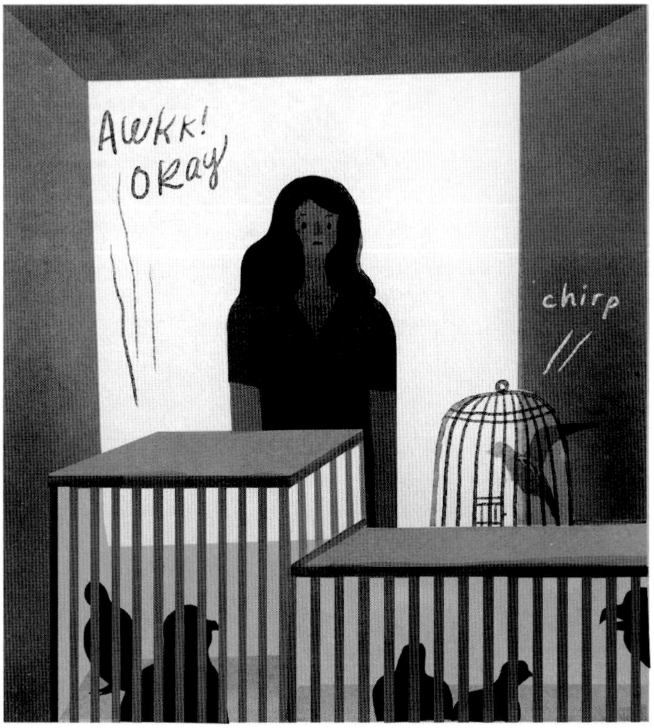
AWKK! OKAY
chirp

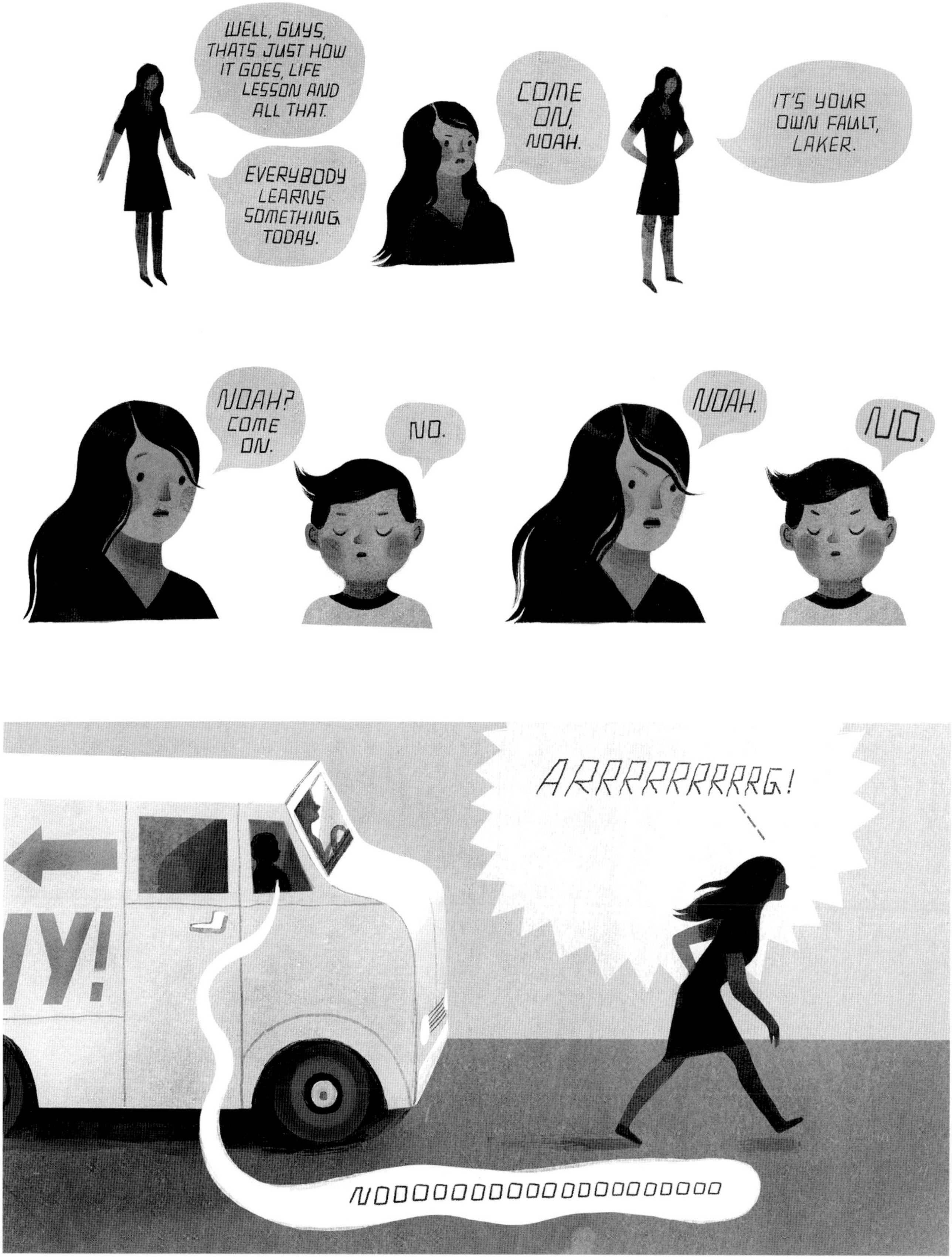
WELL, GUYS, THATS JUST HOW IT GOES, LIFE LESSON AND ALL THAT.
EVERYBODY LEARNS SOMETHING TODAY.
COME ON, NOAH.
IT'S YOUR OWN FAULT, LAKER.
NOAH? COME ON.
NO.
NOAH.
NO.
ARRRRRRRRRG!
NOOOOOOOOOOOOOOOOOOOOOO

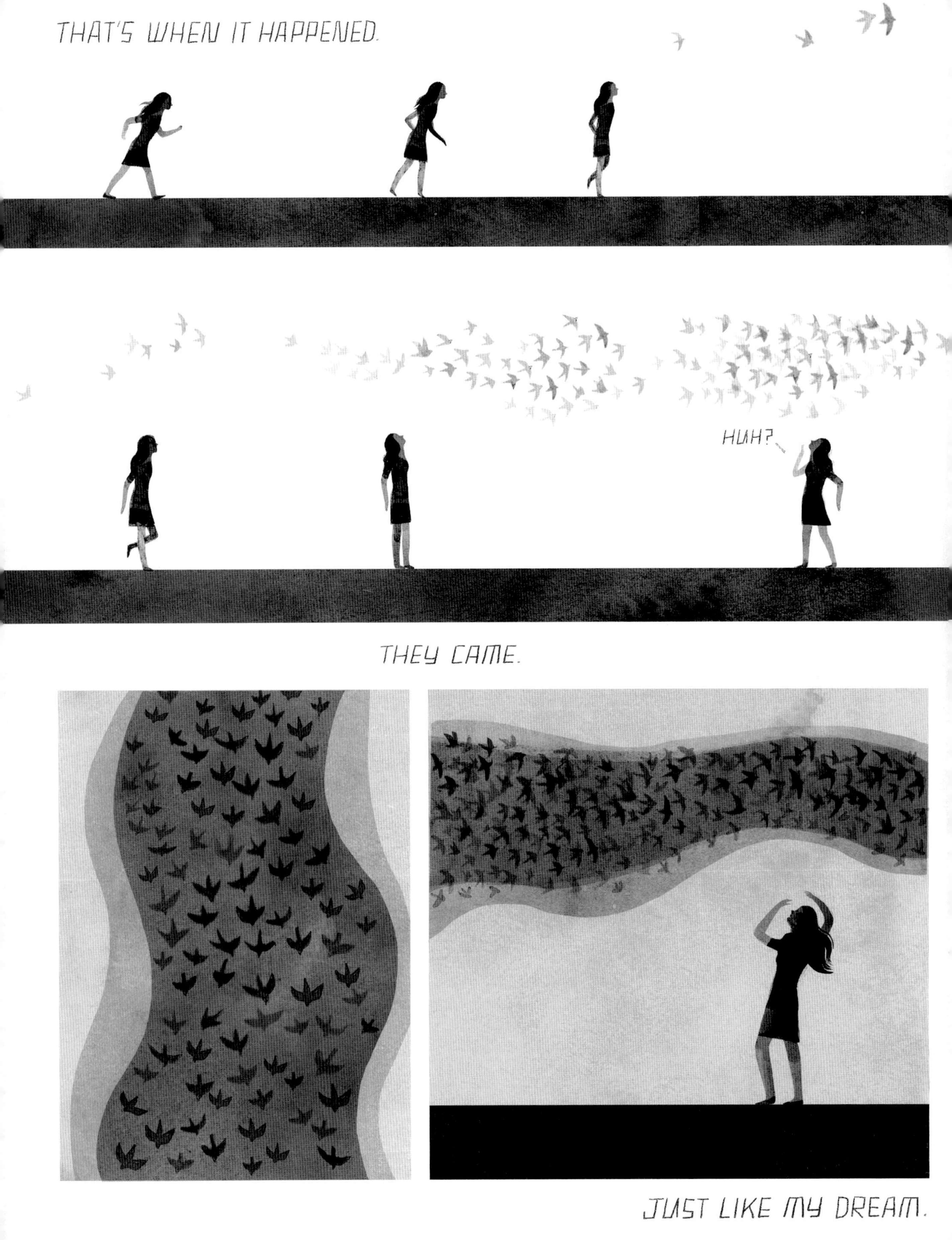
THAT'S WHEN IT HAPPENED.
HUH?
THEY CAME.
JUST LIKE MY DREAM.

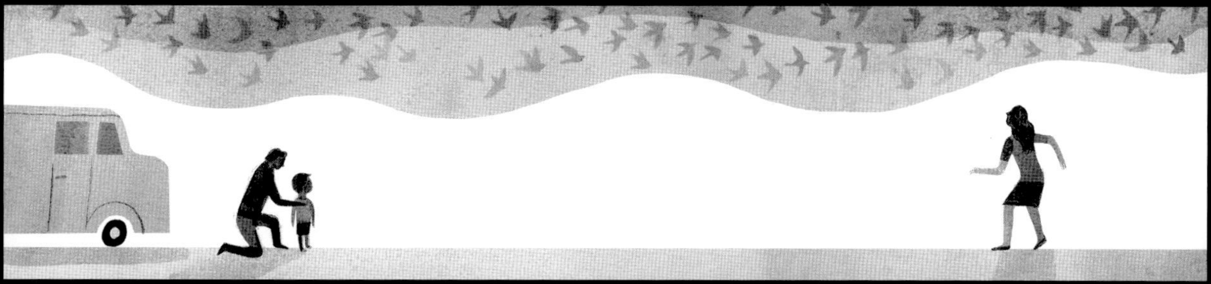

I WAS TIRED OF THE KIND OF REASONING THAT HAD BROUGHT ME TO THIS POINT. IT HAD DONE NOTHING FOR ME EXCEPT SLOWLY STRIP AWAY AT THE FEW THINGS THAT BROUGHT ME JOY.

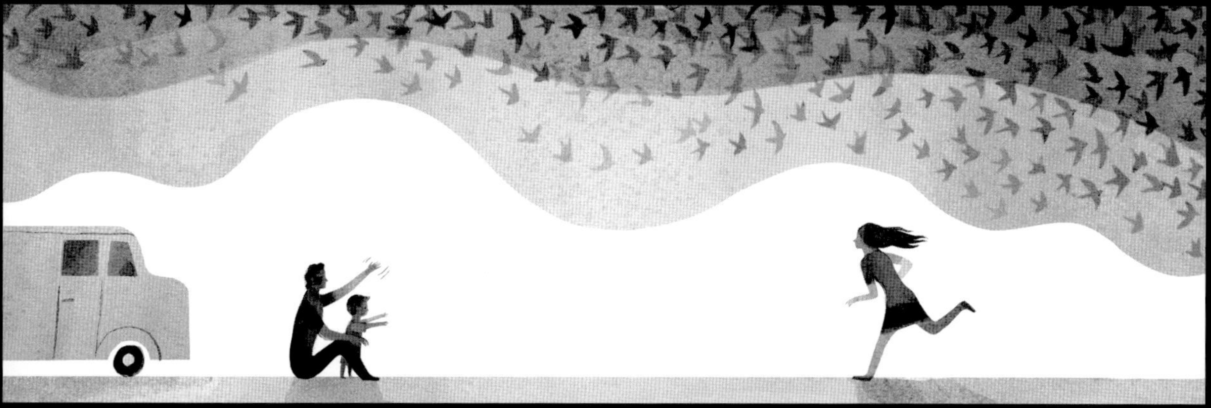

THE ENTIRE CIVILIZED PROJECT SEEMED BASED ON AN ERROR.

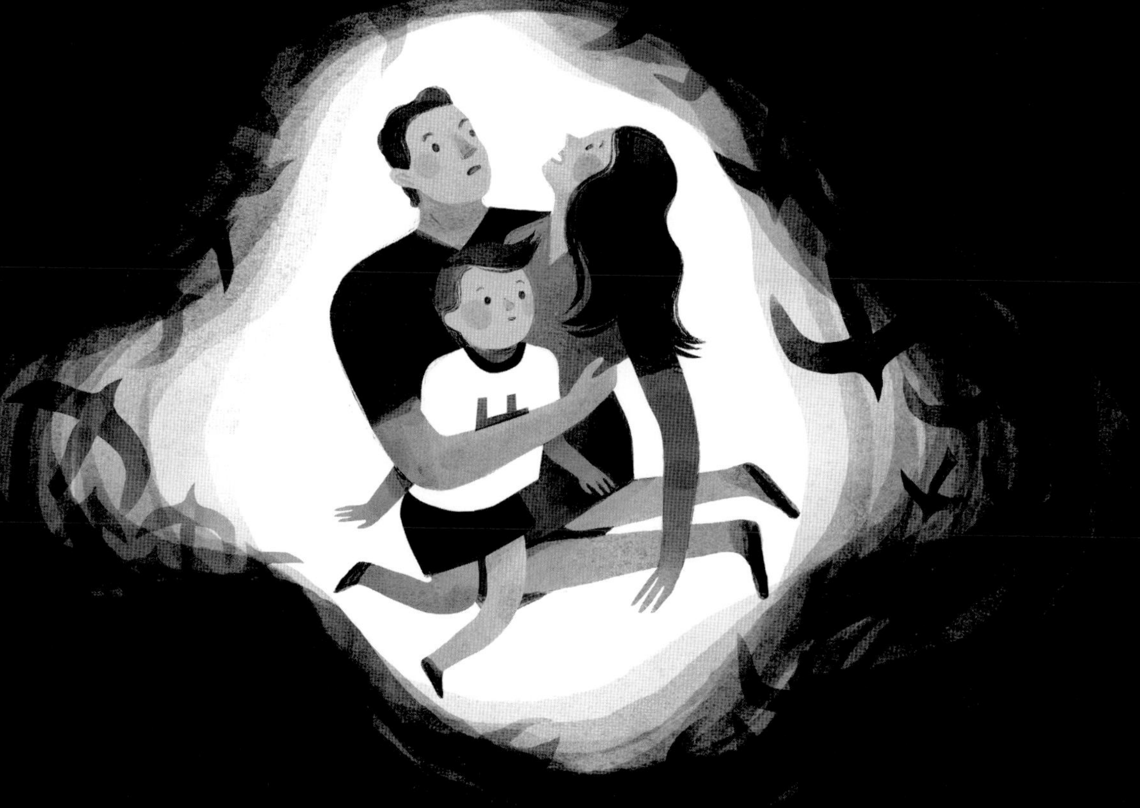

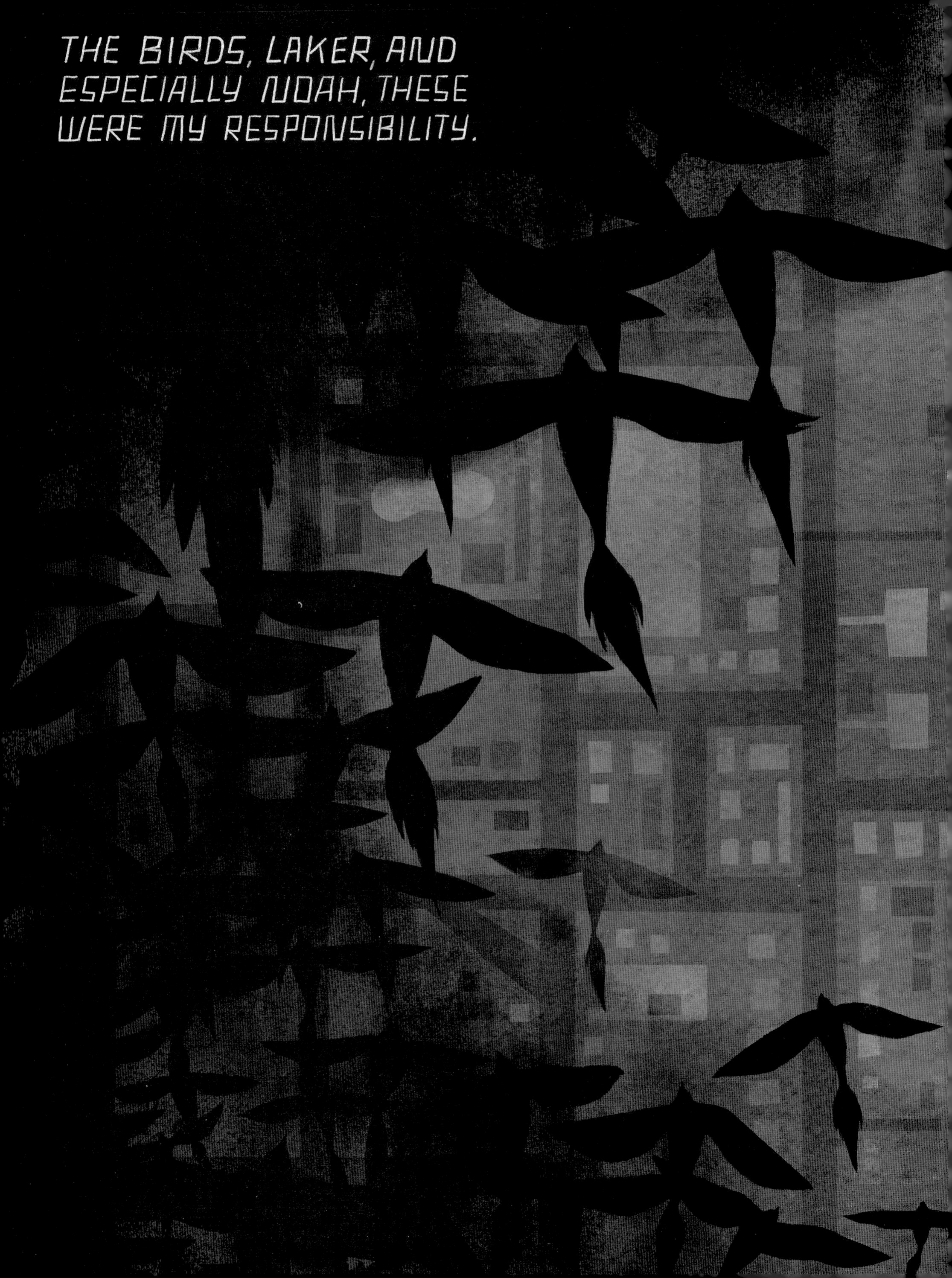
THE BIRDS, LAKER, AND ESPECIALLY NOAH, THESE WERE MY RESPONSIBILITY.

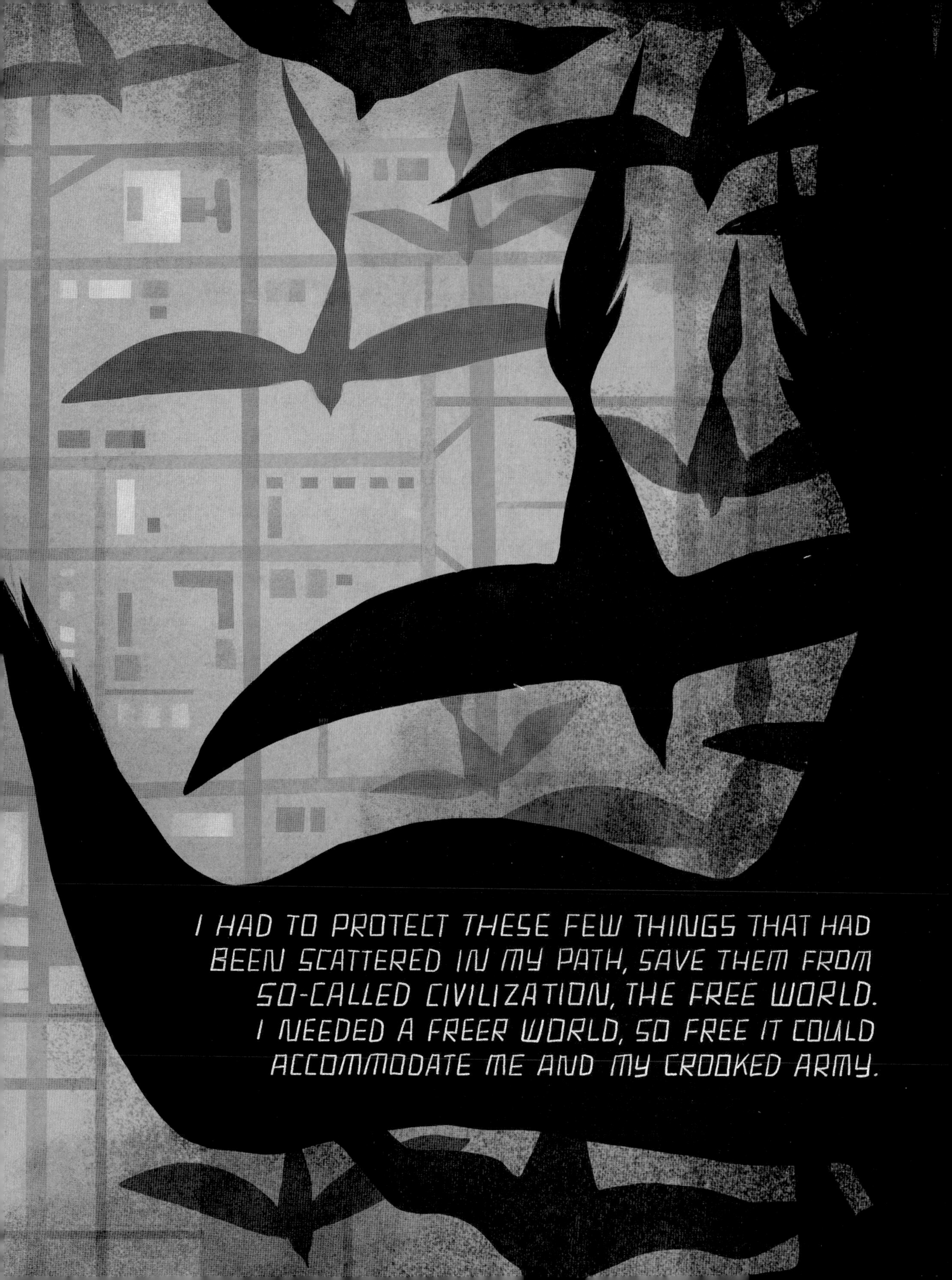
I HAD TO PROTECT THESE FEW THINGS THAT HAD BEEN SCATTERED IN MY PATH, SAVE THEM FROM SO-CALLED CIVILIZATION, THE FREE WORLD. I NEEDED A FREER WORLD, SO FREE IT COULD ACCOMMODATE ME AND MY CROOKED ARMY.

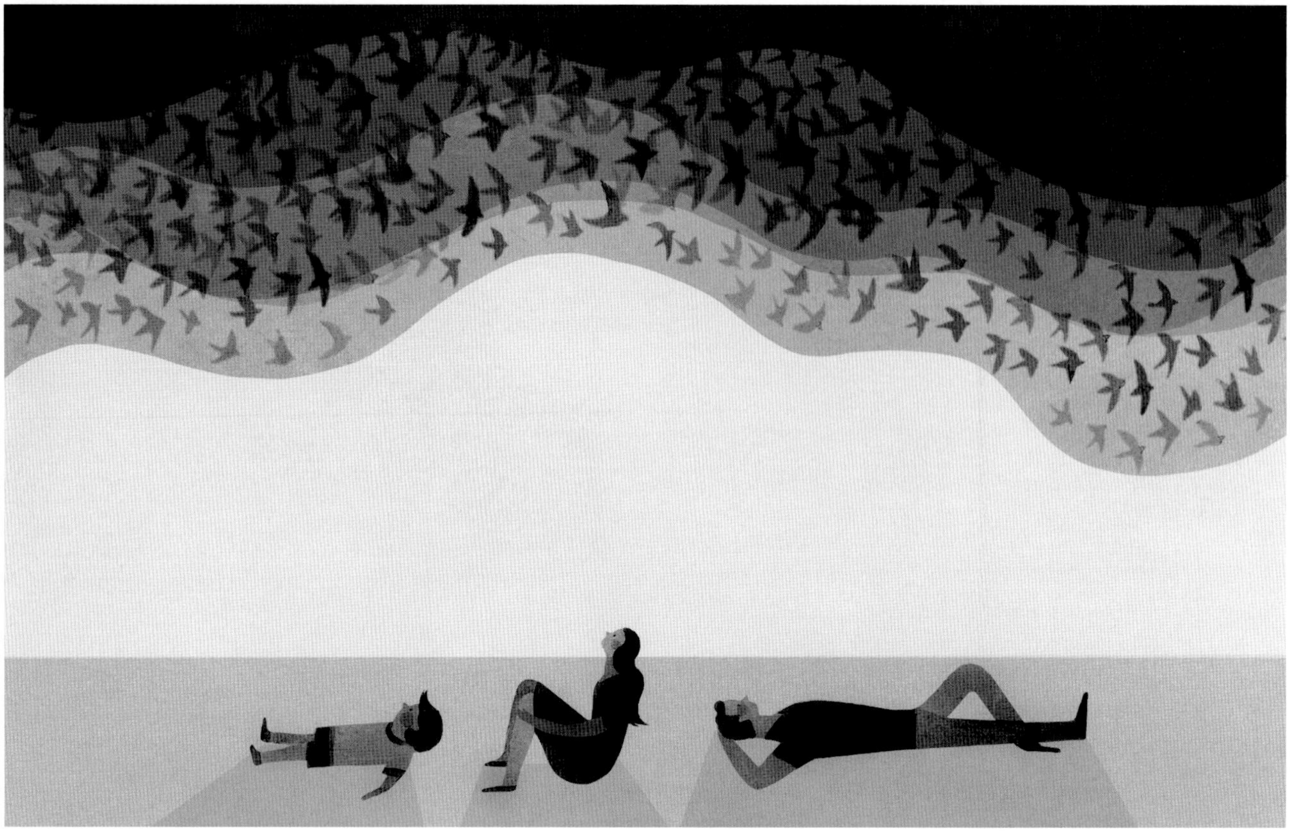

AND BY THE TIME THEY'D PASSED OVER, I KNEW.

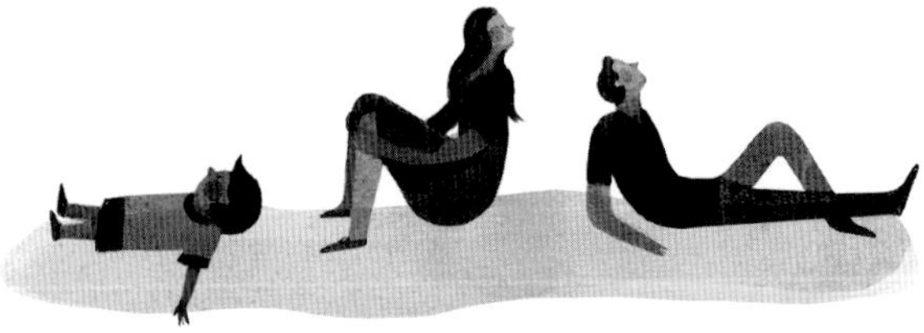

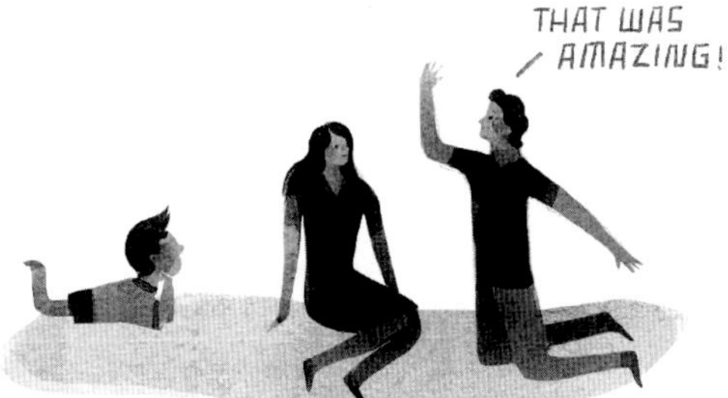
THAT WAS AMAZING!

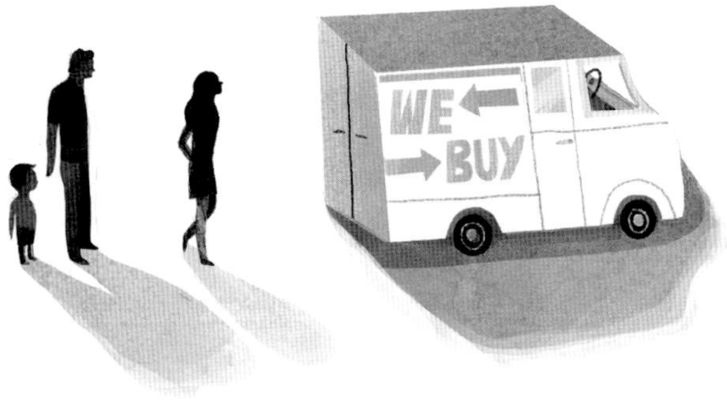
WE
BUY

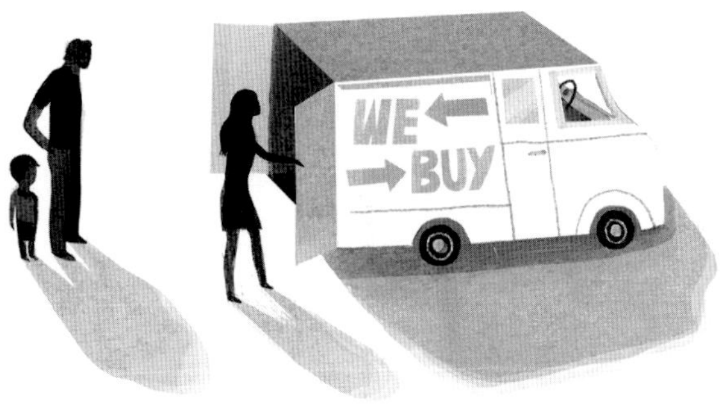
WE
BUY

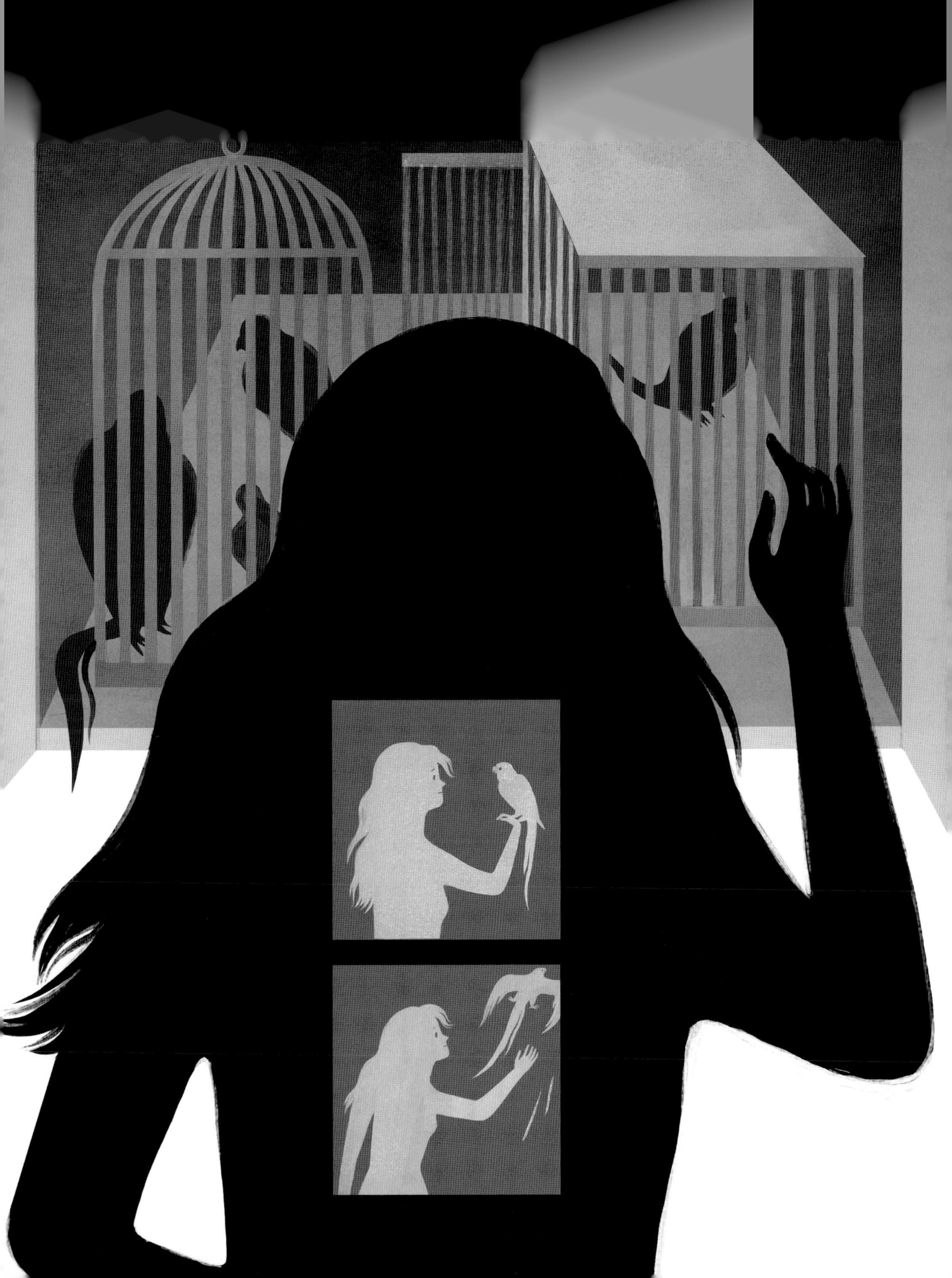

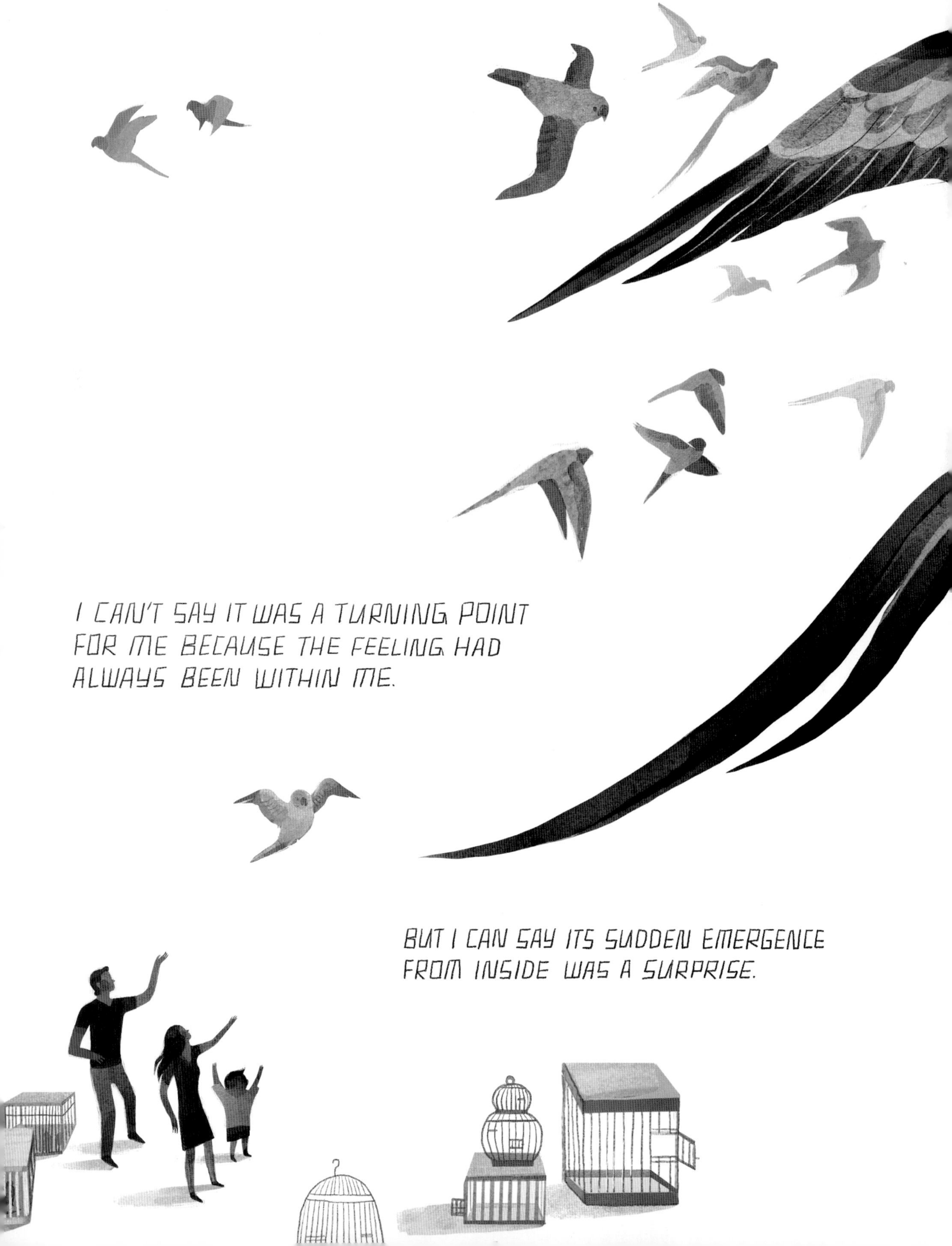
I CAN'T SAY IT WAS A TURNING POINT FOR ME BECAUSE THE FEELING HAD ALWAYS BEEN WITHIN ME.
BUT I CAN SAY ITS SUDDEN EMERGENCE FROM INSIDE WAS A SURPRISE.

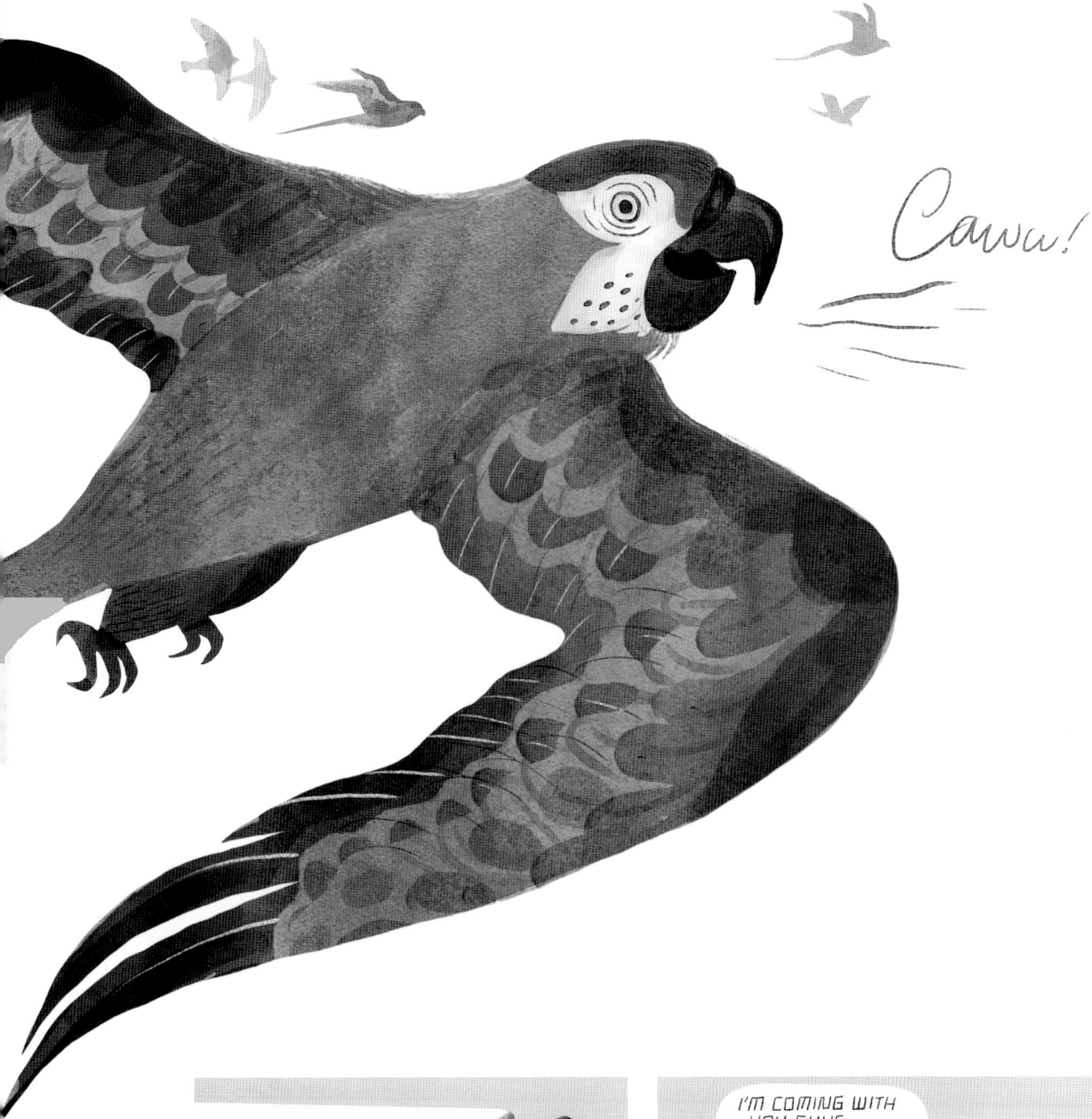
Caww!

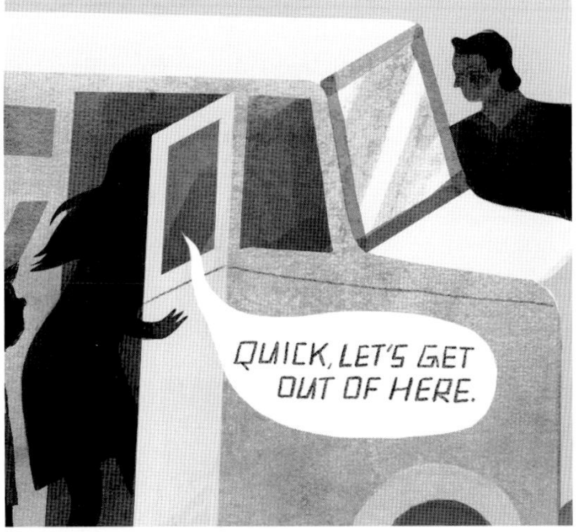
QUICK, LET'S GET OUT OF HERE.

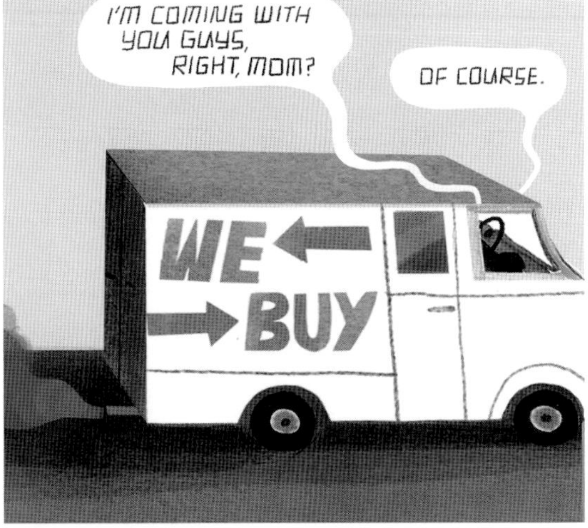
I'M COMING WITH YOU GUYS, RIGHT, MOM?
OF COURSE.
WE BUY

AND AS FOR THE BIRDS...

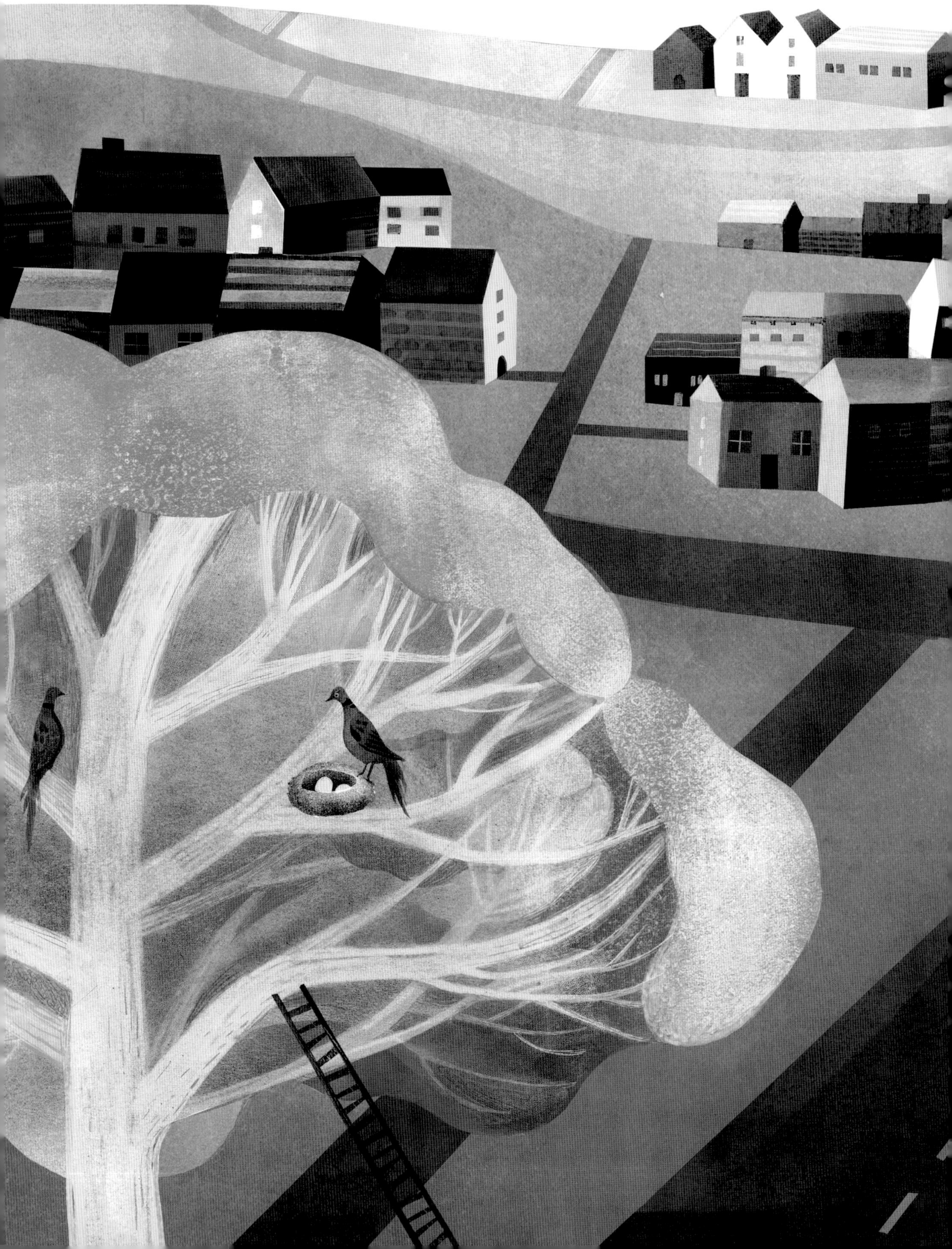

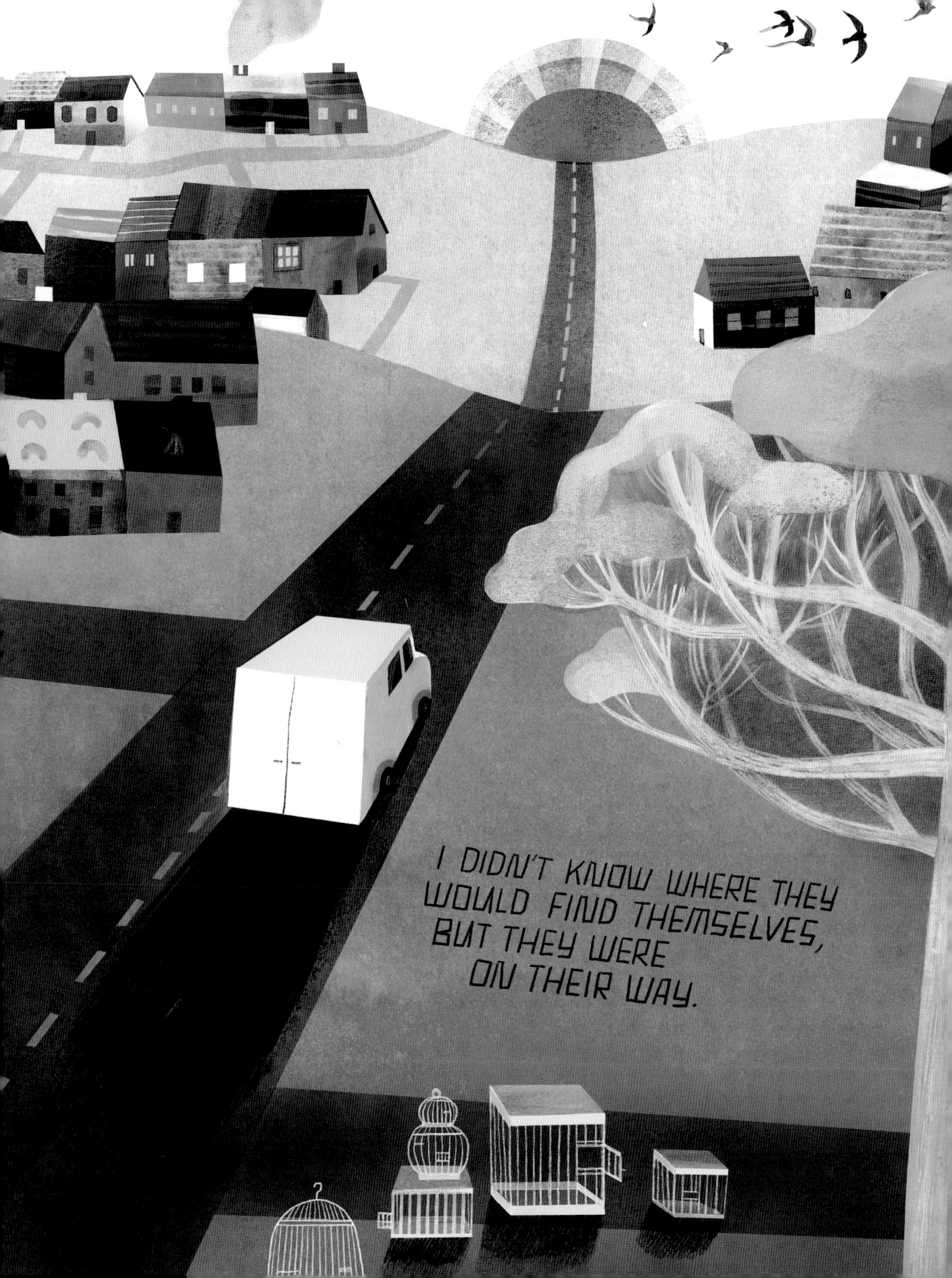
I DIDN'T KNOW WHERE THEY WOULD FIND THEMSELVES, BUT THEY WERE ON THEIR WAY.

ACKNOWLEDGMENTS

GRATEFUL THANKS TO
Matt Evans, Nikki Moustaki,
Bob and Nancy Unferth,
David and Helen Haidle,
Jonathan Haidle, Paul du Coudray,
Tom Devlin, Chris Doyle,
David McCormick, Andy Hunter,
Casey Gonzalez, all the folks at
Catapult, and, above all,
Leigh Newman.

ABOUT THE AUTHOR

DEB OLIN UNFERTH IS THE AUTHOR OF FOUR BOOKS,
MOST RECENTLY, THE STORY COLLECTION *Wait Till You See Me Dance*.
HER FICTION HAS APPEARED IN *Harper's Magazine*, *The Paris Review*,
Granta, *Vice*, *Tin House*, *Noon*, and *McSweeney's*.
SHE IS A CREATIVE CAPITAL FELLOW AND WAS A FINALIST
FOR THE NATIONAL BOOK CRITICS CIRCLE AWARD.
AN ASSOCIATE PROFESSOR AT THE UNIVERSITY OF TEXAS IN AUSTIN,
SHE ALSO RUNS THE PEN-CITY WRITERS, A CREATIVE-WRITING CERTIFICATE
PROGRAM AT THE JOHN B. CONNALLY UNIT, A PENITENTIARY IN SOUTHERN TEXAS.

ABOUT THE ILLUSTRATOR

ELIZABETH HAIDLE IS A FREELANCE ARTIST LIVING IN PORTLAND, OREGON.
HER WORK HAS APPEARED ON A RANGE OF PROJECTS, INCLUDING
COOKBOOKS, COMICS, VIDEO GAMES, & MUSEUM EXHIBITS.
SHE IS CURRENTLY CREATIVE DIRECTOR AT *Illustoria Magazine*
AND WORKING ON A GRAPHIC NOVEL SERIES ABOUT FAMOUS AUTHORS AS KIDS.
SHE IS ALSO THE ART DIRECTOR AT PEN-CITY WRITERS.
SHE CAN BE FOUND PLAYING SAW IN A JUG BAND WHEN SHE HAS SPARE TIME.